NATURAL

REEF AQUARIUMS

Simplified Approaches to Creating Living Saltwater Microcosms

Front Cover
Tridacna clam and *Pseudanthias squamipinnis* basslet; photograph by Paul Humann
Back Cover
Top: Purple Firefish (*Nemateleotris decora*); photograph by Scott W. Michael
Middle: Spotted Cleaning Shrimp (*Periclemenes yucatanicus*) on Florida Pink-tipped
Anemone (*Condylactis gigantea*); photograph by Norburt Wu
Bottom: Spanish Hogfish (*Bodianus rufus*) with Common Sea Fan
(*Gorgonia ventalina*); photograph by Foster Bam

T.F.H. Publications, Inc.
One TFH Plaza
Third and Union Avenues
Neptune City, NJ 07753
www.tfh.com

NATURAL

REEF
AQUARIUMS

Simplified Approaches to Creating
Living Saltwater Microcosms

JOHN H. TULLOCK

With a Foreword by Martin A. Moe, Jr.

Principal Photographers: Paul Humann and Scott W. Michael

MICROCOSM

t.f.h.

PROFESSIONAL
SERIES™

T.F.H. Publications
One T.F.H. Plaza
Third and Union Avenues
Neptune City, NJ 07753
www.tfh.com

First printing 1997. Revised and reprinted February 1999, October 1999, January 2001.

ISBN 1-890087-01-7 (hardcover); ISBN 1-890087-00-9 (pbk.)

Library of Congress Cataloging-in-Publication Data

Tullock, John H.
Natural reef aquariums: simplified approaches to creating living saltwater microcosms / John H. Tullock.
p. cm.
Includes bibliographical references (p.) and index
ISBN 1-890087-01-7 (hardcover). — ISBN 1-890087-00-9 (pbk.)
1. Marine aquariums. 2. Coral reef animals. I. Title.
SF457.1.T87 1997
639.34'2—DC21 97-1440

Color separations by Horsman, Williston, VT and Bergman Graphics, Colchester, VT
Designed by Eugenie Seidenberg Delaney
Co-published by
Microcosm Ltd.
P.O. Box 550
Charlotte, VT 05445
www.microcosm-books.com

Dedicated to my best friend and business partner, Jerry Yarnell,
without whom much of what I know I could not have learned.

"It were happy if we studied nature more in natural things,
and acted according to nature,
whose rules are few, plain and most reasonable."
—WILLIAM PENN

Contents

Foreword

COME, LET US VISIT AN ALIEN WORLD, a world filled with mysterious and beautiful life forms that flourish in an environment inimical to our own life processes. It is a world of strange part-plant and part-animal creatures whose stony skeletons form vast and complex structures; of sleek legless animals of wondrous color and shape that glide weightless through a dense and fluid medium; of colorful animals of soft amorphous form; and of cumbersome, strangely shaped beasts with hard external skeletons that protect their soft tissues from fierce predators. All these organisms are engaged in a savage battle for biological survival, and they war with each other with poison darts and spines, grasping tentacles, brute force, needle-sharp fangs, and crushing teeth, and here even slow but inexorable growth is also a weapon. They feed upon each other, they compete with each other for sustenance and solar energy, they form strange alliances for mutual protection and energy acquisition, and they reproduce in incredible abundance. This is a coral reef, a place of awesome beauty of form and color and a place where the primeval evolutionary forces that shaped the life of Earth still perform the elaborate dance of mindless competition and survival.

Your grandfather, perhaps 100 years ago or so, could only imagine what wonders the world beneath the sea might contain. Your father could follow the exploits of the first explorers of the undersea realm and could just begin to see and experience the explosion of life on a coral reef. But you and I, we can not only visit this world whenever we wish, but we can also capture a small part of it in an oceanic microcosm of our own making in our own homes. But if you lack the knowledge to create this undersea world in a little glass box, then your road will be rocky and impassable, a venture filled with weeping and wailing and gnashing of teeth, with failure as your most likely destination. Fortunately, there are scientists and hobbyists, and very rarely one who is also a teacher, who can smooth this road and bring you to a destination of marvel and delight. John Tullock is such a teacher, and he has written a very good book.

A DECADE AGO, authors of marine aquarium books, myself included, worked at ways to say the same things differently, or more simply, or with greater clarity. Then, suddenly, technological capability and biological understanding clasped hands and led marine aquarists into a new era. The old books no longer told the whole story. There were new avenues to explore, new creatures to husband and grow, new systems to engineer and build, and new books to write. We have learned a great deal in the last ten years about creating marine aquarium systems, about the collection, compatibility, and husbandry of marine organisms, and about the inhabitants and ecology of coral reefs and the nearby tropical aquatic ecosystems. I use the collective "we" here, and this includes marine hobbyists, professional aquarists, retail and wholesale dealers of live marine organisms, manufacturers of aquarium equipment, collectors of marine life, marine scientists, environmentalists, and even the city-bound general public, who can now admire the complexity of a coral reef in the window of the corner aquarium store.

Reef tanks, marine aquarium displays that reflect the complex beauty and ecology of the coral reef environment, have been the cornerstone of these advances. Keeping marine fish was, and is, an exciting hobby that links us with the mysterious world beneath tropical seas, but when we keep a reef tank, then we actually build and grow a complex reef environment, a microcosm of a coral reef within our own home. After years of experimentation and development, we now know what basic elements of life are required by most of the invertebrate inhabitants of coral reefs, and many ways to provide these essential elements to the denizens of our captive reefs. John's book brings us up to date with these many advances. Through his experience as a retailer to the hobby, he distills the science that is the foundation of reef technology into specific recommendations for building various sizes and complexities of reef tanks that reflect particular marine environments. The "how, why, who, and what" of reef tank creation is described in detail with the insight of a professional and the passion of a teacher — a rare combination.

WILLIAM OF OCKHAM was an English philosopher who lived in the early 1300s during the very early dawning of the scientific age. His most important observation, the one that placed his principal of parsimony or "Ockham's Razor" into the heart of science, is simply, "What can be done with fewer, is done in vain with more," or in other words, the simplest solution that adequately solves the problem is most likely the correct solution. Simplicity is at the core of nature's complexity, and so it is with marine aquarium systems. This tenet is also the core of John Tullock's captive aquatic philosophy. "Tullock's Razor," More Biology, Less Technology, defines the structure of the aquarium system by the vitality and ecology of the organisms, and by following his recommendations, an aquarist can be sure to avoid unnecessary technical complexity.

OUR PASSION, AND OUR SUCCESS, has not gone unnoticed. It is not unusual to see coral reef fish and invertebrates, and marine aquariums, featured in print ads, TV commercials, documentary and educational TV programs, in movies, and, of course, on many and varied posters, art works, T-shirts, and coffee cups. This is good because it raises public awareness to the great beauty and biological complexity of tropical aquatic flora and fauna, and stimulates people to learn more about this unique ecosystem and to become actively involved in the hobby of keeping marine aquarium systems. This is also bad because, as awareness of the environmental plight of one of the most productive and delicate ecosystems on Earth pervades public consciousness, the high public profile of captive marine life focuses concern and blame for environmental degradation on this very small component of the exploitation and stress that humanity places on these coral reef ecosystems.

The aquatic world is complex and it is made much more complex by our harvest of its renewable resources. The key word here is "renewable." If the taking of a particular marine organism for food, industry, or aquariums can be managed and regulated so that such harvest does not degrade the environment and is below the point where natural reproduction maintains normal population levels, then harvest of that resource, at that level, is a reasonable and valuable use. Unfortunately, reasonable harvest through sustainable fishing methods and protection of coral reef resources is not the customary practice in most remote tropical environs.

Huge fishing vessels loaded with cyanide and blast fishing equipment do not leave Asian ports seeking tropical aquarium fish. No, they are after food fish for Asian markets. The silt and nutrients that blanket some tropical reefs are not created by fishers of live tropical fish. No, this is the result of improper agriculture, mining, road building, and waste disposal by burgeoning human coastal populations. All the coral exported as live organisms for marine hobbyists is but an insignificant fraction of that that has been, and is being, destroyed by coastal dredging, agricultural run-off, road building, large vessel anchorage, dried curio collection, and industrial and sewage waste outfall. These activities negatively impact the populations of reef fish, corals, and other invertebrates to a far greater extent than does the collection of organisms for marine aquariums.

This is not to say that collection for public and private marine aquariums is without fault. Destructive, reprehensible methods of collection have been and still are in use in some areas. Improper care during collection, holding, and transport of specimens also occurs far more often than is excusable. To most of the world, the marine aquarium hobby is the educator, and the messenger, of our misuse of coral reef ecosystems. It is very important that we not kill the messenger, and that we nurture the educator. The best weapon against such abuses is knowledge, and finding ways to organize within the hobby and the industry to disseminate this knowledge. The end result will be to effect changes that will benefit the hobbyists, the professionals, and most important, the coral reef environment that is the foundation of this fascinating pursuit. John Tullock addresses these problems and knows the subject well, for he is at the forefront of these endeavors.

Back in 1977, at the same time that John was experiencing the inky end of a nudibranch on Pigeon Key, I was a mere 10 miles up the road on Fat Deer Key struggling to squeeze eggs from the rear end of a French Angelfish. We did not know each other then and had no idea that our paths and philosophies would cross in future years. John was studying to be a marine scientist and a teacher, and I was struggling to carve out a niche in the fledgling marine aquaculture industry by breeding marine tropical fish.

Marine aquaculture, or mariculture, is often claimed to be the future of the hobby and the industry. And so it will be, but it will be only a fraction of that future. Its import will increase with time, but marine aquaculture will never be able to produce more than a small percentage of the many thousands of species of fish and invertebrates that are required by the natural diversity of reef aquariums. The hobby and the industry must protect the natural environment that is the foundation of the hobby and foster a sustainable harvest of marine life for the aquarium trade.

To be profitable, commercial marine aquaculture must concentrate on those species that have high value and are relatively easy to culture. Hobbyists, however, can culture any organism that claims their interest, and distribute these cultured species, and their interest in them, to other hobbyists all over the world. Then, through both these channels, commercial and hobby, the pressures on natural populations of popular species will lessen, the hobby will expand into the new horizon of captive propagation, and the message of environment, ecology, economy, and "Less Technology, More Biology" that John espouses will help to preserve the hobby — and the coral reef environment — well into the next century.

— *Martin A. Moe, Jr.*
Fort Lauderdale, Florida

Acknowledgments

No book is solely the work of its author, and this one is hardly the exception. Many people have assisted my efforts throughout the years, each contributing in some way to my evolution as a scientist and author. My late father, Hardin Tullock, kindled my interest in science when I was very young, and my gratitude to him for this (among all the other wonderful things that come from a good relationship between father and son) is boundless. I regret that he did not live to see this book in print.

As for teachers and professional associates, among the first to come to mind is the late Dr. J.O. Mundt, a mentor who possessed not only scientific eminence, but also an enormously keen ability to give good advice without seeming to direct. Drs. Susan Reichert, Mel Whiteside, Gary McCracken, Gerry Vaughan, and especially Dave Etnier helped me become a serious scientist without taking myself too seriously. My colleagues, with whom I share many fond memories of Pigeon Key and the old marine lab there, include Gerry Dinkins, J.R. Shute, Peggy Shute, Pat Rakes, and Jim Beets.

After some ten years in the aquarium industry, I have had the opportunity to learn from a host of people, including Dr. Jaime Baquero, Stan Brown, Dr. Bruce Carlson, Bruce Davidson, Charles Delbeek, Dr. Bob Goldstein, Roy Herndon, Teresa Herndon, Bob Hix, Bill Hoffman, Lance Ichinotsubo, Mikki Ichinotsubo, Stuart Keefer, Lynne Laurita, Andy Lee, Rick Oellers, Dr. Peter Rubec, and Julian Sprung. Thanks to each of you for your valuable insights.

Special thanks are due to Martin Moe, a treasured friend and author of several great books on marine life and aquarium keeping, for taking time out from his hectic schedule to write the Foreword to this book.

Paul Humann, whose excellent books about the reef fauna of Florida and the Caribbean should be in the library of every serious aquarist, and Scott Michael, whose latest book, *Reef Fishes*, is scheduled to debut soon from Microcosm, deserve an accolade for supplying between them virtually all the images that illuminate these pages.

My publisher, James Lawrence, an avid aquarist and editor par excellence, deserves all the credit for turning my manuscript into something accessible and useful for hobbyists. Thanks also to the staff of Microcosm for producing such a beautiful book.

Finally, I am grateful to all the businesses who have gotten behind this project by supplying much of the equipment and other materials for the photography shoots, and by supporting the finished product in the best possible way — by stocking it. You will find their names, along with some others, in the Selected Sources at the back of the book.

Preface

I T WAS A DAY IN LATE WINTER in rural eastern Tennessee, brilliantly sunny but chilly and wet from several days of rain, when my father and I went for a stroll through the wooded barn lot and across a pasture to the tiny pond that served to water my grandfather's small herd of milk cows and also harbored a few fish. My grandfather allowed cattails, sedges, alder, willow, and sycamore to clothe the banks undisturbed, and one might discover a writing spider or a green snake living there. We even had a muskrat, although looking back, I am amazed it found enough to eat. For an 8-year-old boy, it was a wilderness oasis within our carefully tended but monotonous fields of tobacco, corn, and pasture.

Dad said we were on a collecting expedition. Our gear consisted of a quart Mason jar, the kind my mother and grandmother filled with tomatoes, pickles, or green beans. At the edge of the pond, Dad knelt and filled the jar half full of water, scooping up some decaying tree leaves that had collected in a cow's footprint in the mud. I was a bit baffled but unimpressed. What could possibly be interesting about a canning jar of mud and pond water and rotten leaves? We stayed a few minutes, hoping to see the muskrat come out of his hole at the water's edge, the remains of his dinner scattered in front, but he was sleeping in. As we returned to the house, I asked about the jar, and Dad said

cryptically, "Wait and see." He loved to surprise me.

Back at the house, Dad carefully took down a wooden case from its place on a shelf in his basement workshop. From it, he removed a microscope, the first such device I had ever seen. He had been given it by his own father when a teenager, but his keen hopes of studying to become a scientist were swallowed in the abyss of the Great Depression. Showing me how it worked, Dad placed a drop of the pond water on a slide, deftly tipped a coverslip on top, and placed the slide on the stage of the scope. After adjusting the focus a bit, he invited me to have a look. I could scarcely believe my eyes. The water drop was teeming with tiny creatures of many kinds, all appearing to have been blown from tinted glass.

My hands were clumsy at first, but I soon got the hang of moving the slide around to follow the course of one protozoan — move the slide left and the image moved right, "up" meant "down" — it required some practice. Then I saw the stentor. A giant among protozoans, this ciliate is shaped like a large funnel. It had attached itself by the narrow end to a bit of rotten leaf, and a circle of beating cilia around the wide end created a current that drew tiny prey into its gullet. Details of the stentor's internal structure were clearly visible because it is transparent, and this one was blue, my favorite color! I watched the stentor for an hour or more that day, and in the 37 years that have passed between then and now, I've spent as much time as possible peering into microscopes and otherwise observing, reading, and writing about the myriad manifestations of life on our planet.

In due course, I became a biologist and teacher. I have been fortunate to meet many brilliant people along the way, from whom I have managed to learn a little. I have also been lucky to travel and do fieldwork in my favorite part of the world, the southeastern United States. A rich tapestry of life is spread before us here, even yet, despite the encroachment of concrete and asphalt.

Yet no discovery can match the thrill of first peering through the eyepiece at a world of wonder in a drop of pond water, seeing creatures as seemingly alien as a stentor, crafted delicately as if from cobalt glass. A dazzling reef aquarium is yet another window on worlds long hidden from human eyes. In this book, I hope to share with you my lifelong obsession with nature's ebullience.

For me, it started with a drop of pond water and someone who took the time to help me see it. Thanks, Dad.

— *John H. Tullock*
Knoxville, Tennessee

Introduction

The "Natural" Aquarium

*A Personal Journey and a New Approach to
Captive Reef Keeping*

THE HUSTLE AND GLARE OF MIAMI faded quickly behind us. We were headed south, beyond the reach of the Florida Turnpike, stopping only briefly in the farming town of Florida City for gas and produce. I marveled that the tomatoes, vine ripe in early May, tasted no better than those trucked to the grocery shelves back home in Tennessee. Rolling south on A1A, we crossed the bridge over Card Sound and were in the Keys. Dense tangles of mangroves edged the road, osprey nests perched on the tops of telephone poles, the ocean was visible on either side of us. We were barely two miles from the mainland and life was different already.

The Florida Keys stretch from Biscayne Bay, curving south and west nearly 400 miles to terminate in the uninhabited Dry Tortugas. About

**Florida Keys reef scene with gorgonians, sponges, and a Rock Beauty Angel
(*Holacanthus tricolor*). Top: Hawaiian Potter's Angel (*Centropyge potteri*).**

midway along this thread of coral rock outcrops — with the Gulf of Mexico on our right and the Atlantic Ocean barely 50 yards to our left — lies the old Seven Mile Bridge. This motorway bridge, built on the trestle after the original railroad bridge was destroyed in the great hurricane of 1935, spans the broad, shallow channel that separates the Upper and Lower Keys. At the northern end is the town of Marathon; to the south lies Big Pine Key. And smack under the middle of the Seven Mile Bridge is Pigeon Key. This dot, scarcely two acres in size, held our destination, the University of Miami marine laboratory.

The dozen or so white clapboard buildings scattered about the island had been constructed as barracks for the crew that built the railroad in the early 1900s. I arrived there that day in 1977 with 20 other students, a couple of graduate assistants, and Dr. Sue Reichert, Professor of Zoology at the University of Tennessee. The course was Invertebrate Zoology. I hardly suspected that my dormant fascination with the sea and its creatures would waken to shape my future. The expanse of coral rock dotted with Australian pines, with the sea visible from every direction, held for me then nothing more exciting than the anticipated week of field work requisite for completion of the course.

Our accommodations could charitably be called "basic." The barracks, built of whitewashed wood and elevated a few feet off the coral rubble, had a porch at each end. Bedrooms with military-style cots and bunk beds flanked the central hallway. Bathroom facilities were unisex. My colleagues and I avoided most difficulties that might have arisen from these arrangements by showering in two shifts, according to gender. Other minor details of coed living were dealt with by signs left there by generations of students before us. Identical 3x5 cards above each sink said, "Rinse sink or don't shave." The door to the water closet was marked in capital letters on the peeling paint: "KNOCK FIRST, DAMN IT!" Another sign was posted in the hallway by the back door of our barracks, next to the pay phone: "On July 12, 1857, this structure received the distinction of being the first building in North America to be condemned."

The ramshackle nature of Pigeon Key's fading physical plant enhanced the feeling that the Keys were a rustic wilderness not yet invaded by the

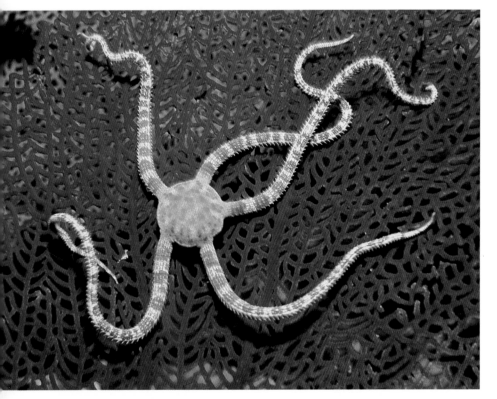

Ruby Brittle Star (*Ophioderma rubicundum*), a nocturnal scavenger and desirable aquarium species, draped over a sea fan on a Cayman Islands fore reef.

hordes of tourists that thronged to Orlando and Miami. This string of islands, thrusting out from the tip of the Florida peninsula like a giant sense organ extended to sample the warm waters to the south, is as rich in history as it is in subtropical flora and fauna. Pirates, gunrunners, and dope smugglers, who in succession had plied the Straits of Florida, all had left their marks on the local culture. There were seedy little taverns near the docks in Marathon full of old sailors: brown leather faces, gray stubble, and endless talk of Cuba or fishing or how America had gone to hell since Ike left office.

On my first night at Pigeon Key, I wandered alone down to the Gulf side with a flashlight. Wading out into the warm, virtually motionless water, I played the light back and forth across the bottom, anticipating nothing in particular. The clear water and pale-colored coral rock on the floor of the lagoon made visibility perfect. Brittle stars slithered away from the light, quintets of arm-legs flailing like Marine recruits belly-crawling under barbed wire and live fire. Eyes shone back at me from dark recesses. Snapping shrimps fired warning shots, audible even above the surface. And in a patch of *Caulerpa*, the largest sea slug I had ever seen undulated along. It was too busy eating seaweed to take notice of the terrestrial creature in tennis shoes towering above it. It was a sea hare, *Aplysia*, a close relative of the sea slug *Tridachia*. To find such a fascinating creature at the water's edge, almost without a search, crystallized my desire to make this path of graduate study successful. I resolved, standing there in the Gulf of Mexico in the middle of the night, that this warm, shallow sea would give up at least a few of its secrets to my inquisitions.

Thinking I would take this first discovery up to the lab and put it in one of the water tables for closer observation, I scooped up the sea hare in my right hand. At once, a lurid shade of purple ink emerged from its body, trickled between my fingers, and ran down my arm and onto my swim

The ink-spewing Spotted Sea Hare (*Aplysia dactylomela*), a species encountered by the author at Pigeon Key, Florida.

trunks. Startled, I dropped the creature into the sea. The secretion, I later learned, is thought to create an olfactory smoke screen to thwart the efforts of predators who hunt the sea hare by smell at night. At the time, for all I knew it would raise blisters on my skin. Fearing the worst, I splashed around frantically, trying to wash the ink away. At length, satisfied that the purple dye was harmless, I mused that this response from the sea hare had been quite effective in deterring me from interrupting its evening meal. The ink, which had for millions of years protected generations of sea hares from predators, would perhaps protect it from the ultimate predator — man.

Soaking wet, I waded back to shore and headed for the lab. Over the water table was another of Pigeon Key's ubiquitous signs: "No *Aplysia* in water table. Ink gums up filters." I had so much to learn.

The days and nights spent snorkeling, wading, and collecting marine life in the waters around Pigeon Key re-

A large Volitans Lionfish (*Pterois volitans*) hovers over a Pacific reef. Voracious predators like lionfishes are poor choices for reef aquariums with smaller fishes.

onfish that had rapidly grown from a 2-inch baby to a foot-long eating machine and who demonstrated no inclination toward a slowing of its growth rate. Partly because the food bill for this fish was beginning to tax my meager stipend from the university, I gave him to a dentist who had a much bigger tank and presumably a better income. Sultan was replaced by a collection of invertebrates, macroalgae, and rocks collected in the Keys. Over the next ten years, I would make many more visits to Pigeon Key. Each time, I came back with new specimens and new ideas for my aquarium. Looking back, I consider this to have been my first "reef tank," because the goal of its design was to duplicate the natural habitat I had observed in Florida.

warded me repeatedly with new insights about the marine environment. For one, it was apparent that even as small an outcrop as Pigeon Key was encircled by distinct ecological zones. Marine organisms from one area were seldom found in the other. I would go out into the ocean and collect specimens from a certain spot until I had filled two buckets, returning to the lab to empty the contents into their own aquarium or water table. I soon began attempting to arrange each aquarium to mimic what I had seen in the ocean just beyond the door. It wasn't long before it occurred to me to try to take home one of these collections and rework my marine aquarium to reflect what I had seen at Pigeon Key.

Like other aquarium hobbyists in the '70s, my marine tank consisted of dead bleached coral skeletons and large, showy fish. Its main attraction was "Sultan," a Volitans Li-

A REEF TANK IS A DISPLAY of tropical marine invertebrates and, often, fishes that approximates the appearance of a small section of natural coral reef habitat. It is arranged according to its creator's intent to achieve an aesthetically pleasing effect, and its development and management involve both art and science. I will try to provide the science in the chapters on technique that follow. To create art, however, requires an understanding of the reef environment on a level that goes beyond the technical specifications for the life-support system. The art expressed by a reef tank, like that of a Japanese tea garden, results from the juxtaposition of living and nonliving elements in an

A colony of Red Vase or Cup Sponges on a Florida reef above a profusion of macroalgaes growing on a rocky substrate.

arrangement that imitates nature, but fits into an unnaturally small space. When the gardener is successful, the observer is unaware of the confinement, and the view seems as encompassing as a mountain vista. Similarly, aquariums are not real ecosystems; by definition an aquarium is an artificial creation. Yet when thoughtfully executed by an aquarist mindful of ecological relationships, a reef tank deceives the eye into believing it is looking through a window to the sea, teeming with life and awash in color and flowing movement.

Unfortunately, marine aquariums, even large public displays created at great expense, are often anything but naturalistic. Big fishes, displayed in population densities that test the limits of elaborate filtration systems, against a backdrop of bleached coral and uniform, shiny white gravel, are still around, indeed are often showcased, in hotel lobbies and doctors' waiting rooms. Such aquariums no more resemble a coral reef habitat than a florist's arrangement of *Anthuriums* resembles a Hawaiian rain forest. Sometimes, especially in public aquariums, an effort is made to make the exhibit appear more "natural" by replacing dead coral skeletons with plastic reproductions dyed to approximate, with varying degrees of success, the colors of living corals.

In fairness, I acknowledge that a few public aquariums are beginning to craft exhibits with living invertebrates and seaweeds. Dr. Bruce Carlson's stony coral exhibits at the Waikiki Aquarium come to mind, and a similar exhibit for the National Aquarium in Baltimore is planned. Though impressive from the standpoint of sheer size, the best efforts of most public aquariums — if the goal is to create a visually appealing display that reflects some aspect of reef ecology — are easily outdone by the majority of home hobbyists whose reef tanks I have observed.

Perhaps the benefits of the natural approach to aquarium keeping will be revealed to the public aquarium community as successful exhibits, such as those at Waikiki and Baltimore, are discussed at scientific meetings and in the literature. Given that one benefit of the natural approach can be significant maintenance-cost savings, when compared to traditional methods, these natural techniques may continue to win converts.

Philosophy of the "Natural" Aquarium

My approach to keeping marine organisms in captivity emphasizes the duplication of nature in as many details as possible. First and foremost, providing a physical and chemical environment closely similar to that found in nature is essential if coral reef organisms are to remain alive for any length of time. In this sense, any aquarium must duplicate nature to a certain degree. My methods attempt to go further than this, seeking to duplicate the *biological* environment found on a real coral reef. This might at first seem like a difficult task, but it can actually be done rather easily, if one will pay attention to what is known about the biology of the organisms that inhabit the aquarium.

The existence of coral reefs has been known for centuries, but not until the development of scuba diving methods did we really begin to learn very much about them and the organisms they harbor.

Reefs develop only in areas of the ocean where specific conditions prevail. Light, in particular, must reach the coral organisms, because all reef-building corals harbor photosynthetic, symbiotic algae. Thus reefs form only where water clarity is sufficient to allow adequate light penetration. Sediments, usually transported from the coastline by rivers, not only reduce light penetration but also can smother and destroy coral growths. Clear, sediment-free water is the primary geological requirement for the development of coral reefs. To a lesser extent, salinity, temperature, the availability of nutrients, water movement, and underwater topography all play a role.

A well-established natural reef aquarium microhabitat displaying a diversity of soft, stony, and encrusting corals growing on a realistic jumble of Pacific live rock.

were not continually held in check).

"As far as the corals themselves are concerned, each species has its own array of growth strategies, food requirements, and reproductive capacities. Each has its own response to disruption by storms or predators, diseases and plagues. Each species competes with others for space, light, and other resources. The net result of all these interactions and balances . . . is to make coral communities among the most diverse of any communities on earth."

UNDERSTANDING THAT such a complex web of ecological interactions exists on the reef helps to explain why specific conditions have to be met in the aquarium before reef species will survive. Many of the species of marine invertebrates that are offered for sale in aquarium shops do not actually come from coral reefs proper. Some species, such as Open Brain Coral (*Trachyphyllia geoffroyi*), occur shoreward of the reef in the quieter, more nutrient-laden waters of the lagoon. Tolerant species like this can be included in an aquarium designed to duplicate that inshore habitat.

We must accept the fact that we cannot recreate the ocean in our living rooms. The best we can hope for is a representation, a display of species that are characteristic of a tiny portion of the ocean realm — a microhabitat. Creating a microhabitat display for invertebrates is a project with a higher chance of success than doing the same for most fishes. This is because fishes move around, and habitat types overlap, while invertebrates by and large remain fixed in place and often occupy a rather limited range of habitat types.

Reefs have developed, generally speaking, only in the Tropics, because of optimal temperatures, and primarily on the eastern coasts of the continents, because of the effects of prevailing currents on water temperature and clarity.

While the geographic distribution of reefs is due mostly to local physical conditions, the biological structure of the reef ecosystem is the result of factors that students of the reef have only begun to elucidate. As the noted coral biologist J.E.N. Veron has explained:

"This diversity can only exist after a series of ecological balances is achieved: not only balances between the corals themselves, but between the corals and other organisms, including predators and parasites, and also between other organisms that have little to do with corals directly, such as the balance between herbivorous fish and macroalgae (the latter would rapidly overgrow most coral communities if it

There are three major features of my approach to keeping "microhabitat displays" of tropical shallow-water invertebrate species. The first of these I will call "less technology, more biology." The husbandry of marine life must be performed in light of the specific ecological needs of the species of interest. Granted, system design cannot be overlooked, but one must begin the thinking process about any aquarium by asking questions about the needs of the species that will occupy it. This principle is easily illustrated. An understanding that most tropical cnidarians (formerly known as coelenterates) require intense, wide-spectrum lighting as an energy source for their symbiotic zooxanthellae made it possible to keep these species alive in aquariums. In the past, hobbyists were told that anemones, for example, needed everything from carbon filtration to trace element supplements to survive, when what they actually were missing in the aquarium environment was appropriate light.

One of my favorite analogies is the comparison between a tankful of marine invertebrates and a flower box full of terrestrial plants. I am an avid gardener. Those familiar with gardening literature know that when one opens the pages of *Horticulture* or *National Gardening* one is not likely to see articles about the latest advances in the design of rototillers or greenhouse heaters. What one finds is articles about plants. The priority in gardening is responsiveness to the needs of the plants, not the needs of the gardener. More of this kind of thinking would benefit the aquarium hobby.

Reef tanks established by the "natural" methods outlined in this book are the most successful, easiest to maintain, and most likely to provide what species need to complete their life cycles. The common features of such aquariums are: 1) ample quantities of "live rock" and "live sand"; 2) high-intensity, broad-spectrum lighting; 3) filtration

A thriving reef aquarium: bringing us face-to-face with the living beauty of tropical marine fishes, corals, and invertebrates.

equipment that focuses on removal of organic wastes rather than mineralization of them; 4) husbandry efforts focused upon limiting quantities of inorganic nutrient ions, while insuring a supply of other inorganic ions in concentrations that match or exceed those found in the ocean; 5) replication of the physical characteristics of the microhabitat, in terms of substrate type, current patterns, diel cycles, and temperature; and 6) attention to the specific community relationships of the species housed together in the same aquarium. In other words, one must try to copy Mother Nature.

Not all technology is undesirable, of course. One would be foolish to reject it entirely. The challenge is to learn to apply the required technology with finesse. One of the best new advances is in the area of more accurate measurements of the aquarium's physical and chemical parameters. Electronic meters have begun to supplant color-change test kits for the measurement of pH, for example, because such instruments are faster, more accurate, and easier to read. This is an example of an appropriate application of technology to aquarium management.

On the other hand, one cannot reduce the dynamics of an ecosystem, even the small and relatively uncomplicated ecosystem of an aquarium, to a table of numerical parameters. The aquarist who nods in satisfaction at a correct pH reading or a high redox potential, yet fails to heed the message conveyed by a disintegrating gorgonian or a *Xenia* that has stopped its rhythmic pulsations, is missing the point altogether. The natural approach requires you to become an observer of nature, not of digital readouts.

The result will be an aquarium that is realistic, with healthier, more colorful animals that survive better than their counterparts in traditional tanks. In addition, the abandonment of technical props that were once thought to be essential components of the "filtration system" can result in significant cost savings. By following the natural approach, one can dispense with wet/dry filters, ultraviolet sterilizers,

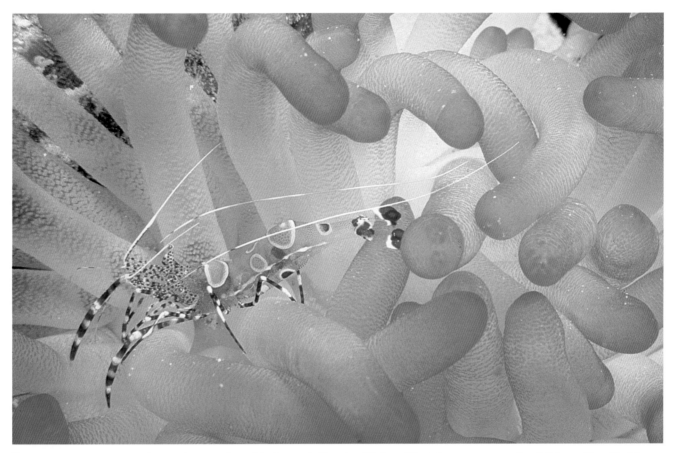

Fascinating interspecies relationships, such as this Spotted Cleaning Shrimp (*Periclimenes yucatanicus*) living with a Florida Pink-tipped Anemone (*Condylactis gigantea*), can be observed in a well-planned and properly stocked natural reef aquarium.

ozonizers and redox controllers, reaction chambers, artificial media to remove nitrate, phosphate, silicate, and other ions, denitrators, and a host of other expensive paraphernalia. The equipment one does require — lighting, pumps, protein skimmers — is uncomplicated in design and straightforward to operate. The essential biological elements — live rock and live sand — are interesting in their own right and add to the aquarium a touch of realism that artificial decorations or the skeletons of dead corals cannot convey.

The second major feature of the natural approach is reliance upon an understanding of biology. The ecological relationships among species and between individuals and their habitats are most easily expressed in the terminology of biology. The language of science lends great precision to discussions and helps to make sense of the bewildering diversity of marine life and marine habitats. I was educated as a scientist, and I will use many scientific terms in the pages that follow. I have attempted to explain unfamiliar terms where appropriate.

Having said all this, I nevertheless agree with Stephen Spotte's assertion (1992): "Science alone has little practical application, and works dealing strictly with technology omit information necessary to foster understanding." Maintaining reef aquarium displays owes much to the application of science. However, we must not ignore the importance of circumstantial or anecdotal information concerning organisms and their behavior in the aquarium. Most of these observations will have been made by nonscientists, but this does not imply that the information is not useful to those who desire to own a reef aquarium and who hope to profit from the experience of others. One should never be too quick to accept the testimony of observers as gospel. On the other hand, these observations, if carefully made and offered up with an honest intent to convey helpful information, are every bit as useful as those of professional scientists.

I feel strongly that amateur aquarists have important contributions to make concerning mankind's knowledge of the intricacies of coral reef ecology, and that the efforts of dedicated hobbyists should be encouraged by professional marine biologists. Aquarists who share this view must make an effort to learn the lingo, however. The reward for this effort is freedom from the depredations of gimmick promoters and snake-oil salesmen who sometimes enrich themselves at the expense of the hobbyist. Access to information is the surest defense against useless products and false claims.

The last feature of my approach is perhaps the most important one to the future of our hobby. The development of techniques for keeping an ever-widening variety of marine life in home aquariums has fostered an awareness of the marvelous richness, diversity, and beauty of the marine realm, even among those who are not themselves aquarium owners. Reef tanks are often displayed prominently, in the living room, for instance, in their owner's homes. As a result, large numbers of "ordinary" people — friends and relatives of the aquarist, primarily — have the opportunity to examine, say, a *Tridacna maxima* giant clam face-to-face.

Without aquariums, the vast majority of people would never see coral reefs up close, except on television. In their quest for large audiences, television producers spend a lot of time and videotape on sharks and other large, spectacular sea creatures. Rarely does television present us with the delicate beauty of an anemone or allow us to glimpse the daily life of the cleaning shrimp that lives among the anemone's tentacles. Naturally, being able to experience reef creatures in a way that not even the best television documentary can duplicate influences how people who view reef aquariums think about coral reefs. This awareness, in turn, increases the desire to see reef resources preserved and protected.

I see some interesting parallels between reef aquarists, divers, and other nature enthusiasts of today with their counterparts of a hundred years ago. Nature study was a popular pastime among our Victorian ancestors. The microscope was their primary tool for investigating the natural world. The structure of an organism, in that it was considered to reflect the precise, clockworklike design of a Divine Plan, was their primary interest. Today, the aquarium has become a tool that permits even an urban apartment dweller to investigate nature. A reef tank is as affordable for many Americans as a good microscope was for Victorian ladies and gentlemen. We, however, are less interested in how organisms are constructed than in their relationships with each other.

When we create these miniature worlds encased in glass or acrylic, we are not seeking to affirm the presence of a greater power (although such affirmation is a commonplace reaction of spiritually inclined aquarists). Rather, by observing the day-to-day existence and interactions of creatures that are like us in so many ways, and yet so startlingly different, we are attempting to comprehend our place in a universe that is proving to be more chaotic, complex, and awe-inspiring than anything the Victorians could ever have imagined.

Chapter One

"Less Technology, More Biology"

The Challenge of Aquarium Keeping:
An Evolution of Equipment, Styles, and Approaches

ONE REASSURING FACT about a marine aquarium is that the constituents and characteristics of seawater that are of importance to invertebrates and fishes are, for the most part, constant throughout the ocean. Although physical parameters such as temperature, dissolved oxygen, and the degree of water movement may vary geographically, or even on opposite sides of a reef crest, the basic medium, seawater, is the same everywhere, or at least everywhere from which one might wish to procure specimens for display in a home aquarium.

Consider how this contrasts with the situation for the freshwater aquarist, who must decide what sort of water he will work with: An Amazonian tank needs soft, acid water and a deep substrate of gravel and sand to provide root space for several species of *Echinodorus* and *Vallisneria*. A tangle of driftwood offers shelter to a school of Cardinal Tetras. How dissimilar is the Rift Lake aquarium with its hard, alkaline water. Limestone forms a labyrinth of caves, each carefully guarded by one of the *mbuna*, the rock-dwelling cichlids of Lake Malawi, that are at home in this habitat. On the upper surfaces of the rocks where strong light plays,

Marine aquarium keeping in the Victorian style: minimal technology but notoriously poor survival rates for livestock.

green filamentous algae grows so abundantly as to maintain itself despite continuous cropping by the fish. Otherwise, no plants can grow. Duplicating either of these environments requires recreating sharply contrasting sets of water chemistry. Duplicating any portion of the marine environment does not. Why, then, does the general impression linger that marine aquarium keeping is such a difficult proposition? Only some of the reasons have to do with the peculiar characteristics of the marine environment. In part, the explanation lies in how marine aquarium keeping has evolved historically.

Early Aquariums

ANCIENT HUMANS probably first kept sea creatures alive in captivity as a means of having fresh seafood close at hand. Fish and invertebrates have been held in various containers for purposes of study or exhibition for centuries. According to Sterba (1983), there are accounts dating back to ancient Egypt. In Rome, fish-holding tubs called *piscinae* have been found in the gardens of the wealthy and powerful. In the New World, containers for both fresh and marine fish adorned Montezuma's gardens. In China, fishkeeping dates to the tenth century.

Everything a natural aquarium is not: a traditional marine tank with too many fishes, no invertebrates, and decorated with dead coral skeletons and plastic plants.

though not as the system of choice for maintaining a diverse ecosystem of coral reef invertebrates. Any aquarium with with a high-density fish population, whether it be a decoration behind the desk at a plush hotel, such as the giant tank at The Mirage in Las Vegas, Nevada, or a multi-tank holding system, such as the live inventory area at my place of business, can be operated with an efficient mineralization or biological filter system. Regular partial water changes of about 20% per month must be carried out, and organic matter must be reduced through the use of activated carbon filtration and, ideally, protein skimming. With proper hygiene and feeding, many fishes can thrive in such a

The Saltwater Aquarium in the Home was the title of a popular little book written in 1959 by the late Robert Straughan, and it marks for us the first attempt to offer suggestions for maintaining a marine aquarium to hobbyists in the United States. Home marine aquariums first became a possibility for the average consumer when the utility of biological filtration, the conversion of ammonia to nitrate via beneficial bacteria, was recognized. Although biological filtration occurs in any aquarium as a result of microorganisms growing on the glass, plants, substrate, and all other surfaces that receive sufficient oxygen, the first device used in an attempt to optimize this process was the undergravel filter. This simple filter can still be used successfully on marine systems for fish and hardy invertebrates.

"Mineralization filters," a term I use to refer to any aquarium filtration system that relies primarily on optimization of biological filtration, have abundant uses, al-

system, but for more demanding species, better methods are required. Fortunately, many advances in marine aquarium filtration have come about in recent years as hobbyists have surged beyond fish-only systems into the challenging world of reef aquarium keeping.

From Fishes to Reefs

IN THE EARLIEST DAYS of marine aquariums in the United States, the business was driven by fish. Not that fish are an unimportant part of any aquarium business, but with marine fish, it was different. Emperor Angels, Clown Triggers, Naso Tangs, all big, boldly colored fish that came from halfway around the world were suddenly appearing, and they sold themselves. Dealers offered what collectors shipped to them, and all were housed in aquariums fitted with undergravel filters and decorated with dead coral skeletons. Crinkly blue florist's foil was the most familiar backdrop. Such eerie, dimly lit aquariums drew inspiration from nature only in the sense that an art-deco table lamp might be molded after a lily bloom.

Hobbyists purchased what was available for sale. On rare occasions, interesting little blennies, strange invertebrates, or a piece of living seaweed would find its way into a shop. In my case, I lived in a small city. Only one shop stocked marine species, and few other local customers shared my interest in occasionally seen curiosities such as a colony of zoanthids. Not until new equipment gave dealers something to sell along with the animals did interest in the business of selling marine invertebrates begin to affect the offerings in holding tanks.

Over the last ten years, marine aquarium keeping has had its horizons expanded many times over. Life forms available to aquarists now come from a tremendous range of geographic locations and an even wider variety of microhabitats. New understanding makes maintenance of appropriate conditions less hit-or-miss. Because of new capabilities, marine tanks have become more than mere displays of fishes. We have moved into the realm of creating a tiny segment of a specific biotope in the aquarium, complete with a cross section of appropriate, diverse life forms. What was once called a "reef tank" or "minireef" can now begin to qualify as a "reef biotope" aquarium, as we are now better able to build realistic habitats rather than throwing together species that would never, ever meet in nature.

Several methods or "styles," more or less standardized ways of establishing and maintaining biotope aquariums, have evolved over the past decade. The goal of each style is the same: to maintain an artificial community of organisms, mimicking in as many details as possible a natural community in a closed aquarium system. The details of each style differ, although they all share certain features. I identify each by the location in which it originated. Thus, the aquarium may be Dutch-style, Berlin-style, Smithsonian-style, Monaco-style, or a hybrid combining elements of several styles.

The Traditional Aquarium

FOR DECADES, THE QUINTESSENTIAL AQUARIUM system for both freshwater and marine hobbyists in North America has been based on submerged, aerobic filtration using internal or external mechanical filters and/or the undergravel filter. Oxygenated aquarium water flows continually through these filters, and biological activity occurs in the filter media or the gravel. Early versions relied on airstones to lift and circulate water, while most contemporary equipment is powered by compact water pumps or powerheads. Such filters are simple and workable for lightly stocked aquariums, but, unless carefully maintained, are prone to clogging with detritus and sometimes dramatic fluctuations of water quality when cleaning sessions remove or disrupt the colonies of beneficial bacteria in the media.

The Dutch-Style Aquarium

I CALL SYSTEMS featuring a trickle or wet/dry filter Dutch-style aquariums, and there is no doubt that these relatively complex setups ushered in a revolution in marine husbandry. The introduction by Dutch proponent George Smit of the "wet/dry" filter, adapted from wastewater treatment technology, resulted in a new wave of interest in minireef aquarium keeping. This new filter system was much more efficient than the undergravel filter and bypassed many of the former system's drawbacks (Smit, 1986a, 1986b). The filter media, kept wet but elevated above the water level of a sump, could support large populations of nitrifying bacteria that seldom or never had to be disturbed by cleaning sessions. The trickling flow of water provided an excellent situation for gas exchange and oxygenation of the system water. The Dutch method also relied largely upon fluorescent lamps as a light source and frequently employed additional techniques, such as ozonization, to cope with organic matter.

Unfortunately, wet/dry filter systems relied on exactly the same biological approach as the old undergravel models: mineralization of nitrogenous wastes through bacterial activity. This eliminates problems with ammonia toxicity, but creates a new set of problems related to accumulation of nitrate and reduction of pH due to the generation of hydrogen ions. Fish are not particularly sensitive to nitrate, even in high concentrations, and their osmoregulatory systems can function over a range of pH. As long as marine aquariums were constructed of artificial materials and stocked only with an appropriate assortment of fishes, water chemistry resulting from biological activity could be satisfactorily maintained with an undergravel filter and a program of regular partial water changes. When invertebrates and seaweeds were included, however, only the hardiest species — hermit crabs, sea urchins, and predatory starfish, to name some popular examples — could survive for long, unless the system was built along the lines described by Smit. His success was attributed to the supposed improvements embodied by the wet/dry filter. Smit's aquariums were beautiful displays of invertebrates, with much live rock and abundant macroalgae growth. Owing to the presence of these important factors, they sustained diverse communities of organisms, perhaps despite their utilization of the wet/dry system.

Smit's original designs were marketed in the United States by International Seaboard, in Cicero, Illinois. In 1987, my partner, J.R. Shute, and I made the eight-hour trek to Chicago to visit the factory and see Smit's aquariums for ourselves. We had just begun a tiny business called Aquatic Specialists and were interested in bringing this

COMPONENTS OF A BERLIN-STYLE AQUARIUM

1. Biological filtration and denitrification is accomplished by the use of a large quantity of cured live rock.

2. Chemical filtration is accomplished through the use of a protein skimmer and activated carbon.

3. Lighting is usually accomplished with metal halide lamps, in combination with blue (actinic) fluorescent lamps.

4. Nothing in the way of organic nutrients is added to the tank, except for feedings for the fish, and inorganic nutrients are limited by using phosphate-free water and sea salt mixes.

5. Limewater, as well as strontium and iodine supplements, are regularly added, with pH, alkalinity and calcium concentration being monitored by testing. In practice, limewater or Kalkwasser is added daily to replenish all evaporated water.

new technology to our customers. We had read Smit's articles, too, and we thought that new opportunities might be opening for our business. We enjoyed meeting Smit and his corporate sales people. We bought a poorly made filter, possibly a factory prototype, and some less than satisfactory European-made fluorescent end caps, and brought them back to Tennessee. We spent about $300, as I recall. Looking back, I can admit to myself that Smit's tanks looked pretty much like the ones I had been doing for the last several years. The only difference was that mine were stocked with Florida Keys inshore species I had collected myself or purchased from collectors I met in Florida. Smit's aquariums had a variety of Indo-Pacific invertebrates. In retrospect, J.R. and I were a couple of rubes, accepting the idea that the filter was the key to success, paying out our money and refusing to accept the evidence of our own experience — that our aquariums were doing just fine the way they were.

The Berlin-Style Aquarium

IN THE 1970S, Peter Wilkens, working in Germany, was approaching aquarium design from a different angle. His systems relied on live rock for biological filtration and denitrification; there was no undergravel or wet/dry filter at all. Organic matter was removed by protein skimming and activated carbon.

Recognizing that calcification was a fundamental life process for the stony corals that were the focus of his interest, Wilkens also advocated the use of limewater additions for maintenance of pH, alkalinity, and calcium concentration. Wilkens was perhaps influenced by the work of Lee Eng in Indonesia, 20 years before, who created "miniature reef" aquariums based on live rock, with only an airstone for water circulation. Eng collected all of his live rock, specimens, water, and natural foods near his home. His aquariums were pictured in the popular literature of the time, but the details of his methods were sketchy; he kept few notes and published little. Peter Wilkens, on the other hand, made accurate measurements, kept copious records, and published his findings in the European and American aquarium literature. His work has been expanded upon and disseminated through the efforts of many people, including, most notably, Alf J. Nilsen in Norway, Charles Delbeek in Canada, and Julian Sprung in the United States. Today, the Berlin method and variations on the live rock theme are the most widely used approaches to the creation of closed-system aquariums for diverse communities of both invertebrates and fishes.

A wonderful example of a successful Berlin-style aquarium, with spreading groups of mushroom anemones and many healthy large-polyped stony corals.

The Smithsonian-Style Aquarium

TO MAINTAIN AQUARIUM water that is low in nutrient compounds, Dr. Walter Adey of the Smithsonian Institution places heavy emphasis on the role of specially cultivated "turfs" composed of various species of algae (Adey and Loveland, 1991). This is commonly known as the Algal Turf-Scrubber approach, and it is currently more common in institutional aquarium installations than in the hobbyist world. Periodic harvesting of a portion of the algae growth serves to export accumulated wastes. In other words, such systems rely heavily upon encouraging the assimilation process.

A stunning live rock and live sand reef system created by Karl Coyne exhibits a minimal fish load and dense stocking of many types of soft and stony corals.

ing available, and they have enthusiastic advocates as well as equally vocal detractors. The latter argue that the large population of algae present in these systems leach significant amounts of terpenoids and other compounds, causing yellowing of the water and — it has been argued — poor survival of stony corals.

The Monaco-Style Aquarium

THIS APPROACH has been closely investigated by Dr. Jean Jaubert at the national aquarium of Monaco, world-renowned for its displays of captive corals and its coral biology research. Its immediate appeal is the prevention of an accumulation of nitrate in the system by enhancing natural denitrification. (Various "denitrifying filters" have been developed and marketed over the years but have failed to gain wide acceptance because they typically require careful monitoring and supplemental feeding for the anaerobic bacteria. A recent version employs electronic-control technology to monitor and adjust critical parameters. Hobbyists report that these units, though expensive, do lower nitrate concentration to near zero.)

Adey's systems also use natural live rock, natural seawater, and natural plankton.

A very interesting point is Adey's contention that centrifugal pumps, almost universally used by hobbyists, are very destructive to microorganisms in the aquarium. The destruction of larvae by these pumps, he suggests, is one reason why instances of reproduction by aquarium invertebrates are seldom reported. The Smithsonian system employs modified pumps that work like bellows or syringes, drawing up water by suction and then expelling it in the desired direction of flow. These pumps, along with the natural seawater and wild-caught plankton Adey uses, are outside the easy reach of the average hobbyist. (Simple suggestions for encouraging the survival of invertebrate larvae are discussed in Chapter Thirteen.)

Algal turf scrubbers for home systems are now becom-

The Jaubert, or Monaco, method of using live sand does the same thing but with a minimum of expense and virtually no maintenance. As described by Dr. Jaubert, a thick layer of aragonite (a more soluble form of $CaCO_3$ than calcite) sand is seeded with a layer of live sand from the ocean floor and supported above the aquarium bottom on a plastic grid. A plenum of anoxic water develops underneath the sand. Small organisms present in the live sand help to keep the substrate healthy, while denitrifying bacteria thrive in the low-to-zero oxygen conditions at the bottom.

It appears that this technique not only results in denitrification, but also that the dissolution of calcareous sand returns important ions — calcium and carbonate in particular — to the water. Jaubert reports extremely low levels of nitrate and phosphate, high levels of calcium and alkalinity, along with exceptionally fast coral growth rates, without the use of skimming, large water changes, or calcium additions.

The live sand approach is analogous to the Berlin method in that it relies on natural processes occurring in low-to-zero oxygen conditions, either within the rock or in the undisturbed sand bed. (Unlike an undergravel filter, there is no forced water flow through the live sand layer, but rather a very slow diffusion.)

Jaubert's work has been introduced to American aquarists by such authors as Tom Frakes, Charles Delbeek, Julian Sprung and Bob Goemans. Goemans, along with other hobbyists, has adapted Jaubert's methods to home aquariums with initially encouraging results.

A layer of plastic light-diffuser grid, commonly known as eggcrate in the electrical trade, is supported above the bare aquarium floor by sturdy, inert plastic spacers, such as PVC pipe sections. This creates a plenum, or water space, roughly 1 to 2 inches in depth. A layer of fiberglass or plastic screening is placed on top of the eggcrate and this is covered with a layer of aragonitic coral sand or gravel with particles ranging in size from about 1 to 3 mm.

This material may be procured from reef collectors as "live sand" or may start out as clean, dry aquarium sand and allowed to take on a life of its own. Jaubert places a second sheet of screening on the bottom layer of sand to prevent burrowing fishes and other organisms from disturbing the bacteria that will develop deep in the bed. A top layer of substrate — composed of aragonite sand, coral pebbles, shell fragments, or similar materials of reef origin — is added. If dry sand layers are used, the system is typically "inoculated" with desirable bacteria and other organisms found in wild reef substrates by mixing in a portion of live sand or allowing the organisms to migrate from healthy, recently collected live rock.

From this point, the aquarium is constructed along fairly conventional lines. Jaubert has employed powerful airstones to induce water movement. This style is more fully discussed in Chapter Three.

One of California coral breeder Steve Tyree's 180-gallon reefs: proof that previously unkeepable small-polyped stony corals can thrive in captive systems.

The Natural Style: A Euro-American Hybrid

COMBINING THE BEST of various reef aquarium techniques and approaches, a growing number of North American aquarists are reporting unprecedented success with reef organisms, including previously hard-to-keep corals. Typically, the new natural-style system incorporates live rock, a bed of live aragonite sand — with or without a plenum, strong, chaotic water movement, efficient protein skimming, and intense lighting.

Aquariums heavily stocked with growing corals and tridacnid clams also rely on limewater additions and/or the use of calcium reactors that extract calcium and other ions from aragonite sand in the presence of carbon dioxide. Several serious coral keepers have reported matching the known wild growth rates of *Acropora* in home systems, and many species of small-polyped scleractinian corals (also called stony corals) are now being propagated in aquariums with one variation or another of this natural approach.

Common Features of Captive Ecosystems

FRAKES (1994) COMPARED each of the methods discussed above and concluded, "Several methods have been shown to be successful with certain organisms when properly applied." Martin Moe[1] has pointed out to me that this is simply attributable to each approach providing an "adequate substitute" for the natural environment of the organisms that have been successfully maintained. The fact that these approaches all have drawbacks simply serves to demonstrate that man cannot create a perfect copy of a true ecosystem. But all types of captive ecosystems share common features. This universality of underlying principles applies not only to marine aquariums, but to freshwater aquariums and

[1] Personal communication.

various types of artificial terrestrial habitats as well.

As the marine side of the aquarium hobby returns to its roots through its current fascination for aquariums dominated by invertebrates, undoubtedly among the earliest of marine tank subjects, so has the freshwater hobby seen a resurgence of interest in the oldest kind of aquarium, the planted freshwater tank.

Aquarists have long known that vascular plants, while actively growing, remove pollutants from aquarium water. This is, in fact, the oldest form of aquarium "filtration." Displays of tropical fish were created during the Victorian era, for example, in enormous planted aquariums, long before the advent of the kinds of equipment so familiar to aquarists today. Dutch-style planted freshwater aquariums may have inspired the aquascapes of Smit's Dutch-style minireefs, with their lush growths of seaweeds.

Fifteen years ago, when the fish display with dead coral was the only type of marine aquarium most people had ever seen, I wrote about, and published photographs of, high-biodiversity marine aquariums featuring photosynthetic invertebrates, macroalgae, and live rock (e.g., Tullock, 1982). In particular, I emphasized the role of photosynthesis in maintaining the aquarium ecosystem and recommended high light intensities, about four times what was typically being used at the time. I offered, however, no new technical aid (apart from shoplights that could be bought at any hardware store) and certainly nothing as flashy as the wet/dry filter that Smit was to write about later. As a consequence, little note was taken of my work.

The early history of invertebrate aquarium keeping, at least in its manifestations as a new segment of the aquarium industry, is a history of escalating attempts to find a technical solution (wet/dry filters, redox controllers) to every

Natural reef tank with an impressive vertical grouping of leather corals (*Sarcophyton* sp.) propagated by cutting.

problem. In short, just as the marine business was driven by fish sales in the early days, in the last ten years it has been driven by sales of technology. And all the while, as Lee Eng in the '60s and I in the '80s had demonstrated, better results could be had more easily by facilitating, rather than attempting to constrain technically, the natural rhythms — chemical, physical, and biological — that evolve in the aquarium if suitable natural sources of microorganisms and small invertebrates are implanted. Lately, aquarists have welcomed this saner, more holistic approach.

To return to the question I posed earlier, why then does the general impression linger that marine aquarium keeping is such a difficult proposition? I suggest that too many would-be marine aquarists see only the artificial, big-fish, big-tank aquarium that many shops still offer as a "real" marine aquarium. Obtaining satisfaction from a system such as this can be both expensive and time-consuming. If a store sells "reef" systems, too often a costly, complicated array of equipment and technological aids, in the outmoded style of the '80s, is presented as the only way to achieve results. Sometimes, people are told to start with the "easier" under-gravel-filter "beginner's" system for fish. Later, they may "graduate" to the supposedly greater challenge of the reef tank. The truth is, a natural marine aquarium with a diverse community of organisms can be the least difficult sort of marine aquarium to maintain.

Richly populated reef system with a Rainford's Goby, one of many species that do best in established, natural systems.

The history of marine aquarium keeping in the United States can be divided into four general eras. An early, experimental era preceded the commercial era, during which better air-cargo service made marine fish widely accessible. When the introduction of the wet/dry filter ushered in the technological era, the business climate (these were the Reagan years, remember) was ripe for an explosion in the industry. New products, new ideas, and many new aquarium stores sprang up.

With some hobbyists and businesses, the high-tech era is still in full swing. An English hobbyist magazine recently featured an example of such a system (Dakin, 1995). The aquarium's owner, Rick Allen, had the 270-plus gallon tank custom-built and outfitted it with a sump, two trickle towers, three skimmers, two carbon reactors, two oxygen/ozone reactors, a denitrator, a chiller, two UV sterilizers, seven electronic test/control devices, two reserve vats (for a daily 2-gallon water change and automated evaporation replacement with RO water), four metal halide light fixtures, three 750 gph pumps and six powerheads! Water-quality data and stocking levels for this aquarium are also reported. Both are in the range of aquariums (mine and

Not a nuclear plant, just the full-tech approach to reef keeping: a schematic diagram of British aquarist Rick Allen's 270-gallon successful but expensive and heavily gear-dependent system.

those of others whom I have personally observed) maintained with simple, natural methods and scarcely any equipment. I'm not boasting, merely asserting that there is a better, simpler, and cheaper way. Dr. Paul Loiselle once quipped to me at a conference that some marine aquarium hobbyists appear to be afflicted with "acute apparatophilia!"

A new era of marine aquarium keeping has begun — the biological era. If the commercial era was driven by flashy fish and the technological age pushed by glittering acrylic boxes of colorful biomedia, the biological era will be propelled by the discovery that a host of beautiful marine species will not merely survive, but grow and reproduce, in home aquariums created through a variety of simple techniques. Not that technology has been consigned to the dustbin. Artificial lighting, temperature management, and water movement must all be supplied; equipment will continue to evolve to do this work better, more simply, and with greater energy efficiency.

What is really new is the notion that living organisms, with appropriate encouragement, actually create water conditions suitable for themselves and other species in the same ecosystem. Welcome to the new era.

Chapter Two

Systems: The Choices & the Basics

Planning and Equipping the Natural Marine Aquarium

BY BOTH TRAINING AND NATURAL INCLINATION, I am a taxonomist — a classifier and categorizer of living things. Accordingly, when faced with the challenge of trying to make a living in the aquarium business, one of my first responses was to categorize the various customers that came into our store and to focus my sales approach accordingly.

The fish business, if you will pardon the pun, is either sink or swim. If one enters this unique niche, one must use every resource to succeed, largely because the market is so specialized. My classifications of customers were rather arbitrary at first, but I came to realize that finding common traits allowed me to concentrate upon the needs and aspirations of each client. While each aquarium is as individual as its owner, I have found that there are three basic reasons people want to own aquariums. Understanding your own primary motivation for having a marine aquarium can make the process of planning and acquiring the system much less confusing or stressful.

A window to undersea life: a segment of Indo-Pacific shallow-reef habitat in the enhanced 20-gallon starter system described on pages 64-71. (Scarlet Cleaner Shrimp on Fiji live rock, with Fox Coral and *Pachyclavularia* colony, lower right.)

The Aquarium As Decoration

I VIVIDLY RECALL THE VISIT one Saturday of a gentleman of about 50, accompanied by a younger man, whom I later learned was both the gentleman's son and the person responsible for the interior design work on his father's residence. Sizing up the situation and instinctively zeroing in on the manager of the shop as his target, the older man strode right up to me. I was, at that moment, standing in front of our magnificent 135-gallon reef display tank. It had only recently received maintenance and the addition of some new specimens, and it looked marvelous that day. "How much to duplicate this in my living room?" he inquired. I told him. He didn't blink. "Will you come and maintain it for me?" Of course we could arrange for that. Dad did all the talking, only occasionally engaging in a whispered consultation with Son. He wanted this fish, that coral, and those anemones. He allowed a flicker of annoyance to show in his face when I suggested that predators and prey might not fare well in the same tank together. And at least one Purple Tang was a requirement, because the aquarium had to match the purple living room drapes. Accordingly, we structured the fish population around Purple Tangs.

Eventually, a beautiful reef tank was installed in this

The reef aquarium as architectural focal point: oak cabinetry housing a 270-gallon glass system created by Exotic Aquaria.

man's splendid mountain retreat. Everything, from the custom-built filtration and metal halide lighting systems enclosed in hardwood cabinets (done by the family carpenter) was of first-class quality. But it proved to be a disappointment. No one in the family wanted to take responsibility or even get their hands wet. Between weekly cleanings by the maintenance service, algae grew on the glass. Feeding the fish, once the owners learned that their diet must consist of more than flake foods tossed in every few days, became a hassle. There were repeated requests to rearrange the live rock to make the tank look "more artistic." The system was never allowed to develop its potential.

Less than two years later, it was all redone. The marine system was removed and a freshwater aquarium with plastic plants now occupies the space, augmenting a panoramic view of the Smoky Mountains. Why? Because the point in having the aquarium for this family was not to own a living reef, but rather to have a colorful, low-maintenance decoration for their living room. When it became apparent that the aquarium would require not only regular visits from the maintenance person, but also a degree of attention — and understanding — from its owners, the aquarium became less appealing, and, of course, considerable money was wasted.

My advice for readers of this book, then, is to ask yourself if you are looking solely for a decoration. While a natural marine aquarium can enhance any home, if your main interest is in the decorative aspect, I strongly urge you to hire a competent business to carry out the installation and maintenance. Be prepared to pay a handsome weekly, biweekly, or monthly fee for this service.

There is an old saying, "If you can't spend money, you must spend time." Most aquarists, of course, fully intend to care for their own aquariums, but it is vital to recognize the commitment that this represents and to plan for it. Undeniably, a natural marine aquarium can be a spectacular focal point for any room. The degree to which your efforts in caring for it are rewarded will be in large measure dictated by how carefully the theme of the aquarium is chosen. The simplified designs of the systems described in this book result in lowered maintenance, especially after the first year or so. This makes the aquarium much like a landscape project, another way in which people often enhance the appearance of their homes with natural objects and living organisms. Wise choices of species will result in a relatively worry-free, yet visually stunning, exhibit.

The Aquarium As Educational Tool

SOME FAMILIES BUY AN AQUARIUM as an educational tool for the benefit of their children. Not a parent myself, I find that I am observing from afar, as it were, the results of this approach, as I see kids visiting the store with Mom or Dad or both over the course of several years. My conclusion: sometimes the desired result is achieved and sometimes not. I know at least one future marine biologist who is developing his proposed career in this way. There is little doubt that children of all ages are drawn to aquariums. I know that having an aquarium as a child served to increase my interest in school biology. The use of aquariums to teach children about nature is a laudable goal. If the aquarium belongs to the child who is responsible for its maintenance, a simple,

reliable system is needed. The natural approach described here satisfies that need. As an added benefit, including many elements in one ecosystem stimulates other avenues of interest, from chemistry to fluid mechanics to nutrition, that a child might want to explore. Contrary to popular belief, a young person's first tank need not be freshwater; there are a growing number of young aquarists in the marine aquarium hobby who started in with saltwater and have never owned a guppy or goldfish.

The Aquarium As Hobby

HOBBYISTS COMPRISE the third customer category. These are people who are interested in something for the sake of diversion, curiosity, personal challenge, and a rewarding use of nonworking hours. Personal fulfillment comes in spending one's leisure time in developing expertise, whether the pursuit be marine aquarium keeping, tennis, or the poetry of Milton. It is no accident that a hobbyist may refer to himself as an "amateur chef" or an "amateur scientist"; the word "amateur" can be translated as "one who loves." One reason for the current popularity of marine aquariums is the deep attraction many people feel for nature and natural history. This is a hobby that breeds passionate amateurs with a lifelong commitment to their salty pursuits.

Creating a natural marine aquarium cannot be accomplished without utilizing a certain repertoire of tools and skills. This chapter will cover basic tools, such as the aquarium tank itself and the other equipment needed to maintain coral reef species. Some gear saves time by automating routine work, but such equipment, if of good quality and reliable performance, can be prohibitively expensive. Fortunately, all of the necessary maintenance tasks can be performed manually. It is important to bear in mind that no equipment, no matter how sophisticated or costly, can substitute for the good judgment and technical skills of a care-

course. Even matching the color of the drapes with a Purple Tang is acceptable, as long as this results in an aquarium that reflects the natural habitat of this fish, which happens to be the Red Sea.

After you have created a Must Have list and a Goes With list, inspect the lists carefully, perhaps doing a bit of research and note-taking, to identify the one Pivotal Species in your scheme. The Pivotal Species is the one that will make the greatest demands upon the system for its long-term survival. (The Must Have and Pivotal Species are not always one and the same.) The system must be designed with the needs of the Pivotal Species clearly in mind. If attention is given to this aspect of marine aquarium keeping, success with the rest of the community of species within the aquarium is virtually assured.

For example, among the more popular aquarium subjects are clownfishes and their host sea anemones. Every beginner who has ever inquired of me about keeping these species asks first what size tank will accommodate them. Subsequent questions often involve filtration and the addition of nutrient supplements to the water. Seldom am I asked about providing adequate light for the anemone, which is the key to succeeding with this plan. Even less often am I asked about the distinctions among the different species of host anemones, which range from one species nearly impossible to keep to another species that can be readily propagated. If the anemone does not survive, and a high percentage of them do not, the whole point of this aquarium is lost. Obviously, once you are aware of this, the anemone becomes the greater challenge and is thus the Pivotal Species in the plan.

Practicality will dictate that choices be made with a budget in mind. The relationship of the cost of the completed system to the size of the tank becomes readily apparent when one prices aquariums. Although the tanks themselves are often sold at very low margins (most dealers subscribe to the theory that a person who does not own a tank has little use for anything else in the store), the capacity of the tank will influence the cost of the complete system more significantly than any other factor. Achieving a natural marine aquarium within a given tank requires thinking about the space requirements of the proposed inhabitants. Thus, if a shark is something you are longing to own, consider that its need for space at its adult size will probably require a larger tank than most people can provide at home. Another common example of size consideration is the Volitans Lionfish, which easily reaches 12 to 18 inches in length and can live to be 20 years old. Trying to shoehorn this species into a 50-gallon tank is inappropriate and will shorten the fish's lifespan significantly. Species that grow large will often be your Pivotal Species.

Tank Size

IN GENERAL, BUY THE LARGEST AQUARIUM that your available space and budget can accommodate. With any aquarium system, the bigger, the better. Consider how immense is the structure that you are trying to recreate. For example, a small patch reef in the Florida Keys can be larger than a two-story house. One can have a very small tank, but one must be prepared to limit the inhabitants to a selection of species whose size and behavior are compatible with this restriction. One must consider, further, the total cost of the complete system and not just that of the tank itself. I suggest an allowance of about $30 to $50 for each gallon of tank capacity as the final cost of a completed system. This includes not only the tank and the equipment to run it, but also the biological components, such as live rock, seawater, and the inhabitants, whether fish or invertebrates. Any size aquarium can be simple to maintain, if it is populated appropriately.

On a counter at my store, Aquatic Specialists, we have

had, for several years, a 10-gallon aquarium that has evolved into a remarkable representation of a rocky Indo-Pacific habitat. Soft corals and false coral polyps are the dominant species. There are two fish. A tiny blenny, scarcely an inch in length, occupies a tubelike hole in one of the rocks, and a 2-inch Jordan's Fairy Wrasse glides in and out of the many small caves created from chunks of live rock. There are dozens of small, encrusting invertebrate species that have grown in the tank. Most of the larger specimens, such as small colonies of leather corals, have been propagated from bits and pieces deliberately or accidentally detached from larger colonies in the store's inventory. Every Christmas, we are asked repeatedly to quote a price for recreating this system. At the time of this writing, it amounts to $300 and several years of patient attention. Care, however, is minimal and straightforward. I would like, once and for all, to dispel the myth that a marine aquarium must be big to be successful.

Since "big" and "small" can mean different things to different people, it is useful to define these terms as I use them in this book. A "really big" aquarium is anything larger than about 300 gallons, the upper limit to commercially available, standard tanks. Anything above 100 gallons, but less than 300, is "big." Tanks in the range of 30 to 75 gallons are the most popular with marine aquarists and are of "average" size. Anything less than 30 gallons is "small." The lower limit, in my experience, is about 1 gallon.

Julian Sprung, a noted author and well-versed expert on reef tanks, has helped foster the notion that anyone can create a fully packed reef tank in 15 gallons, as he has done so splendidly. To do this successfully, however, takes considerable skill and attention to an appropriate maintenance routine. Most beginners add a massive overload of fish and invertebrates and thus end up with a mess. Approached correctly, however, small tanks can be quite rewarding and are a relatively low-cost way for a beginner to become involved in the marine aquarium hobby. Later chapters in this book will be of great help in setting realistic stocking goals. Depending upon what one has in mind in terms of space and money, I suggest that beginners choose a small to average tank: a 20-, 30-, 50-, or 75-gallon system. If the plan is to go for a big tank, then 120 gallons is a good choice for a reef system. (See suggested setups, pages 64-79.) All of these sizes provide a reasonable ratio of surface area to water volume, standard lighting equipment works well with them, and the broad base design (18 to 24 inches front to back) of the larger tanks allows for easily installed and visually appealing decoration. For systems intended to feature many, or larger, fishes, a really big tank will be needed.

Let's get back to why people are often told that small tanks won't do. An oft-cited problem is temperature control, with the suggestion that a small tank will be subject to severe temperature fluctuations. The high heat capacity of water tends to stabilize the temperature of the tank, as compared to the fluctuating temperature of the surrounding air. This tendency is constant, regardless of the size of the tank. Much depends upon the shape of the tank in relation to its volume. Tall, narrow tanks with relatively little surface area are the most difficult to cool in dangerously hot weather. To be sure, evaporation of water from a smaller tank will change the salinity more quickly than would be the case for a larger tank housed in the same room, although evaporation rate depends upon many factors.

Possibly the greatest misunderstanding arises in regard to bioload. Overstocking the smaller water volume will not, as is often erroneously suggested, result in a faster decline in water quality than would be the case with a larger tank. The rate at which pollutants are released into the system will be a function of the metabolism of the animals present. If two systems are stocked with the same biomass, or grams of fish, per gallon, the pollution rates will be the same. In other words, the mere number of animals present is not

THE LURE (AND PERIL) OF THE SMALL MARINE AQUARIUM

NOVICE MARINE AQUARISTS should think twice before starting a too-small tank, despite the lower cost. I have had many an inexperienced person tell me that the only reason dealers recommend larger tanks is that they want to make a bigger sale. Having been a dealer, I can refute this categorically. The successful hobbyist is most likely to be a repeat customer, and any good dealer's basic philosophy is to cultivate successful hobbyists. The consensus among experienced hobbyists is that the greatest likelihood of success with a first-time marine aquarium is to be had with a system of around 40 to 100 gallons. The stability of a larger system works in your favor. Therefore, it is good business to encourage people to buy something that will give them satisfaction. It is not good business, however, to try to talk a customer into something that is clearly outside the realm of what they are able, or willing, to pay. When only a small system will do, I try to encourage success by pointing out that the rules are rather strict for a tiny reef tank. Here are the most important points to remember if considering a marine aquarium of less than 40 gallons:

1. Absolutely rigorous attention must be paid to maintenance chores, such as water changes and evaporation replenishment. Neglecting topping off for one day in a 2-gallon desktop tank, for example, can result in a salinity increase that will kill starfish.

2. Choose appropriate invertebrate specimens.

A small but obviously successful 10-gallon acrylic setup designed as the Micro-Mini Reef by Coral Reef Eco-Systems of Windsor, CA.

Stick with shallow-water species, such as leather corals and mushroom polyps, that are tolerant of less than pristine water quality. No beginning marine aquarist should start with SPS (small-polyped scleractinian) corals under any circumstances. Spend time developing aquarium-keeping skills to avoid the needless sacrifice of demanding species.

3. For best results, do not put fishes into a small reef tank. Fish put the greatest demand on any aquarium system. In a small volume of water, pollution levels can rise

Filtration components: back-of-tank power filter, hang-on venturi skimmer-filter, and hidden under-sand plenum.

rapidly when fish are present and being fed. A single diminutive fish might be the limit for a tiny tank; if you must have more, it may be best to make yours a small fish tank and limit the invertebrates to hardy species like shrimps, fanworms, and small hermit crabs.

4. Overfeeding the fish always leads to trouble. Few experienced hobbyists, much less beginners, have the patience and restraint necessary to provide several marine fish housed in a small aquarium with an adequate diet, while at the same time avoiding an accumulation of excess nutrients in the water. One of the characteristics of a seasoned talent is the ability to make an inherently difficult achievement appear simple. Novices would be wise to note that the most celebrated small marine reef aquariums are the creations of expert aquarists.

important, their mass per unit of water volume is. (We are assuming here that the metabolic rates of the animals are the same. Say all the animals in the tank are the same species, a school of blue damsels, for example.) In this regard, the problems most often seen with small tanks result from a lack of restraint on the part of the aquarist, rather than an inherent defect of the system. Like a small garden, a small aquarium can be as rewarding as a large one. What is required is understanding and finesse on the part of the aquarist or gardener and a controlling hand to rein in the exuberance of nature confined. Bigger tanks offer more leeway, perhaps, in stocking and design capabilities, but also require more resources to maintain effectively and are no more forgiving of gross carelessness than smaller systems. If you are willing to practice the techniques for success with a marine aquarium, it matters little what size you choose.

Using $30 per gallon as your cost estimate, decide what you can afford to install and stock, remembering that not all of this investment will be required immediately. About one-third of the expense will go for the tank and equipment, another third for live rock, and the remaining third for additional live specimens. Your budgeting efforts should also take into consideration the ongoing costs of food, seawater, and replacement parts such as lamps. These costs increase in proportion to the size of the aquarium.

Overflow Box

ONCE THE TANK SIZE IS DECIDED, most aquarists will select a predrilled tank with an internal overflow box. The overflow box normally consists of a rectangular plastic chamber, a little taller than the maximum water level, installed in one corner or along the back wall of the tank. Two such boxes are recommended in tanks over 4 feet long. The box is notched near the top to create a "fence," preventing fish from being swept over the edge. The overflow

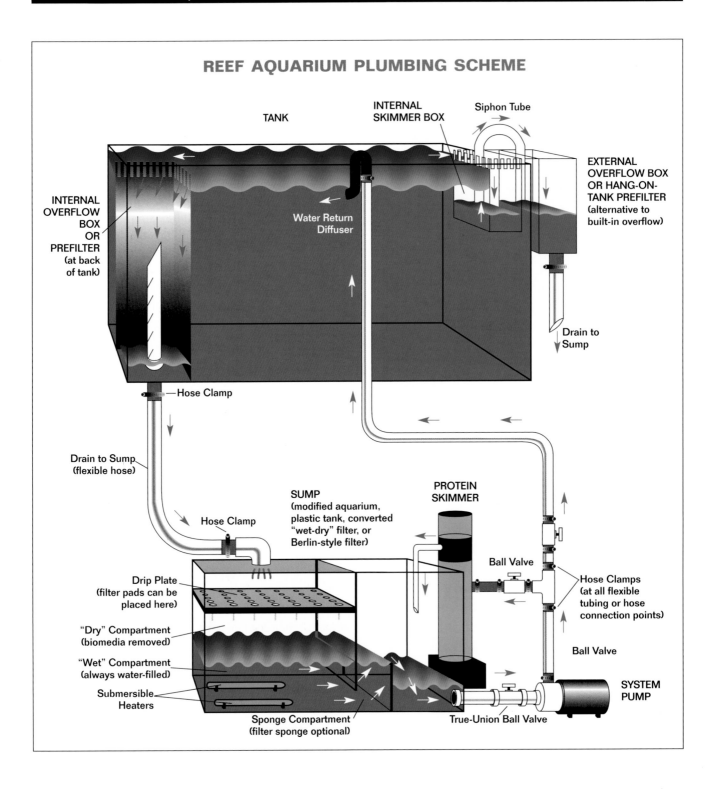

REEF AQUARIUM PLUMBING SCHEME

TANK

INTERNAL
SKIMMER BOX

Siphon Tube

EXTERNAL
OVERFLOW BOX
OR HANG-ON-
TANK PREFILTER
(alternative to
built-in overflow)

INTERNAL
OVERFLOW
BOX
OR
PREFILTER
(at back
of tank)

Water Return
Diffuser

Drain to
Sump

Hose Clamp

Drain to Sump
(flexible hose)

Hose Clamp

SUMP
(modified aquarium,
plastic tank, converted
"wet-dry" filter, or
Berlin-style filter)

PROTEIN
SKIMMER

Ball Valve

Hose Clamps
(at all flexible
tubing or hose
connection points)

Drip Plate
(filter pads can be
placed here)

"Dry" Compartment
(biomedia removed)

"Wet" Compartment
(always water-filled)

Submersible
Heaters

Ball Valve

SYSTEM
PUMP

True-Union Ball Valve

Sponge Compartment
(filter sponge optional)

box serves two functions. One is to allow for removal of surface water from the tank and to direct water into a sump below the tank. The other is to trap large debris in a spot from which it can be conveniently removed and discarded. Some aquarists use the overflow box itself as a debris trap, while others let the water flow unimpeded through the overflow and catch the waste in the sump. (See diagram at left for a typical design with overflow box and simple sump.)

If the tank is not predrilled, any competent aquarium shop can arrange to have it drilled and outfitted with an appropriate overflow chamber. Do-it-yourselfers like acrylic aquariums because they can be drilled by any person handy with power tools. But glass tanks should always be drilled by the manufacturer lest the warranty be voided. Even professional glass-cutting shops will refuse to assume responsibility when asked to drill an aquarium. Letting the manufacturer do the job will mean waiting a couple of extra weeks for the tank, but it will avoid a costly disaster.

Installation of the overflow box must be done carefully to insure that the seams will not leak, which would allow the tank to drain completely. In most tanks, a standpipe centered in the overflow box is screwed into a bulkhead fitting that passes through a drain hole drilled in the bottom of the tank. The standpipe is perforated to admit air and prevent the slurping sound that the water makes as it descends. Some designs have a second hole in the bottom of the overflow box to facilitate installation of the return plumbing. This is a good idea, as nearly all of the pipes are thus hidden from view. The overflow box should be easily accessible for service, as it should be cleaned about once a week if it contains any mechanism or media to trap debris.

Another method of getting water out of the tank involves an over-the-side overflow installed on the outside of the tank. Such a device is used to remove surface water and to provide a drain when drilling the tank is not an option. There are potential problems with this arrangement, as it can lose siphon and thereby shut down the flow through the system. (Devotees of these systems swear they can operate for years without loss of siphon; others just swear at these systems as being disaster-prone.) Another drawback is the necessity for several inches of clearance between the tank and the wall behind or to the side to allow room for the external overflow box. While an external overflow may be the only option for some aquarium owners, it is one to be avoided if there is any other choice.

The Sump

WATER LEAVING THE AQUARIUM via either type of overflow drains into a sump, or reservoir, located in the cabinet below the tank. The sump is drained by the main system pump, which returns water to the tank. As the pump raises the water level in the tank, water passes over the top of the overflow box and into the sump again. This is the basic flow cycle for any aquarium system.

State-of-the-art ETS acrylic sump designed by Gary Lohr to be the water-handling center of a sophisticated reef system.

Besides being an integral part of the plumbing, the sump provides a convenient place to install additional equipment that may be needed. Commonly, a heater, if used, is placed in the sump. Activated carbon, an optional filtration medium that will be discussed in more detail later, can simply be put in a mesh bag and placed in the sump. A protein skimmer may draw water from, and return it to, the sump, as might a chiller. Probes for electronic measurement of pH and temperature, if placed in the sump, will be slower to accumulate a coating of algae, being hidden away in the dark of the cabinet. Carefully consider the size of the sump in relation to that of the display tank. The sump must not overflow if power is shut off to the pump and all plumbing is allowed to drain into it. A prudent design will allow for plenty of sump capacity. One of the silliest mistakes I have seen repeated over the years is the installation of a sump too small for the system. The number one resulting problem is the overflow of seawater onto the surrounding floor when the electricity is interrupted. This always seems to happen when the family is away, maximizing the potential for damage to the floor finish and furnishings. A large sump also effectively increases the capacity of the system by providing additional water volume. A 75-gallon display tank with

a sump holding 25 gallons is really a 100-gallon system.

For small tanks, the sump can be dispensed with, although having one is a nice attribute. In its place, one can install a hang-on-the-back outside power filter that incorporates a protein skimmer. This arrangement, which I first described many years ago in *Marine Fish Monthly* (Tullock, 1989), accomplishes two things at once. The protein skimmer is moved outside the tank, and neither it nor an overflow box is seen inside the display. Second, good water movement can be achieved in tanks of up to about 30 gallons by using the largest possible outside filter unit. Placing a powerhead at a right angle to the water flow from the main filter helps to create chaotic water movement, or turbulence. In larger systems, the primary source of directional water movement is the main system pump, augmented by additional small pumps or powerheads.

Pumps & Plumbing

SELECTION OF A MAIN SYSTEM PUMP will be predicated on three factors: the desired flow rate, the amount of head pressure, and the cost/performance specifications for the particular brand of pump being evaluated. The main pump should deliver at least five times the system's water volume per hour at the point of discharge into the display tank. Most pumps are rated in gallons per hour at 1 foot of head pressure. Head pressure is the distance from the inlet of the pump to the discharge point in the display tank. For most home aquarium systems, this will be about 4 feet. However, other factors affect working head pressure. Each 90-degree bend in the plumbing will add about a foot of head because of

A good aquarium pump should be reliable, quiet, energy efficient, and have the capacity to turn over the entire volume of system water at least five times each hour.

the friction of the water moving around the bend. Also as a result of friction, each 10-foot horizontal run of pipe will add a foot of head pressure. If part of the pump discharge is shunted off, to a protein skimmer for example, this will also rob the display tank of flow. Once all of these effects are totaled up, one needs only to choose a pump that will deliver the required flow, or more, at the calculated head pressure for the system. Finding a pump to meet these specifications is simple — inspect the manufacturer's literature on the pump to find the information. Selecting a pump on the basis of its cost/performance ratio, however, is more difficult. Among several brands of pumps meeting the basic specifications, one may cost much more than the others. Presumably, this is a better pump. But is it worth it? Good pumps cost more than poor-quality ones, of course, but one can only be assured of a particular brand's performance through direct testing. This is one area where the experience of other aquarists or a trusted retail dealer can be invaluable. The best advice I can offer is this: Even if you are on a very tight budget, do not scrimp on the pump. This is the most important component of the system, and its failure can spell disaster.

The plumbing necessary to connect the overflow box to the sump, and the pump to the tank, must be carefully designed. A sketch of the plumbing, showing the location of bends, valves, etc., is essential. Using graph paper, prepare a scale drawing, taking measurements from the aquarium, sump, and cabinet. Inexperienced plumbers should seek the advice of a friend, professional plumber, or qualified aquarium system dealer when designing and installing the plumbing. Schedule 40 PVC pipe, flexible vinyl hose or a combination of these, with appropriate fittings, is most often used for aquarium installations. While the tools required are simple and the techniques for assembly of these materials are not difficult, neat, professional-looking work can only be achieved with practice. (Be aware that neatness can

be carried to extremes in aquarium plumbing: every 90-degree elbow in a plumbing loop will significantly slow water flow and can reduce needed pressure dramatically. In many instances, less elegant sweeps of tubing may be superior to a series of tight bends.) The plumbing is one part of the system that needs to be done only once and so should be done carefully and correctly. I recommend testing the completed plumbing connections by filling the tank with freshwater and running the system for a few days before adding seawater mix. This will afford a chance to check that everything is working properly and that there are no leaks. Also, flushing the system with freshwater will remove dust and dirt that may be present.

Water Movement

YOU MUST INSTALL ADDITIONAL EQUIPMENT to create water movement in the display aquarium. Such movement is important to sessile species that must rely on moving water to bring them food and dissolved gases and to carry away wastes and reproductive cells. Fish also benefit from the exercise they get swimming against the currents. There are devices available that will allow automatic switching be-

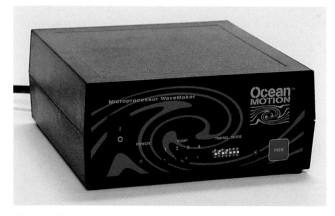

Wavemakers provide constant, random switching of power-heads to create the water turbulence required by reef life.

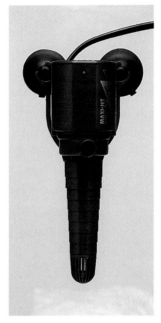 

Essential circulation is created by an in-tank powerhead, left; ever-changing currents are provided by the Osci-Wave, right, which rotates, sweeping its output 90 degrees back and forth.

tween two pumps to produce a pulsed flow simulating tidal currents. Alternatives include using a larger system pump and directing the return flow through various outlets to create turbulence. Submersible centrifugal water pumps may also be used for this purpose. Many public aquariums employ "dump buckets" to produce random surges, but this method may prove too messy for a home installation. As long as turbulence and good water movement are present, how this is achieved is important only in terms of the reliability of the equipment and its cost.

Temperature Control

TEMPERATURE CONTROL may require a heater or, more commonly, a chiller unit. Tropical marine organisms do best at temperatures within the range of about 70 to 80 de-grees F, with the optimum being 75 degrees. The role of temperature in the maintenance of aquatic organisms is significant. The metabolic rate (the way in which the body obtains energy from foods) in fishes is highly dependent on temperature. Keeping coral reef fishes at the optimum temperature of 75 degrees results in better health, fewer disease problems, and longer life spans than if they are kept at higher temperatures.

To determine if heating or cooling will be needed for a particular aquarium installation, the best route is an empirical one. Place the tank in the desired location, fill it with water, and record the temperature over a period of time. If you're only at the planning and shopping stage, use a big plastic trash can or similar container with a capacity close to that of the tank you envision. Depending upon where you live and the temperature fluctuations you expect in the area where the tank is to be located, you should elect to make these observations when the ambient temperature is most likely to deviate significantly from the desired aquarium temperature of 75 degrees F. The use of central heating, air conditioning, fans, etc. will all affect not only the temperature of the aquarium but also the rate of water evaporation. Because of its weight and fragility, any aquarium, once in place and full of water, is an effort to relocate. It is therefore important to choose the location of the aquarium carefully. As simple a choice as placing the tank on an inside, rather than an outside, wall of the room made it possible for me to maintain the temperature of my first 10-gallon aquarium at 75 degrees. Perhaps the stable temperature contributed to my limited success in rearing the offspring of a female Dwarf Octopus (*Octopus jouboni*) that brooded a string of egg clusters in the aquarium shortly after I obtained her from a local shop (Tullock, 1980). In the long run, it is worth it to take actual temperature measurements in the proposed location of the tank under various conditions. The larger the tank, the more important this aspect of planning will be. Heating and cooling water can be profligate of electricity and a significant cost issue, depending upon where you live. Probably the ideal location, and precisely where my next aquarium will be built, is in an enclosure away from the outside walls of the house. From the living space of the home, only a front or corner view of the aquarium will be apparent. All of the equipment, hidden behind a wall, will nevertheless be easily accessible in a closet. If one is willing to make the commitment, the sky's the limit with a large, built-in system.

An average temperature that departs significantly (say by 2 degrees) from the desired range will require artificial adjustment. Lighting systems and pumps produce heat. This additional heating should be taken into account in evaluating the temperature stability of the system. Especially for large systems that require hefty pumps and many watts of artificial lighting, cooling the water by means of a fluid chiller will be required.

If additional heat is required to maintain the temperature of the aquarium above 70 degrees F, select a good-quality heater, preferably of the submersible type, and install it in the sump. (Many residents of northern states have timed thermostats controlling their home heating in winter. If you are programming your furnace to run at 72-74 degrees during the day and then drop to 65 degrees or lower at night, the aquarium will definitely require a heater to avoid a daily temperature shift that will destabilize marine creatures.) Allow about 3 watts of heating capacity per gallon of water in the system. A 75-gallon system would normally have a 250-watt heater installed, since this is the heater size nearest the required capacity. But it would be better to use two 150-watt heaters for this setup, rather than one 250-watt. That way, if one heater fails, there will still be some heating capacity. The likelihood of both heaters failing simultaneously is small. There is no benefit in installing a heater significantly larger than the required capacity. If a

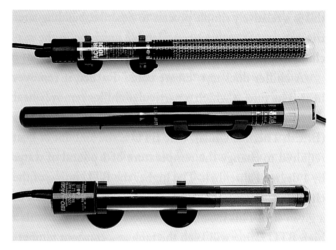

Submersible heaters are self-contained, adjustable, and completely waterproof; allow 3 watts per gallon of system water.

100-watt heater will raise the temperature of the tank 5 degrees in two hours, a 200-watt heater will simply raise the temperature of the water by the same amount in only one hour. Rapid changes in water temperature are not the rule in aquatic habitats. The high specific heat of water results in the moderation of temperatures. In fact, this is one reason why an aquatic habitat can be more biologically diverse than the adjacent terrestrial habitat.

An aquarium chiller (also called a fluid chiller) operates in essentially the same manner as a refrigerator or air conditioner. Refrigerant gas, commonly Freon, is compressed by an electrically driven compressor. This results in the gas losing energy (its temperature goes down). The compressed gas flows through a heat exchanger, where it picks up heat from the surrounding medium, in this case water from the aquarium that is being pumped through the exchanger. The gas carries heat back toward the compressor, but on the way it encounters an expansion valve, which allows the pressure to drop suddenly. As the pressure drops, the gas gives up heat to a radiator, which dispels the heat into the surrounding air with the aid of a fan. Although the need for such media, except in highly specific applications under unusual circumstances. For example, there is an ion-removing resin-bead product that extracts copper ions. Useful, if one has this specific need.

Activated carbon is a mixed blessing. There are many types and grades of activated carbon and much confusion regarding its use. For one thing, some carbons may leach phosphate into the water, contributing to the load of nutrients that one must keep under control. Careful testing of the product you plan to use is the only way to determine if this is going to be a problem. To test, a sample of the product is placed in seawater overnight, and the water is then tested for phosphate. Any detectable amount, using a phosphate test kit with a lower detection limit of 0.05 ppm, is too much. Considering the primary benefit of activated carbon — the removal of yellowing agents that eventually discolor the water — this ongoing testing for phosphates may be too much effort. Yellowing can be eliminated by changing water, and depending upon the dynamics of your system, yellow coloring may only be apparent after a long period without water changes.

The use of activated carbon in reef aquariums is likely to remain a controversial topic for some time. Peter Wilkens, who helped develop and popularize the Berlin method, continues to advocate continual use of pharmaceutical-grade activated carbon to serve as a site for bacterial growth, to remove dissolved organics, and to remove toxins released by captive corals. Wilkens, speaking at the Western Marine Conference in San Francisco in 1996, strongly advocated the use of multiple mesh bags of carbon, with one of the packets being replaced every three to four weeks.

Others, including the noted Norwegian aquarist Alf Jacob Nilsen, have stated a suspicion that continual use of activated carbon can lead to stony coral bleaching if replenishment of trace elements such as iodine is not done on a regular basis (Western Marine Conference, 1995).

Protein Skimming

OF THE MANY POSSIBLE METHODS for reducing levels of organic matter in aquarium water, one of the simpler and more convenient is foam fractionation, or protein skimming. In a process analogous to the production of sea foam in surf, injection of air bubbles into the aquarium water creates a meringuelike foam when organic molecules collect at the air-water interfaces of the bubbles. Protein skimmers are designed not only to produce this foam but also to facilitate its collection in a reservoir from which it can be periodically discarded.

Foam fractionation is an important part of the successful maintenance of a marine aquarium. It is the only method available that physically removes organic pollutants from the water. All other techniques simply sequester pollution within filter media, which are then removed and replenished with fresh media. Meanwhile, pollutant molecules may be constantly exchanged between the media and the aquarium water, reducing the overall effectiveness of the filtration system. For marine aquariums, foam fractionation is a practical and simple way to control this organic pollution.

There is a bewildering array of skimmer designs and sizes. If in doubt, choose one that is larger than necessary; most reef-keeping experts agree that it is not possible to "overskim" the aquarium. There seems to be no definite answer to the question, "Which skimmer should I buy?" Many authors, including Moe (1989) and Spotte (1992), have discussed skimmer design and selection. Experience has taught me two things about choosing a skimmer: 1) any skimmer is better than none at all, as long as foam is being collected; and 2) use common sense — don't put a tiny skimmer on a giant tank or vice versa. Although any protein skimmer will remove organic matter from the tank, for maximum efficiency, choose one designed for the amount of water your aquarium system will contain.

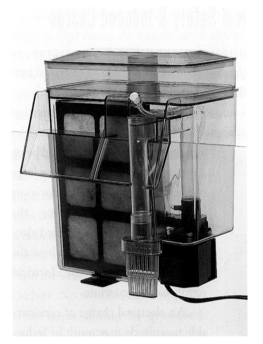
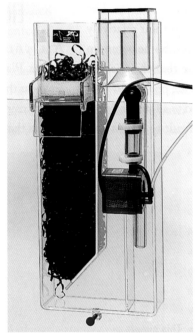

Constantly evolving, protein skimmers are available for every level of reef keeping. The Supreme Skilter, left, is a beginner's model; the CPR BakPak, center, is popular for smaller tanks; the ETS, right, is a high-end favorite of advanced hobbyists.

The advantages and disadvantages of the different types of protein skimmers can be summarized as follows: Columnar skimmers that are designed to go inside the tank are simple, foolproof, and relatively inexpensive. They are, however, bulky, and their presence in the tank detracts from the overall natural appearance. External columnar skimmers are more expensive, because they must be made leakproof. In addition, such a skimmer, especially for a large tank, must have a tall column to maximize the contact time between the air bubbles and the water. Thus the skimmer may be too bulky for a particular application. For example, the skimmer may not fit under the aquarium cabinet, out of sight. Many skimmers rely on air diffusers to create a stream of very fine bubbles. These will need periodic replacement. Further, as the diffusers begin to clog with use, the air supply will require adjustment in order to keep the skimmer op-

erating properly. Venturi skimmers, on the other hand, do not employ diffusers, but rather use a venturi valve to produce a mix of water and fine bubbles. Therefore, there is nothing to replace, and adjustments may not have to be made as frequently to keep the skimmer working correctly. Some venturi skimmer designs do, however, seem to require constant adjusting. Some old hands prefer the simplicity of replacing reliable limewood airstones every four weeks to fiddling with ill-tempered or ill-designed venturi types. Venturi skimmers are also often designed to create a spinning vortex of water and air inside the skimmer to maximize contact time between the air and water without the necessity of a tall column. Thus a venturi skimmer for a given size tank will always be smaller than a comparable columnar skimmer. The small size means that the venturi skimmer can easily be hidden underneath the tank and will

that filters out most of the pollutants, producing a product that is suitable for aquarium use.

As a rule of thumb, assume that any contaminant in the feed water will be reduced by about 90% by the RO unit. The degree of actual contaminant removal depends upon a number of factors, including the type of RO membrane, the pressure, temperature, and dissolved solids content of the feed water, the use of prefiltration of the feed water to remove gross contamination, and the specific contaminant. In some areas of the country, excessively high content of algae nutrients in the feed water may require additional purification of the RO water in order to eliminate algae blooms in the aquarium. Passing RO water through a mixed-bed deionization filter will produce nearly distilled-quality water. (Deionization media are synthetic resins that chemically bind specific contaminants.) Deionization can be employed to purify tap water directly, but pretreatment by RO to lower contaminant levels significantly prolongs the life of the (rather expensive) deionization media.

Synthetic Seawater

THERE ARE MANY BRANDS of synthetic seawater mix. Formulas for synthetic seawater have been a part of the scientific literature for a long time. Experienced marine aquarists who read the following passage from Spotte (1979) will find it has a familiar ring:

"McLanahan (1973) wryly notes that the number of formulas [for artificial seawater] nearly equals the number of investigators. The result has been a bewildering array of recipes, some touted as the best available for culture of a particular animal or plant. But McLanahan further pointed out that such claims are rarely supported by sufficient data."

I have had experience with about ten different synthetic seawater formulas. All were satisfactory for aquariums housing fishes only, and only a few were unsuitable for aquariums

COMPONENTS OF SEAWATER OF INTEREST TO AQUARISTS

Element	ppm	Ionic Form
Chloride	19,500	Cl^-
Sodium	10,770	Na^+
Magnesium	1,290	Mg^+
Sulfur	905	SO_4^{2-}, $NaSO_4^-$
Calcium	412	Ca^{2+}
Potassium	380	K^+
Bromine	67	Br^-
Carbon [1]	28	HCO_3^{2-}, CO_3^{2-}, CO_2 gas
Nitrogen [2]	11.5	N_2 gas, NO_3^-, NH_4^+
Strontium	8	Sr^+
Oxygen	6	O_2 gas
Silicon	2	$Si(OH)_4$
Phosphorus [3]	0.06	PO_4^{3-}, HPO_4^{2-}, H_2PO_4
Iodine	0.06	IO_3^-, I^-
Molybdenum	0.01	MoO_4^{2-}
Iron	0.002	$Fe(OH)_2^+$, $Fe(OH)_4^-$
Copper	0.0001	$CuCO_3$, $CuOH^+$

[1] CO_2 gas is found in coral reef waters at about 2 ppm. Dissolved organic carbon in surface seawater is seldom higher than 2.0 ppm and is generally much lower in coral reef habitats.

[2] Coral reef habitats typically have the lowest concentration of total inorganic nitrogen found in the ocean, in the range of only 1 to 2 parts per billion (ppb).

[3] In the water that bathes coral reefs, orthophosphate concentrations are frequently no higher than 0.1 to 0.2 ppb. The figure given is the average for the entire ocean.

with sessile invertebrates, primarily because of excessive phosphate content. The majority of brands, however, are essentially interchangeable. Hobbyists with whom I have spoken and corresponded report good success with a variety of synthetic mixes. Aquarium spawnings of both fishes and invertebrates of a variety of species have occurred in all of the brands for which I have personal experience. It would therefore appear that brand selection may depend rather more upon personal preferences and availability than upon any real differences in the results obtained with any particular brand versus another.

Aquarium salt mixes include 11 major ions that occur in the same proportion in all of the world's seas, along with minor and trace elements essential to marine life.

Seawater is composed of 11 major ions. These constituents make up 99.9% of the dissolved substances in seawater. They are: chloride, sulfate, bicarbonate, bromide, borate, fluoride, sodium, magnesium, calcium, potassium, and strontium. These major ions are "conserved," an important concept regarding the chemistry of seawater. While the total amount of these ions can vary locally, i.e., the salinity of the water can be different in different locations, the relative proportions of these ions remain constant. The importance of this fact is that organisms such as corals are adapted to a specific set of chemical conditions in the seawater that surrounds them, and this is why the maintenance of any marine aquarium involves testing and adjusting the chemical conditions of the water in the tank. Besides these major ions, all of which are present at a concentration of 1 part per million (ppm) or more, two other groups of ions are found in seawater. Minor elements are those that are present at a level greater than 1 part per billion (ppb), but less than 1 ppm. Trace elements are those that are present in concentrations less than 1 ppb. (For our purposes, the terms "ions" and "elements" can be used interchangeably. Chemists would refer to "ions," but aquarium hobbyists usually say "elements.")

An important distinction between the major elements and the minor and trace elements is that while the ratios of the concentrations of the major elements are constant and therefore unaffected by local conditions, the concentrations of minor and trace elements *are* affected by chemical or biological processes. This is why adding certain ions to, or removing them from, the aquarium has definite biological effects. Examples of minor ions that produce a demonstrable effect when added to the tank are iodide and phosphate. Iodide is important to all organisms, but especially so to corals, crustaceans, and seaweeds. It is also apparently removed by protein skimming. Iodide supplementation can result in accelerated growth of corals and coralline algae, for example. Adding phosphate ions to the aquarium will typically result in an algae bloom, a decidedly unwanted effect. An example of a trace ion with significant concentration-dependent effects is copper. At a concentration of 0.2 ppm, copper is therapeutic for common parasitic infestations of fishes. At greater than 0.3 ppm, however, it is toxic to fishes, and any amount detectable with a hobbyist test kit is lethal to most invertebrates. Yet copper is an essential element for many life forms; the quantity needed is extraordinarily minute.

In my opinion, the best way to select a salt mix is to prepare a small batch, using RO water, and then run a few tests. In a suitable container, prepare a small batch of the salt mix according to the manufacturer's instructions and allow it to sit overnight with an airstone or powerhead to provide agitation and aeration. This will assure complete dissolution of the salts and equilibration of the pH. (Note: synthetic seawater should never be used immediately after rehydration. Always aerate it overnight before use.) Temperature and specific gravity should be within the proper range, corresponding to the parameters of the aquarium in which the water is to be used. Check pH first; it should be 8.2 to 8.5. Next check alkalinity. It should be in the range of 2.0 to 5.0 milliequivalents per liter. For natural seawater, a pH of 8.2 and alkalinity of 2.1 to 2.5 milliequivalents per liter are reported values. Tests for both nitrate and phosphate should be below the range of most test kits, i.e., less than 0.1 ppm for phosphate and less than 10 ppm for nitrate. Test the sample for calcium also, which should be 400 ppm or a bit more. (See the table on page 60 for a list of the major components of seawater and some of the minor and trace components that aquarists often talk about. See Chapter Five for more information about water analysis.) The average hobbyist will be unable to test for some components, such as trace elements, although a private analytical lab will perform such analyses for a fee. One should bear in mind that a perfect synthetic seawater has not yet been devised. If one can acquire the real thing — natural seawater — by all means use it.

Natural Seawater

NATURAL SEAWATER can be purchased from supply services if you happen to live in a large coastal city. Biological-supply houses will ship natural seawater, but the cost of freight can be prohibitive. You can collect your own seawater when traveling by car, however, and even a small addition of this substance can have beneficial effects on a marine tank. I have collected seawater in 5-gallon plastic buckets with snap-on lids, which I obtained for free from a local bakery.

After washing the buckets well, I stow them in the trunk of the car. Once they are filled with seawater, I leave them in the trunk of the car, then in a cool, dark basement, for about two weeks. This causes planktonic organisms to die and settle to the bottom of the buckets, along with sand and mud. The water is then decanted and added to the aquarium, after warming it to the aquarium's temperature with an immersion heater.

Choose a seawater collecting site carefully, to avoid possible pollutants. Close to shore, this can be more of a problem than at sea, so a boat is of great help. I have, however, lowered buckets off fishing piers by rope in order to take water from the channel. Clean ocean water has no smell of decay or hydrogen sulfide and should have no oily surface

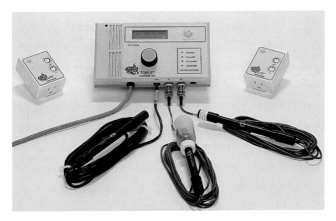

The Octopus computerized water-quality monitor and controller with probes for marine aquariums, by Aquadyne.

film. One way to check for "healthy" seawater is to place some surface water in a clean glass jar and observe it in bright light for the darting motes of planktonic organisms, many of which are just visible to the naked eye. (Microscopic examination is, of course, also a desirable way to check.) The presence of such organisms generally indicates unpolluted water. Water that is bright green, teeming with phytoplankton, may have a high nutrient load, however. Aquarists have expressed concern about introducing harmful organisms along with natural seawater. In my experience, it is more likely that parasites will enter the aquarium with their hosts, rather than via other sources. Dire warnings about the hazards of using natural seawater are unfounded. Properly prepared as described, natural seawater is used by professional marine biology labs worldwide.

If you decide to collect natural seawater on your next vacation trip, I suggest that you also make a separate collection of a gallon or two. Keep this water gently aerated (just stir it with your hand every few hours or use a battery-operated air pump) and in an insulated container, such as a beverage cooler. Add it to the aquarium immediately upon your return home. The purpose of this is to introduce natural plankton to the system. I have done this, even with plankton concentrated by towing a plankton net and transporting the harvest in a few gallons of aerated water, without the introduction of harmful species.

TO SET UP A NATURAL REEF AQUARIUM, you must have a tank, a sump, water pumps, plumbing, appropriate temperature control, a protein skimmer, and a lighting system. I cannot overstate the importance of planning before you start spending money. Design the system on paper, visit shops and private aquariums to see what fish and invertebrates catch your fancy, and gather all the information you can about species and equipment. Determine how you will provide an appropriate supply of seawater. Never lose sight of the fact that equipment selection is only half the process. Even with the best equipment, problems will surely develop if attention is not paid to water quality and to the special needs of the life forms that will inhabit the aquarium ecosystem. (For suggested setups, see the Step-by-Step section on pages 64-79.)

Natural rewards: beautiful, healthy fishes and invertebrates repay the aquarist's planning and attention to water quality.

A marine aquarium can be an enhancement to your personal living space. Observing your captive sea can help you relax, teach you and your children something about the world of nature, and delight you with unexpected and unpredictable events and discoveries. Without a sound overall design, without some thought as to how this glass box filled with strange, beautiful creatures will fit into your home, your available leisure time, and your budget, or without a commitment to appropriate, long-term care, a marine aquarium can be a real nightmare and a source of frustration. My goal is to help you avoid that outcome.

Step-by-Step

Starter Reef

*Setting Up a First Marine Aquarium or Young Aquarist's
Tank Using a Simplified, Natural Approach*

OFTEN PERPLEXING FOR THOSE who haven't tried it before, setting up a new aquarium can be simple when done in logical, unhurried steps. The accompanying photographs illustrate a straightforward sequence one might use to create a simple reef system, using the techniques discussed in this book. The theme we have chosen is a bit of Micronesian deep fore-reef habitat, which will be housed in a 20-gallon aquarium — a tank size that offers enough room to create an interesting ecosystem but is small enough to fit a beginner's space and budget, with no expensive lighting or filtration equipment required.

Step 1: Assemble the Equipment

AFTER VISITING THE LOCAL AQUARIUM SHOPS and developing a plan and budget for your system, you will first acquire the necessary tank and equipment. Under no circumstances will you buy the gear (hardware) and livestock (software) on the same first trip. Unlike the typical setup for a child's goldfish bowl, you must have a marine aquarium up and running, with the water quality stabilized, before you bring home the first live organism.

ESSENTIALS:

From Aquarium Shop

Aquarium

Lighting hood and bulbs

Small skimmer/external filter

Small powerhead

Heater

Thermometer

Hydrometer

Basic marine water test kit

Salt mix

Natural coral sand (aragonite)

Background film or paint and brush (optional)

Other

Stand (or other stable, level surface)

5-gallon clean plastic bucket(s)

Carpenter's level

Transparent (Scotch) tape

Duct tape

Single-edged razor blade

Light timer

Ground-fault interrupter extension cord

Step 1: Essential components of a basic, inexpensive, beginner's natural reef system, including 20-gallon glass aquarium, simple light hood, external skimmer, small powerhead, thermometer, hydrometer, test kit, salt, and aragonite or coral sand.

Step 2: Prepare for Filling

• Rinse the tank with freshwater. Never use soap or commercial cleaners to clean an aquarium. (If you need to remove a stubborn deposit, use a little white vinegar. A single-edged razor blade can be used on a glass aquarium, never on acrylic, to remove anything adhering to the glass. Rinse again with freshwater after cleaning.)

• Apply the background. Before the aquarium is positioned against a wall, take the time to install a background, which will obscure any distracting wires, filtration gear, or man-made wallcovering behind the tank. Pet shops carry waterproof paper or plastic background materials in sheets or rolls; there are many decorative choices, but I recommend a simple black or dark blue as the best choice for a novice. First, clean the outside of the tank glass thoroughly. Fingerprints or splotches will be remarkably apparent against the background when the tank is set up and illuminated. Use small pieces of tape to hold the background in place, then use duct tape to completely seal the background to

TYPICAL EQUIPMENT LIST

STARTER SYSTEM: Perfecto 20-gallon aquarium (24 x 12 x 17 inches) and light hood; Supreme Skilter 250 skimmer and filter; Rio 600 powerhead; Ebo-Jager LZ 75-watt heater; fasTesT saltwater test kit; SeaTest hydrometer; Hagen glass thermometer; Intermatic light timer; Leviton ground-fault interrupter extension cord; Tropic Marin salt mix; CaribSea Florida crushed coral.

ENHANCED SYSTEM: Coralife fluorescent and actinic lights (4 x 20-watts) in oak hood; CPR Cyclone BakPak skimmer; Tsunami HD wavemaker; additional powerhead.

Step 3: Once properly located and leveled on a stable surface with background film or paint applied, the tank is filled with freshwater to check for leaks and test equipment.

the top frame of the tank. The idea is to prevent water from finding its way between the background material and the glass, where it will evaporate and make a salt stain that will detract from the appearance of your captive reef. Next, seal the other three edges to the tank in the same manner. Trim the tape with a single-edged razor blade. Properly done, the background should last a long time. It is a nuisance to attach or replace the background once the tank is filled, so make the effort now to do it correctly. (Some experienced aquarists prefer a more permanent solution and paint the exterior of the back glass with quick-drying latex enamel, usually black or a shade of blue.)

• Locate and level the aquarium. Place the tank in its permanent position, and use a carpenter's level, side-to-side and front-to-back, to be sure it is on a perfectly flat surface. You may need to add shims under the legs of the tank stand, or you may need to choose another spot. If the tank is not level, chances of an eventual leak are increased dramatically. (Needless to say, the stand should be rock-solid; if there is any chance of tipping, whether caused by children playing or by earthquakes, the stand should be firmly anchored to the wall or floor.)

Step 3: Add Water

• Fill the tank with cold tap water, dry all exterior surfaces and seams, and check for leaks. Leaks are not common, but do happen. Most manufacturers provide an appropriate guarantee, and a reputable retailer will quickly replace a defective aquarium for you. Ask about this before you buy, and keep your receipt. If the tank does not show any leaks within 24 hours, it probably never will.

• If the tank appears watertight, unpack, assemble, and install the skimmer, the powerhead, and the heater, following the instructions that are packed in the boxes with the equipment. Do not connect power at this time.

• Being careful to first wipe up any spills, plug in all the equipment. (For shock prevention and peace of mind, connect everything through a ground-fault interrupter power cord, available at any good hardware store.) Check to be sure that the skimmer and powerhead are working properly. Don't expect the skimmer to produce foam at this point. It won't. Adjust the thermostat on the heater, following the manufacturer's instructions. Unless you are attempting to duplicate a special environment, 75 to 78 degrees F is a good starting range for a typical marine tank. (If the heater does not provide temperature settings, you will have to check and readjust the thermostat several times over the first day or two until the correct water temperature, as shown by your thermometer, is achieved.)

• Cover the tank, install the light strip, and connect the light to the timer. Set the timer and check its operation.

• Allow the system to run overnight. The next morning, check to see that the temperature is on target and that no slow leaks have appeared.

Step 4: Add Salt Mix

MOST SALT MIX FORMULAS require a little more than 2 cups of dry mix to produce 5 gallons of synthetic seawater. Add the appropriate amount, about 9 cups total for this 20-gallon system, to the tank. The water will turn cloudy. Not all of the salt will dissolve immediately. The circulation created by the skimmer and powerhead will help get the salt into solution.

• After allowing 24 hours for the salt to dissolve completely, check the water with an aquarium hydrometer. A typical glass hydrometer reading should be 1.022-1.024 at 75 degrees F (24 degrees C). Temperature affects the reading. Use the table on page 121 to correct for temperature

Step 4: Aquarium salt mix is added and water is allowed to circulate for 24 hours; then check and adjust the density.

variations. For example, a hydrometer reading of 1.0240 at 24 degrees C calls for a correction factor of +0.0021. Thus the corrected density reading is 1.0261. The salinity, from the table on page 122, is 35 ppt, the same as full-strength seawater. (Some hydrometers intended for marine aquarium use have the scale already adjusted for a temperature of 75 degrees F, and thus read directly in specific gravity units.) If the specific gravity is too low, add more salt mix and wait three or four hours for it to dissolve before checking again. If the density is too high, take some water out and replace it with freshwater. After the density is adjusted properly, mark the water level in an inconspicuous spot, using a bit of tape or a permanent marker. This will make it easy to tell when the water level changes due to evaporation.

• Next, using your test kit, check the pH of the synthetic seawater. It should be in the range of 8.2 to 8.3, plus or minus 0.1 pH unit. In any case, make certain the temperature, specific gravity, and pH are correct before you proceed to the next step. (Rather than mixing the salt solution in the aquarium, you may prefer to use a large vat or a new plastic trash can. Such a reservoir will be extremely handy in the long run, providing a place to mix and age saltwater. A small powerhead or an airstone to keep the water circulating in the reservoir is a good adjunct, as is a submersible heater in cooler climates.)

Step 5: Add Live Rock

AFTER THE AQUARIUM WATER HAS BEEN ADJUSTED to the correct beginning parameters, it is time to add live rock. We are placing the rock first, before adding sand, to create a completely stable rockwork structure, with no pieces precariously balanced or in danger of tipping or sliding out

Steps 5 & 6: Once the proper water conditions are achieved, 15-20 pounds of cured live rock are assembled in a stable structure and approximately 2 inches of sand added.

of place. Some aquarists prefer to place the sand bed first, but additional care must be exercised to ensure that the burrowing of livestock does not undermine and topple the rocks. If the base rocks are resting firmly on the bottom of the aquarium, this should never happen.

During aquascaping, the addition of rock, sand, and your hands and arms will cause the water level to rise. Remove excess saltwater to a storage bucket and set it aside for future water changes; be sure not to let the pumps or heater run dry if the water level falls. As a precaution, you may wish to unplug everything while doing Steps 4 and 5.

You will need to have acquired about 20 pounds of live rock, usually in pieces ranging from the size of a baseball to that of a cantaloupe. (You may wish to use fewer, larger pieces, which may fetch a premium price.)

• Starting with the bigger, heavier, and/or less interesting pieces, build up a reef structure, using any arrangement that suits your fancy. Assuming you select cured live rock, all you will need to do is remove it from the container in which it was transported and place it directly in the tank. Try to have an open arrangement that allows for water movement around each piece, rather than a solid "brick wall" effect. Use your imagination. Since the habitat we have chosen for this tank is a deep fore reef, try to create a cave, arranged so that a view into the cave will be the focal point of the tank. Here is where your fishes or shrimp will likely retreat to avoid disturbances or to sleep.

• If possible, position the powerhead and skimmer so they will be hidden by the rockwork, and direct their currents to flow either across or through the reef structure.

Step 6: Add Substrate

• Pour aragonite sand from the bag in which it is supplied into a clean 5-gallon plastic bucket until the bucket is about one-third full. (You should buy a new bucket or two to use only for aquarium chores. Never use buckets that have held any commodity other than food intended for human consumption. Sometimes restaurants and bakeries will have such buckets free for the asking.) Run tepid freshwater from a tap or garden hose into the bucket, swirling the sand around with your hand. The water will become cloudy, due to the fine particles that have accumulated in the sand during shipment and storage. Pour off the water and repeat the washing process a time or two. This step is not absolutely necessary — the dust is harmless — but the aquarium water will clear up more quickly if the sand is rinsed in this fashion. As each batch of sand is rinsed, add it to the tank, creating a uniform layer on the bottom. Don't worry if the tank becomes cloudy; this is virtually inevitable at this stage and it will clear up in a day or two.

Step 7: Once the rock and sand are placed, introduce hardy livestock, including hermit crabs, snails, and perhaps a damselfish or two.

• Now add, without rinsing, a pound of purchased live sand or sand obtained from a long-established, healthy reef aquarium. Spread this in a layer on top of the aragonite sand.

• Restart the powerhead, skimmer, and heater and turn on the tank lighting. Double-check to make sure everything is working — although the skimmer will still be producing very little or no foam. Recheck the temperature, specific gravity, and pH. If all seems well, leave the tank alone for a day or two, or until the water is completely clear. If something is amiss, correct the problem, and let the tank again sit for a day or two. Now is a good time to begin a log of your water quality parameters (see pages 138-139).

Step 7: Add Livestock

OVER THE NEXT FEW WEEKS, the tank will begin to grow algae. You may want to clean the front and side panels with a brush or razor blade, but the appearance of algae is a clear call to bring in biological helpers. I believe that the most appropriate first inhabitants are herbivorous species that will industriously attack the algae growing on the rock and tank walls. For this tank, 10 snails and four tiny hermit crabs would be good choices. You may be able to order Pacific species of both kinds of organisms, but if necessary, make do with *Astraea* snails and Blue-legged Hermit Crabs (*Clibanarius tricolor*), which are native to Florida. After obtaining specimens, float them (in their plastic bags) in the tank for about half an hour, then release the animals, but not the bag water, into your aquarium. Wait a week before adding any other specimens. If no algae growth is apparent yet, add a tiny pinch of fish food for the benefit of the hermit crabs.

Many, if not most, marine systems are started with rugged little damselfishes to feed the nitrogen cycle. This is still an acceptable approach, but not necessary, and you may want to think twice before adding fishes with scrappy tendencies, especially if later inhabitants will be shy or easily harassed. Remember that any fish you place in a reef tank can be difficult to remove later without upsetting or removing the rockwork. To my mind, the emerging life on good quality live rock and the hermit crabs will provide suf-

Step 8: The completed reef, with Fiji live rock, Golden or Canary Wrasses, a Blue Devil Damsel, and a selection of easy-to-keep Feather Duster Worms.

ficient show for the first weeks. You will be amused at the antics of the crabs as they scurry for the food, and the rock can easily provide living surprises of its own.

Step 8: Complete the Ecosystem

AFTER THE TANK HAS BEEN HOME to snails and hermit crabs for a week or more, you can complete the system with additional invertebrates and fishes.

Because of the modest lighting used on this system, confine your selections to hardy, nonphotosynthetic invertebrates. An excellent choice for the beginner is the Feather Duster (*Sabellastarte indica*; *S. sanctijosephi*), and several specimens can be placed attractively in crevices in the live

rock. A Scarlet Cleaner Shrimp (*Lysmata amboinensis*) would also be at home in this reef environment. The Feather Dusters are filter feeders, and the Scarlet Cleaner is a scavenger, so feeding need not be too frequent. Once or twice a week, a very small amount of frozen fish food can be added for the shrimp. The Feather Dusters will feed on bacteria and other small particles stirred up during maintenance of the tank. Plan on doing a 20% water change about 30 days after the live rock is first added and each month thereafter. Check the nitrate level each week and start doing partial water changes if it rises above 20 ppm. This may be more or less often than every month, depending upon the individual circumstances of your tank. Check and record the pH every week, and check the temperature each time you observe the tank. Add water, preferably distilled or purified, to compensate for evaporation. It is best to do this as soon as you notice that evaporation has occurred. If you forget, and the water has evaporated far below the mark you made earlier, add distilled water a little at a time to correct the specific gravity by no more than 0.001 units per day. Use your hydrometer to determine how far the specific gravity has shifted and to determine the rate at which your corrections are proceeding. Your motto should be "test, then tweak." Trying to correct a problem too quickly may cause more harm than the problem itself.

When you feel comfortable with the maintenance routine, it is time to add the fishes. The choices available are many. The photograph on this page shows a system with a trio of delightful Golden or Canary Wrasses (*Halichoeres chrysus*), which are commonly available and make an interesting, active display. Also shown is a Blue Devil Damsel (*Chrysiptera cyanea*), the classic beginner's fish and an ultra-hardy selection. An alternate choice might be a pair of cardinalfish, also quite content in a small tank.

Remember that any new specimen will require a few days to become accustomed to its surroundings, so do not become alarmed if the fish hide and/or fail to eat for a brief period. Healthy specimens should start feeding within three or four days. If there appear to be problems, consult with the dealer from whom you purchased the fish.

Purchase a selection of frozen foods at the same time you obtain the fish. Feed a small amount each day, observing carefully to make sure that all the food is consumed within an hour of feeding. Watch for normal behavior and check tank conditions (including temperature and equipment functioning) at each feeding.

Congratulations! You have now succeeded in establishing your first natural reef aquarium.

Enhanced four-bulb lighting, upgraded skimming, and increased circulation allow for the addition of mushroom polyps and other relatively hardy "beginner's" corals.

Upgrading the Hardware

WITH ONLY A COUPLE OF MODIFICATIONS, the 20-gallon system just described could easily become a typical Indo-Pacific fringing reef, representing a shallower habitat between the shore and lagoon. First, install a four-lamp fluorescent lighting system instead of the single strip light in the previous example. I would also recommend installing a second powerhead, directing the outflow perpendicular to that of the first powerhead (to the extent permitted by the rockwork) and control both powerheads with a wavemaker.

Upgrading the "Software"

AFTER YOUR STARTER REEF SYSTEM is established, it will begin to exhibit periodic algae blooms. If you follow my advice on pages 136-138, however, the algae blooms should abate after about six or eight weeks, and small patches of purple and mauve coralline algae should begin to appear here and there. Once this coralline algae growth develops, you can add an assortment of soft corals and mushroom polyps. A variety of these might be found in any shallow, fringing reef habitat. You may choose to populate this reef with different or more exotic fish species, but use caution: a 20-gallon system with this filtration system will support only a light load of fishes and/or mobile invertebrates.

As you gain confidence with your skills as a reef aquarist, you will likely want to set up a larger system, and to try your hand at keeping a wider variety of species. Relax and enjoy. You are well on your way to a lifetime of learning and pleasure as you gain experience with the denizens of Earth's most interesting ecosystem, the living coral reef.

50-Gallon Clam Lagoon

Overhead view of a shallow-water clam and coral nursery, typical of an Indo-Pacific patch reef in a lagoon area, featuring captive-propagated *Tridacna* clams, young stony coral colonies, neon-green and orange zoanthids, and a scattering of fishes.

HERE IS AN EYECATCHING AQUARIUM that reflects a small patch of Indo-Pacific back reef or shallow lagoon where baby *Tridacna* clams and various stony coral colonies have settled out. It demands intense lighting and excellent water conditions, but returns the investment in a display that is equally captivating when viewed from front or top — the full coloration of the clams is best seen from above. All clams, corals, and most of the other stock in this tank were propagated in Palau or Hawaii by Gerald Heslinga's Indo-Pacific Reef Farms. The relatively small foam fractionator suits a system that should not be overskimmed, according to clam experts. Regular calcium supplementation is a must.

Aquarium: All-Glass (36 x 18 x 19 inches)

Lighting: Coralife metal halide pendant fixtures: two 175-watt 10,000 K

Temperature Control: two Ebo-Jager 100-watt heaters

Skimming: CPR SR2 in-sump skimmer

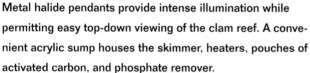

Metal halide pendants provide intense illumination while permitting easy top-down viewing of the clam reef. A convenient acrylic sump houses the skimmer, heaters, pouches of activated carbon, and phosphate remover.

A dazzling spectrum of colors in the fast-growing coral fragments and young clams compensates for a small fish population. The small size of this system dictates that some specimens be relocated to larger aquariums as they develop.

Primary Circulation: Eheim 1060 pump
Other Circulation: Accurate Acrylic Osci-Wave with Maxi-Jet 1000 pump (as powerhead)
Sump: Amiracle Maxi-Reef 200 (biomedia removed)
Control Devices: Intermatic Time-All light timer; Ocean Motion wavemaker
Plenum: Reef Renovators' Eco-Sand Filter Plate used under the bed of aragonite sand
Reefscaping: 30 pounds Marshall Islands live rock (Aquatic Specialists); 50 pounds aragonite sand (CaribSea)

Livestock: Invertebrates: giant clam species *Tridacna maxima, T. squamosa, T. crocea, T. derasa, T. gigas*; various species of *Acropora* started from fragments; neon-green soft coral (*Nephthea* sp.); zoanthids on "polyp rock" (all clams and corals captive-propagated; from Reef Science Intl.). **Fishes:** small Clown Wrasse (*Coris gaimard*) for pyramidellid snail control; False Percula Clownfish (*Amphiprion ocellaris*) captive-bred by C-Quest; Yellow Tang (*Zebrasoma flavescens*) for algae control. **Aquascaping:** 30 pounds Marshall Islands live rock; 50 pounds aragonite sand.

60-Gallon Gulf of Mexico Patch Reef

Full of surprises for those unfamiliar with the beauty of reef organisms from North American waters, this Gulf of Mexico display makes attractive use of a cube-shaped acrylic aquarium.

Rear view of the system shows the integrated sump that easily accommodates a venturi skimmer, system pump, heater, and chemical filtration media in nylon pouches.

Side view of the reef, showing the stable structure of aquacultured live rock and numerous sponges, gorgonians, small colonies of coral, and a spreading spray of *Caulerpa*, top.

WONDERFUL REEF ORGANISMS can be found in our own backyards, as seen in this microhabitat display from the waters off western Florida, not far from Tampa. A dominant mound of live rock demonstrates the promise of aquaculturing, with proliferating colonies of sponges and small stony corals. The aquarium itself, delivered as a complete system, with lighting, stand, and all filtration equipment included, is a good example of an acrylic tank with integrated filtration built into the back of the unit, including an ample skimmer and chambers for heaters, probes, water return pump, and any filtration media.

Aquarium: US Aquarium acrylic UltraReef Combo system (24 x 24 x 24 inches) with granite-gray cabinetry

Lighting: Power Compact fluorescents: two 96-watt 6,700 K Ultra Daylight; two 96-watt 7,100 K Blue; two Intermatic timers for dawn-midday-dusk cycle.

Primary Circulation: Rio 1700 submerged pump

Temperature Control: two Ebo-Jager 100-watt heaters

Skimming: Rio 600 Pro-Twin pump (integrated)

Reefscaping: 60 pounds aquacultured Gulf live rock (Sea Critters); 40 pounds aragonite sand (CaribSea)

Livestock: Invertebrates: Tube Coral colonies (*Cladocora* sp.), Arrow Crab (*Stenorhynchus seticornus*), Common Sea Star (*Echinaster sentus*), Porous Sea Rods (*Pseudoplexaura* sp.), Knobby Sea Rod (*Eunicea* sp.), Star Shell Snails (*Astraea tecta*), Murex Snail (*Murex* sp.), numerous other sponges and invertebrates. **Fishes:** Neon Gobies (*Gobiosoma oceanops*), High-Hat Reef Drum (*Equetus acuminatus*). (All livestock from Sea Critters.)

120-Gallon Stony Coral Reef

A visual feast of coral colonies and captive-grown fragments from the Solomon Islands, Fiji, Palau, Djakarta, and other locales.

HIGH ENERGY IS THE KEY to this pleasing 120-gallon stony coral system. Simulating a section of upper fore or back reef, this is an area subjected to vigorous water movement and intense light, both of which must be supplied by the aquarist who wants to succeed with these demanding corals. The circulatory heart of the system is an ETS state-of-the-art sump and skimmer, the control nexus for water handling, with dual rotating water returns, that creates desirable, chaotic water flow patterns. Lighting, temperature, and other systems are run by an Octopus computerized controller. Heavy feeding demands of the corals are met by an MTC calcium-carbonate reactor, with a chiller to prevent overheating by the metal halide and actinic lighting.

Aquarium: Perfecto glass with oak trim (48 x 24 x 24 inches)

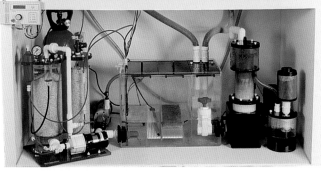

Relatively compact by stony-coral aquarium standards, the under-the-cabinet equipment for this system includes a hard-working sump and skimmer (note several days' accumulation of waste), a calcium reactor and electronic controller.

Aquarium or wild reef? With a shoal of Black-Axil Chromis and a Sailfin Tang at home in the growing corals, this aquarium succeeds as a small but complex microcosm that is not easily distinguished from the real, unfettered biotope.

Lighting: Coralife metal halides and fluorescents, in fan-cooled oak hood: two 175-watt 10,000 K Radium metal halides; two 40-watt actinic fluorescents (Energy Savers Unlimited)

Temperature Control: Aquanetics ASC-2 ⅓ hp chiller (not shown); two Ebo-Jager 200-watt heaters

Skimming: ETS 500 Environmental Tower Scrubber (A.E. Technology); Quiet One pump

Primary Circulation: GenX PC 40X pump

Other Circulation: two AquaGate oscillating water return modules (Aquatic Vision)

Sump: ETS (A.E. Technology)

Control Devices: Octopus Controller monitors and controls lighting, temperature, pH, ORP (Aquadyne)

Other: Marine Technical Concepts Pro Cal calcium reactor

Reefscaping: 100 pounds Fiji Islands live rock (Marine Center); 50 pounds aragonite sand (CaribSea)

Livestock: Invertebrates: colonies of *Acropora, Montipora, Pocillopora, Hydnophora, Pavona, Seriatopora, Porites, Cynarina, Lobophyllia* and others (from Exotic Aquaria, Dynamic Ecomorphology, Marine Center, Reef Science International, Scientific Corals, Tropicorium). **Fishes:** Sailfin Tang (*Zebrasoma veliferum*); Black-Axil Chromis (*Chromis atripectoralis*); Copperband Butterflyfish (*Chelmon rostratus*); Six-Line Wrasse (*Pseudocheilinus hexataenia*).

230-Gallon Red Sea Shallow Fore Reef

Twin peaks of live rock allow ample swimming room for an impressive collection of fishes from the waters off Saudi Arabia.

The behind-the-tank utility room has a large downdraft skimmer, UV sterilizer and heavy-duty chiller, all fed from a 90-gallon sump via a 150-gallon live-sand refugium.

A lack of invertebrate life is balanced by the electrifying colors of the fishes, such as the Masked Butterflyfish, Sohal Tang, and Lyretail Anthias, in an elegant, active aquascape.

NATURAL METHODS can be readily adapted to traditional "fish-only" systems, as in this dramatic Red Sea tank with a stony fore-reef aquascape. More than 400 pounds of live rock and sand serve as a huge biological filter, with some 250 small hermit crabs and snails scavenging waste and algae in the rockwork and in the 150-gallon live-sand refugium behind the aquarium.

Aquarium: Inter-American glass (72 x 24 x 30 inches)

Lighting: Hamilton Technology 72-inch fan-cooled aluminum hood with three 400-watt 20,000 K metal halides and two 160-watt Super Actinics

Temperature Control: four Ebo-Jager 250-watt heaters; Aquanetics ⅓ hp chiller

Skimming: ETS Gemini 800; Iwaki 70 RLT

Primary Circulation: Iwaki MD 100 RLT; water returns through two Aquagate oscillating wavemakers

Sumps: Primary/refugium: Rubbermaid 100-gallon stock watering trough catches detritus from tank and contains Monaco-style live sand bed. **Secondary:** US Plastics 90-gallon polyethylene tank serves skimmer, chiller, return pump.

Other: Aquanetics 25-watt UV sterilizer

Reefscaping: 200 pounds western Pacific live rock; 100 pounds Samoa Pink coral sand (Worldwide Imports)

Livestock: 250 "reef janitor" hermit crabs and snails of mixed species—these are subject to some predation by the fishes in this system and may be periodically replenished (Geothermal Aquaculture Research); Masked Butterflyfish (*Chaetodon semilarvatus*), Half-Moon Angelfish (*Pomacanthus maculosus*), Checkerboard Wrasse (*Halichoeres hortulanus*), Purple Tang (*Zebrasoma xanthurum*), Sohal Tang (*Acanthurus sohal*), Lyretail Anthias (*Pseudanthias squamipinnis*), Golden or Red Sea Mimic Blennies (*Escenius gravieri*) (all from Al-Sawaee Red Sea Marine Fish via Global Marine and Marine Wholesale Inc.).

Chapter Three

The Living Filter

Natural Cycles:
The Simple Beauty of Live Rock and Live Sand Systems

EARLY IN MY COLLEGE DAYS at the University of Tennessee, long before I had any training in marine biology, I was lucky enough to be assigned as an advisee to Dr. J.O. Mundt of the Department of Microbiology. Dr. Mundt (now deceased) was a great mentor who kindled my interest in microorganisms and their biochemical virtuosity by demonstrating a remarkable capability in the area of controlled fermentation to produce beverage alcohol. In layman's terms, he made great wines.

His skill extended to other foodstuffs that were prepared with the aid of bacteria, yeasts, and molds, and I shall never forget the taste of his strawberry vinegar. It was not made by steeping the fruit in white wine vinegar, as the commercial product is produced. Rather, ripe strawberries were first transformed into wine by the action of yeast, and this was subsequently turned into vinegar by the introduction of appropriate bacteria. The result had the sweet/tart tang of wild strawberries. Dribbled on garden fresh lettuce, the effect of this concoction was Elysian.

Dr. Mundt was the first microbial ecologist I ever met, and he taught me how the bacteria inhabiting all of Earth's

Festooned with mushroom anemones and other life, live rock forms the biological foundation of a natural reef aquarium.

environments contribute fundamentally to the characteristics of those environments. Oddly, 30 years later, I have come to associate the clean ocean smell of live rock with Dr. Mundt.

This characteristic odor, rather like that of freshly dug earth, is due to volatile organic molecules produced by bacteria. As a marine aquarium retailer, I have handled, literally, tons of live rock. Some of it has been a source of discovery, while some of it has brought with it little more than foul silt and bad smells. Good-quality live rock, however, is absolutely essential to the successful establishment of a natural marine aquarium in the shortest possible time.

Chief among the helpful microorganisms colonizing live rock and live sand are nitrogen-dependent bacteria. To Dr. Mundt, this would have been obvious. To the novice aquarist, it is perhaps less so. The management of the nitrogen from these essential microorganisms is vital to the survival of all higher organisms in the aquarium ecosystem.

The Nitrogen Cycle I

MUCH HAS BEEN WRITTEN about one group of aquarium bacteria in particular, the nitrifiers. Two genera, *Nitrosomonas* and *Nitrobacter*, have long been recognized for their importance in the process called biological filtration. Every aquarist must comprehend fully the process of biological filtration. In brief, this important ecological cycle is as follows: Ammonia that is excreted by fish and invertebrates is converted first to nitrite and then to nitrate by the metabolic activities of nitrifying bacteria. Ammonia and nitrite are highly toxic to aquatic organisms, while nitrate is much less so. Biological filtration consumes oxygen and produces acidic compounds as a by-product. Both these facts are important to the overall water quality of the aquarium. These chemical conversions are mediated by *Nitrosomonas* and *Nitrobacter* and a few other types collectively known as nitrifying bacteria. (Most sources credit *Nitrosomonas* and *Nitrobacter* with playing the key roles in aquariums, but some recent research suggests that this may need further study.) Whatever the bacterial forms at work, they are essential to the process in nature known as the Nitrogen Cycle. This process is crucial to aquarium systems as well.

Aquariums designed to exhibit coral reef fishes are commonly equipped with biological filters designed to encour-

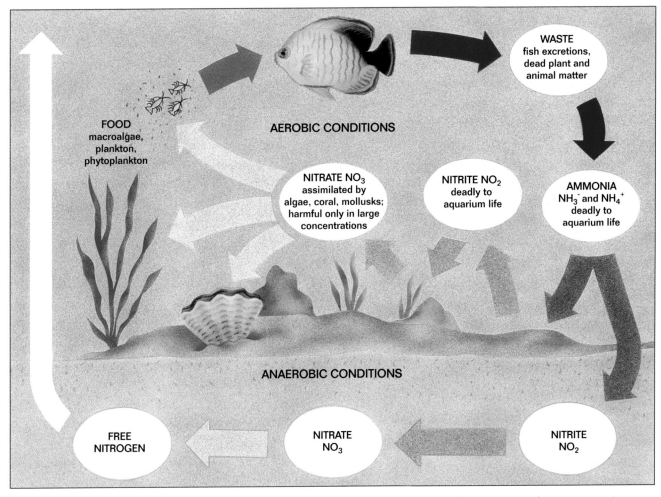

The Nitrogen Cycle in nature: an understanding of these nutrient pathways is fundamental to success with marine aquariums.

age colonization by nitrifying bacteria. Hobbyists will be familiar with equipment ranging from undergravel filters to many types of wet/dry filters. All focus upon rapid conversion of ammonia to nitrate. In these systems, the process of "mineralization" of nutrients occurs. Nitrogen that enters the system as complex organic molecules (proteins) in food is reduced to its simpler "mineral" components by biological activity. Not all of this biological activity comes from animal metabolism. In fact, only a small part of the food energy entering the hobbyist's tank is captured by the fishes. Much more probably feeds bacteria than feeds the fishes. Even fish fecal pellets and other organic "wastes" can be utilized by some form of simple bacteria or other microorganisms residing in the aquarium. These organisms are collectively termed "heterotrophs."

The substances upon which heterotrophs feed may be, like fecal pellets, preprocessed by another organism or group of organisms before the heterotrophs get a crack at it. Large invertebrates, including annelids, mollusks, echinoderms, and arthropods, may feed on food not consumed by fishes, for example. The excretory products of these organisms are then further acted upon by microscopic life forms, such as microcrustaceans, nematodes, worms, fungi, and protozoans, and thus finally reach the heterotrophs.

All along the way, gases, minerals, trace elements, and various organic compounds are being spewed out, recycled, converted, and reconverted in a dizzying frenzy of biochemical activity. The end result consists primarily of "inorganic minerals," such as ammonia, phosphate, sulfate, and carbon dioxide gas. The ammonia is utilized by *Nitrosomonas*, which uses oxygen dissolved in the surrounding water to oxidize ammonia to nitrite, extracting energy in the process. *Nitrobacter*, in turn, oxidizes nitrite to nitrate and thereby also gains energy.

All of these processes require oxygen, and all are said to be "oxidizing" reactions. What remains of the complex food molecules at the end of this process is about what would be left after burning them in a fire: water, carbon dioxide, and minerals.

The Nitrogen Cycle II

THERE ARE OTHER IMPORTANT biochemical processes that occur in the aquarium and must be taken into account by the aquarist. One of these involves bacteria and the absence of oxygen. This process is called denitrification. Denitrification is a reduction process. Denitrifying bacteria reduce nitrate to nitrogen gas, which escapes to the atmosphere. In the simplest terms, we can think of nitrification — the detoxification of deadly ammonia — taking place in aerobic conditions on the extensive surface area of live rock and live sand in the aquarium. Denitrification, the breakdown of nitrate to elemental nitrogen, occurs within the porous rock or deep in the sand bed. While artificial media can offer some of the benefits of these live materials, for most of us attempting to create a natural reef aquarium, live rock and live sand are attractive, interesting in their own right, and provide many benefits to system health and well-being.

Live Rock

WHAT IS "LIVE ROCK"? For the keeper of a tropical marine aquarium, it is fragments of stony reef material, often coral rubble, broken off in storms and scattered in piles in the lagoon, shoreward of the reef. Taken from the ocean with various species of encrusting organisms attached, live rock reaches the retailer in much the same way that vegetables reach the grocer's shelves. Sometimes, the product arrives freshly harvested, glistening with clean water; perhaps with an interesting arthropod or mollusk tagging along, still ambling about as if basking under a warm sky. At other times, the journey has been arduous, and the rock,

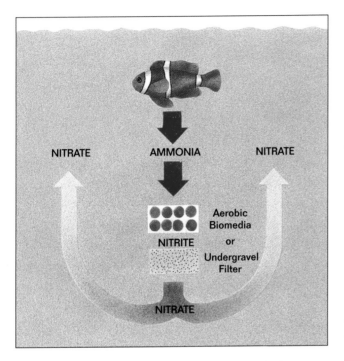

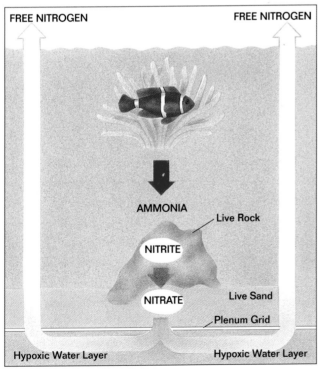

Top left: the Nitrogen Cycle in a conventional marine aquarium — nitrate accumulates as the end product of waste conversion. Bottom left: a natural system with a Monaco-style plenum — denitrification yields elemental nitrogen.

smelly with an odor of putrefaction, is coated with slime. Mobile animal life either lies dead at the bottom of the box or struggles feebly to avail itself of whatever moisture and oxygen might yet remain.

Among the earliest discussions of reef tanks, George Smit's (1986) articles make repeated references to the use of live rock in creating the aquarium environment:

"I believe that most hobbyists would agree, however, that the picture of a complete 'miniature reef,' complete with living rock, thriving algal plants such as *Caulerpa* sp., invertebrates that do not just 'exist' for a short period of time, but actually grow and multiply, along with healthy specimens of fish, would be the ideal goal to achieve. Yet how many aquarists are actually aware of the fact that live rock is not just a decorative alternative to coral skeletons, but as necessary to the long-term survival of the miniature reef as the correct quantity and quality of light?"

Smit recognized the value of microorganisms associated with live rock and suggests, in the caption of one of the illustrations that accompany his articles, that live rock bacteria may even produce antibiotic substances with beneficial effects. He describes carefully how live rock may be used to "seed" the system with nitrifying bacteria. It apparently never occurred to Smit that live rock could be used to filter the aquarium all by itself. Perhaps this was because his primary focus was on the wet/dry filter system that he was introducing to American hobbyists. It was perhaps from Smit's writings that the notion of "seeded" live rock came to exist. The word "seeded," if used to mean cleaned and held after collection, is inappropriate and misleading in this context. It suggests that the rock begins its development

Encrusted with coralline algae and calcareous macroalgae, Caribbean live rock can be exceedingly colorful.

A section of premium Pacific zoanthid rock from Fiji, covered with *Palythoa* polyps and a sprig of *Caulerpa racemosa*.

during the handling it receives before being put to its final use in a reef tank. It is more correct to say that the rock must "cure," or complete its development (like prosciutto or Stilton) after its having been "seeded" by nature. To appreciate the process of curing live rock and the effect this has on the aquarium environment, it is necessary to understand how this material reaches the aquarium marketplace.

Before restrictions were placed on the collecting of live rock in Florida, collectors might take specimens in only a few inches of water, just below the low-tide mark. At the extreme, road fill, barely wetted with each turn of the tide, but harboring a few tree oysters and blobs of filamentous algae, was boxed up and shipped to unsuspecting aquarists. As the unhappy recipient of one of these shipments, I cautioned employees not to cut themselves hauling the rock to the dumpster. I had visited spots in the Keys where rocks like this could be found, filthy coves where Styrofoam cups and broken glass were the most common species; I was concerned about the potential for infection.

Aquaculture efforts in Florida are placing substrate rock at depths ranging from 10 to 110 feet (Frakes, 1995). In

the Indo-Pacific, rock is harvested at shallower depths, in part because collectors often lack equipment. In any case, collectors bring in as many chunks of rock as they can carry, and store them in tubs or baskets on the deck of the dive boat. Ideally, the rock is kept covered by wet blankets or tarps to prevent drying under the harsh tropical sun. When the boat returns from a collecting excursion, the rock is packed in boxes, usually surrounded by wet newspaper, and shipped via air freight to the dealer. This may be a retailer, as is often the case with rock collected in Florida and shipped to a store east of the Mississippi. If the rock originates in the Indo-Pacific, it will first arrive in the hands of a broker who takes care of the import paperwork before shipping the rock along to the retailer. If the retailer is only able to purchase a small quantity of rock, another middleman, a wholesaler who supplies many dealers with both rock and other specimens, will be part of the picture. Along the way, the rock remains in the original packing container, so much depends upon how expeditiously the journey from some tiny island 15,000 miles out in the Pacific to the retailer's holding tanks can be completed. Variations in transit time can have pro-

tions. At the time of this writing, as I understand the situation, live rock harvest in Florida has been phased out completely (as of January 1, 1997, collection of any type of live rock product was banned). Thus, rock colonized with Florida False Coral (*Ricordea florida*) is now seldom available, although these specimens were once quite common. The Green Sea Mat (*Zoanthus sociatus*), and other species of sea mats, as well, are now seldom seen in Florida collections. Cultivated, or farmed, rock is likely to be the only Florida live rock available, and this will consist of coral rubble or rock collected from land and deposited in aquaculture zones to be colonized by marine algae, organisms, and bacteria. The Indo-Pacific remains the primary source for specimens of mushroom polyps, sea mats, and other assorted cnidarians that are supplied as colonies attached to a chunk of rock. Rocks such as these are often adorned with brightly colored sponge colonies, macroalgae, assorted fanworms, tunicates, and other small organisms, in addition to the dominant invertebrates.

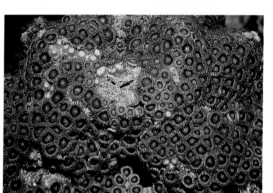

Well-established zoanthid rock, almost completely covered with a green sea mat, *Zoanthus* sp.

Types of Live Rock

PLANT ROCK is simply live rock upon which one or more species of macroalgae predominate. There may, of course, be additional organisms present on the rock, but plants are the primary colonizers. Such material generally does not come from the reef itself. While certain macroalgae are found on reefs, plant rock is most often collected in shallow, back-reef areas, where the absence of herbivorous fishes permits many types of seaweeds to flourish. Macroalgae add a desirable, natural appearance to the aquarium. Introducing macroalgae via plant rock is one of the best ways to establish these species in the aquarium. Some very beautiful specimens once came from the Florida Keys. Plant rock is sometimes available with healthy growths of species such as *Dictyosphaerium*, *Valonia*, or *Codium* present. More often, however, only *Caulerpa*, a more widespread genus, is present. Calcareous macroalgae such as *Udotea*, *Penicillus*, and *Halimeda* often do best if obtained attached to plant rock. Many other species of macroalgae may be found on plant rock, and these may vary considerably in their adaptability to the aquarium. The aquarist can spend many fascinating hours in establishing a tank devoted primarily to macroalgae, and such a project is to be encouraged. A macroalgae tank can contain many organisms besides the algae themselves: seahorses, slugs, and certain anemones that are found in heavily vegetated shallow-water habitats.

ZOANTHID ROCK comes from both Atlantic and Pacific sources. This material, mostly collected from shallow water, is dominated by the presence of one or (rarely) more than one species of zoanthid, or "sea mat." By far the most commonly available specimens once were colonies of the Green Sea Mat, *Zoanthus sociatus*, from Florida and the Caribbean. Less commonly seen were the golden sea mats, *Palythoa* sp. and *Isaurus duchassaingi*, a related species. From Hawaii, seven species of sea mats were once available. The most attractive is *Isaurus elongatus* with polyps about 2 inches in length. In *Isaurus*, the dime-sized crown of tentacles is usually a lovely greenish blue color. *Palythoa vestitus*, *P. psammophilia*, *P. toxica*, *Zoanthus pacificus*, and *Z.*

kealakekuanensis are also found on Hawaiian live rock specimens. While these specimens are no longer collected in Florida or Hawaii, similar species may be found on specimens from other localities in the Indo-Pacific.

Living as they do in shallow waters, sea mats require bright light, but they are otherwise hardy and undemanding, usually spreading readily throughout the aquarium. Specimens are sometimes heavily laden with fine silt, and these should be rinsed in seawater to remove as much silt as possible before being exhibited. Other zoanthids, including *Palythoa caribaeorum*, *P. tuberculosa*, "*Parazoanthus gracilis*" (not a true scientific name), and *P. swifti*, are deep-reef organisms and thus are not found on sea mat rock from shallow water. These species also make good aquarium inhabitants.

FLORIDA FALSE CORAL (*Ricordea florida*) is a favorite species of mine. Like the mushroom polyps imported from the Pacific, *Ricordea* polyps are flattened disks, averaging about an inch in diameter, that occur in scattered colonies in waters up to 60 feet down. The tentacles are round knobs about 1/16-inch across and are usually bright blue-green in color, although specimens are rarely orange, pink or blue-gray in color. The more green pigment present in a given speci-

Brazilian rock, displaying an appealing irregular shape and good coralline growths.

Aquacultured Florida rock with macroalgae and small colonies of stony corals.

men, the greater the likelihood that it came from shallow water. *Ricordea* needs plenty of light. With the closure of the Florida Keys to all live rock harvest at the end of 1995, false coral rock is now seldom available, but if one can locate a specimen, it makes a striking addition to the aquarium. Like all mushroom polyps, it is easy to keep. Mushroom polyp rocks from the Indo-Pacific are readily available and make fine aquarium specimens. They propagate themselves easily under good conditions.

BASE ROCK is a term used to denote material that is mostly devoid of living organisms. This stuff tends toward heavy, rounded pieces that are neither attractive nor particularly easy to stack to create an open framework. Advances in the production of aquacultured live rock, using porous artificial substrates, together with the ban on collection of Florida live rock, will probably eliminate "base rock" from the aquarium trade. Good riddance, in my view.

Organisms on Live Rock

THE VARIETY OF LIFE PRESENT on a live rock specimen, and the state of health of that life, turns upon one important issue: was the rock collected, packed, and shipped without prolonged exposure to the air? In other words, was each individual piece handled separately and treated like a shrimp or fish specimen, or was the rock harvested in bulk and shipped "dry," i.e., covered with wet newspaper? "Dry" shipment results in rock that has to be cured before it can be used in the tank, as a result of significant die-off of the fauna on the rock. I have discussed the curing process in detail above. Cured live rock is therefore not heavily encrusted with a multitude of life forms. These may appear later, though, after the rock has been in an aquarium for several months. By contrast, live rock that has been kept submerged often has no die-off at all. As a result, delicate species like sponges and tunicates survive to become part of the aquarium fauna. Such rock needs no curing.

One frequently seen type of live rock deserves special consideration. Rocks from the Gulf of Mexico, harboring colonies of the serpulid annelid *Spirobranchus giganteus*, the Christmas Tree Worm, are regularly seen in the aquarium trade because of their multicolored beauty. While these specimens are not appropriate subjects for the tropical reef aquarium, they do deserve the interest of aquarists who might create a tank focused upon their unique habitat (see Chapter Seven).

The fact that highly successful reef systems can be created using live rock as the sole source of biological nitrification and denitrification — Berlin-style reef aquariums — is strong evidence for the important role of live rock microfauna and flora. Julian Sprung has suggested to me that biological denitrification occurring within anaerobic areas of live rock removes nitrates from the system as they are produced, with little or no accumulation in the tank. My own observations support Sprung's contention. One aquarium of mine in particular never had a measurable level of nitrate in three years' time, despite a typical "load" of invertebrates and fishes.

What role, if any, other live rock organisms may play in the ecology of the aquarium has yet to be determined. One can suggest several possible benefits, however, from rock that has a full, natural complement of life forms present. First, the encrusting fauna of live rock assist in nutrient management in the aquarium by sequestering nutrients within biomass rather than having these same compounds available as particulate or dissolved substances in the water. Second, many of these organisms aid in detritus removal. Certain worms, for example, accumulate little piles of debris near the holes in which they live, facilitating its removal by the hobbyist. This represents another form of nutrient management. A third possible benefit is the production, almost continuously in some species, of larvae that constitute the tank's "plankton." A fourth benefit, less tangible than the others, is the inherent stability created in a system that is highly diverse. It is an axiom of ecology that very diverse ecosystems are better able to weather stress than simpler ones. While the typical tank may contain 30 or 40 species of algae, invertebrates, and fishes, the number of species on a single piece of live rock, when all the bacteria, protozoa, and microinvertebrates are counted, can number in the hundreds. The live rock fauna thus contributes significantly to the biodiversity of the aquarium. From the foregoing, it would seem obvious that one wants live rock with as many organisms as possible present. However, there is a catch. Preserving the maximum number of species requires that the rock be kept in water during the journey from the point of collection to the aquarium, as mentioned before. I have verified this observation repeatedly on collecting excursions. Air freight is a big part of the cost of live rock, and shipping the rock in water will add significantly to its weight. Because the cost of air freight is determined by weight, rock shipped in water will ultimately be much more expensive to the consumer than rock shipped "dry." Thus, the choice, as usual, becomes one of ecology versus economy.

What about my contention that Florida "base rock" is

not as useful as live rock from the Pacific? My thinking results from two sets of observations. The first of these I call the "boring sponge" argument. Certain sponges, chiefly species of *Cliona*, actually bore into carbonate rocks and infiltrate the rock mass with their bodies. This infiltration can be very extensive, with perhaps 25% of the rock replaced by sponge tissue. Like most other sponges, *Cliona* tends to die when removed from the water. The dead sponge decays very slowly, and the resultant pollution is produced over a very long period of time. When this happens, the rock frequently sports a growth of filamentous algae that is virtually impossible to control. This scenario might explain why, in an otherwise pristine tank, one tenacious patch of algae defies all attempts at eradication.

The other argument I call the "shape" argument. Consider first that the primary object in using live rock is to aid in nutrient management in the tank. Remember that nitrification, an aerobic process, occurs on the surface of the rock, and denitrification, an anaerobic process, occurs in the interior of the rock. This arrangement facilitates coordination of these two processes, as envisioned by Sprung. If these assumptions are correct, processing of nitrogen compounds from the water will occur most efficiently when exposure of the water to rock surface is at maximum. So a rock that is branched and porous, with lots of crannies, crevices, and holes, is more desirable than a rock that is relatively solid and shaped like a brick or rounded lump. This is the same reasoning that is applied to the selection of plastic widgets for filling the biological chamber of a trickle filter. Rather than using Ping-Pong balls, trickle filters employ a variety of spiked, perforated, and ornamented doodads in an effort to provide the maximum amount of surface area for bacterial colonization.

By these two arguments, then, the optimum choice is for live rock that is highly branched, porous, and free of embedded boring sponge growth. Generally speaking, these traits are the ones consistently found in rock imported from the Western Pacific, from locations such as the Marshall Islands. Porous, attractive rock is being aquacultured in large quantities on the Gulf side of Florida, and new sources of wild rock from Panama, Central America, and Brazil are also emerging. (The last year for any wild live rock collecting in the waters off the United States was 1996.)

Gulf of Mexico rock with hangers-on: *Murex* snail, limpets, sea cucumber, Clinging Crab, urchin, and tiny brain corals (at right).

Some of the organisms on live rock belong to taxonomic groups encountered nowhere else in the aquarium trade. I shall briefly mention each of these minor groups here, since many aquarists want to know what is inhabiting their live rock specimens.

SPONGES are often imported for the aquarium and may do very well in the reef tank. Live rock specimens may harbor a variety of sponges in an array of colors. Sponges can be distinguished from the remainder of the organisms listed by virtue of their porous structure and the absence of tentacles of any kind. As mentioned earlier, beware of fouling from sponges that have been exposed to the air.

Fanworms on coral-encrusted rock in the Caribbean: many such organisms can emerge from high-quality live rock.

Fan bryozoans and Encrusting Red Sponge in Biscayne Bay: Florida rock now comes only from licensed aquaculture sites.

ANNELIDS AND OTHER WORMS. In addition to embedded fanworms of various types, the fauna of live rock may include cirratulids — a family of annelids with long, spaghetti-like tentacles. A bewildering variety of motile annelids with scales, spines, and bristles may disclose themselves once the rock is in your tank. Only large or numerous bristleworms pose any threat of harm to other reef tank organisms, however. Minor worm groups, usually found within the rock's crevices, include sipunculids, also called peanut-worms, and the rare echiurids. Sipunculids are usually drab in color and have a long, extensible proboscis. Echiurids are often brown or gray, but occasionally are lavender, pale green, or other pastel shades and may be distinguished by a flattened, triangular proboscis. Sipunculids and echiurids are detritus feeders. I have often found sipunculids as a result of the breakage of a piece of live rock. At Aquatic Specialists, it has become routine to feed dying invertebrates found in rock shipments to the fish. When an employee recently did feed a little brown sipunculid from a shipment of Tongan live rock to a mixed tank of fish, the results were quite unexpected. Only two fish in the tank

nibbled at the worm, and both were rapidly and dramatically affected. Coloration became pale, and overnight the fish exhibited signs of extreme dehydration. Dehydration probably occurs as a result of kidney failure, and the resulting emaciation of the fish happens rapidly. The fish are literally "pickled" by the salty water surrounding them. A common feature of toxic reactions in higher vertebrates is the shut down of renal function. If these observations indicate that the skin slime of the sipunculid is toxic to fishes, the toxin must be a potent one. No damage at all could be found on the worm, meaning that none of its flesh was tasted by the fish. Thus, only a minute amount of secreted material induced the effects, and no other fish in the same aquarium was affected in any noticeable way. After about two days, during which they hid and refused to eat, the two affected fish emerged from hiding, apparently good as new. Moral: feed not that which you do not know for sure is safe! Sipunculids are rarely seen outside their retreats in the rocks, but apparently when they do venture forth, they do so well armed in the face of danger from predatory fishes.

Nemertean worms are flattened, ribbonlike, and very

elongated. They may be variously colored and patterned. Nemerteans feed on small invertebrates, but pose no threat to the inhabitants of the reef tank. Flatworms may also be quite colorful and can be recognized by their smooth, very flattened bodies. They are seldom more than an inch or two in length. Most flatworms are predatory and feed on other invertebrates. If you find one, observe it closely to determine its feeding preferences; remove it from the tank only if it seems to have a taste for something you plan to protect.

BRYOZOANS. The bryozoans are all colonial, and many resemble plants. In fact, the name "bryozoan" means "moss animal." These are filter feeders that may encrust large areas of live rock, forming colonies that are often rather stiff and hard, owing to a skeletal structure composed of calcium carbonate or tough protein material. They can be recognized by a circle of tentacles that is just visible to the naked eye and appears much like a tiny fanworm. Most are quite colorful.

TUNICATES. Many species of colonial tunicates may be found on live rock specimens. They are beautiful animals, usually colorful and quite delicate-looking, appearing to be constructed of translucent glass. Larger tunicates, about the size of a grape or marble, can clearly be seen to possess a pair of body openings, side-by-side. Water is drawn into one of these, the food material is strained out, and the water is expelled through the other opening.

Regardless of its source or the nature of the organisms attached, live rock is an essential component of the natural marine aquarium. I compare live rock to the soil in a fertile garden because of its significance to the living processes taking place within the captive ecosystem. Most important among these processes are nitrification and denitrification, which are both mediated by bacteria.

Live Sand

THE MONACO-STYLE AQUARIUM is analogous to the Berlin-style in that it relies on natural, bacteriological processes occurring within the aquarium. Dr. Jean Jaubert of Monaco has exploited this approach using the natural properties of reef sand to create inexpensive, effective filtration for reef aquariums. Jaubert's methods were described for the benefit of American hobbyists by Sprung and Delbeek

Often overlooked, delicate tunicates are relatively common on live rock that is shipped with care and kept in good water.

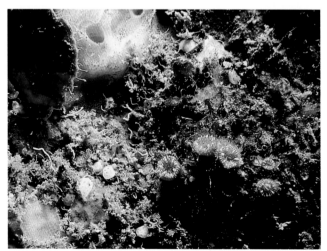

Dwarf Cup Coral, *Astrangia solitaria*, a hardy stony coral frequently seen on rock from Florida and the Caribbean.

(1990) and by Frakes (1993a, 1994). In brief, this technique relies upon a thick layer of sand on the aquarium bottom to provide an appropriate home for denitrifying bacteria. Either a bed of live reef sand or, more commonly, a layer of aragonite sand seeded with a quantity of live sand collected from the ocean floor is used. Small organisms present in the live sand help keep the substrate biologically active, while denitrifying bacteria thrive in the low-to-zero oxygen conditions in the deepest layer of the sand. This technique results in denitrification, and the dissolution of the aragonite returns both calcium and carbonate ions to the water. Dr. Jaubert has been successful in maintaining high levels of calcium and alkalinity in his systems, together with low levels of phosphate and nitrate, through reliance on these natural processes alone. The tremendous surface area within the sand bed apparently adds significantly to the biological filtration capabilities of a captive system, and many reef aquarists who have augmented their former Berlin-type systems have reported better nitrate control and increased coral growth with live sand *and* live rock, rather than with live rock alone.

Natural substrate materials of coral reef origin assist greatly in maintaining a proper chemical balance and can be used to create authentic and unusual aquarium microhabitats.

Establishing a Monaco-Style System

FOR TANKS OF UP TO 200 GALLONS, here is a step-by-step explanation for establishing a Monaco-style system:

1. A false bottom of plastic light-diffuser grid, called eggcrate, is suspended about 1 inch off the bottom of the aquarium tank. The plastic must cover the entire bottom securely and should be made in two pieces to facilitate installation. Straight couplings for ¾-inch (ID) PVC pipe, which are about 1 inch in outside diameter, can be used to support the plastic grid. Place each coupling on its side and secure it to the grid with plastic cable ties. Use about one coupling every 6 inches in each direction to be sure of adequate support. Off-the-shelf grid systems are also available, including undergravel filter plates available from any aquarium shop. Simply remove and cap the lift tubes to create an enclosed plenum under the sand. Other commercial models, such as the Eco-Sand Filter Plate (shown on facing page), provide further options.

2. On top of the eggcrate, one or more layers of plastic window screening are used to prevent the sand from falling through to the plenum, the area underneath the grid where water, but no sand, is present. This is important, as the plenum must remain unobstructed and contain only water. (Before adding any live substrate, the system should be filled with saltwater and circulation systems activated.)

3. Enough sand to create a layer 1 to 2 inches deep is placed on the screen. This should be silica sand, crushed coral, or other material that will not

PEN PLAX
UNDERGRAVEL FILTER

REEF RENOVATORS'
ECO-SAND FILTER PLATE

PERFECT-A-FLOW
UNDERGRAVEL
FILTER

HOMEMADE
JAUBERT-STYLE PLENUM

Simple grids that can be used in Monaco-type systems, in which a layer of hypoxic water is formed under layers of sand. Homemade versions are easily constructed using plastic eggcrate and fiberglass screening, with off-the-shelf options also available.

readily dissolve. Aragonite should not be used for this layer, or it may eventually turn into a chunk of "concrete." This is the denitrification layer and should remain undisturbed. Aragonite can be used in the upper layer, where the activities of burrowing organisms will prevent solidification.

4. A second layer of screening is placed atop the first sand bed. On top of this, another 1 to 2 inches of substrate is placed. This looks and works best if composed of aragonite, live sand from the ocean, crushed coral, and crushed shell fragments, with about half the total amount being aragonite and/or live sand. This material will slowly dissolve and be replaced by small amounts of new aragonite as the system matures. The live sand portion is to provide a seeding of beneficial organisms (see below for how to determine the weight of materials needed).

5. There should be vigorous water movement created by pumps, powerheads, airstones, or some combination thereof. Lighting can be minimal or none at this stage. Dr. Jaubert's original systems do not employ protein skimming, but have very low loading of dissolved organics, primarily, in my view, because of their small fish populations. If the aquarium does have a large bioload, protein skimming can and should be used to minimize the water's organic content. Early discussions (Frakes, 1993a, 1994) of the Jaubert method suggested, incorrectly, that protein skimming would be detrimental, as it might deprive beneficial organisms of a needed energy source. Dr. Jaubert has publicly corrected this misinterpretation of his work, however (Jaubert, 1995).

6. Enough ammonium chloride solution is added to give 3.0 ppm on a good ammonia test kit. Commercial preparations are available, or use a 6% (w/v) solution of reagent

grade NH_4Cl in distilled water. This is added along with the live sand.

7. Nitrite is measured with a test kit, beginning about a week after the ammonium chloride is added and continuing every few days. You will see a peak of nitrite, followed by a decline to zero. At this point, about 30 days after the live sand/ammonium chloride was first added, you will have enough nitrate in the water to be detected by a test kit. The pH will have fallen during this time. It can be maintained by adding limewater during the whole process, enough to compensate for all evaporated water, or by using a commercial pH buffer. Sodium bicarbonate (household baking soda) can also be used as a buffer additive. A solution containing about 1 teaspoon (5 gm) of soda in 1 pint (500 ml) distilled water can be added to the tank for each 10 gallons of water and the resulting effect on pH noted. It is then possible to determine how much of the solution to add to move the pH to the desired reading. Changing the pH of the aquarium by additions of chemical should always be done slowly, so that a few tenths of a pH unit of change occurs over several days time. Maintaining the pH during this phase of the aquarium's development is not crucial but will make life easier later on.

8. Nitrate is now measured every few days. As anaerobic bacteria grow in the lower sand layer, the nitrate is converted to nitrogen gas, which escapes into the atmosphere. When the nitrate level is down to zero, perhaps 3 to 4 weeks later, the bacterial populations of the tank are established and stable.

At this point, live rock is added to create the reef structure, the lights are turned on, and the system is developed like a Berlin-style reef tank. If maintenance of pH, alkalinity, and calcium were not done during the cycling period, they are adjusted now, and a regular routine of maintenance is established. The tank will undergo a series of algae blooms for the next six to eight weeks, during which time only mo-

bile organisms, and especially those that help with "housekeeping" such as *Astraea* snails, brittle stars, hermit crabs, fish, etc., are added. When the algae blooms stop and the tank starts growing coralline algae, photosynthetic invertebrates can be added. As long as the water chemistry is maintained, the system will grow and develop from this point with little effort (apart from maintenance duties, of course) on your part.

Additional Considerations in the Monaco-Style Aquarium

1. Adding the live rock along with the live sand will speed the nitrogen cycle along considerably. Some people prefer to add the live rock periodically in small amounts, because of the cost. This is also acceptable.

2. To figure out how much substrate you need, calculate the volume of the sand bed in cubic inches, using the following equivalents:

1 pound of live sand = 14 cubic inches

1 pound of aragonite, live rock fragments, or shell fragments = 23 cubic inches.

Example: Let's say we want a 2-inch layer of sand in the bottom of a 75-gallon tank that has a base of 4' x 1½'.

48" x 18" x 2" = 1,728 cubic inches.

If you use all live sand, you will need

1,728 ÷ 14 = 123 pounds of sand.

For a half-and-half mix, about 40 pounds of rock fragments and 60 pounds of sand will be required.

3. To construct the reef itself, you will need about 1 pound of cured Pacific Islands live rock for each 1 gallon of water capacity, if the aquarium is constructed in a standard, rectangular tank. This much live rock makes a stack about three-quarters the height of the tank and running the full length of the tank, allowing plenty of room for water flow.

4. While Dr. Jaubert relies on the dissolution of the

aragonite alone to replenish both calcium and carbonate ions in his systems, you will probably find that a densely populated home system needs either additions of limewater or more aragonite and additional maintenance. I would rather add the limewater than do other maintenance. The end result will be the same in either case.

5. Add substrate sifting animals as soon as tests indicate that the development of bacterial activity in the sand bed is complete. This would be at the same time that live rock and algae-eating organisms are added. The idea is to establish the community of "utilitarian" species that will help to maintain the environment for the Pivotal Species to occupy the aquarium later.

The live sand system in action: note the gas bubbles, blue-legged hermit crab, and sand-sifting goby, all part of the working environment.

The Simplified Live Sand Approach

THE NOTION OF HAVING A PLENUM with a layer of "dead" water at the bottom of the aquarium strikes some hobbyists as either unnatural or too complicated. A number of Americans have modified the Jaubert method simply by adding a layer of live sand several inches deep to reef aquariums already containing significant amounts of live rock. Virtually all believe that the sand provides valuable denitrification and helps provide calcium and buffering capacity to their systems.

Speaking at the Western Marine Conference in San Francisco in 1996, hobbyist Larry Jackson advocated building one's live rock structure directly on the bottom of the aquarium and then filling with aragonitic sand (live or dried) to a depth of two to three inches. Jackson uses only

one layer of sand, but keeps it physically active with the presence of small sea cucumbers and other burrowing organisms. His own recipe for creating live sand is to mix oolitic aragonite with coarser "Samoa Pink" reef sand and let this bed become colonized with beneficial bacteria, worms, and other organisms through contact with healthy live rock.

"I like to keep things simple, and I've had good luck without going to the trouble of building a plenum," Jackson said. "Why bother?"

In exchanges on Internet aquarists' forums (see Selected Sources, page 307), others have reported similar success without the use of a plenum, but some hobbyists have also experienced the development of pockets of hydrogen sulfide gas in live sand beds that do not have the benefit of a plenum. Jaubert and others suggest that the plenum allows a very slow diffusion of water and gas through the sand, thus avoiding noticeable hydrogen sulfide problems.

Some hobbyists have found that placing the bulk of their live sand over a plenum in the sump, rather than in the display tank, makes for easier maintenance and fewer problems with fishes disrupting the deeper sand. For those with established reef tanks, a remote sump allows one to add the advantage of live sand without tearing down the aquarium. Such a sump, devoid of predatory fishes, can also become a haven for delicate organisms and a settling basin for larvae of various species.

Until controlled experiments are done, these various creative methods of employing live sand will remain within the realm of home aquarists developing their own tech-

CORALLINE ALGAE

HOBBYISTS INTERESTED IN REEF TANKS and live rock certainly hear a lot about coralline algae. Most are aware that this is something good to have in a marine aquarium, but not many know what coralline algae are and how to encourage them to grow.

Classification of the marine algae is a subject for experts, although the corallines form a distinct group. They are red algae (Rhodophyta, Order Cryptonemiales) scientifically identified by certain microscopic details of their reproductive structures. The coralline species, which are distinguished from all other red algae by the production of

Strikingly beautiful, coralline algae also prevent the growth of undesirable forms of microalgae on live rock.

a calcified skeleton, constitute the Family Corallinaceae. The body, or thallus, of a coralline species may be crustose, covering rocks like a lichen on a stump, or erect and segmented. The reproductive structures are produced in special cups, called conceptacles. These are sometimes evident to the eye or touch and are a useful clue to the identity of some species. The corallines comprise one of the largest and most important families of the red algae and are found in all seas from pole to pole. They tolerate temperature extremes and are found at great depths, owing to the ability of some species to survive on very low light intensities. While coralline algae are impor-

tant components of the flora of cold seas, they can be significant in tropical habitats as well. In Hawaii, for example, the living reef crest is often composed of coralline algae, not coral growth. Ecologists designate this portion of a Hawaiian reef the Porolithon Ridge, named for the dominant genus of coralline algae in this zone of turbulent surf. *Lithophyllum* is another species found in heavy surf.

In shallow-water habitats, articulated coralline algae may be found. These branching, jointed forms include *Amphiroa*, densely bushy *Corallina* in reef flats and tidepools, and common, shrublike *Jania*, found in many habitats. These types are capable of overgrowing stony corals. Tidepools and shady areas of the back reef may be home to *Galaxaura*, which has distinctive hollow branches that may be flattened, bushy, or even fuzzy, depending upon the species. In open, more wave-swept habitats, unusual *Liagora*, only partially calcified and therefore more flexible, is found.

Aquarium keepers are more likely to encounter the encrusting coralline algae. Many can be tentatively identified by noting the color and the pattern of growth. Growing on shells and rubble in shallow water and often seen on the shells of *Astraea* snails is *Titanoderma prototypum*. It looks like a patch of mauve paint. Related *Titanoderma* and species of *Fosliella* grow only on the surfaces of green macroalgae such as *Dictyosphaerium*. (These are not the only corallines that live on other organisms. Some are parasites.) Knobby, pale bluish clumps with sharp projections scattered over the surface are colonies of *Neogoniolithon spectabile*, which might also be confused with the lavender, rough-surfaced *Hydrolithon*. Smooth, maroon, distinctly botryoidal encrustations are *Sporolithon*, found in the intertidal zone to 90 feet and common on live rock. Another common genus is *Peyssonnelia*, looking like a dark reddish or maroon coat of paint on rocks down to 600 feet. Uncommon pinkish

Platelike coralline algae: one of many forms and hues that can thrive in aquariums receiving calcium supplementation.

purple *Tenarea* has pretty spiral sculpting on its surface, making it easy to identify. It is most often found on rocks taken from about 30 feet, but sometimes occurs in shallower waters. The genus of coralline algae I see most often established in hobbyist aquariums is *Mesophyllum*. It is a medium purple, forming lovely shelflike plates and crusts on rocks, decorations, equipment, and glass in old, established reef systems. Careful analysis of the coralline algae growth on live rocks could be used to make a good guess about the approximate depth from which the rock was collected, because the algae's habitat preferences may be rather specific.

Coralline algae thrive under aquarium conditions that are conducive to good growth in stony corals, i.e., well-oxygenated water, correct pH and alkalinity, ample calcium, strontium, and iodine. Most encrusting corallines grow under moderate light conditions and will not be found in the brighter areas of the aquarium. *Mesophyllum* is perhaps the most light-loving species.

After initially adding all of the live rock to a new aquarium, the system is likely to experience blooms of microalgae for several weeks. If the aquarium is maintained during this time as if stony corals were already present, the corallines will usually begin to appear in small patches on the glass about six weeks after the initial introduction of live rock. This may be taken as a good sign that the system is maturing properly and will soon be a suitable environment for stony corals. The presence of coralline algae on a particular site often inhibits the development of other types of algae in the same spot.

Coralline algae are ubiquitous in the marine environment. In the aquarium, their presence is an indicator of good conditions. Their growth discourages competing algae. They are also colorful, attractive, and easy to obtain on live rock. Like many of the less noticeable species that contribute to the aquarium's biodiversity, coralline algae provide important benefits.

niques and making their own informal observations. Clearly, however, the use of live sand beds both to maintain a better chemical balance and to provide habitat for beneficial organisms offers both environmental and aesthetic improvements over the bare tank bottoms that were widely advocated only a few years ago.

Assimilation by Photosynthesis

THE OTHER VITAL BIOCHEMICAL PROCESS that occurs in all ecosystems — assimilation — is carried out by photosynthetic organisms. Photosynthesis is essential to many of the species that will be exhibited in a reef aquarium. Some photosynthetic organisms, however, can be a major problem for the aquarist. Photosynthetic organisms utilize light energy to power the reverse of the oxidation process: reduction. During photosynthesis, carbon dioxide (one of the end products of mineralization or decomposition) is "reduced" to carbohydrate molecules in the presence of light. After nightfall, the energy stored in the carbohydrate molecules is liberated once again, using oxygen, in the same metabolic process used by nonphotosynthetic organisms to carry out decomposition. The energy liberated from the carbohydrates is ultimately used by the photosynthesizer to create complex molecules for growth, development, reproduction, and other important biological tasks. When photosynthesizers are in turn eaten by animals, or decomposed by bacteria or fungi, the energy stored in their carbohydrates is liberated for the benefit of the consumers. Photosynthesis thus channels the sun's energy into the ecosystem.

The role of bacteria in nitrate utilization is important to the stability of the aquarium ecosystem, but is likely to be quickly overshadowed by photosynthesis when nutrients required for photosynthesis are abundant. Many corals and their relatives, although technically nonphotosynthetic animals, depend upon photosynthesis because they contain symbiotic algae, called zooxanthellae. These have important functions in the life of the coral, one of which is the assimilation of waste products of the coral's metabolism. Much nutrient recycling thus occurs in reef organisms such as these. Probably very little ammonia is actually excreted into the water column by organisms harboring photosynthetic symbionts. Tridacnid clams, for example, are known to extract ammonia and nitrate from aquarium water (Heslinga, et al., 1990).

The bulk of the living material (biomass) of the natural reef aquarium will consist of species that are photosynthetic or that have photosynthetic symbionts. Nonphotosynthetic invertebrates will also be present in significant numbers, as will heterotrophic bacteria. All will release ammonia and other compounds into the water. Owing, however, to their comparatively minuscule food requirements, these organisms will not contribute much to the pollution load in the aquarium. It will most likely be fishes, with their greedy appetites and high levels of activity, that provide most of the waste products for processing by the system. This is one reason why the fish population of the natural reef aquarium should be kept low, although such systems are able to support a population density of fishes per gallon of water that is much higher than the density that occurs in the ocean.

Interest in maintaining large numbers of fishes no doubt led early marine aquarists to focus on the oxidation of ammonia to nitrate as the most important detoxification process that should take place in the aquarium system. To the modern aquarist seeking to maintain a natural reef aquarium, biological filtration (mineralization) must be balanced with its counterparts — assimilation and denitrification. Artificial methods for achieving such a balance in the aquarium usually look good on paper but are impractical because they must necessarily focus on limited aspects of the total ecosystem. Hence, wet/dry filters, for example, are wonderful at achieving mineralization, but a tank so equipped may experience excessive algae growth if additional effort is not expended to reduce the accumulation of algae nutrients in the water.

In the natural reef aquarium, artificial methods are employed largely to remove organic compounds before they are mineralized. The technique that accomplishes this is foam fractionation, also known as protein skimming. In addition, husbandry practices in the natural reef aquarium are directed toward limiting the input of nutrients from outside the system. Bacteria present in live rock carry out both mineralization (nitrification) and denitrification, thus taking care of any excess material that escapes the protein skimmer. Finally, growth of certain types of algae (usually coralline algae species) is allowed to develop naturally, permitting assimilation to occur. In this manner, the natural reef system develops its own balance.

Colorful but secretive, sometimes troublesome, and covered with stiffened, stinging hairs, bristleworms routinely appear in reef aquariums, imported unseen in live rock.

Interactions & Equilibriums

To SELECT AN APPROPRIATE SUITE of techniques for a particular installation, the marine hobbyist must consider the reason for the aquarium's existence. To readers of this book, that reason may be the enjoyment of a relaxing hobby, the challenge of learning about coral reefs and their inhabitants, or the pleasure derived from having a special kind of decoration in the living room. Other good reasons for aquariums include creating an artificial ecosystem to study the effects of change on natural ecosystems or the production of marine organisms for sale or for restocking the ocean.

In any aquarium, however, regardless of the techniques employed to create it, a complex collection of interrelated organisms will develop over time. The biological processes mediated by each of them will affect all of the others. Consider the equilibrium that is achieved in a system that has been running for a year or more with no additions of new animals. Apart from the growth of the original specimens, there may be little change in the biomass. A stable population of nitrifying bacteria will convert to nitrate any ammonia not collected by photosynthetic organisms. As soon as it is produced, the nitrate is converted to nitrogen by the denitrifying bacteria. When such an equilibrium exists, the net amount of nitrogen measurable in the water, whether as ammonia, nitrite, or nitrate, will therefore be zero. This is a fundamental observation that has been overlooked in

Herbivorous cleaners, such as this Red Reef Hermit (*Paguristes cadenati*), are essential allies in fighting algae in the reef tank.

the past. Nitrate is not toxic at low concentrations, but it should not be present in the marine aquarium for precisely the same reason that it is not found in the waters around the coral reef: recycling of nitrogen by biological activities results in a low level of free nitrogen compounds in the surrounding water. Similarly, stability of other water parameters that are influenced by biological activity — pH, alkalinity, and calcium concentration — occurs when an equilibrium condition is reached. Now consider what happens when, let us say, one Royal Gramma Basslet dies unnoticed. The fish's biomass is rapidly transformed. Hermit crabs and small bristleworms living in the substrate quickly reduce the basslet's carcass to small bits, leaving only the tiny, hairlike bones. Microinvertebrates complete the physical breakdown of the fish, and heterotrophic bacteria and fungi begin the chemical dissolution process. The nitrogen stored in the gramma's flesh over several years of growth is now released all at once into the system. Ammonia, nitrite, and nitrate may all appear in the water, as the bacterial population always experiences a lag in adjusting to the newly available food supply. Organic matter and phosphate are also released, and some of the latter is quickly consumed by algae, which experience a noticeable surge in growth. The inexperienced aquarist may react to these changes with panic, taking all sorts of measures to restore the system to its former state. Removing any undecayed portion of the dead fish, changing some water and persevering with routine care are all that need be done, however. A healthy system will return to equilibrium on its own. Just be patient.

Together with the interplay among all of the living species present, one must also consider the interaction between the organisms and the physical conditions maintained by the aquarist. In my frequent correspondence with marine aquarists the world over, I am surprised at the number of things that are added to, or done to, aquariums with a view toward circumventing natural processes in favor of quick results, or a somehow "better" system. Undefined mixtures touted with vague claims of efficacy against a variety of problems or as miraculous growth stimulants are dumped into tanks by unsuspecting hobbyists, changing the environment in unknown ways and creating a new set of parameters with which the specimens in the aquarium must cope. The result of these interactions is totally unpredictable, because there are so many possible variables. Each system is slightly different in design, each collection of species unique. Thus, while we can describe methods and practices that seem to give us the results we desire, we can never create entirely predictable systems. Mother Nature herself is unpredictable, but all alone, even in a glass box of synthetic seawater, with minimal prodding, she will organize an ecosystem that maintains itself as surely as she delivers plankton to the waiting tentacles of a soft coral with each turn of the tide. But she must be given a chance to work her magic.

That said, evidence is slowly emerging that, given sufficient time for the development of appropriate flora and fauna, natural marine aquariums can be created without the use of large quantities of material harvested from the ocean. For example, systems that rely on a "live sand" bed for biochemical stability are typically built using dry, dead sand that eventually develops into a living community. Given time and the proper circumstances, dead rock and coral skeletons can be turned into cultivated versions of live rock, either via natural or artificial means. In all cases, however, a seed stock of organisms must come either from a previously established aquarium or from the sea, but only a small quantity of such material is necessary to inoculate a system.

A significant component of any ecosystem, whether natural or confined within an aquarium, is a complex, not fully characterized community of microorganisms we introduce with live rock and live sand: bacteria, fungi, algae, protozoans, and tiny invertebrates. Just as certain essential processes mediated by soil microorganisms sustain terrestrial communities of plants and animals, so does an invisible community of microorganisms sustain the artificial ecosystem of the aquarium. We add fertilizer to the garden in the form of manure or compost. Bacteria and other organisms in the soil then transform nutrients that were consumed by the animal that excreted the manure or accumulated in the plants that comprise the compost, performing chemical alterations that make the nutrients available to the plants in the garden. Organic gardeners appreciate this relationship between dead and living organic matter. Fostering this interaction in the natural marine aquarium requires one to become an organic aquarist. Learn to be nice to the bacteria that live in your aquarium, and they will be nice to you. Dr. Mundt, I think, would have been pleased that you learned this.

Chapter Four

Aquarium Lighting

Solar Substitutes for the Reef Aquarium

WITHOUT THE CONSTANT INFUSION of powerful energy from the sun, the ocean would be a stagnant environment, starved of life. Our local star warms the water, gives rise to winds and currents, and, with the moon, commands the tides. It feeds the biosphere through photosynthesis. Take away the fueling function of the sun and the oceans would die, taking the rest of the biosphere with them. One of the greatest catastrophes ever to occur on Earth may have been the impact of a giant meteorite off the Yucatán Peninsula about 65 million years ago. According to theory, this object, about 6 miles wide, threw up so much dust by its impact that solar energy was blocked for a long time, affecting photosynthesis in the ocean and weakening the ecosystem so severely that major portions of Earth's fauna died out forever. Although the evidence is compelling, this theory remains unproved, but its hypothetical scenario demonstrates clearly how solar energy powers the biosphere.

Aquariums are equally dependent on the life-sustaining input of light, and much of the history of keeping captive systems has involved the search for a better substitute for real sunlight. Apart from good water conditions, the single most important factor in the success of any aquarium containing photosynthetic organisms is the quantity and quality of the light provided. One must supply a minimum of 10,000 lumens of light per square meter of aquarium surface in order to meet the needs of most aquatic organisms commonly kept in aquariums. One cannot fully compensate for insufficient overall intensity by increasing the period of time that the lights are on (photoperiod) or by using wide-spectrum lamps (lamps that emit light over a broad range of visible wavelengths).

Still, marine organisms are marvelously adaptable creatures that can subsist on less than the optimum amount of light. After all, it is not always sunny in the Tropics, the water is not always crystal clear, and it is not always necessary for zooxanthellae to be photosynthesizing at their maximum rate. If organisms that depend upon photosynthesis grow and reproduce in their artificial habitat, then the lighting obviously is adequate.

I have been asked repeatedly about the relative merits of various types of lamps and lighting systems for aquariums. In my opinion, there are many choices that give satisfactory results. The last word on aquarium lighting has hardly been written, but there are some basic guidelines.

Gorgonians and a school of Blue-striped Grunts (*Haemulon sciurus*) in the sunlit waters of a reef in the Florida Keys.

Photobiology

PHOTOBIOLOGISTS, scientists who study the interactions between living organisms and light, measure light intensity in terms of photon irradiance. Simply put, this is a measure of the number of light-energy units (photons) falling on a given area in a given period of time. The standard measurement is a unit of energy (microeinsteins per square centimeter per second). Why use such a measurement? Because energy drives living systems. For photosynthetic organisms, the amount of light energy reaching them determines how well the vital engine of photosynthesis runs. This situation can be compared to the relationship between the accelerator pedal (light intensity) and the speed of a car engine (photosynthesis). Press down on the pedal (increase the light intensity) and the engine revs up (rate of photosynthesis increases). Just as a car runs best at moderate as opposed to very slow or very high speeds, there is an optimum level of "acceleration" for photosynthesis. Photobiologists have learned that the total number of photons (intensity) falling on a given organism is more important than the energy level (wavelength) of the individual photons.

How then, is the aquarist going to insure that this energy requirement is met? Natural daylight is the best lighting source, but it is an impractical one for most of us today. To utilize natural daylight for aquarium lighting, a greenhouse or special window arrangement is required in most climates. More and more advanced reef enthusiasts are experimenting with the use of natural sunlight in such situations to enhance growth rates or coloration of stony corals, but these systems almost invariably require both supplemental lighting and a water chiller. Even in the most northerly regions, an aquarium placed in direct sunlight can overheat. Aquarists should avoid placing the aquarium in a sunny window, as seasonal fluctuations in temperature in such a location will make maintaining the correct water temperature a challenge. Artificial lighting, for most home situations, is the better choice, being more controllable, predictable, and programmable for the most convenient viewing period.

Providing Sufficient Light Intensity

BEFORE INSTALLING A LIGHTING SYSTEM, one must make certain that the resulting levels of illumination over the aquarium will be sufficient. Simple approaches are given below, but many aquarists enjoy the challenge of planning their own lighting schemes. Ideally, one could carry out direct measurements in the tank with an underwater lux meter. This is more difficult to do accurately than one might think, even assuming one has the rather expensive instrument available.

One way to estimate intensity is to rely upon the old-style method of measuring intensity in lumens and irradiance in lux (lumens per square meter). Over tropical seas, irradiance can exceed 150,000 lux, far more intense than any aquarist can hope to achieve with artificial light. Fortunately, 10,000 lux is sufficient for most aquatic organisms, although more than this is certainly not harmful. Thus, to determine the light intensity required, first calculate the surface area of the tank in square meters. One square foot equals 0.093 square meters. So the surface area of a 55-gallon tank (about 4 square feet) is about 0.37 square meters. Multiplying this value by 10,000 lumens per square meter yields 3,700 lumens for the minimum amount of light that must reach the organisms in the tank.

How can one determine which lamps will provide this much light? Major lighting manufacturers provide this data in the specification sheets they publish for every type of lamp they make. For example, according to the Phillips Lighting catalog, one of their 40-watt Ultralume fluorescent lamps (F40T12/50U) has an initial lumen output of 3,300 lumens. Therefore, two of these over a 55-gallon tank should provide plenty of light. Unfortunately, the specified lumen output of the lamp does not accurately represent the light intensity that can be expected in actual use. All lamps decrease in intensity with use, so the average lumen output over the life of the lamp, not the higher initial lumen output, must be taken as the starting point. This varies with different lamp types, but is usually somewhere around 60% of the initial output. That would be 1,980 lumens for the Ultralume lamp in this example. Two Ultralume lamps would therefore have an average output of 3,960 lumens. It still seems like a high enough output for the 55-gallon tank in our example, but other factors must be considered.

Up to this point, we have assumed that all of the light emitted from the lamps will reach both the water surface and the bottom of the tank, but the laws of physics are against us. In order for the total output of the lamps to reach the surface, we would need a reflector over the lamps that was 100% efficient, casting all of the light output onto the tank. Of course, no such perfect reflector exists. Estimates of reflector efficiency, coupled with allowances for reflection from the water surface and other factors, reveal that, at best, roughly 50% of the light emitted from the lamps will reach the tank. That means we will actually need four of the 40-watt lamps in this example to provide a total of 3,960 lumens at the water surface.

In order for the light to reach from the surface to the bottom of the tank, we must next take into account a principle of physics called the Inverse Square Law. This states: "The intensity of light falling upon an object decreases in proportion to the square of the distance between the object and the light source." For our purposes, this can be translated, "If you double the distance between the lamps and a photosynthetic organism growing in the tank, you'll need four times as many lamps in order for the organism to continue to grow at the same rate." It would be difficult, therefore, to provide too many of the 40-watt Ultralume lamps,

but the minimum would be four for a 55-gallon tank, 20 inches deep, to provide reasonably bright light. As we will see, even this is insufficient for many reef organisms.

Fluorescent Lighting Systems

FLUORESCENT LAMPS are the most affordable and convenient solution for most beginning reef systems, and they come in standard output, high output (HO) and very high output (VHO) types. Brighter than standard lamps of the same length, HO and VHO lamps consume correspondingly more electricity. They also lose output faster, but this may be offset by periodic replacement. Output ratings for fluorescent lamps discussed in the aquarium literature seldom refer to the efficacy of the lamp, i.e., the lumens of light produced per watt of electricity consumed. While it is generally true that "the higher the wattage, the brighter the lamp," the suitability of a particular lamp design for aquarium use has mostly been determined by trial and error. This makes giving precise watts-per-square-foot estimates of the amount of light needed for an aquarium of photosynthetic invertebrates a frustrating, difficult exercise.

As a starting point, select fluorescent lamps of the maximum wattage that can be easily accommodated over the aquarium. For example, if the tank is 4 feet long, use lamps that are also 4 feet long. Standard lamps in this length are 40 watts and provide about 2,000 to 3,000 lumens each, depending upon the lamp type. For moderate light in tanks up to 18 inches deep, two standard lamps are the minimum. (The single-bulb lighting strips commonly sold with "starter aquarium packages" are virtually useless for all but very dimly lit, nonphotosynthetic or fish-only systems.) Four lamps are needed for bright light, such as a lagoon tank. For a deeper tank, or to illuminate a tank more brightly with fewer lamps, HO or VHO lamps can be used.

For tanks up to 18 inches deep, use the following guidelines for determining the total wattage needed when using standard fluorescent lamps:

Tank Dimensions L x W x H (inches)	Watts Needed of Standard Fluorescent Lamps	
	Minimal Reef Light	Moderate Reef Light
20 x 10 x 10	15 watts	30 watts
24 x 12 x 16	40 watts	80 watts
36 x 12 x 16	60 watts	120 watts
48 x 12 x 18	80 watts	160 watts

These are modest lighting levels, with the "minimal" wattage appropriate for fishes and nonphotosynthetic invertebrates. The "moderate" level can be sufficient for the less demanding soft corals such as *Lobophytum, Pachyclavularia, Sarcophyton,* and even such large-polyped stony corals as *Fungia, Plerogyra* (Bubble Coral), *Trachyphyllia* (Open Brain Coral), *Turbinaria* (cup corals), and the *Actinodiscus* (mushroom polyps). Realistically, this calls for four fluorescent bulbs above the tank, and even with this amount of light, many of these corals will suffer if the bulbs are not replaced frequently.

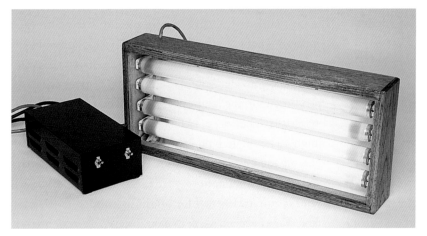

Good starter fluorescent lighting unit for a small reef tank, with oak hood enclosing two full-spectrum and two actinic-blue bulbs and a remote ballast unit.

In order to thrive, virtually all soft corals and most stony corals will require multiples of this wattage, dictating the use of HO or VHO fluorescents, high-intensity compact fluorescents, or metal halide lighting. Additional illumination will always permit the maintenance of a wider range of shallow-water species.

The nature of the phosphor coating on the inside of the white tube is what gives fluorescent lamps their spectral-output characteristics. Photosynthetic organisms have pigments that absorb strongly in the red and blue regions of the spectrum, although accessory pigments allow energy to be gathered from light of many wavelengths. It is wiser to provide a balanced white light for shallow-water species and to emphasize the blue wavelengths in aquariums for species that come from greater depths. Most of the brand-related claims for fluorescent aquarium lamps revolve around their special spectral qualities. Hobbyists should remember that many combinations of fluorescent lamps have been successfully used to culture photosynthetic marine invertebrates and macroalgae. It is much more important to use enough lamps to provide proper light intensity before fretting over minor differences in the spectral distribution curve of one brand of lamp versus another.

The fluorescent lighting system of choice among experienced reef keepers, assuming no budgetary constraints, would probably be two or three VHO full-spectrum or "reef" bulbs and one or two VHO actinic tubes for a 75-gallon tank, 24 inches deep.

Metal Halide Lighting Systems

THE NEED FOR HIGH LIGHT intensity, especially for larger aquariums or those featuring invertebrates that demand plenty of light, is one reason I advocate the use of metal halide lighting. A single 175-watt metal halide lamp generates about 15,000 lumens and is smaller than a football. I know of no other practical light source for the aquarium that will provide this intensity in so small a space. A single-bulb metal halide pendant such as the one shown in the accompanying photograph is sufficient light to illuminate an aquarium of about 24" x 24" x 24" (about 60 gallons). A tank of this size, so illuminated, could be called a "brightly lit" or "shallow-water" tank, suitable for specimens accustomed to intense solar radiation. I have observed that many species of photosynthetic invertebrates grow and reproduce successfully in this level of illumination.

If you expand the cube to a rectangular shape 36" x 24" x 24" (about 90 gallons) using the same lighting, the level of illumination could be called "moderately lit" or "middepth." I have found that mushroom polyps, for example, will reproduce under these conditions, some other species will grow slowly, and many species are able to maintain themselves but do not grow or reproduce.

Finally, if you increase the size of the tank to 48" x 24" x 24" (120 gallons), still using a single 175-watt metal halide

Metal halide bulbs, ranging widely in shape, size, and output, yield the most intense practical light for the home reef.

Simple and attractive with a remote ballast unit, a single-bulb metal halide offers intense lighting with good heat diffusion.

bulb for lighting, you would have a "dimly lit" or "deep" tank in which, for example, mushroom polyps would survive, but growth, if any, would be very slow.

The gold-standard reef lighting package today typically includes two 175-watt metal halide bulbs and two 110-watt VHO fluorescent tubes that can be operated independently. Placed over a 4-foot-long tank 18 inches deep, this lighting configuration will allow the aquarist to

Excellent reef tank lighting package, with two actinic-blue fluorescent bulbs and two 175-watt full-spectrum metal halides.

succeed with most soft and stony corals. Deeper tanks and more demanding stony corals, such as *Pavona*, *Goniopora* and certain *Acropora* species, need 250- or even 400-watt metal halides for success.

What about assertions that metal halide lamps will always "burn" invertebrates? This, in my opinion, is hogwash. I have placed literally hundreds of specimens beneath metal halide light sources and have never had this problem. Even metal halide lighting will not be as bright as the sunlight that may have fallen upon these animals in nature. So where do these stories about burning come from? I suspect there are three sources for the confusion:

1. Some gorgonians and alcyonarians that are regularly sold as tank mates for photosynthetic corals come from areas where light intensity is naturally low. Placing such animals under intense lighting could well have detrimental effects. Try growing a forest fern in full sun and you will see by analogy what I mean.

2. Some suppliers may not provide proper lighting for specimens kept in their holding tanks. If deprived of light for a sufficiently long period of time, polyps may shed their zooxanthellae, taking on a "bleached" appearance. When such specimens are subsequently reexposed to bright light, the remaining zooxanthellae begin to photosynthesize at a high rate and to multiply rapidly. This results in a high rate of oxygen production. While oxygen is essential for all forms of life, too much is harmful. Charles Delbeek has suggested that the detrimental effects of placing a bleached specimen under high-intensity lighting may be due to this oxygen poisoning.[1]

3. When corals and other polyps are held under conditions of inadequate light, or when the specimens happen to have been collected from shaded waters, changes in the pigmentation of the zooxanthellae result. Zooxanthellae are marvelously adaptable. They produce, in addition to chlorophyll, a host of other photosynthetic pigments. Some of these "accessory" pigments permit the utilization of light wavelengths that chlorophyll does not absorb, enabling the zooxanthellae to capture more of the sun's energy and to take advantage as much as possible of the light spectra available at different depths, on cloudy days, etc. Other pigments are produced by the host polyp in response to ultraviolet light and probably serve to shield the zooxanthellae from the harmful effects of this radiation.

Therefore, two things can happen when organisms harboring zooxanthellae are shifted from one lighting regime to another. The proportion of the different accessory pigments may change as the zooxanthellae accommodate themselves to the new light situation. This may be evident as a color change in the coral and be interpreted as burning by aquarists unaware of the phenomenon. Alternatively, organisms from deeper waters, or specimens that have languished for too long in dim light, may have ceased production of protective pigments. When these specimens are then placed under bright lights, the effect is similar to that experienced by someone who, having spent a long winter indoors, rushes out on the first sunny day and spends an afternoon sunbathing. I believe that the alleged burning of corals by metal halide lights can be attributed to a lack of understanding of how these organisms respond to light and not to any inherent detrimental effect of the lights themselves.

When in doubt, experts typically do not place newly acquired specimens close to the surface and directly under strong metal halide lighting. Rather, the new coral or other organism is started lower in the tank and gradually, over a period of days or weeks, worked up to the position where it will be permanently placed. (Vegetable gardeners who start their own seedlings will see the similarity to the "hardening off" process used when indoor plants are first exposed to full outdoor sun. This is done over a period of days,

---

[1] Charles Delbeek, personal communication.

as even sun-loving tomatoes can be seriously "burned" by sudden, day-long exposure to unfiltered sunlight. As with metal halides, it is not the source of the light that is the problem here, but rather the lack of experience of the human manipulating the plant or animal.)

On the other hand, overheating is a real potential threat whenever metal halide lights are used. With good air circulation over the surface of the tank (usually provided by silent "muffin" fans that come on automatically with the halides), and a cool or air-conditioned house, increased water temperatures may not result. But metal halides do throw prodigious amounts of heat, and many owners of such lighting systems have found the need to incorporate chillers to prevent routine overheating or disasters during hot spells. Whenever installing a new lighting package, make frequent water temperature checks to ensure that a problem isn't developing. (Even HO or VHO fluorescents in a tight, unventilated hood can overheat certain systems.)

Spectral Characteristics

WHAT ABOUT THE QUALITY OF THE LIGHT, its spectral characteristics, or, if you prefer, its "color"? Sunlight is composed of many wavelengths (colors) of light. To meet the needs of photosynthesis and to create a natural appearing aquarium, a light source that duplicates the spectrum of sunlight as closely as possible is desirable. There is a relatively simple way to compare the spectral output of various light sources to that of sunlight. This is called the Kelvin temperature scale. Noonday sun under clear skies has a rating of 5,500 degrees Kelvin (K). This is a bluish white light. Lower Kelvin temperature ratings will be progressively more red in color, while higher temperatures are progressively more blue. Thus, the nearer the Kelvin temperature of an artificial light source is to 5,500 degrees K, the more closely this source mimics the color of sunlight. Kelvin tempera-

ture data on virtually any lamp can be obtained by checking the specification sheet for that lamp type, available from the lamp's manufacturer. The Phillips Ultralume fluorescent lamp used in the example earlier has a rating of 5,000 degrees K. The aquarist should use lamps that have a high Kelvin-degree rating, at or above 5,000 degrees K, if possible. (Bulbs intended for other uses are often inappropriate: horticultural lighting is typically in the 4,000 to 4,500 K range — "redder" or "warmer" than the ideal for reef tanks.)

It is possible to combine different types of fluorescent lamps to achieve both high intensity and a suitable spectral rating. High output (HO) and very high output (VHO) fluorescent lamps are very bright and come in many suitable types. These lamps require special ballasts and the bulbs will need to be changed more frequently (about every 6 months) than standard fluorescent lamps. Standard lamps should be changed every 9 to 12 months, owing to shifts in the spectral output of the lamps during prolonged use. The point is that many fluorescent lamps and combinations of lamps will work as aquarium light sources. The list of available lamp types is seemingly endless. Only by experimentation can one determine if a particular combination is going to be satisfactory for the organisms in any given aquarium, taking into account both the needs of the organisms and the appearance of the tank. Different types of lamps also give different biological results. For example, I find that macroalgae seem to grow better under illumination that is higher than 5,500 degrees K. Various genera, including *Caulerpa* (several species), *Penicillus*, *Halimeda*, *Udotea*, *Cymopolia*, *Valonia*, *Dictyosphaerium*, *Gracillaria*, *Hypnea*, and several others, grew in my aquariums under fluorescent lighting. All of these species, however, as well as corals and anemones, do as well or better under metal halide lighting.

As many people may be aware from extensive discussion in the aquarium literature, sunlight's colors are progressively filtered out by the water as one descends deeper into the

#1. Expert aquarist Michael Paletta's large reef system under four different lighting schemes, starting with 6,500-degree K metal halides.

#2. The same section of Paletta's stony coral aquarium with all-actinic fluorescent lighting, clearly displaying a distinctive blue cast.

ocean. Many stony and soft corals grow at depths where all of the light is in blue wavelengths. (The longer red wavelengths are absorbed near the surface, while the shorter blue wavelengths penetrate most deeply.) Lighting systems with lamps rich in blue wavelengths are often included for the benefit of these specimens, although the effect, while it is a realistic depiction of the appearance of the reef at these depths, may appear unnatural or eerie to some observers. Also, the beautiful colors of some deep-water species are only apparent when they are exposed to full-spectrum illumination. This is why many hobbyists, as well as public aquariums, use white rather than blue light for the majority of their displays.

Shallow-water species, of course, should always be illuminated with white light. Red wavelengths are absorbed by green pigments, and specimens with bright green pigmentation probably came from shallow waters where red wavelengths penetrate. Golden-yellow pigments, found in zooxanthellae, absorb blue light. These pigments are found in all photosynthetic invertebrates, suggesting that providing blue light is beneficial. Many species produce pigments that fluoresce in blue light, a sure sign that the light is interacting with the pigment but not necessarily an indication of any biological effect of the light. (The vibrant fluorescent greens and blues seen under actinic-blue or so-called 03 actinic lights account for their inclusion in the mix of bulbs over many reef setups.) Ultraviolet (UV) protective pink or purple pigments are produced by many species of cnidarians exposed to high levels of UV in shallow, brightly illuminated locations. Such specimens may lose their colorful pigments if transferred to another light regime.

Safety

SAFETY IS AN IMPORTANT CONSIDERATION for any aquarium lighting system, only in part because of the potentially deadly combination of water and high voltages. One must pay attention to other important safeguards. Never look directly at the filament of a metal halide lamp; all produce at least some UV radiation, which can damage the eyes. Locate the lighting transformer, or "ballast," in an area where it will be well ventilated — all lamp ballasts produce heat — and protect it (and all other electrical equipment around the aquarium) from contact with seawater. Never place a ballast on the floor of an aquarium cabinet where it can be reached by spilled water. If there is a spill near the ballast, disconnect the power before cleaning up. Finally, suspend metal halide lamps sufficiently high above the water to provide ample room to work on the tank without bumping into the light fixtures (they're hot!) and make sure the fixtures are securely mounted and ventilated. Keep the acrylic UV shield provided with your light hood or pendant in place to prevent the hot bulb from being splattered by cool water; metal halides can and do explode on occasion.

Photoperiod

A PHOTOPERIOD IS THE LENGTH of the "daylight" period to which organisms are exposed. Changes in photoperiod have important regulatory effects in the life cycles of marine invertebrates and fishes. Regardless of the type or arrangement of the lighting system, it is desirable to have automatic timers in place to switch the

#3. Paletta's system under 20,000-degree K metal halide bulbs, showing better balance than the pure actinic approach in photograph #2.

#4. Finally, a combination of fluorescent actinics, 6,500-degree K, and 20,000-degree K metal halides that many consider most pleasing.

Sophisticated new aquarium lighting controllers can time dawn, high noon, dusk, phases of the moon, and seasonality.

Simple timers, available at most hardware stores, are essential in establishing regular lighting cycles for all aquariums.

lights on and off on a preset schedule. This will allows precise control of the photoperiod of the aquarium.

Operate the lighting system for a maximum of 12 hours per day to mimic the day/night cycle in the Tropics. Having fluorescent lamps that come on an hour or two before the metal halide system and remain on for an hour or so afterward simulates the changing intensity of sunlight from dawn to dusk. Fluctuation in light intensity may benefit some photosynthetic organisms. Daylength may also be an important regulator of seasonal cycles of growth and reproduction in some species. Coral reefs occur at latitudes both north and south of the equator, where there are seasonal changes in sunlight. Computer-controlled timing systems, capable of simulating such changes with an eye toward stimulation of coral spawning, are now available from several sources specializing in electronic controls for reef systems. Lunar periodicity plays an important role in the reproductive cycles of many marine organisms, and specialized lighting equipment designed to mimic moonlight is also on the market. Using a variety of lighting effects may produce interesting results in the culture of invertebrate and plant species in aquariums.

Once thought impossible to keep in captivity, sun-loving corals and giant clams can now prosper in home aquariums.

IN SUMMARY, AQUARIUM LIGHTING must be very intense and should have a spectral output appropriate to the water depth frequented by the species on display when photosynthetic invertebrates or algae are the aquarium subjects. Metal halide lighting, perhaps in combination with fluorescent lamps, is currently the best choice for most applications, although satisfactory results can be obtained with fluorescent lamps alone if enough of the right kinds of lamps are used. New, high-intensity compact fluorescent systems have recently been introduced and appear to offer a solution for smaller systems that tend to overheat quickly under full-scale metal halide lights.

Lamps should be on for no more than 12 hours a day and should be regulated by a timer. One must take every precaution to insure that any aquarium lighting system is installed and operated safely. Unless you are willing to move to the Tropics and put the tank on your back porch, you will still have to resort to artificial illumination to duplicate the nuances of natural lighting. Many different lighting systems facilitate the reproduction of corals and other species, proving that artificial lighting can and does work for a variety of organisms.

But then again, for the committed aquarium hobbyist, moving to the Tropics might not be such a bad idea.

Chapter Five

Maintenance & Troubleshooting

Testing, Tweaking, and Keeping Water Quality High

THE RAIN DID NOT MERELY FALL, it was hurled, sometimes nearly parallel to the ground, with force sufficient to drive the raindrops through the canvas walls of our tent. The storm came up after sunset, and most people had crawled into their sleeping bags before the clouds started eating the stars out at sea. Within minutes, the squall was upon us. Lightning portrayed the campground — ironically, Sunshine Key — in a series of tableaux: people running and scrambling to move gear under cover. The lightning came again and again, while thunder and the howling downpour made communication impossible. One of our group had been sleeping in the bed of his pickup truck when the storm hit. He was a sound sleeper and there was an inch of water under his sleeping bag before he awoke. And then the storm passed on, out into the Gulf of Mexico, and we were left, muddy and cold, flashlights bobbing in the dark. It was my only visit to the Florida Keys as a camper. Landlubbers who have never experienced a tropical thunderstorm can scarcely imagine the naked power unleashed.

The storm's energy cleansed the inshore flats, rearrang-

ing rubble and scouring silt from deep pockets. Everywhere, the morning after the storm, one could see natural selection in its most basic manifestation: winnowing populations of animals and plants. Clumps of algae that managed to hang onto the submerged rocks would endow a new generation with the genes for a stronger holdfast. Coral colonies that settled on large, stable boulders would remain, those that had landed on smaller stones had been ground to powder as the storm winds churned the sea. Storms like this, along with earthquakes, volcanoes, and the constant action of the tides are but a few examples of the many ways nature employs tremendous amounts of energy to sculpt the biosphere.

To grow and develop as an artificial biosphere, an aquarium, too, must receive a constant input of energy. This will come from two sources. One is electricity; the other is you. Virtually all of the real work will be done by electricity: lighting, pumps, timers, meters — and perhaps an automated top-off system or a doser for adding limewater. No fair complaining, then, about the small amount of work you will need to do on a regular basis — with an occasional storm session for good measure.

Basically, your chores consist of simple tasks that do not demand a great deal of time but that do require consci-

A healthy natural reef aquarium: pristine water provided by good skimming and occasional "storms" to remove detritus.

entious attention. You must test and record water conditions, correcting any found to be out of range, about once a week. You must see that food and supplements are added to the system according to the needs of the organisms present. Periodically, prefilter pads must be cleaned, the skimmer cup must be emptied, algae must be removed from the front glass, debris must be siphoned out, and equipment must be serviced. If all goes as planned, corals or seaweeds will eventually require pruning or harvesting. This may sound like a lot of work. It can be, but a well-organized person should be able to handle all of these routine chores in about an hour or two a week. Scheduling a monthly maintenance session that occupies an afternoon will be necessary for less frequently needed ministrations.

One should spend a lot of time, however, just looking at the aquarium and thinking analytically about the course of its development as it unfolds. The pace of change in a new system is much more rapid than that of an older one. In an established aquarium, the ecosystem has had sufficient time to achieve equilibrium. Learning to recognize the signs of sudden change in an established system is the surest way to avoid catastrophe. Occasional problems can certainly crop up. You may lose a specimen or two; minor setbacks are to be expected. But a real disaster — the kind too often heard in horror stories told by disappointed former hobby-

Open (top) or closed polyps, as in this *Palythoa* colony, can be an indicator of water conditions. Constantly closed polyps are a sign of trouble.

ists — a total wipeout, complete system failure, should be a relatively uncommon event. In every case of marine aquarium disaster of which I have been aware, the problem could easily have been avoided by the application of simple, widely discussed techniques and common sense.

Recently, a customer returned to my store with a Purple Tang he had purchased. All water conditions, he advised the clerk upon questioning, had tested out normally. The fish was doing poorly, and he assumed it was sick. This he regarded as our problem, since the fish had been purchased only a few days before. But when the water from his aquarium was tested, the ammonia level was nearly off the scale. Further questioning revealed that another dealer had advised him that pH and nitrate were the only parameters that needed investigation, so these were the only test kits the hobbyist owned and the only tests he was able to perform. The tang recovered completely after transfer to good water. I could not help but wonder, though, why someone would spend more than $100 for a fish and not even bother to read a book about aquarium care. In my experience in the retail aquarium business, this kind of self-imposed ignorance of the simplest tenets of aquarium keeping is widespread.

Acceptable ranges for various parameters of the coral reef habitat are shown in the Water Quality Parameters

WATER QUALITY PARAMETERS FOR TROPICAL MARINE AQUARIUMS

Temperature	75 degrees F (optimum; natural range is about 68 to 84 degrees)
Hydrometer Reading	1.022 to 1.0240
pH	8.15 to 8.4
Alkalinity	2.5 to 5.0 meq/L
Ammonia (NH_3)	zero
Nitrite (NO_2^-)	zero
Nitrate (NO_3^-)	< 10 mg/L* (ion)
Phosphate (PO_4^{-3})	< 0.05 mg/L
Calcium (Ca_2^+)	400 to 475 mg/L
Dissolved Oxygen	> 6.90 mg/L
Carbon Dioxide (CO_2)	< 2.0 mg/L

*May depend upon individual circumstances.

table, above. The numbers are for fore-reef conditions; organisms from this habitat are the most demanding, especially of oxygen. In the back reef, lagoon, and inshore zones, salinity may be lower, currents variable, and the concentrations of nutrient ions much higher than around a "blue water" coral reef. Many "reef" organisms considered especially tolerant of aquarium life are actually from near-reef zones.

Evaluating Aquarium Tests

TO ASSURE THAT APPROPRIATE CONDITIONS are met, one must test various parameters from time to time and make adjustments as required. Proper technique is funda-mental to obtaining accurate test results. Here, then, are some general guidelines:

ACCURACY: Accuracy is the degree to which a test result reflects the real state of the sample being tested. Say the true concentration of calcium in a sample is 400 mg/L, for example. For aquarium purposes, an accurate test kit might give a reading of 380 mg/L on a single test. For an analytical laboratory, however, a much more accurate test might be needed, which would give a reading for the same sample of 399.8 mg/L. The cost of a test kit increases as accuracy increases. An instrument or test that is accurate to within ±10 units of the true state of the sample may only cost a fraction as much as a similar instrument that is accurate to within ±0.1 units (a 100-fold increase in accuracy).

For some purposes, a highly accurate test is not necessary. For example, one needs to know only if ammonia is present at all, not the exact amount, since finding any amount of this toxic compound in aquarium water is cause for concern. On the other hand, when copper is used for the treatment of parasitic infestation in fishes, a difference of 0.1 ppm can spell the difference between a successful cure and loss of the specimen. In common parlance, a synonym for what chemists mean by "accuracy" is "reliability" — how well one can rely on the test result's being "true."

PRECISION: Precision refers to the amount of difference a test or instrument will permit the observer to distinguish between two similar tests. The smaller the increment, the greater the precision and, consequently, the higher the cost. For example, to measure the difference between 0.010 and 0.015 units may be much more difficult (and expensive) than determining the difference between 10 and 15 units. Tests, therefore, for the major components of seawater are much more easily carried out than tests for minor or trace components. For maintaining a reef aquarium, one must have a phosphate test of rather high precision (±0.05 ppm), for example, because the difference between having an algae bloom and not having one can be 0.05 ppm of orthophosphate. An imprecise test might give the same value for samples taken from two otherwise identical tanks, one with and one without an algae bloom.

Thus it is necessary to consider not only the nature of the test being performed, but also the level of accuracy and precision needed for successful aquarium keeping. This book is directed at the operation of a marine aquarium display as a hobby rather than for purposes of scientific research. The ranges of tolerance for most marine organisms commonly kept in home aquariums are comparatively broad; therefore, one does not require laboratory-grade instruments or test kits. One does, however, need tests that can be relied upon to give results sufficiently correct for reasonable judgments to be made concerning the husbandry of the aquarium. Hobbyist publications have conducted test-kit evaluations, and these should be consulted for comparisons among the several available brands.

A basic marine test kit to check levels of ammonia, nitrite, nitrate, and pH.

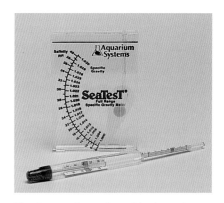

Floating or dip-and-read hydrometers give quick readings of specific gravity.

Specific Gravity, Salinity & Temperature

SPECIFIC GRAVITY IS DEFINED as the ratio of the weight of one liter of seawater to that of one liter of pure water at a specified temperature. Since it is a ratio, there are no units. Specific gravity can be measured with a hydrometer. Laboratory hydrometers are made of glass tubing, weighted so that they will float at different levels in solutions of different densities. A scale on the tube is marked off in specific gravity units. To take a reading, the observer notes the point on the scale corresponding to the water level at which the tube floats. This is the specific gravity. If the temperature of the sample is also measured, the salinity of the sample can then be determined.

Specific gravity is an indirect measurement of the quantity of dissolved salts in the water. Average ocean water has a salinity of 35 parts per thousand, or 35 grams of dissolved salts per 1,000 grams of seawater. This corresponds to an observed hydrometer reading of 1.0240 at a temperature of 75 degrees F. Marine aquariums are often maintained at a lower specific gravity in the belief that the lowered salinity reduces stress on fishes and makes the survival of parasites less likely. I am aware of no evidence to support this practice; I recommend a reading of 1.0240 at 75 degrees F.

Hobbyist hydrometers may not be accurate. To calibrate a glass hydrometer, measure the specific gravity of a sample of distilled freshwater. It should be 1.000 after correction for the tank temperature. If the hydrometer reads higher or lower than 1.000, simply determine how much to add or subtract as a correction factor. For example, if the pure water sample reads 0.999, that means 0.001 must be added to any subsequent reading to correct for the error. Thus, if a seawater reading is 1.023, the corrected reading is 1.024.

ESTIMATING SALINITY FROM SPECIFIC GRAVITY

WHEN THE SPECIFIC GRAVITY of aquarium water is measured with a hydrometer, the salinity of the water can be calculated if the temperature is also known.

First, convert the temperature reading to Celsius, by using the following formula: °C = 0.56 (°F–32)

Next, read across to find the temperature in the first table below, Conversion of Observed Hydrometer Readings to Density. Read down that column to the row corresponding to the hydrometer reading. The number in the table is a con-

version factor, which should be added to the hydrometer reading. The result is the density reading of the water. For example, if the temperature in your tank is 22 degrees Celsius and your hydrometer reading is 1.0230, the conversion factor (0.0016) should be added to your hydrometer reading, resulting in a density reading of 1.0246. Then refer to the table on page 122, Conversion of Density to Salinity. There you find that your density calculation of 1.0246 gives a salinity reading of approximately 33.

CONVERSION OF OBSERVED HYDROMETER READINGS TO DENSITY

| | TEMPERATURE (°C) | | | | | | |
HYDROMETER READING	20°	21°	22°	23°	24°	25°	26°
1.0170	.0010	.0012	.0015	.0017	.0020	.0022	.0025
1.0180	.0010	.0012	.0015	.0017	.0020	.0023	.0025
1.0190	.0010	.0012	.0015	.0018	.0020	.0023	.0026
1.0200	.0010	.0013	.0015	.0018	.0020	.0023	.0026
1.0210	.0010	.0013	.0015	.0018	.0021	.0023	.0026
1.0220	.0011	.0013	.0015	.0018	.0021	.0023	.0026
1.0230	.0011	.0013	.0016	.0018	.0021	.0024	.0026
1.0240	.0011	.0013	.0016	.0018	.0021	.0024	.0027
1.0250	.0011	.0013	.0016	.0018	.0021	.0024	.0027
1.0260	.0011	.0013	.0016	.0019	.0022	.0024	.0027
1.0270	.0011	.0014	.0016	.0019	.0022	.0024	.0027
1.0280	.0011	.0014	.0016	.0019	.0022	.0025	.0028
1.0290	.0011	.0014	.0016	.0019	.0022		

CONVERSION OF DENSITY TO SALINITY

DENSITY	SALINITY (in parts per thousand)	DENSITY	SALINITY (in parts per thousand)
1.0180	25	1.0240	32
1.0185	25	1.0245	33
1.0190	26	1.0250	34
1.0195	27	1.0255	34
1.0200	27	1.0260	35
1.0205	28	1.0265	36
1.0210	29	1.0270	36
1.0215	29	1.0275	37
1.0220	30	1.0280	38
1.0225	30	1.0285	38
1.0230	31	1.0290	39
1.0235	32	1.0295	40
		1.0300	40

Natural salinity is 35 in the vicinity of most coral reefs, unless the ocean is diluted from a nearby freshwater source. The acceptable salinity range for invertebrates is 34 to 36, while fishes can tolerate lower salinities.

temperature. Mercury thermometers, often used in photographic darkroom work, are useful, as are red alcohol thermometers. Select one with the degrees engraved into the glass, rather than on a scale attached to the thermometer, which can shift and produce inaccurate readings. Liquid crystal thermometers that adhere to the outside aquarium glass are popular with hobbyists because they are easy to read, but should be calibrated with a glass thermometer before relying upon the measurements so obtained. After installing a liquid crystal thermometer, take the temperature of the aquarium water with a glass thermometer immersed in the tank for at least five minutes. Note any variation between the two readings and remember this correction factor when relying upon the liquid crystal thermometer for routine measurement. Any glass thermometer may be calibrated in either an ice bath or in boiling water. These will be 0 degrees C/32 degrees F and 100 degrees C/212 degrees F, respectively, at sea level. At higher altitudes, the variation is small, but measurable. Standard references can be used to determine the boiling point and freezing point of water at specific altitudes, but these variations are not important unless one lives high in the mountains.

Electronic devices for measurement of both temperature and salinity are available and are usually accurate in proportion to their cost. Salinity may also be determined chemically, by means of titration. Electronic temperature controllers that can operate both heating and cooling equipment to maintain the aquarium within a tight temperature range (± 1 degree F) are available.

Dissolved Oxygen

EVERY LIVING ORGANISM in the aquarium, from nitrifying bacteria to fish, requires oxygen to sustain life. Oxygen depletion, even slightly below saturation, can create significant stress. Seawater at 75 degrees F contains about 6.8 milli-

Plastic "dip and read" hydrometers are popular. These may be calibrated by comparing their readings to a glass hydrometer of known accuracy. One cannot check a sample of pure water with the "dip and read" unit, because the scale of measurement does not give a reading in that low range.

Temperature measurement is of obvious importance for any aquarium because bodies of water exhibit temperature stability. The high specific heat of water results in a strong moderating effect, even with wide fluctuations in air

grams per liter (mg/L) of dissolved oxygen at 100% saturation. An aquarium should have sufficient aeration to achieve this concentration or higher, as levels of "super-saturation" (125%) can occur in the reef environment. If there is plenty of water movement and the aquarium provides a large amount of surface exposed to the air, sufficient dissolved oxygen is likely to be available. Dissolved oxygen (DO) measurement can be useful to advanced aquarists, but this particular test is not essential for the successful maintenance of a reef aquarium. If you do decide to use this test, check the dissolved oxygen concentration when the tank is initially set up and after any new specimens are added. (Wait about 24 hours after adding new animals before checking DO.) "Wet" chemical DO tests require careful attention to the collection of the sample and proper use of several test chemicals in order to produce accurate results. Electronic DO meters are significantly more reliable than chemical methods for hobbyists unfamiliar with the appropriate laboratory techniques.

Dissolved oxygen test kits, one of many diagnostic tools for advanced aquarists.

Nitrogen Compounds

AFTER THE INITIAL RUN-IN PERIOD, tests for ammonia and nitrite need not be carried out routinely, but one should check them promptly if there is any reason to suspect that a problem is developing. The test result for both compounds should always be zero. If either is detected, a partial water change must be carried out immediately and an effort made to determine what has interrupted the biological filtration process. Some common causes of this kind of problem are:

1. Too many animals in the tank.

2. Uneaten food or a dead animal decaying.

3. Insufficient oxygen in the system.

4. The nitrifying bacteria have been weakened or killed by the addition of undesirable chemicals (including many "medications").

Obvious signs calling for an ammonia check include stressed, dying, or dead fishes or invertebrates, cloudy water, or any whiff of foul odor coming from the tank.

Unfortunately, there is no quick fix should the nitrifying bacteria die. These bacteria are relatively slow-growing, and it may take up to a month for the system to recover. Therefore, one of the most important aspects of aquarium maintenance is to make sure that none of the problems described above has a chance to occur.

Nitrate, ideally, should be at zero concentration in a coral reef aquarium, although relatively high levels of this compound are tolerated by many species of fishes and invertebrates. Using most aquarium test kits, the water around a coral reef would test zero, despite the fact that traces of nitrate are actually present. Successful reef aquariums with 20 to 40 ppm of nitrate have been maintained by many hobbyists. One should, however, test the tank for nitrate on a weekly basis and attempt to maintain nitrate levels below 10 ppm, if possible. This can be accomplished by frequent partial water changes. Fish are significantly more tolerant of nitrates than many invertebrates seem to be, and the level of nitrate ion in a fish-only tank can be allowed to reach 40 ppm before corrective measures need be taken. Tangs, however, may stop eating if nitrates are too high.

Frakes (1993b) has recently pointed out that nitrate itself may not be directly harmful to marine life, but its presence in the aquarium may be an indicator of declining water quality due to other factors. He tends to dismiss the idea that reef aquariums should be maintained with the low nitrate levels I have recommended. Nevertheless, the natural reef environment is low in nitrates, and there is abundant anecdotal evidence that partial water changes, to lower nitrate or for other reasons, are beneficial to the aquarium.

Confusion can occur in the interpretation of test results for ammonia or ammonium, nitrite, and nitrate. This is because there are two ways of expressing the concentrations of these substances. Concentration of ammonia or ammonium ion (NH_3 or NH_4^+), nitrite (NO_2^-), and nitrate (NO_3^-) may be expressed either as the total concentration of the ion or as only the amount of nitrogen present. Note that nitrogen (N) appears in the chemical formulas for each of these compounds: ammonia contains one atom of nitrogen and three atoms of hydrogen; ammonium, one atom of nitrogen and four atoms of hydrogen; nitrite, one atom of nitrogen and two atoms of oxygen; nitrate, one atom of nitrogen and three atoms of oxygen. Each contains nitrogen but is different from the others because of the additional atoms (oxygen or hydrogen) present. Some test kits for ammonia/ammonium, nitrite, and nitrate measure the ion, and some measure only nitrogen, so it's important to know the difference when

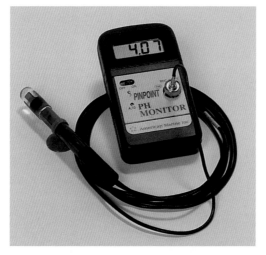

A digital pH meter is one of a growing selection of electronic monitors for aquarium keepers.

comparing readings taken with two different test kits. Making the conversion from one to the other is a matter of knowing the conversion factor and doing some simple arithmetic. If the test kit measures total ammonia/ammonium (NH_3 or NH_4^+), then divide by 1.3 to obtain ammonia nitrogen ($NH_4^+ - N$). If the measurement is of nitrite ion (NO_2^-), then divide by 3.3 to obtain nitrite nitrogen ($NO_2^- - N$), and if the kit records nitrate ion (NO_3^-), divide by 4.4 to obtain nitrate nitrogen ($NO_3^- - N$). To convert nitrogen readings to ion equivalents, multiply by the appropriate conversion factor.

pH, Alkalinity & Calcium

pH. The degree to which a solution is acid or alkaline indicates the pH of the solution. This is calculated as:

$$pH = - \log [H^+]$$

meaning "take the logarithm of the hydrogen ion concentration in moles per liter, and multiply by minus one." Since pure water, the standard reference point for many chemical measurements, including pH, contains 10^{-7} moles of hydrogen ions per liter, it has a pH of 7 and is said to be neutral. A solution with a pH less than 7 has more hydrogen ions than pure water and is said to be acidic, while a solution with fewer hydrogen ions than pure water has a pH greater than 7 and is said to be alkaline, or basic. Hydrogen ions are among the most important chemical factors involved in reactions that take place in aquarium waters.

Ions are charged molecules. Hydrogen ions carry a positive charge, as signified by the chemical shorthand for this ion, H^+. Ions can exist individually only in the minds of chemists. In a hypothetical sample of absolutely pure water, ions would exist as pairs, with each positively charged ion matched by a corresponding negatively charged one, so that the overall charge would always remain at zero. In this water, the hydrogen ions would be balanced by hydroxyl ions (OH^-). Adding hydrogen ions to the water would cause the pH to decrease, adding hydroxyl ions would have the opposite effect, making the solution more basic. In aquarium terms, rarely is there a perfect balance that would yield a pH of 7.000, but rather there are continual ionic imbalances that aquarists must measure and track with test kits or electronic monitors. Natural seawater on a coral reef is mildly basic, with a pH of 8.0 to 8.4.

Reliable digital pH meters are now available at prices hobbyists can afford and are, in my view, a vast improvement over color-change-based chemical pH kits. When considering one of these units, remember that it is essential to be able to calibrate the instrument easily against standard buffer solutions of known pH. Purchase a small amount of these calibration buffers (pH 7.0 and 10.0) along with the pH meter. Carefully read and follow the manufacturer's instructions to calibrate and use any electronic pH meter.

ALKALINITY. The degree to which a solution maintains its pH when acid is added is the alkalinity of the solution. Related terms used in reference to aquariums are "carbonate hardness" and its German equivalent KH (degrees of hardness, expressed as dKH, with K being "Karbonat"). In practice, these terms are used interchangeably, but in reality, total alkalinity in seawater is slightly higher than carbonate hardness. This is because the latter is a measure of only the contribution of carbonate (CO_3^{-2}) and bicarbonate (HCO_3^-) to total alkalinity. In seawater, various other negatively charged ions, such as borate (BO_3^{-3}) and hydroxides (OH^-) contribute to the total.

In the metric system, alkalinity is measured in milliequivalents per liter (meq/L). To understand the derivation

DEVELOPING GOOD LAB PROCEDURE

PROPER TECHNIQUE results in accurate, reproducible test results. The best test kit will give bad information if not used correctly or if the aquarist's technique is sloppy. Some tips for proper testing:

1. Read the instructions carefully and make sure all equipment is handy before beginning test procedures.

2. Use a timer when a test specifies a certain waiting period.

3. Wash test tubes and other equipment carefully, rinse in distilled water, and drain dry after each use.

4. Rinse test vials and pipettes with the water to be tested immediately prior to carrying out the test.

5. For very accurate results, perform the test in triplicate and average the readings.

6. Parts per million (ppm) and milligrams per liter (mg/L) are the same thing, for practical purposes. To be completely technical, multiply mg/L times specific gravity to obtain ppm.

7. Don't go to all the trouble to buy test kits, learn good techniques, and make regular tests unless the results are recorded in a notebook for future reference. (Pages 139 and 140 are log sheets that can be reproduced on a copier or used as a guide to help make record keeping easier.)

of this term and to better understand the concept of alkalinity, return to the discussion of neutralization reactions. The general formula for a neutralization reaction is written as follows:

$$H^+ + OH^- \rightarrow H_2O$$

Note that equivalent amounts of both hydrogen and hydroxide ions are involved. Next consider that different chemical compounds will yield up different amounts of hydrogen or hydroxide ions when dissolved in water. Nitric acid, HNO_3, yields only one hydrogen ion per molecule, while sulfuric acid, H_2SO_4, yields two. This can be determined by inspection of the formula. Similarly, calcium hydroxide, $Ca(OH)_2$, yields two hydroxyl ions per molecule, and sodium hydroxide, $NaOH$, yields only one. The number of hydrogen or hydroxyl ions available per unit of a solution of a compound is the number of equivalents per unit of that solution.

MOLAR SOLUTIONS. Chemists long ago recognized the need for a standardized way of making solutions so that experiments could be consistently repeated. Combinations of ions are important to chemists, so it was natural that they would develop a standard solution that is defined in terms of the combining ratios of the ions in the solution. When a compound such as salt (sodium chloride, or $NaCl$) is added to water, it breaks up into ions (Na^+ and Cl^-). When these ions combine with others added subsequently, they do so in precise ways, each negative charge matching exactly with a positive charge. We often need to know exactly how many individual ions there are in a solution, so we can add precisely enough of something else to achieve some desired result. This is accomplished through the use of molar and normal solutions.

To prepare a molar solution, it is first necessary to total up the molecular weight of the compound in question. For the salt, $NaCl$, in this example, the atomic weight of sodium is 23, and that of chlorine is 35, so the molecular weight is 58. If we weigh out 58 grams of salt, we will have a gram-molecular-weight, or mole, of this compound. In the case of water, two atoms of hydrogen, atomic weight 1, are combined with one atom of oxygen, atomic weight 16, so one mole of water is 18 grams.

Why is this important? A chemist named Avogadro proved a few centuries ago that one mole of anything will contain exactly the same number of individual particles, whether atoms, molecules, or ions. The number is 6.02 x 10^{23}, or 602,000,000,000,000,000,000,000 particles.

Avogadro's number is not really important by itself. What is significant is that a mole of anything contains this same number of particles. When one mole of a compound is dissolved in an aqueous solution to make a total volume of one liter, we have a standard solution, called a molar solution, abbreviated as 1 M.

Note that in a molar solution of sodium chloride there will be one mole each of Na^+ and Cl^- ions present. Similarly, in a molar solution of nitric acid, we have one mole of hydrogen ions (H^+) and one mole of nitrate ions (NO_3^-). This is a solution of acid, and it receives special consideration because it contains one mole of those very important hydrogen ions. Chemists call such a solution a normal solution (1 N). A 1 N solution delivers one equivalent of either acid or base. In other words, one teaspoon of a 1 N solution of acid will neutralize exactly one teaspoon of a 1 N solution of base. It does not matter which acid or base is the source of hydrogen or hydroxyl ions, because all that is important is the combining ratio, based on Avogadro's number. The combining ratio, or equivalency, of a normal solution is a constant.

Returning to the measurement of alkalinity, then, we are determining how many equivalents of acid must be added in order to combine completely with the bicarbonate, carbonate, borate, hydroxide, and other ions present in the water sample, without adding an excess of hydrogen ions. We do this by performing a titration, adding a standardized acid solution drop by drop and noting when the endpoint is reached by means of an indicator that changes color in response to different pH levels. As it happens, the endpoint of the total alkalinity titration is reached at a pH of 4.5, and the indicator used, for example phenolphthalein, changes color at this pH. Phenolphthalein changes from colorless to bright red, while bromthymol blue, an indicator often used in carbonate hardness (KH) tests, changes from blue to yellow at the endpoint. Determination of the endpoint can be done precisely using a pH meter. If one does this, recording the solution's pH as each drop of acid is added, the results appear as in the accompanying titration graph.

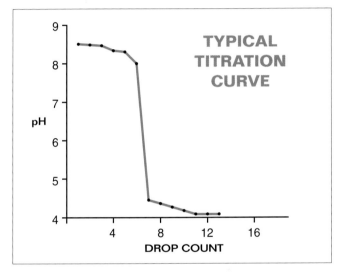

Note that the pH remains stable for the first few additions of acid and then drops precipitously as the endpoint is approached. The initial stability of the pH reflects the fact that the solution (in this case seawater) is a buffer. Buffers are solutions that resist pH changes. This is why you will sometimes hear alkalinity or KH referred to as "buffering capacity."

The alkalinity of natural seawater is around 2.0 to 2.5 meq/L. To convert to the German degrees of carbonate hardness (dKH), multiply this number by 2.8, to yield about 6 to 7 dKH. It is generally recommended that a marine aquarium be maintained at an alkalinity somewhat higher than that of natural seawater, between 7 and 10 dKH. The higher alkalinity offsets the accumulation of acids typical of a closed-system aquarium. These acids come from several sources, the primary ones being carbon dioxide from respiration, nitric acid from biological filtration, and organic acids from metabolic wastes.

CALCIUM. Another dancer in the chemical ballet going on in the marine aquarium is calcium. Corals, crustaceans, mollusks, and calcareous algae all extract calcium from seawater, using it to construct their skeletons from calcium carbonate. Early efforts at maintaining the proper chemical environment for these organisms focused too narrowly on calcium alone, largely ignoring the role of alkalinity. This is unfortunate, because the availability of carbonate, the other essential component in skeletal structures, mostly depends upon the pH and alkalinity of the water. In fact, when the alkalinity is high, skeleton building can still occur, even when calcium is present at a level significantly below that of natural seawater. However, when both alkalinity and calcium concentration are low, corals do not thrive. Conversely, raising the calcium level above about 550 mg/L will result in precipitation of calcium carbonate as chalk, with a concomitant drop in alkalinity, and calcification is made more difficult. "Calcium hardness" is the term used to describe the calcium content of the water, which for natural seawater is about 380 mg/L. Note that this is a simple weight/volume measurement; each liter of seawater contains about 380 mg of calcium. Maintaining this level is a relatively simple matter, as any soluble compound containing calcium can be added to the water to compensate for a deficit. However, remember from the discussion above that ions always come in pairs. Any compound containing calcium also contains a partner ion, and the nature of this partner can have important implications for aquarium chemistry. For example, using calcium chloride as a calcium source may result in the need for a "buffer additive" to restore the alkalinity. Sodium carbonate or sodium bicarbonate alone can be added to increase alkalinity, but better buffer additives contain other ions, such as borate, that participate in the alkalinity reactions of seawater.

Julian Sprung (1994) enumerated a number of benefits from adding limewater (or "Kalkwasser" in the parlance of German-speaking aquarists) to the aquarium, only one of which is to maintain the calcium concentration, but all of which have to do with the needs of the organisms being kept in the aquarium. Using limewater for calcium maintenance also helps to maintain the pH and alkalinity of the aquarium, because the hydroxyl ions from the limewater neutralize some of the acids accumulating in the system. In effect, this prevents the alkalinity from being "used up" and the pH therefore remains more stable. The ideal pH for calcification is about 8.40 to 8.45, and according to Sprung, aquariums should be maintained so that the pH does not rise above 8.45 during the day, except for a temporary rise (never more than 8.6) when a dose of limewater is added. Allowing the pH to go higher than this will, ironically, impede calcium maintenance, as calcium carbonate will spontaneously precipitate as the pH rises, once again robbing the system of both calcium and carbonate ions. Maintaining the proper balance is best accomplished through the use of an automated system for dosing the limewater, and an electronic pH meter. Adding the limewater by hand and evaluating pH with a color-change-type test kit can be done, albeit with more room for error.

The relationship between pH, calcium, and alkalinity is particularly noticeable in a tank devoted to macroalgae cultivation. Two opposing principles are at work in such a tank, and the combined result may explain why calcareous macroalgae, such as *Penicillus,* have been regarded as very difficult aquarium subjects. In the first place, these organisms remove calcium from the water profligately, compared to corals, owing to their much more rapid rates of growth. Secondly, photosynthesis carried out by macroalgae during the daylight hours also removes carbon dioxide from

the water, driving the pH above 8.5. When the free CO_2 is used up, the macroalgae start utilizing bicarbonate ions. The overall result is a lowering of both calcium concentration and alkalinity and an increase in pH, all of which inhibit the calcification process essential to the plants' growth. That this can happen in a matter of days in the confines of an aquarium makes one appreciate what an inexhaustible supply of calcium and carbonate ions are available in the ocean. In a reef tank containing many colonies of the pink and purple calcareous algae prized by reef enthusiasts, macroalgae growth can be self-limiting, even though conditions appear favorable.

Just as the problem of fine-tuning limewater additions can be aided through the use of a dosing system and an electronic pH monitor, so can the problem of too-high pH be met through the use of a carbon dioxide system controlled by an electronic pH controller. Such systems must be designed, however, to insure that overdosing the system with CO_2 does not happen should a malfunction occur. Carbon dioxide is toxic to fish in too high a concentration, and an excess will cause the pH of the tank to fall to disastrously low levels.

Besides aiding in the maintenance of pH, alkalinity, and calcium concentration, the addition of limewater to the reef aquarium has other benefits. Limewater addition, according to Sprung, also enhances protein skimming. This, he maintains, "promotes a cleaner, healthier aquarium environment, impeding the growth of filamentous and slime algae while encouraging the growth of calcareous algae and corals." According to Wilkens (1994), an important benefit of limewater addition is the near-total precipitation of phosphate (PO_4^{-3}) from the water. Phosphate interferes with calcification because it is a "crystal poison" (see Simkiss, 1964, as referenced in Sprung, 1994) and has been shown to be detrimental to corals under natural conditions if present in excess (Burke, 1994). Also of great concern to the aquarist, undesirable algae growth is almost always a consequence of excess phosphate. (Phosphate is a biolimiting nutrient, meaning that algae cannot grow if starved for this nutrient. Interestingly, another biolimiting nutrient, nitrate, is always found in the sea in a precise 15:1 molar ratio with phosphorus. Not surprisingly, this is the exact ratio in which these nutrients are required by living organisms. Perhaps this observation helps to explain why limiting the phosphate, rather than the nitrate, concentration of the aquarium seems to be a more effective means of algae control. Due to its removal through chemical and biological processes, virtually no phosphate is found in the water around a coral reef.)

Other Factors Affecting Calcium & Alkalinity

WE POINTED OUT EARLIER that acid production is characteristic of biological filtration. Acid production depletes both calcium and alkalinity from the aquarium water, probably via the neutralization reaction and ion-pair formation. Systems, therefore, that accumulate nitrate will experience problems with maintenance of pH, alkalinity, and calcium hardness as well. The tendency to accumulate nitrate can be overcome by carrying out frequent partial water changes, a chore that many aquarists find especially bothersome, or by denitrifying the aquarium.

Denitrification is carried out by beneficial bacteria in several genera, including *Bacillus*, *Denitrobacillus*, *Micrococcus*, *Pseudomonas*, *Thiobacillus*, and others. These bacteria must have anaerobic (oxygen-free) conditions in order to carry out their chemical conversions. They are able to extract energy from the nitrate molecule, converting it to other chemical forms and, most importantly for our purposes, into nitrogen gas that ultimately escapes from the aquarium into the atmosphere. The overall reaction for this process is:

$$2NO_3^- + 12H^+ \rightarrow N_2 + 6H_2O$$

Note that six moles of hydrogen ions are used up for every mole of nitrate ions converted. As a result, the denitrification process also helps to retain alkalinity. In addition, denitrifiers consume carbon compounds (organic matter) to obtain energy. This process releases carbonates and bicarbonates, further enhancing the buffering system in the aquarium water.

Denitrifying bacteria probably reside within the interior of live rock. One of the most important aspects of the Berlin-style reef tank design is the reliance upon this source of denitrification. While many aquarists report low or even zero levels of nitrate in aquariums maintained exclusively by this technique, others report that in these systems, a stable, low level of nitrate, in the range of 10 to 20 mg NO_3^- per liter, is continuously maintained after the system has been operating for several months. But naturally occurring nitrate levels in coral reef waters are much lower than this, approaching zero, probably due to bioaccumulation. As a result, aquarists have sought methods of reducing nitrate concentrations to near zero levels without carrying out frequent or massive water changes.

Two different methodologies presently exist for enhancing denitrification. One approach, which has been a topic for discussion in the aquarium literature for years, is the use of a "denitrifying filter." Analogous to the wet/dry filter, this device seeks to optimize conditions for the growth of denitrifying bacteria. Recent versions employ electronic-control technology to monitor and adjust critical parameters. Hobbyists report that these units, though expensive, do work well.

The second approach has been closely investigated by Dr. Jean Jaubert in Monaco. In brief, this technique relies upon a thick layer of sand on the aquarium bottom to provide an appropriate home for denitrifying bacteria. A layer of aragonite sand is seeded with a layer of "live sand" collected from the ocean floor. Small organisms present in the

in the tank. Carbon is also present in the form of carbonates, ions that participate in the pH buffering system and are measured by an alkalinity test. The third form of carbon is dissolved organic carbon (DOC). Measuring the level of DOC in seawater is difficult to carry out, but values that have been reported range up to a maximum of about 2 parts per million. Control of microalgae growth in the aquarium consists primarily in keeping the concentrations of nitrate, phosphate, and DOC as close to zero as possible.

Algae Control Tips

INSTALL A PROTEIN SKIMMER. DOC is not one but many different compounds. Methods to reduce DOC include the use of protein skimmers, activated carbon, chemical resins, and ozonization. Removal of DOC by means of a protein skimmer is one of the simplest techniques. Besides removing DOC, protein skimmers lower the concentration of carbon dioxide in the water. The protein skimmer also lowers the concentration of nitrate (see below) indirectly, because the DOC would eventually be decomposed into nitrate by bacteria if it were allowed to remain in the tank. Unlike other forms of filtration, protein skimming physically removes the pollutants from contact with the water. Using activated carbon or chemical adsorption media does trap DOC, but water continues to flow over these media, and bacteria growing in them decompose the DOC, returning pollutants to the tank. Step one, then, in any plan to prevent algae from taking over, is to install a protein skimmer — and make sure it gets periodic maintenance.

REDUCE NITRATE. Limiting the concentration of nitrate is not as simple as installing a piece of equipment. Nitrate accumulates in the aquarium as the end product of biological filtration. Roughly 90% of the nitrogen in foods added to the tank winds up as nitrate in the water. Regular partial water changes are one means of controlling nitrate.

The amount and frequency of water changes will depend on the particular circumstances of each individual aquarium. Thus, one should perform a nitrate test weekly and change water when the concentration of nitrate ion rises above a predetermined level, depending upon the circumstances of the individual aquarium.

LIMIT SILICATE. Silicate (SiO_2^-), is essential for the development of the golden-brown films that spread across the glass, substrate, and decorations: diatoms. Under the microscope, the glass cases that these algae create for themselves are beautiful, but a massive diatom bloom in an aquarium is not so aesthetically pleasing. Silicate enters the aquarium most often in tap water. To eliminate it, the only satisfactory solution is to use reverse osmosis (RO) water, not tap water. Fortunately, diatom blooms may be short-lived, as other algae compete and as the diatoms exhaust the supply of silicate. Using tap water for water changes, however, will replenish silica, and the diatoms will return.

EXPERIMENT WITH LIGHTING. As one might expect, light also plays a role in algae growth in the aquarium. The sudden appearance of a "bloom" of diatoms, red slime algae, or blue-green slime algae is often indicative of the need to correct the aquarium's lighting. As lamps age, for example, their intensity diminishes and their spectral output changes, and this may trigger a growth of undesirable algae. The type of lamp can also strongly influence the development of an algae bloom. Proper selection of a lighting system depends upon the size and shape of the aquarium and the kinds of organisms that will live in the tank. The relationship between light and marine life is complicated and poorly understood, however, so experimentation with different lighting systems may be necessary to eliminate a particular algae problem.

CHECK CARBON DIOXIDE. Algae need carbon dioxide in order to grow. Aquarists rarely think about carbon dioxide, but it is often a source of problems. One of the basic

Chemical media choices are many, including activated carbon and other formulations to scavenge dissolved organics, phosphates, and copper from system water.

causes of carbon dioxide accumulation is low output from pumps or powerheads. This can occur because too small a unit was chosen or because the pump has slowed down due to age or lack of maintenance. Vigorous water movement is characteristic of most marine environments and is important in the aquarium to prevent carbon dioxide buildup. Check the pH and alkalinity of the tank regularly. If either is chronically below normal, check to see if carbon dioxide is accumulating in the aquarium. This can be done simply. Remove a half-gallon sample of water from the tank and aerate it vigorously overnight. After 24 hours of aeration, check the pH of the sample. Check the pH of the tank at the same time. Compare the two readings. If the pH of the tank is more than 0.2 pH units below that of the aerated sample, the tank is probably accumulating carbon dioxide. Correcting the problem will greatly reduce algae growth and is essential for fish and invertebrate health.

CLEAN THE FILTER SYSTEM. Accumulations of detritus may contain very high nutrient concentrations. Siphon detritus from the entire system every week. I like to use one of the commercially available siphon hoses that come with an elongated funnel on the intake end, permitting fine, lightweight detritus to be siphoned out without also removing sand or gravel from the substrate. Purchase a plastic turkey baster and use it to direct a gentle stream of water to dislodge debris that may accumulate in crannies and crevices. Be especially careful to remove debris that has settled on sedentary invertebrates. Using a powerhead to direct a vigorous stream of water to dislodge debris is another satisfactory technique. These occasional disruptions mimic what happens in natural environments when a storm occurs. A small accumulation of detritus is not harmful, so one need not be overly meticulous about removing such accumulations.

ADD HERBIVORES. Many species of marine life feed on algae, and some of these should be in every aquarium. Tangs, angelfishes, some blennies, rabbitfishes, sea urchins, hermit crabs, and many kinds of snails are in this category. These species will benefit from being able to graze on algae growth and will keep the aquarium from looking "overgrown." Some of these species are suited to smaller tanks, while others are more appropriate for large tanks with many fishes. Still others are most useful in "blue water" reef tanks.

IN SUMMARY, UNDESIRABLE MICROALGAE GROWTH in the aquarium can be controlled by: using live rock rather than dead materials; using a protein skimmer; taking measures to keep nitrates, phosphate, silicate, and DOC to a minimum; preventing the accumulation of carbon dioxide; removing detritus regularly; and adding herbivorous organisms to the aquarium. Algae are found everywhere one looks on a natural reef and will always be present in marine aquariums. No one would deny that in the aquarium, as in nature, the presence of algae is important to maintain a high level of biodiversity. Excessive algae growth, however, is neither natural nor desirable.

Record Keeping

ONE SHOULD KEEP RECORDS of all water tests carried out. Include the date, time, and any comments needed to describe conditions in the aquarium at that moment. In this way, you develop a history of conditions in the tank that can be of great value in diagnosing problems later. Such a log can also help identify trends in water-quality fluctuations, enabling corrective action to be taken before such fluctuations become serious. One can purchase record books with printed forms for aquarium records, or use a simple loose-leaf binder. Include in the record the date and amount of water changes and the name, size, and date of introduction of each specimen placed in the aquarium. Other important data are such things as date of lamp replacements, feeding schedules and type of foods preferred, and events such as spawnings or deaths of animals. Also record purchase dates for equipment for warranty purposes (staple the receipt to the page as proof of purchase in case a warranty repair or replacement should become necessary). Two sample Aquarium Log pages (one for water tests, one for livestock) are reproduced on pages 139 and 140; they may be photocopied or used as the basis for creating your own versions. Even notes jotted in a desk calendar or diary are better than nothing and often very helpful in tracking down the start of a problem or an improvement in the system. (For example, more than one aquarist has been able to correlate the onset of dismaying algae blooms with the addition of certain "reef stimulants," vitamin supplements, or other ad-

ditives.) Periodically adding a snapshot or Polaroid photograph to the Aquarium Log is another useful way to track the growth of your specimens and the general progress of your reef.

Water Changes

IN THE EARLIEST MARINE AQUARIUMS, changing water was the only way to maintain water quality. Long ago, I read about a Victorian Englishwoman whose personal passion was sea anemones. (It was quite fashionable, in that era, for the upper classes to have an interest in natural history, and many a beau, apparently, was kept a-waiting by ladies too enamored of their microscopes.) She collected a specimen from a tidepool along the Cornwall coast and kept it in a bowl on a table in her sitting room. She aerated the water by stirring it with her hand after breakfast every morning. Every month, the anemone received a piece of fish, shrimp, or cockle meat. Each week, she replenished the seawater in the bowl with water taken from the ocean. The anemone, according to the story, survived for so many years that the lady's friends marveled at its longevity. This lady had a lot going for her. The temperature in her home by modern standards would have been decidedly cool, providing the anemone an appropriate temperature for a creature from the shore of the chilly Celtic Sea. Her maintenance routine could be successfully duplicated by any modern hobbyist having ready access to the ocean, substituting a simple airstone and pump for the lady's dainty hand. I've done this myself, even without an air pump, while camping along the South Carolina coast. I was able to maintain several Sea Pansies (*Renilla mulleri*) for over a week in a plastic busboy's tub filled with seawater and a layer of beach sand. (A colonial cnidarian of the temperate Atlantic coast, *Renilla* is related to the sea pens of the Tropics. It flashes with bioluminescence when disturbed.)

MARINE AQUARIUM WEEKLY LOG   TANK:____

DATE & TIME	pH	NITRATE	CALCIUM	ALK	SG	TEMP °F	PO₄	LW(ml)	Sr(ml)	I(ml)	OBSERVATIONS	% W/C
[Targets]	8.3	<10 ppm	>400 ppm	>2.5	1.024	75	0	*	*	*	Spawnings, deaths, etc.	5%/wk

LEGEND: ALK = alkalinity (meq/L), SG = specific gravity, LW = limewater, Sr = strontium additive, I = iodine additive,
W/C = water change   *These amounts must be determined by trial and error for each individual tank.

MARINE AQUARIUM ANIMAL LOG   TANK: _____

SPECIES	DATE	COST	ACQUIRED FROM	NOTES AND OBSERVATIONS	REMOVED
Ex: Clownfish, Ocellaris	1/15/97	$7.00	local aquarium store	Hatchery produced (Bahamas), 1" long, eats a variety of foods	

Although the matter of water changes is sometimes a controversial subject, it remains my view that no filtration system, regardless of its complexity, can permanently eliminate the need for regular partial water changes in a marine aquarium. The more "artificial" the system, the larger and more frequent such changes must be. Periodically, one must remove some water from the aquarium and replace it with freshly prepared synthetic seawater. How much water should be changed and how often? Ideally, change small quantities of water frequently, perhaps 2 to 3 gallons every three or four days in a 100-gallon tank. This would work out to roughly 5% per week, a reasonable goal in my view. The idea is to keep fluctuations in overall water quality to a minimum, and this can best be accomplished through smaller, more frequent changes, rather than by changing a huge amount of water on an infrequent schedule. (The old freshwater method of changing 20% to 50% of the aquarium's water once a month is far too traumatic for a reef aquarium.) In addition to partial water changes, additions of pure water must be done to compensate for evaporation. Salinity fluctuations that occur as a result of evaporation and the subsequent addition of freshwater can be quite large if topping-up is neglected for too long.

For example, consider a tank of 100 gallons. Dissolved in the water in this tank are some 29.4 pounds or 13.3 kilograms of salt (at a salinity of 35 parts per thousand). If 1 inch of water evaporates, the same quantity of salt will now be dissolved in 95.6 gallons of water, giving a salinity of 36.6 parts per thousand. This represents a 5% increase in salinity, a huge fluctuation compared to the changes that occur in the ocean. As a general rule, top up the tank on a schedule that results in only 1 gallon or less being required per 100 gallons of tank water.

It can be very convenient to install an automatic top-up system. Such a system can be pump-operated or gravity-fed. A pumped system requires the following equipment: a plastic reservoir tank, a pump, an electric float switch that controls the pump, and plumbing to run from the pump to the sump. The float switch is installed in the sump and adjusted so that it will energize the pump when the water level in the sump drops a bit due to evaporation. (The exact level for a particular tank is determined by trial and error.) Make sure the float switch is safe for saltwater use and has electrical specifications that match those of the pump. The system operates as follows: when the water level in the sump drops, the float switch closes and turns on the pump. The pump moves water from the reservoir of purified water to the sump, restoring the original level. This causes the float switch to open again, shutting off the pump. By adjusting both the float switch and the pumping rate, water can automatically be added to the system when even a small amount evaporates. For a gravity-operated system, the reservoir is located above the sump, and a plastic float valve controls the flow from the reservoir. This method works on the same principle as the plumbing inside a toilet tank. Such a top-up system can be employed to add limewater automatically to the tank. Many reef aquarists use limewater for replenishment of all evaporated water, with excellent results. When this is done, care must be taken to prevent accumulated lime from plugging the plumbing. Keeping the limewater fresh and minimizing its exposure to air are important considerations in the design of such an automated system.

A MARINE AQUARIUM is a dynamic system in which the living components interact with the nonliving ones in predictable but complex ways. Being a closed system, the aquarium tends to deviate from the ranges needed by living organisms, even when the artificial ecosystem is in equilibrium. The only way to offset this tendency is to monitor conditions and make suitable adjustments. That, in a nutshell, is the aquarist's lifestyle — test, then tweak.

Introduction

Reflecting the Wild Reef

*The Biotope Approach to Replicating
Nature's Microhabitats*

AN OPPORTUNITY TO RETURN TO PIGEON KEY came precisely one year after my first visit. Dr. David Etnier, who was to influence my professional development profoundly over the next several years, was offering a new course, "Coral Reef Ecology." Students would attend a series of lectures dealing with the reef ecosystem, identification of invertebrates, and, especially, the biology of the fishes found around coral reefs. The course would culminate with a field trip to the Florida Keys. I signed up immediately.

Pigeon Key was supervised by a crusty caretaker — dubbed by one of us The Meanest Man in the World — who lived with his wife and two children in a house at the center of the island. The Key was his exclusive domain, and he ran it with the brusque manner of an irritable ship captain

Teeming Pacific diversity, with a large leather coral (*Sarcophyton* sp.) and a shoal of Peach Anthias (*Pseudanthias dispar*). Top: *Tubastraea coccinea*.

143

whose vessel was constantly in danger of breaking down. The Key was not supplied with electricity from the mainland, but there was a diesel generator in a shed on the northwest corner of the island, just above the reach of high tide. The drone of the generator's engine was forever in the background, along with the whoosh of passing cars above us on the bridge. When the generator went down one night, the sudden hush, not to mention the darkness, caught us all off guard. About ten of us were sitting on the T-shaped dock on Pigeon Key's Gulf side after dinner. Evening entertainment consisted of fishing, looking at the ocean, and drinking beer. To improve our chances in the fishing department, we had turned on a big floodlight mounted on a pole at one end of the dock, hoping to attract a swarm of little fish, crustaceans, and plankton that would in turn lure bigger fish within range of our nets. It was a near-perfect night, the air so clear the stars seemed low enough to touch. The moon, recently full, was not yet up. I was halfway through

Steep fore reef in the Pacific with a kaleidoscopic stand of feather stars (*Crinoidea*) and soft corals (*Dendronephthya* sp.).

my third beer when the generator went out. As it happened, no cars were passing overhead; the island was wrapped in silence. Then the caretaker's screen door slammed shut with a bang. We watched his bobbing flashlight as he stomped across the sandy lawn, cursing, toward the generator shed. His loud imprecations shortly after entering the shed suggested repairs might take a while. A few minutes passed during which no one said a word. We were enthralled by the unexpected quiet and the splendor of the glorious sky.

"What was that?" said a voice to my left.

"What was what?" As I turned, I could just make out the lanky frame of one of the other grad students.

"That. See, there it is again. And there again." His arm was outstretched toward the expanse of the Gulf of Mexico. There were flashes of light at the water's surface, like fireflies courting in the trees on a summer's night back home. As we watched, the flashes became more numerous, and the intervals between flashes grew shorter and shorter, until it seemed as if the ocean were a mirror of the Milky Way's ragged path across the night sky. Entranced by this unknown and wholly unexpected phenomenon, we hesitated for a few long moments. Then, realizing that the flashes of light

Indo-Pacific fore reef wall that an advanced reef aquarist might attempt to simulate.

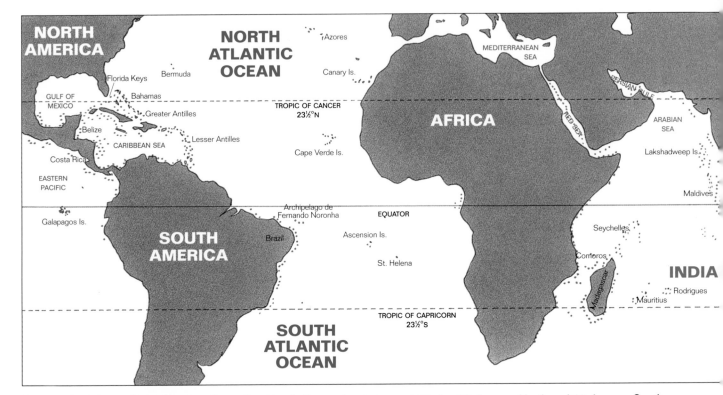

Coral reefs of the world (pink): primarily confined to shallow waters between latitudes 30-degrees North and 30-degrees South.

must be coming from sea creatures swimming at the surface, we bolted for the lab, grabbed nets and jars and buckets, and raced back, lest the swarm of oceanic fireflies retreat to the depths as suddenly as they had arrived.

Our efforts were quickly rewarded. The comparison to fireflies did not hold up, once we examined our catch, but firefly larvae, or glowworms, would have been a better analogy. A centimeter or two in length, the flashing creatures were segmented worms, annelids, of the most common marine group, the polychaetes. Many of the thousands of species of marine polychaetes are blind, but these had large, numerous eyes, obvious under the low-power microscope. The rear portion of the body of each worm was completely filled with ripe gonads, glowing with the eerie yellow-green of bioluminescence. Every few seconds, as we watched, male

and female worms would shudder and contract, spewing out a cloud of phosphorescent eggs or sperm. We were witnessing pyrotechnic orgasms of the sort that happen, in human experience, rather less often than one might wish.

Later, I learned that the creature we observed that night was the Bermuda Fireworm, *Odontosyllis enopla*. It is thought to spend most of its time feeding on organic sediments in the shallow, gravelly bottoms of protected coves. Its spawning behavior is timed to coincide with lunar phases. In summer, when the Bermuda Fireworm's reproductive cycle reaches its peak three days after the full moon, females appear at the surface about an hour after sunset and begin discharging clouds of glowing eggs. Smaller males, attracted by the flashes of light emitted by the females, soon join the orgy. Their luminescent sperm, in turn, attracts more of the

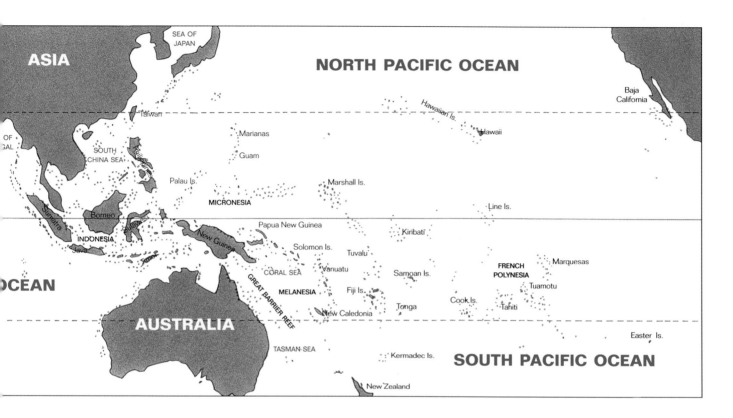

worms, and the spawning swarm increases in size and activity level.

As if the displays of bioluminescence associated with spawning were not sufficiently strange to warrant interest, *Odontosyllis* is among the many species of marine worms that also exhibit the phenomenon of epitoky. The epitoke, or sexually reproducing form of the worm, differs in significant ways from the nonsexual form that spends its time grubbing in the mud on the bottom. The epitoke may exhibit loss or major alteration of internal organs and muscles, alteration of appendages to facilitate swimming as opposed to crawling, and development or enlargement of sense organs, such as the conspicuous eyes of *Odontosyllis*. Swarming at the surface is the sole job of the epitoke and insures that both eggs and sperm will be discharged into the water simultaneously, increasing the likelihood of successful fertilization. After

fertilization, the egg develops into a larval form that remains in the plankton for a while before settling to the bottom to metamorphose into an adult.

Given that the larval form is small, that the adult feeds on detritus, and that the spawning display of bioluminescence occurs several times throughout the year, the Bermuda Fireworm might easily be included in the reef aquarium. Although I have never tried to accomplish this, it occurs to me that one could throw quite a party with the worm's spawning display being the main attraction. Guests could enjoy their drinks and snacks while observing the corals and fishes, until the lights on the aquarium, and finally the room, were slowly dimmed to simulate sunset. An hour of romantic twilight would allow the drama to build, and then the room lights would be darkened completely, as the fireworms swam up, one by one, from the rubble at the bottom of the tank. Moon-watching parties are popular in Japan. Why not a fireworm fest?

The Bermuda Fireworm is a good example of a species that is associated with a specific microhabitat. Its remarkable spawning behavior only occurs in shallow water, over a substrate of pebbles and gravel, in coves that are sheltered from the force of heavy waves. In this respect, it is like the majority of reef organisms, and the aquarist who really wants to accommodate reef species will want to take their idiosyncrasies into account.

Specialization is the rule, not the exception, to the lifestyles of the organisms of the coral reef. While a precise re-creation in the aquarium of the environment from which an organism is taken is not absolutely necessary to its survival, key elements of the organism's ecology — a specialized diet, for example — must be provided. This means that it is important not only to know something about the environment from which a specimen is taken, but also to identify the organism with accuracy (see "No Fear Taxonomy," page 249. The organism's scientific name (genus and species, when known) can often be used as a key word when using references to locate information about its lifestyle. A species that lives among rocks at the water's edge may be closely related to another species living in deeper water with a very different lifestyle. Such information is essential to the design of an appropriate aquarium habitat.

Creatures for an unusual temperate marine biotope: Clown Shrimp (*Lebbeus grandimanas*) and Crimson Anemone (*Cribinopsis fernaldi*) off British Columbia, Canada.

Creating a Reef Environment

IF WATER CONDITIONS are as indicated in Chapter Five, the aquarium should be suited to any of the organisms found on or around coral reefs. If you have become a novice marine aquarist, no doubt you are anxious to add some of these beautiful creatures. But before you begin stocking up on reef organisms, you should do some careful planning and a bit of research. The fish, invertebrates, and macroalgae you will find in your dealer's tanks come from a wide variety of locations and habitats in nature. In the confines of an aquarium, you can hope to reproduce only a tiny segment of a real habitat. Thus, concentrate upon one particular type of habitat (microenvironment), and attempt to replicate this habitat as faithfully as possible.

There is really nothing new in this approach; serious freshwater hobbyists have been keeping "species tanks" and "habitat tanks" for years. All the marine hobbyist needs, in order to emulate these tried and true methods, is information. In Part 2, we will explore detailed examples of marine habitats and the types of organisms that populate them. Conditions of lighting, current, etc. will be similar for organisms that live together in nature (sympatric species). This makes it possible to create an optimum setting for a community of organisms, rather than settling for an average set of conditions that diverse organisms all will tolerate but that are not really ideal for any one species.

Another major reason for keeping sympatric species together in the same aquarium is that organisms from one part of the ocean have had no opportunity to develop a natural immunity to parasites and bacteria that are harbored by those from another part of the world. One may also be surprised by unusual behavioral interactions between species that would not normally encounter each other. If one is unsure of the original habitat of a particular species, references should be consulted. There are many excellent field guides and picture books available that will aid greatly in distinguishing species from Florida, Hawaii, the Sea of Cortez, Australia, etc. Dealers should be able to provide locality information about the specimens they stock, but many do not. (You'll likely find that the dealer who knows or is willing to track down source information for you is also a purveyor whose business is built on healthy livestock and good service rather than low prices and fast turnover.)

When considering a setup from a particular locality, remember that some species are readily available only from certain parts of the world, although they may also occur elsewhere. The Scarlet Cleaner Shrimp (*Lysmata amboinensis*), for example, is found on coral reefs throughout the world and is collected from many locations. For aquarium purposes, the Atlantic-Caribbean species, *L. grabhami*, is

Fringing reef off Oahu, Hawaii: the aquarist has a wealth of geographical areas and habitats that can be replicated.

identical. Most algae-eating snails available to aquarists, on the other hand, are collected either in Florida or Mexico, even though similar species are found worldwide.

Don't plan on a Florida or Hawaii tank, however, and expect to put true stony corals in it. All corals found in U.S. waters are currently protected by Federal law, and any spec-

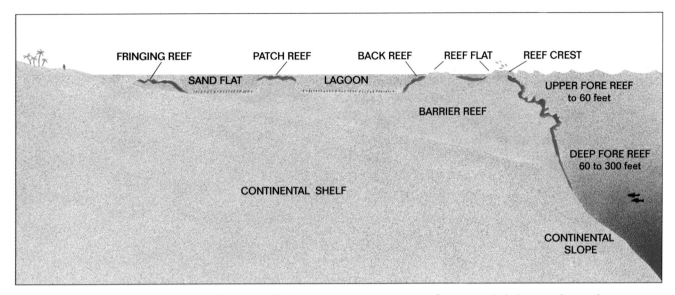

FRINGING REEF   PATCH REEF   BACK REEF   REEF FLAT   REEF CREST
SAND FLAT   LAGOON   UPPER FORE REEF
to 60 feet
BARRIER REEF
DEEP FORE REEF
60 to 300 feet
CONTINENTAL SHELF
CONTINENTAL
SLOPE

Reef Zonation: a cross-sectional map of the natural habitats a marine aquarist can choose to mimic in a captive setting.

imens offered for sale were illegally collected. The same holds true for Australia. Given the growing success of stony coral propagation at the hands of a number of pioneering marine aquarists, it is possible that captive-grown specimens of currently banned Caribbean species will be available. The tons of cultured live rock now being readied for harvest off the Florida shoreline will also harbor small corals that have settled out naturally during the rock-farming process. These corals are expected to be exempt from the usual regulations. In my experience, the shallow-water stony corals found in the waters around Pigeon Key and elsewhere in the Florida Keys grow abundantly under rather adverse conditions of high water temperature and heavy nutrient load. Small specimens brought into aquariums at the University of Tennessee fared well. Finger Coral (*Porites porites*), Yellow Mustard Coral (*P. astreoides*), Starlet Corals (*Astrangia* sp.) and Rose Coral (*Manicina areolata*) were the species we worked with. The first three are found on hard-bottom areas, usually along with *Halimeda* algae and frequently accompanied by the Upside-down Jellyfish

(*Cassiopea*). Rose Coral is found on silty or sandy substrates, where its pointed base helps to keep it stable. It is the Caribbean analog of *Trachyphyllia geoffroyi*, Open Brain Coral, with respect to its mode of life in the lagoon.

The availability of species from some regions can make setting up accurate biotope tanks more of a challenge, but therein lies the great joy of moving beyond the typical marine aquarium that recklessly mixes species that would never, ever be found within the same sea or hemisphere.

Water Depth

HAVING SETTLED UPON a particular ocean and geographic region that you find appealing, next limit the aquarium further, to a more specific microhabitat within that region. We will discuss in more detail later the various life zones associated with coral reefs, but for now let's consider only one aspect of reef ecology: water depth. Water depth greatly affects the distribution of many types of organisms, largely because of its influence on both the intensity and spectral quality of the sunlight that reaches them. Light intensity decreases with depth. Spectral quality changes from broad to narrow, with predominantly blue light penetrating most deeply. Clearly, then, lighting system requirements will be different for a tank of shallow-water organisms as opposed to deep-water species. Aquarium specimens are collected from depths ranging from a few inches to 60 feet or more, so their light requirements vary greatly. Since most aquariums are 24 inches deep or less, organisms with widely varying light requirements will be difficult to satisfy within the confines of a single tank. Much of the confusion and controversy surrounding the issue of aquarium lighting may simply be the result of attempts to keep a wide selection of species under one set of light conditions. The best plan is to select species that occupy roughly similar water depths in nature, then provide the tank with appropriate lighting.

Determining the depth from which a particular specimen was collected may be a challenge, since collectors rarely supply such data. At this time, there is no single source of such information in book form for marine hobbyists. However, many field guides provide a depth range for the specimens they describe, and picture books that depict reef communities may note the depth at which the photograph was made. Such books often provide excellent photos of whole communities of organisms and can give you valuable ideas about how natural reefs actually look. This can be a great help, not only in selecting specimens, but also as a guide to arranging your reef tank decor. There are many such references at your bookseller or library, and more appearing each year. (See Selected Sources, pages 307-308, and Bibliography, page 313.)

A good guess about the relative depth from which a specimen may have come can sometimes be deduced from its appearance. For example, in shallow areas with more water movement, branching corals may be very bushy and upright in body form. In deeper water, the same species may be broad and flattened, forming plates that scarcely resemble the shallow-water growth pattern. By altering its growth form, the coral is able to present more surface area containing photosynthetic zooxanthellae to collect sunlight, light intensity having been attenuated by the water column.

Reef Zonation

WITHIN ANY HABITAT, there are specific zones where particular organisms are most abundant. Bearing in mind that one can duplicate only a tiny area, one can focus on a particular zone and try to make it as accurate as possible.

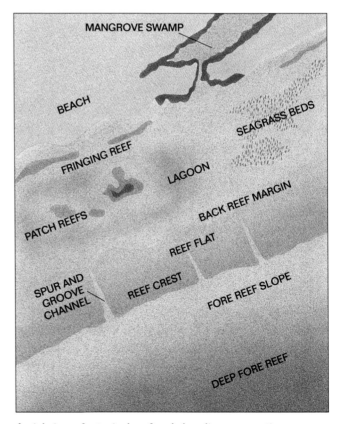

Aerial view of a typical reef and shoreline, suggesting many distinctive microhabitats appropriate for a biotope aquarium.

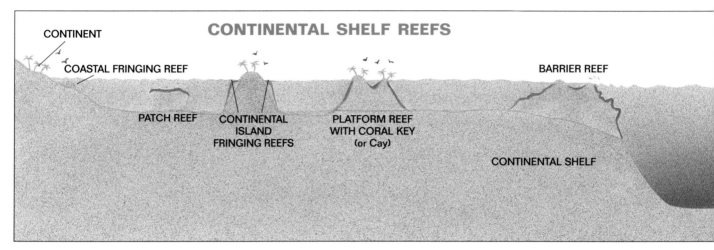

Types of coral reefs, divided between those that have developed along the continental shelves and those that are found in the open ocean. Living corals occur at depths ranging from less than a foot to more than 300 feet in certain exceptional regions.

The illustration on page 150 is a schematic of a typical barrier or fringing reef. The shore is on the left side of the diagram, the open sea on the right, and live corals are shown in deep pink. (Buried or dead coral growth appears in light pink.) The scope of this drawing is somewhat condensed; the lagoon zone may be 5 miles wide in some areas. Breakers form whitecaps at the reef crest, while the shallower back reef and lagoon, protected by the reef from the force of the open sea, are relatively calm. Even in these protected areas, however, tidal surges, currents, and wind-driven wave action create constant water movement. Note the relative amounts of wave and light energy at play in each zone.

In selecting a zone to mimic, you may find that the microhabitat you'd most like to duplicate and your aquarium budget are at odds. The reef crest, or shallow fore reef, with its combination of chaotic circulation, fiercely intense lighting, and absolutely pristine water conditions can be expensive to replicate. The deep fore reef, on the other hand, with calmer conditions and a gentle blue light, can be every bit as beautiful but much less demanding when it comes to pur-

chasing and operating lights, pumps, and other equipment.

Certain species of organisms are frequently, or in some cases exclusively, found with other species of organisms. The relationship between clownfishes and anemones is a familiar example of what biologists call symbiosis. Often, the two symbiotic partners cannot survive without each other in the wild. A tank devoted to keeping specific partners together can be most rewarding.

Species Tanks

DEDICATING AN ENTIRE TANK to only one or two species may seem a bit extravagant, but results in a breathtaking effect. Many kinds of corals, for example, form huge stands of just one species. All other corals are excluded, either because of water conditions or because of successful competition on the part of the dominant coral type. A whole tank of flourishing Colt Coral, for example, can make a magnificent display and a real departure from the menagerie approach. Similarly, some species of fishes live in shoals or

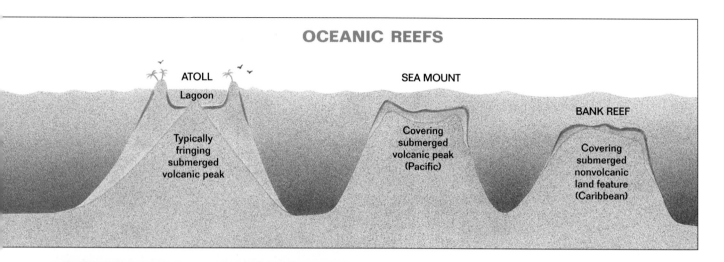

OCEANIC REEFS

ATOLL

Lagoon

SEA MOUNT

BANK REEF

Typically
fringing
submerged
volcanic peak

Covering
submerged
volcanic peak
(Pacific)

Covering
submerged
nonvolcanic
land feature
(Caribbean)

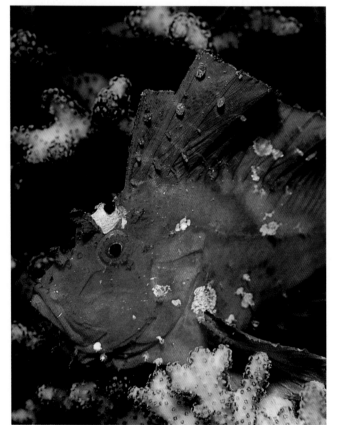

Ideal candidate for isolation in a species tank: Leaf Scorpi-onfish (*Taenianotus tricanthus*), bizarre but all-consuming.

schools, consisting of many individuals of the same species. In the aquarium, a single Green Chromis, *Chromis viridis*, can be a rather lonely looking creature, but a group of seven to ten or more starts to become much more natural and fascinating to observe.

ONE OF THE MOST CHARACTERISTIC FEATURES of the biota of coral reefs is their remarkable specializations for survival. Because the varied topography offers a variety of possibilities for organisms to exploit, particular microhabitats come to be occupied by a particular suite of species. This aspect of reef ecology can be exploited to create a natural reef aquarium. Plan the aquarium to include species that live in the same area of the world and at roughly the same water depth. Choose organisms from a particular habitat zone. Combine species that form symbiotic relationships. Devote a tank to only one or a few species. By attempting to duplicate a specific microhabitat, rather than merely assembling a hodgepodge of unrelated organisms, one can achieve an aquarium that is not only beautiful but also relatively free of commonplace problems. Perhaps you will find inspiration in the chapters that follow as we examine some actual microhabitats and the organisms they contain.

Chapter Six

Marine Habitats of the Florida Keys & Caribbean Sea

Dazzling Biotopes from Our Own Backyard

AMERICANS ARE INTERNATIONALLY KNOWN for shunning our native aquatic species, freshwater and marine, while aquarists in Europe and Asia prize them highly. The Florida Keys are surrounded by the third largest barrier reef system in the world, with at least 62 species of stony corals, 389 reef fish species, and a remarkable diversity of sponges, gorgonians, and macroalgae. The reef life of the Keys and the nearby Caribbean, once you come to recognize and appreciate it, can make for uncommonly beautiful and fascinating biotopes.

While perhaps not the most spectacular of the world's coral reefs, the reef system of the Florida Keys is one of the best studied. Hence, much information about this area and its fauna is available. This is also the area with which I am best acquainted. For aquarists in the eastern United States, the Keys offer the most easily accessible coral reefs to visit. I heartily recommend the experience. The area includes several hundred square miles, from Miami to Key West and beyond to the Dry Tortugas, with some 6,000 patch reefs in

Hawk's Channel. Water depth ranges to over 100 feet. Within the region are numerous scattered areas of bedrock, rubble, sand, mud, and silt; Turtle Grass (*Thalassia*) may cover acres and then abruptly give way to hard bottom dominated by gorgonians and scattered coral outgrowths. In short, the area is ecologically complex, and any attempt to create a generalized depiction of the patterns of life within it will be an approximation. Nevertheless, zonation can be observed, and particular communities of animals and plants are associated with each zone. From such communities, species can be chosen for a microhabitat aquarium.

In areas where Turtle Grass grows, water movement is reduced by the thick carpet of plants. As a result, suspended particles are deposited among the grass blades, and the silt may be several feet deep. Turtle Grass beds thus act as giant filters, efficiently removing the nutrient-laden debris that washes outward from the shore.

Where rocky outcrops occur within the lagoon zone, patch reefs may form when the rocks are colonized by corals and other organisms from the main reef nearby. When patch reefs are distantly isolated from other underwater structures, they may harbor a surprisingly diverse assem-

"Floribbean" habitat: a large French Angel (*Pomacanthus paru*) glides through clear waters on a Florida Keys reef.

Turtle Grass (*Thalassia testudinum*)

Fern Caulerpa (*Caulerpa mexicana*)

Green Grape Caulerpa (*C. racemosa*)

Common Caulerpa (*C. prolifera*)

Sawblade Caulerpa (*C. serrulata*)

Sargassum (*Sargassum* sp.)

blage of fishes. This feature makes some patch reefs quite popular with divers.

Seaward of the lagoon area lies the reef itself, which may be subdivided into four major life zones: the rear zone, the reef crest, the mixed zone, and the fore reef. Each zone has its own characteristics and its own community of species.

The rear zone, like the lagoon lying shoreward of it, is protected by the reef from the pounding of the open sea. Here are found many species of shallow-water corals, soft corals, calcareous algae, and herbivorous mollusks. Sea mats may be locally abundant in the rear zone, so much so that reef ecologists sometimes designate a "zoanthid zone" to emphasize this fact.

The reef crest, scoured by breaking surf, may be devoid of all life apart from algal mats, or may be dominated by branching staghorn and elkhorn corals (*Acropora* spp.) that require turbulence, sediment-free water, bright light, and abundant oxygen.

Seaward of the reef crest, as the reef begins to slope outward and downward to the abyss of the open ocean, one finds the richest diversity of species. In these areas (mixed zone and fore-reef zone), water depth plays a major role in determining what types of invertebrates may be found. Ecologists often further subdivide these zones to reflect the special nature of the communities of organisms that develop at a particular depth or over a particular substrate.

It is readily apparent that a variety of specialized microhabitats occurs both on and around the Keys coral reefs. Each microhabitat contains characteristic species, and these constitute the community to select from for an aquarium. Not all species from any given zone will necessarily be suited to aquarium life, of course, and knowing how to choose the appropriate species from among what is available is an important skill that the marine aquarist develops with study and experience.

The Inshore Zone

ONE OF MY FAVORITE SPOTS in the Keys is a huge, bowl-shaped tidepool just off U.S. 1. Protected from wave action by a sea wall of coral rock rubble, this pool is a giant natural aquarium. Dozens of species of macroalgae occur here. By far the most common are members of the large genus *Caulerpa*. *C. prolifera* has a simple flat blade (botanically, the "assimilator") that often spirals like a loose corkscrew as it grows upward. *C. mexicana* has a blade more reminiscent of a fern frond, that is, it is deeply notched. Less common species include *C. racemosa*, in which the blade looks like a bunch of grapes; *C. peltata*, which has an upright central stem with little lollipop-shaped "leaflets" attached along its length; *C. sertularioides*, with a blade that looks like a bird's feather; and *C. verticillata*, with short blades composed of a central thread bearing tufts of side filaments arranged in whorls along its length. These species of *Caulerpa* are adapted to scrambling over rubble, dead coral heads, and similar hard, irregular substrates. In the aquarium, arrange specimens attractively on top of a rock positioned in good light, and they will soon attach themselves and begin to grow.

Other species of *Caulerpa* are adapted to life in sandy or muddy habitats. These include *C. paspaloides*, which produces a tall, stiff blade crowned with feathery branches that give the overall appearance of a palm tree; *C. cupressoides*, with tough, squarish blades that are toothed along the edges; and *C. lanuginosa*, the blade of which is a fat, rounded rod covered with little projections that give it the appearance of a spruce tree branch. These three species require a fine substrate.

Under optimum conditions, growth of *Caulerpa* can be as much as an inch a day, so pruning will be necessary. The prunings can be fed to herbivorous fish or can be used to start new plants. A single blade of any *Caulerpa* can be partially buried in sand and will form a complete new plant within a few weeks. Natural growths of *Caulerpa* are probably "pruned" regularly by algae-eating animals. Pruning seems to be important in preventing *Caulerpa* from undergoing sporulation, a process in which the internal contents of the blade become reorganized, forming free-swimming reproductive cells. The first time I observed this phenomenon, I was amazed at the speed with which the changes in the seaweed occurred. At first, the blade takes on a veined appearance, as green chloroplasts cluster around cell nuclei and new walls of cellulose partition off the blade into myriad tiny packages. Within a few hours, these spores will be released into the water, each endowed with a flagellum that permits it to swim, leaving behind the dead, translucent husk of the parent.

On the shady side of large boulders in the inshore zone may be found colorful sponges, including *Chondrilla*, the Chicken Liver Sponge, which can be kept successfully in the aquarium. Scattered among rubble and pebbles, the lovely

Giant Fanworm (*Sabellastarte magnifica*): fascinating to behold and one of the best invertebrate choices for beginners.

giant fanworm, *Sabellastarte magnifica* extends its feathery fan, feeding on plankton. These worms, preferring quiet, sheltered locations, are common in boat slips and on submerged pilings. Other species of fanworms, though none as large as *Sabellastarte*, are abundant in such areas as well.

Shallow-Water "Flower Garden"

AMONG THE ANEMONES, *Condylactis*, *Bartholomea* and *Phymanthus* are hardy, colorful, sometimes have interesting symbionts associated with them, and are gloriously abundant in shallow waters surrounding the Florida Keys. I have witnessed vegetative reproduction in *Bartholomea* and sexual reproduction in the other two species (actually, the release of sexually produced offspring from a brooding "female" in each case) in the aquarium, suggesting possibilities for captive propagation.

Curleycue Anemone (*Bartholomea annulata*) with its claw-snapping partner, the Curleycue Shrimp (*Alpheus armatus*).

So-called Flower Anemones from Florida waters occur in a variety of lovely hues and color patterns and include a number of species.

Rock or Flower-Anemones (*Phymanthus crucifer*) live in crevices between the cobbles, often in only a few inches of water. When the rocks are exposed at low tide, or when the anemone is disturbed by inquisitive fingers, it retracts completely beneath the substrate. As a student and in my salad days as a biology instructor, I observed these lovely invertebrates on numerous expeditions to Pigeon Key, directly underneath the old Seven Mile Bridge. At the edge of the island, not quite underneath the bridge, and thus in full sun for about ten hours a day, lay a patch of gravelly sand dotted with *Phymanthus crucifer*. Since collecting around the island was forbidden, this patch had been undisturbed for a long time and covered many square yards. At low tide, the area was left high and dry, the gravel moist and cooling as seawater evaporated under the terrific sun. The anemones would be withdrawn into the gravel, waiting for the sea to return. When it did so, they would slowly emerge, revealing their intricate colors and patterns as they stretched to expose themselves to the sun. The anemones were of every hue possible for this species, and I spent hours wading in that "flower garden," admiring the seemingly infinite variations.

Phymanthus crucifer is a highly variable species, with variegated tentacles located just at the margin of the oral disc and a very short, stubby column, often sporting protective pink, purple, and green pigmentation. Other species called

"Flower Anemones" may be superficially similar in appearance, but the tentacles are smooth, not knobby as they are in *Phymanthus*. All are easy to keep, but coming as they do from very shallow water, they need bright light.

Another anemone that retracts into a crevice when disturbed is the Curleycue Anemone (*Bartholomea annulata*). It is unmistakable. Golden-brown to cream-colored, all specimens have rings of white spiraling around the tentacles, from which trait its common name is derived. This anemone will not only sting other anemones, it can eat them, so beware — although because of its symbiotic algae, it does not need to rely on catching food. Several species of shrimps are often found in association with the Curleycue Anemone, and an interesting aquarium could be set up featuring this community of species. In a burrow at the base of the anemone live pairs of Curleycue Shrimp (*Alpheus armatus*). Males can be distinguished by their striped antennae. Each pair of shrimp stakes out a particular anemone as home turf and will vigorously defend this position against any intruder, even fish much larger than the shrimp. (For this reason, only one pair of Curleycue Shrimp can be kept

together in the aquarium, as males will fight until one is dismembered.) When the anemone is approached by a fish or diver, the shrimp marches boldly from its burrow and emits a loud "Pop!" using a claw specialized for this purpose. The sound is audible from a considerable distance and is apparently enough to frighten away fishes that would otherwise feed on the anemone. In this fashion, the anemone is protected by the shrimp. The shrimp, in turn, receives protection from shrimp-eating fishes, owing to the stinging tentacles of the anemone.

Other shrimps, such as Pederson's Cleaning Shrimp (*Periclimenes pedersoni*), Sexy Shrimp (*Thor amboinensis*), and Spotted Cleaning Shrimp (*Periclimenes yucatanicus*) may seek shelter among the tentacles of the Curleycue Anemone. Their long, white antennae, together with distinctive swaying movements, advertise the services of cleaner shrimps to fishes seeking removal of parasites and dead tissue. Fish approach the shrimp's "cleaning station" and indicate a desire to be cleaned by adopting special postures or color patterns. The shrimp will then leave the protective tentacles of the anemone and alight on the fish's

Spotted Cleaning Shrimp (*Periclimenes yucatanicus*) on a Florida Pink-tipped Anemone (*Condylactis gigantea*).

Atlantic Carpet Anemones (*Stichodactyla helianthus*): attractive, but not recommended as appropriate aquarium subjects.

body, moving about — even inside the mouth and gill covers — extracting parasites, dead tissue, and loose scales. These the shrimp eats, so both fish and shrimp derive benefit from the cleaning relationship.

A hippolytid shrimp, *Thor amboinensis* is probably not a cleaner but is always found in association with anemones. In the Atlantic, it associates with the Curleycue Anemone and the Atlantic Carpet Anemone, *Stichodactyla helianthus.* (The latter anemone species is not a good aquarium subject.) These delightful little shrimp were once readily available, but now are rarely imported. It must, like all other anemone shrimp, be kept with an appropriate host. *Thor* occurs in the Indo-Pacific as well as the Atlantic and Caribbean. In the Indo-Pacific, this shrimp associates with corals such as *Heliofungia,* as well as with various anemones.

Most anemone shrimp species belong to the Family Palaemonidae and to a single genus, *Periclimenes.* One should obtain the shrimp and its host together. Mated pairs of shrimps are sometimes available, and the two will share a single anemone. Otherwise, attempting to keep two shrimp in a single anemone may result in a territorial squabble. Pederson's Cleaning Shrimp (*P. pedersoni*) occurs on several anemone species, perching in the tentacles and swaying back and forth to attract "customers." It rarely leaves the anemone, except to carry out its cleaning services. The body of this shrimp is transparent, with attractive white and purple stripes. Like most cleaners, it has white antennae. It grows to just over an inch in length. *P. yucatanicus* is a bit larger, also transparent, and is marked with distinctive tan and white saddles on the back of its carapace. The legs are banded in white and purple, and there is a series of purple dots, surrounded with white circles, along the sides of the abdomen and on the upper surface of the tail. The antennae are white, but there is no direct evidence that *P. yucatanicus* is actually a cleaner. It may be a false cleaner, mimicking the behavior in order to benefit from the same

protection from predation that true cleaner shrimps enjoy. (Fish rarely eat cleaners, as the latter provide a valuable service.) *P. yucatanicus* associates with *Condylactis gigantea* and with the Antler Anemone, *Lebrunia danae,* as well as with *Bartholomea,* the Curleycue Anemone.

Florida Pink-tipped Anemone (*Condylactis gigantea*): note shrimp hiding deep in the mass of stinging tentacles.

Commonplace in the inshore zone is the tiny Tricolor Hermit Crab, *Clibanarius tricolor*. All hermit crabs protect themselves by making use of the discarded shell of a dead snail, and this species is usually found in the small shell of a common species, *Battelaria*. Hermit crabs are found on all shores, and most species from the Tropics are colorful. The Tricolor Hermit's name derives from the red, yellow, and blue markings on its legs. It is seldom larger than an inch. Being very hardy, hermit crabs are often the first invertebrate to be kept by the beginning aquarist. A few hermit crabs can be included in any marine aquarium and make excellent scavengers. Make sure that the species is not one that grows large, however, since large hermits can be destructive.

American Star Shell (*Astraea tecta americana*): an excellent algae grazer.

Throughout the inshore zone, among rubble, under rocks and in crevices, brittle stars abound. While not particularly popular with aquarists, owing to their secretive habits, brittle stars make a fine addition to the aquarium. Many species sport attractive colors and patterns, and all are excellent scavengers, coming out at night to feed on bacteria, plankton, debris, or bits of dead animal matter. One species, the Reticulate Brittle Star (*Ophionereis reticulata*), is especially abundant among beds of the calcareous alga *Halimeda*. This brittle star has a unique way of defending itself against predators when it leaves the safety of the *Halimeda* to forage at night. When disturbed, its entire body flashes with a brilliant yellow-green light (bioluminescence). This reaction presumably dazzles the would-be predator, allowing the brittle star sufficient time to escape. Brittle stars are so named because they are easily damaged by handling. They will not survive in the aquarium unless provided with shelter into which they can retire to escape the light.

Another useful resident of the inshore zone is *Astraea tecta americana*, the American Star Shell. (Another subspecies, *A. tecta tecta*, occurs in the West Indies.) This mollusk (Gastropoda-Turbinidae) is valued by aquarists for its propensity to consume algal turfs. It also occurs in grass beds and on the back reef. Several species of keyhole limpets (*Diodora*, Gastropoda-Fissurellidae) are also found in the Keys, from shallows to great depths. All of the shallow-water forms feed on algae, and so are often included in aquarium displays for functional, rather than aesthetic, reasons. Limpets are capable of reproduction in the aquarium, a trait which further recommends them to hobbyists.

Fish species appropriate for this biotope would include any of the common shallow-water damsels, such as the Beau Gregory (*Stegastes leucostictus*), various wrasses, such as the colorful Bluehead Wrasse (*Thalassoma bifasciatum*), as well as numerous blennies of the Keys and the Caribbean that appear in the trade, often unidentified. Juveniles of many other species also pass through these shallows, and a young Blue Tang (*Acanthurus coeruleus*), French Angel (*Pomacanthus paru*), Porcupine Puffer (*Diodon hystrix*) or Goldspotted Snake Eel (*Myrichthys ocellatus*) would not be out of place here, although any of these would outgrow a small tank.

Grass Beds

MAJOR AREAS OF THE INSHORE ZONE of the Florida Keys are occupied by beds of Turtle Grass (*Thalassia*) and Manatee Grass (*Syringodium*). These angiosperms (flowering plants) can be grown in the aquarium if provided with a 4-inch-thick substrate of fine silt and sand. Including numerous burrowing organisms that help to keep the substrate stirred up makes it possible to duplicate the Turtle Grass habitat. The nutrient-rich substrate of the Turtle Grass beds is home to hundreds of species. Here one finds the Florida Pink-tipped Anemone (*Condylactis gigantea*) in abundance. Formerly known to many as *C. passiflora*, this is probably the most common and widely available of all anemones. Specimens vary in color, generally shades of pink, cream, white, or a combination of these. (*C. gigantea* is variously called the Florida Pink-tipped, Haitian Pink-tipped, or Giant Anemone in the aquarium business.) Forms vary considerably: the column may be white, pink, or reddish in color, and the tentacles are cream to greenish in color with or without a definite pattern of shading. This species grows both in reefs

Florida Pink-tipped Anemone (*Condylactis gigantea*): common, inexpensive, and relatively hardy.

and Turtle Grass beds, where it tends to be smaller.

The amusing Variegated Urchin (*Lytechinus variegatus*), sometimes called the Carrier Urchin because of its habit of carrying objects as camouflage, and the Lined Seahorse (*Hippocampus erectus*) are other grass bed dwellers. Seahorses have long been popular as aquarium subjects, but the beginner should be warned that they are challenging to maintain. Aside from requiring living foods, seahorses are frequently infected with a variety of pathogens and parasites. Collectors may not handle seahorses properly, and the stress of capture and shipment may cause them to succumb to infections. All seahorses should be carefully medicated upon receipt. A supply of live guppies, adult brine shrimp, and grass shrimps should always be on hand for daily feed-

ings. After becoming acclimated to the aquarium for a few months, seahorses can sometimes be trained to accept non-living foods and may even take food from the aquarist's fingers.

Reticulated sea stars, the "Bahama Star" of the aquarium trade (*Oreaster reticulatus*) and the Five-toothed Sea Cucumber (*Actinopyga agassizii*), which carries its teeth in its anus rather than its mouth, are large, conspicuous inhabitants of the Turtle Grass bed. The Five-toothed Sea Cucumber is sometimes host to the Pearlfish (*Carapus bermudensis*), which lives inside the cucumber's digestive tract, emerging only at night to feed on small invertebrates. Long-spined Sea Urchins (*Diadema antillarum*) and the Queen Conch (*Strombus gigas*) were once common in Turtle Grass, but a decline in their numbers has resulted in these two species being protected in Florida waters. Several small coral species are found in the grass beds, and all, according to researchers, can be kept successfully in the aquarium. None of these are currently available to hobbyists, however, since all corals in American waters are protected. This may change with the advent of live rock mariculture. Some live rock farmers in Florida have already received permits to sell stony coral colonies that develop on their "rock farms."

If genuine Turtle Grass is unavailable, you may want to consider substituting plastic replicas of the freshwater plant *Vallisneria*, commonly sold in aquarium shops. Interplant this with live macroalgae, or include a few scattered pieces of aquacultured live rock, preferably with small stony coral colonies present. To help control filamentous algae, include a few of the cultivated juvenile Queen Conchs now being

Five-toothed Sea Cucumber
(*Actinopyga agassizii*)

Variegated or Carrier Urchin
(*Lytechinus variegatus*)

Queen Conch
(*Strombus gigas*)

offered. Sea cucumbers and brittle stars will help to keep the sand stirred up.

One fish associated with Turtle Grass is the Sergeant Major Damselfish (*Abudefduf saxatilis*). Commonly available and inexpensive, its hardiness is legendary. Other piscine inhabitants for a Turtle Grass habitat tank might include the widespread Slippery Dick (*Halichoeres bivitta-*

Antler Anemones (*Lebrunia danae*): branching tentacles.

tus), an ever-active, attractive wrasse. Two other wrasses usually associated almost exclusively with Turtle Grass beds can usually be obtained by special order if your dealer has access to a good collector in Florida or the Caribbean. These are the Blackear Wrasse (*H. poeyi*) and the Dwarf Wrasse (*Doratonotus megalepis*). The latter lives only in seagrass and alters its coloration to match its habitat. Since the Dwarf Wrasse reaches only 3 inches in length, it is a good choice for a smaller tank. Several wrasses can be kept together and make for a consistently lively display.

Many other larval and juvenile fishes are plentiful in the grass beds, where they find both food and shelter in abundance among the fronds. The choices are broad for this habitat, and a listing of fishes typical of the Keys area is included in Chapter Ten.

The Lagoon

OPEN WATERS OF THE LAGOON ZONE may be dotted with tiny patch reefs, and here an abundance of organisms more commonly seen on the reef proper may be found. Both the Curleycue Anemone and the Florida Pink-tipped Anemone may be seen here. The Antler Anemone (*Lebru-*

nia danae) occurs here and there in the lagoon. *Lebrunia* has two types of tentacles, one set is short and closely circles the mouth, the other set is much larger and branches repeatedly, not unlike the antlers of a deer. This is also known as the "Stinging Anemone" in south Florida. The latter name is descriptive — beware.

Sandy or muddy bottoms with rubble are often carpeted with the Green Sea Mat (*Zoanthus sociatus*). This colorful and hardy species is at home in any aquarium with sufficiently bright light. I have seen Green Sea Mat colonies completely exposed at low tide, baking under the tropical sun at temperatures in excess of 100 degrees F. No wonder this species is hardy in the aquarium! It is less commonly available these days, due to collecting restrictions.

To create a lagoon tank featuring sea mats and other shallow-water invertebrates, an aquarist would be hard-pressed to find a more appropriate and appealing species than the Yellow-headed Jawfish (*Opistognathus aurifrons*), sometimes called the Pearly Jawfish. This burrowing species needs about 6 inches of sandy substrate, including a few smooth pebbles with which it can reinforce the walls of its burrow. The tunnel is often constructed beneath a sheltering rock, and careful placement of a flat piece of live rock, supported an inch or two above the tank bottom by pieces of rock buried in sand and pebbles, will create a perfect site for a rocky cave. Chances are good that the jawfish will be enticed to set up housekeeping here, and with some forethought you

Sea Mat or Mat Zoanthid
(*Zoanthus pulchellus*)

Yellow-headed or Pearly Jawfish
(*Opistognathus aurifrons*)

can coax the fishes to settle down in a spot that makes it easy to observe their behavior. Jawfish are gregarious; a colony of half a dozen or more can be maintained if the tank is large enough and shelter is sufficient. Do not place jawfish in an aquarium with anemones, however, as the fish is prone to becoming a meal for the cnidarian. Instead, populate the aquarium with invertebrates from the grass beds (many of which are found in the lagoon) or with specimens of one or more of the soft corals discussed in the following section.

The Gorgonian Forest

NOT ALL OF THE LAGOON bottom in the Keys is strewn with rubble and sand, which gives rise to the type of microhabitat frequented by Curley-cue Anemones, nor is it all soft, silty pastures of Turtle Grass. In many places, the Key Largo limestone strata are exposed and are largely bare of sediments. It is in this kind of hard-bottom lagoon that a sort of inshore reef occurs, dominated by the soft corals called gorgonians. I like to think of these areas as "gorgonian forests," for they share some similarities with the great belt of coniferous forests that encircles the Earth at the northernmost limits of the temperate zone.

One such forest occurs just beyond a seawall along the western side of U.S. 1. One can easily wade out a few yards and snorkel over the stand of gorgonians. They are very uniformly spaced, and all are approximately the same size. The

**Sea Plumes or Sea Feathers (*Pseudopterogorgia bipinnata*):
commonly available and readily propagated from cuttings.**

Gorgonacea includes sea whips and sea fans; colonies are branched and treelike, with the branches sometimes fused into a net (sea fans), or sheetlike, spreading over the substrate. In either case, they are stiffened by the protein gorgonin, with or without calcified elements called spicules. In the upright species, there is an axial skeleton overlaid with cortical tissue (the colorful part of the creature) in which the polyps are embedded. The axial skeleton is absent in the encrusting types of gorgonians.

There are many families of gorgonians, and individual species may be difficult to identify. Accurate identification is based upon the presence or absence of spicules and upon the shapes and colors of these elements when examined under a microscope.

To prepare a specimen for study, one must place a bit of the cortical tissue on a microscope slide and add a drop of laundry bleach. The bleach dissolves away the soft tissues, leaving the skeletal elements intact. Examination of this preparation to identify the different types of spicules present is required for positive identification, which even then may be beyond the capabilities of all but those who specialize in studying this group. There are some broad generalizations to be made about the commonest types of gorgonians, however. The following is a partial list of families and genera found in the Florida Keys and the Caribbean, which supply most of the gorgonians collected for the aquarium trade.

FAMILY BRIAREIDAE — the encrusting gorgonians (example, *Briareum asbestinum*):

Most gorgonians are branching, upright forms, but there are also spreading types, typified by the pinkish *Erythropodium caribaeorum*. In this species, which is sometimes called Brown Encrusting Soft Coral, the skeleton is sheetlike and rubbery, without calcified spicules, and spreads over rocks and other solid surfaces, often colonizing the dead skeletons of other gorgonians and so appearing to be a branching species. This one has grown quite well in one of

predominant color of these soft corals is deep purple, probably owing to the production of pigments that shield them from the effects of ultraviolet light. The water here is barely 4 feet deep, and the pale-colored limestone bottom reflects the sun, meaning that these organisms are receiving just about the maximum amount of illumination possible. This is the Gulf of Mexico side, and the low waves keep the gorgonians swaying back and forth in constant motion. When the tide turns, the directional flow of the water is quite perceptible. The stiff yet flexible skeleton of the gorgonians seems ideally suited to life in this locale. Each is firmly cemented to the solid rock, and movement is facilitated by several inches of "trunk" protruding straight up from the base before any branches occur. This design apparently works as well for gorgonians as it does for trees, in terms of coping with the forces of moving water or wind.

Gorgonians are cnidarians consisting of colonies of individual polyps with tentacles in multiples of eight. Order

my aquariums, starting from a single polyp attached to a piece of live rock.

As indicated by their golden-brown coloration, the very large tentacles of *E. caribaeorum* are filled with zooxanthellae, but they also show a feeding response, expanding when something nutritious, like brine shrimp juice, is in the water or if the sediments in the aquarium are stirred up. Wilkens and Birkholz (1986) reported a similar response in the nonphotosynthetic gorgonians. Kaplan (1982) suggested that gorgonians may be specialized for photosynthesis as the primary feeding mode, since the polyps are expanded mostly during the daytime, when plankton is less abundant. Determining the dominant source of nutrition for *Erythropodium* would make an interesting research project. In any case, it is a good aquarium species and rather commonplace in Florida, so it should not be difficult to obtain a specimen.

Another species that lacks a carbonate skeleton is *Briareum asbestinum*, also called Deadman's Fingers. The colony is composed of fat, pinkish brown branches with huge, feathery, brown polyps that appear fuzzy. *Briareum* sometimes forms branches, but I have most often encountered the encrusting form in the field. It is probably the most common

Encrusting gorgonian (*Erythropodium caribaeorum*) colony: will spread under good lighting.

Deadman's Fingers or Corky Sea Fingers (*Briareum asbestinum*): readily regenerates.

species in areas where the substrate is unstable, for it can grow quickly and regenerates readily from broken pieces. It is a good choice for the aquarium and can be easily propagated. *Briareum* may be confused with the Brown Star Polyp (*Cornularia*) but this should not be a problem if the source of a specimen is known, as the Brown Star Polyp is found only in the Indo-Pacific.

FAMILY PLEXAURIDAE — the bushy gorgonians (example, *Plexaura*):

The several genera in this family include most of the species that one will see in the aquarium trade. *Plexaura*, with at least three species, shows distinct growth forms depending upon the water depth at which it grows. In the genus *Muricea*, the branches of the colony are spiny or prickly due to the size of the skeletal elements. *Eunicea*, with many species, usually has protruding knobs or bumps from which the polyps extend. *Plexaurella* has tall, sparse, thick, and very fuzzy branches. All are widely distributed gorgonian genera. Collections from shallow water, as opposed to the reef itself, will probably be dominated by species of *Plexaura* and *Muricea*.

FAMILY GORGONIDAE — the sea fans and sea feathers (examples, *Gorgonia*, *Pseudopterogorgia*):

Sea fans (*Gorgonia* spp.) are specialized gorgonians in which the flat branches are very finely divided and fused together to form a net. Sea fans are rarely seen growing inshore from the reef in my experience. Sea fans can be successfully maintained in aquariums suited to stony corals. Sea fans should be oriented so that they are spread perpendicular to the current. In fact, orientation may be an important key to success with most gorgonians.

Sea fans are not regularly available in aquarium shops. On the other hand, sea feathers, *Pseudopterogorgia* and *Pterogorgia*, are frequently to be had. One common name often applied to these gorgonians is Purple Frilly Gorgonian. In these genera, the branches arise in one plane from opposite sides of a central stalk, creating the overall appearance of a feather. In *Pterogorgia*, the branches are flat, with polyps confined to the edges, while in

Bahamian Sea Fan (*Gorgonia flabellum*): can thrive in a reef tank with vigorous currents.

Pseudopterogorgia, the branches are rounded and the polyps are uniformly distributed along them.

Gorgonians from shallow waters in Florida and the Caribbean are commonly photosynthetic and are colored purple, green, or brown, with mostly brownish or greenish polyps protruding from the skeleton. They fulfill the same ecological roles in the Caribbean that the leather corals fulfill in the Indo-Pacific. While sometimes regarded as difficult to maintain in the aquarium, photosynthetic gorgonians respond well to the same conditions provided for stony corals. They demand bright light and vigorous water movement. A well-established natural aquarium suits them, but it should have auxiliary pumps or powerheads controlled by a

wavemaker to provide plenty of turbulence. Water movement is essential for all gorgonians, especially for those that are entirely photosynthetic and absorptive in their feeding behavior. These can be recognized by their tiny polyps in which tentacles are rudimentary or even absent. Clearly, these little guys cannot catch plankton and so depend upon currents to bring nutrients and carry off wastes, while photosynthesis by their zooxanthellae provides calories for growth and development. Upright types grow attached at the base to a rock and should be mounted in this fashion in the aquarium, using waterproof epoxy, unless collected already attached to a suitable base (highly desirable). A number of individuals are now offering propagated gorgonians for sale, usually smaller branches attached to pieces of live rock. Coming from captive stock, these are often hardy and easier to acclimate than wild-collected gorgonians.

Not all gorgonians are constructed according to the same body plan, although the branching ones do appear superficially identical. In some, the branches are round in cross section, with polyps arranged more or less uniformly over the whole surface of the branch. In others, the branches are triangular in cross section, with polyps usually confined to the apices of the triangle, and in still others, the branches are flattened blades, with polyps arrayed only on the edges. These differences probably represent adaptations to environmental conditions that vary in both the degree of exposure to sunlight and in the nature of currents prevailing in the gorgonian's preferred habitat. We know that stony corals alter their growth patterns depending upon ambient light,

Shaving Brush (Penicillus dumetosus)

Rolled-blade Alga (Padina boergesenii)

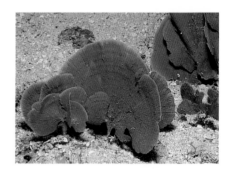

Mermaid's Fans (Udotea spinulosa)

Watercress Alga (*Halimeda discoidea*)

Calcareous Green Alga (*Halimeda* sp.)

Pinecone Alga (*Rhipocephalus* sp.)

becoming flatter and more platelike with increasing water depth. In areas subjected to a great deal of turbulence, as opposed to directional flow, there would seem to be no special advantage to the orientation of the polyps, or indeed of the whole gorgonian, with respect to water movement. In other localities, however, directional flow may predominate, and the polyps might be arranged so that all are "facing into the wind" or, in this case, the current, which brings food and oxygen and carries away wastes and reproductive cells. Sea fans are almost always perpendicular to the prevailing currents, and they are of the flat-stemmed type of gorgonian. Careful inspection of a sea fan with expanded polyps will show that the polyps are only found on the edges of each tiny branchlet and that all seem to stretch toward the incoming water flow. Placement of gorgonians with attention to these specializations should enhance their likelihood of surviving

and growing in the aquarium. Nonphotosynthetic gorgonians are, in my experience, nearly always of the round-branch type, with uniformly distributed polyps, the better to catch food arriving from any direction.

MACROALGAE. Down among the bases of the gorgonians, calcareous macroalgae fulfill roles similar to those of the shrubs and herbs of the forest floor. *Udotea flabelliforme, U. cyathiformis, Penicillus capitatus, P. dumetosus, Halimeda incrassata, H. discoidea, Rhipocephalus phoenix, Avrainvillea nigricans, Cymopolia barbata, Dasycladus vermicularis* and *Acetabularia crenulata* all occur in the gorgonian forest in abundance. *Caulerpa*, interestingly, is not so common, probably because only a few species of this tropical seaweed can make do with smooth, solid rock for a substrate.

There are three major groups into which macroalgae may be sorted. These groupings are based upon pigmentation. Perhaps most familiar are the green algae, (Chlorophyta), with *Caulerpa* being a typical species. Red algae (Rhodophyta) are typified by species such as *Gracillaria*. (The "red slime" algae that sometime reach plague proportions in the aquarium are *not* in this group.) The third group, brown algae (Phaeophyta), includes the giant kelps and numerous other species that live in cool waters, although there are several tropical species, notably *Sargassum*.

Among the most common algae at any depth are several species of mauve or purple coralline, or calcareous, red algae that encrust the undersides of rocks in shallow waters, able to subsist on the sunlight reflected up to them from the sea bottom. Given conditions to their liking, these algae will reproduce in the aquarium, encrusting the glass and other objects. Coralline algae are regarded as being desirable in any aquarium with live rock. Besides being attractive, these species indicate by their presence that corals can grow in the tank as well.

There are two subclasses of Rhodophyta, and one, the Florideophyceae, contains all of the red algae species that are multicellular, capable of both sexual and asexual reproduction, and possessing multinucleate cells with disc-shaped chloroplasts. Pit connections, a distinctive microscopic feature of the cell wall, are prominent. There are nine orders, distinguished on the basis of details of the development of the reproductive organs, with Order Cryptonemiales being

the order in which corallines are placed. All of the coralline species are placed in one family, Corallinaceae, distinguished by the calcified body structure.

Coralline algae are either crustose (thinly encrusting) or articulated (upright and branching) and are found in all seas, although they are most abundant in cold, agitated waters. They tolerate low light intensities and are found at greater depths than other kinds of algae. Genera and species of corallines are separated by studying the details of the sexual reproductive cycles, usually by microscopic examination of specimens grown under laboratory conditions. The average hobbyist will therefore be unable to identify with accuracy any corallines that he or she may encounter. They can be subdivided into two groups: those that undergo sexual reproduction only in the summer months and those that do so either year-round or at a season other than summer. Presumably, the tropical species that are usually found on live rock in the aquarium trade are reproductive year-round.

Among the green macroalgae (Chlorophyta) found on rocks, *Dasycladus vermicularis*, which looks like 3-inch lengths of green pipe cleaners clustered together, and *Batophora*, a relative of *Dasycladus* that looks like clusters of small, green bananas, are frequently present.

For our purposes, the green macroalgae of shallow waters may be divided into two groups: those that produce a

Flat Twig Alga (*Amphiroa tribulus*)

Crustose coralline algae (Rhodophyta)

Lavender coralline algae (Rhodophyta)

MACROALGAE CULTIVATION

AN AQUARIUM BASED ON KEYS OR CARIBBEAN species would be ideal for the many species of interesting and attractive macroalgae available to hobbyists. For the calcium-loving calcareous types, the tank should have a layer of substrate; the upper layer of a live sand bed is satisfactory, perhaps making it a bit thicker than an inch here and there, to better support these algae, which are rooted in the substrate by a holdfast. *Penicillus*, *Rhipocephalus*, *Udotea* and *Halimeda incrassata* are typical and often occur together in the lagoon. *Halimeda opuntia* and *Cymopolia barbata* are not usually rooted in the substrate but are attached to rocks or simply lie on the bottom.

Macroalgae reach their greatest diversity and abundance in shallow habitats with a sandy or muddy bottom. Inshore habitats, too, may harbor all the species just mentioned, along

Green Grape Caulerpa (*C. racemosa*)

with many more, including various forms of *Caulerpa*. The latter is not calcified, and leaks organic matter into the water, so the aquarium housing it needs adequate skimming. Soft corals of the more tolerant varieties, such as *Sarcophyton*, mushroom polyps, and LPS (large-polyped scleractinian) corals, such as *Trachyphyllia*, are at home in a habitat with abundant, noncalcified seaweeds, but SPS (small-polyped scleractinian) corals would not be appropriate. A dense growth of macroalgae dominated by *Caulerpa* also comes close to duplicating a patch denuded of Turtle Grass and sub-

sequently recolonized by the more rapidly growing macroalgae. This is analogous to what happens in a forest when fire destroys a tract of trees. Fast-growing, opportunistic species appear quickly and dominate for a while, but the old growth trees eventually return to prominence. This is also true of Turtle Grass, so an aquarium built around this theme can have another facet of interest, that of capturing a microhabitat at a specific "moment" in time.

The single most important requirement for the cultivation of macroalgae is sufficient light. Refer to Chapter Four for information regarding selection of artificial lighting systems for the aquarium. The optimum light intensity for shallow-water tropical macroalgae is about 16,000 lux (Spotte, 1979). For large-scale algae production, greenhouse culture is probably the most economical route.

The major and minor nutrients required by macroalgae are: nitrogen compounds, phosphate, potassium, sulfate, iron, manganese, thiamine, biotin, and vitamin B_{12}. Nitrogen compounds and phosphate are generally always available in the aquarium, often to the extent that one must take measures to remove them. Other major elements (potassium, sulfate, and manganese) are present in seawater mixes. Iron and iodine, important trace elements for growth, are often added to macroalgae aquariums. If iron supplementation is used, test the water daily with an iron test kit and add sufficient supplement to maintain a concentration of 0.05 to 0.1 mg/L. Iodine supplements should also be used (see Chapter Twelve for more information on supplements). Algae that have calcareous skeletons are especially sensitive to pH, alkalinity, and calcium concentration.

Some fishes and invertebrates are not compatible with macroalgae. Tangs, angelfishes, sea urchins, and many mollusks will readily consume a carefully tended underwater garden. A pair of seahorses would be suitable and quite at home in a seaweed-dominated aquarium environment but are notoriously difficult to maintain in captivity. A better choice, for an Indo-Pacific environment, would be one or more gobies (*Gobiodon* spp.*)* or wrasses (*Halichoeres* spp.). For a biologically accurate macroalgae tank from Florida or the Caribbean, consider including any of the species mentioned in this chapter that are recommended for the lagoon or seagrass habitats.

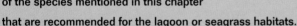

Feather Caulerpa (*C. sertularioides*)

Aquarists are sometimes told that macroalgae are to be avoided because they will invariably die and release harmful compounds into the water, spelling disaster for all of the tank's other inhabitants. This notion is a mix of both fact and fiction. In the first place, apparently only *Caulerpa* species experience mass die-off with any regularity. This phenomenon is associated with the reproductive cycle, or sporulation, of the algae. I have seen it occur only once with a species other than a member of the *Caulerpa* genus; in that instance, the species was *Halimeda discoidea*. In any case, sporulation can be avoided by proper maintenance techniques. It appears that iron depletion (which would never occur in the sea), and lack of regular pruning (which naturally occurs as a result of nibbling by herbivores) may trigger sporulation.

As to the assertion that harmful compounds are released, again, this is only partly true. Macroalgae may indeed produce poisonous alkaloids to deter other organisms from feeding upon them, and the death and decay of any organism will create pollution in the aquarium if the system's capacity is overloaded. However, these phenomena may not be responsible for the disastrous effects upon the other specimens in the tank following a sporulation event by *Caulerpa*. I suspect that the most likely problem is oxygen depletion. The spore of *Caulerpa* is a free-swimming organism that may be considered analogous to a mammalian sperm cell. It swims vigorously by means of a whiplike appendage, the flagellum. This activity demands plenty of oxygen. Since literally millions of these spores may be released at once, enough to tint the water green, oxygen depletion can occur, and fish and other organisms may die as a result.

Another problem that may develop in an aquarium with abundant macroalgae is an elevated pH. This occurs as the growing algae remove carbon dioxide from the water for photosynthesis. Vigorous aeration for increased gas exchange, or control of pH with an automated carbon dioxide injection system, may be necessary.

Macroalgae reward the careful aquarist with the lush, green color of chlorophyll and a beautiful diversity of forms. Wisely chosen and properly grown, they are appropriate additions to any natural reef aquarium.

calcium carbonate skeleton and those that do not. The calcareous varieties are among the most interesting and beautiful macroalgae. This group includes the various species of *Halimeda*, which are found in shallow-water habitats as well as on the reef. The appearance of Merman's Shaving Brush (*Penicillus capitatus* and *P. dumetosus*) is adequately described by its common name. Green Sea Fan is the name most frequently given to *Udotea*. Two species are available, *U. spinulosa*, a flattened form, and *U. cyathiformis*, in which the fan is curved, almost cone-shaped. Sea Paintbrush or Pinecone Shaving Brush are two common names that describe the appearance of *Rhipocephalus phoenix*.

Dictyota is a member of the brown algae phylum (Phaeophyta). Its golden-brown fronds divide repeatedly, producing a loose clump held upright above the point of attachment. *Dictyota* is probably the most commonly seen member of the brown algae family in collections made for the aquarium. Its "cousin" *Sargassum* is only occasionally collected and is rather difficult to cultivate. One other brown alga genus deserves mention. This is *Padina*, which must be obtained attached to a rock if there is to be any hope of keeping it alive. It is abundant in inshore waters, where it forms clumps of ruffled, fan-shaped blades attached to rocks and rubble. The blades are golden-brown in color, with alternating bands of bright yellow-green. It is an attractive species that sometimes does not retain its banded appearance in the aquarium. All brown algae appear to benefit from additions of iodine, and *Padina* is no exception.

My favorite calcareous macroalga is one of the Chlorophyta, *Cymopolia barbata*. It looks like branched strings of white beads with a tuft of green filaments forming a "pom-pom" at the tip of each branch. All of the calcareous macroalgae grow best if obtained attached to a rock, although some may also grow in loose, sandy substrates. Each of the species mentioned above has an upright stalk with a rootlike structure, the holdfast, at the lower end. The hold-

fast anchors the plant in the substrate or to a hard surface but does not function in the assimilation of nutrients, as the roots of terrestrial plants do. Calcareous algae with the holdfast missing will not survive for long. All of these calcareous macroalgae can be included in an aquarium mimicking the gorgonian forest.

Spreading on live rock, compound tunicates appear in many colors and forms and are often misidentified as sponges.

OTHER DENIZENS OF THE GORGONIAN FOREST.

While one can find the usual snails and hermit crabs crawling around on the floor of the lagoon, it is among and upon the gorgonians that the most interesting animals may be found. There are a number of snails and nudibranchs that feed solely upon gorgonian polyps, and these may be found munching their way along one of the branches. One must look closely in order to find many of these, as they are often well camouflaged and look remarkably like their host species. These browsers are never very abundant, however, and do not seem to be doing significant damage to the gorgonian host. In the aquarium, however, such predation might pose a problem, since the supply of gorgonians would be very limited. These organisms are usually introduced into the aquarium inadvertently, along with the gorgonian. Inspect new gorgonian specimens carefully, and if subsequent damage appears, search for and remove any predators.

Gorgonians also harbor barnacles, representatives of a group of crustaceans so curiously modified that Charles Darwin himself devoted a large portion of his scientific studies to them. I am convinced, admittedly with no basis other than an educated guess, that particular species of barnacles grow only upon certain gorgonians. Here again, it appears that no harm is done to the host.

My most memorable find in the gorgonian forest of the Keys came as I snorkeled up to a gorgonian bearing what at first appeared to be a bunch of orange grapes dangling like fruit from one of its branches. This turned out to be a colony of tunicates, filter feeders that are much more interesting organisms than their simple structure would belie. Up close, each member of the colony looked like a glass bottle with two necks; these latter actually were the creature's incurrent and excurrent siphons. Through the tunic, like orange gelatin in its color and transparency, the delicate internal organs were clearly visible. The pharyngeal baskets, used by the tunicate for straining food particles from the water, reminded me of the cradle forks used to gather hay in the days before diesel fuel replaced oats as the primary farmyard fuel. Those simple baskets appeared to be the most complicated organs in an overall body plan that eliminated all but the absolute essentials of structural complexity. I knew from my studies, however, that they represented much more than this.

Tunicates, you see, do not start life stuck firmly in one place. The larval tunicate looks much like a tadpole and is a likely candidate for the type of organism that may have made the transition from invertebrate to vertebrate a few hundred million years ago. We will never know for sure, of course, but those pharyngeal baskets tempt speculation. They are present in the simplest vertebrates and are the embryological precursors of everything from the gill arches of fish to the little bones that make hearing possible in humans. Looking through that beautiful, translucent tunicate hanging there 30 yards from shore, I felt I could see my own biological heritage. One could do worse than to keep an aquarium of these tunicates, together with the other interesting and attractive inhabitants of the gorgonian forest.

FISHES FOR THE GORGONIAN FOREST. While the various Caribbean angelfishes and butterflies would naturally be found in the gorgonian forest, neither group makes a particularly good choice. The butterflies are notoriously hard to keep and are corallivores that will nibble the gorgonians to death. Likewise, the beautiful Queen, Blue, and French Angels are all inappropriate for a reef tank, growing too large and eating everything in sight. Schools of chromis, groups of wrasses, blennies, small drums, the meek cardinals, and the carnivorous basses, such as the Harlequin Basslet, *Serranus tigrinus*, would be good selections.

The Fore Reef

THE GREATEST ABUNDANCE and diversity of life can be found on the fore reef, although many of the species found here can also be found elsewhere — in the lagoon zone, for example. The type of reef tank most often constructed by aquarium hobbyists is based upon conditions found on the fore reef. Although most of the commonly available aquarium species from this zone are from the Indo-Pacific, aquarists wishing to duplicate a Keys fore-reef habitat do have some interesting invertebrates from which to choose.

If the fore reef is especially rich in species diversity, it also offers a profusion of microhabitats. The fore reef begins just beyond the wave-tossed reef crest, at a depth of about 30 feet. There may be a broad, gently sloping fore-reef terrace, of varying width, terminating in a rather steep escarpment that may plunge to 90 feet or so. Sand may accumulate, forming a "moat" at the base of the escarpment, and wave action may cut channels into the reef that then fill with sand, reaching back like fingers, subdividing the face of the escarpment. Beyond the moat, the reef slope gradually dips toward the abyss. Each of these microhabitats has its own characteristic fauna, the distribution of which is often determined by the ability of certain corals to grow with the available light at a given depth. Thus, the branching acroporid corals tend to dominate shallower areas of the reef terrace, while more massive or platelike corals are found on the escarpment.

Among the cnidarians to be found on the fore reef are Florida Pink-tipped Anemones, Curley-cue Anemones, Flower Anemones, sea fans, and gorgonians such as *Pseudopterogorgia*, *Plexaura*, and *Briareum*. There are other cnidarians in this zone, as well, that are legally collected for the aquarium trade. These include false corals and zoanthids.

FALSE CORALS (Order Corallimorpharia). The scientific name for this group of polyps means "coral-shaped animals," but they are also called mushroom polyps, mushroom corals or disc anemones. All are basically flattened discs with very short columns, and most occur in aggregations of several to many individuals. These are usually sold as groups of individuals attached to a rock. *Ricordea florida*, the Florida False Coral, once commonplace, is now difficult to obtain due to collecting restrictions. Polyps are roughly the size of a quarter,

Florida False Coral (*Ricordea florida*)

Deep-water sea mat (*Palythoa grandis*)

with bright green tentacles that are spherical, about 1/16 inch in diameter. Occasionally, bright orange specimens are seen. Given bright light and excellent water quality, this species will reproduce in the aquarium, although it is sometimes reported as being difficult to keep.

Discosoma neglecta is commonly called the Neon Disc Anemone. It lives in inshore waters, usually on hard-bottom areas where branched *Porites* corals and many macroalgae are found, as well as on the fore reef. This species is seldom collected for the aquarium but well worth obtaining for its bright blue-green coloration. Tentacles are completely absent.

SEA MATS (Order Zoantharia). This is an interesting and hardy group that lies somewhere between anemones and corals in the scheme of cnidarian classification. Sea mats look like colonies of small anemones. In the majority of species, the polyps are all joined together at the base by a sheet of tissue that spreads over hard surfaces and gives rise to additional polyps. The shallow-water form, *Zoanthus sociatus*, has already been described (page 164). Other Atlantic zoanthids, including *Palythoa caribaeorum*, *P. tuberculosa*, *P. grandis* and *Parazoanthus swiftii*, are deep-reef organisms and are rarely found on sea mat rock from shallow water. *P. swiftii* is always found in association with sponges and is thought by some authors to be a parasite. More likely, however, the association is a benign one, as I have never observed sponges harboring this sea mat that appeared to be harmed by the association in any way. The various *Palythoa* species are excellent aquarium subjects.

CRUSTACEANS. The Arrow Crab, *Stenorhynchus seticornis*, looks like a spider with its long, spindly legs. The name comes from the arrowhead shape of the body. Two arrow crabs cannot be kept together, as they will fight to the death, with the winner making a meal of the loser. The Arrow Crab may not get along well with Banded Coral Shrimp either (see below). Despite its untrustworthiness in the presence of these other crustaceans, this crab can be a useful addition to the tank, as it will seek out and eliminate bristleworms, which it eats. Its fondness for polychaetes extends to the more desirable species, however, and this crab should be avoided if you intend to keep large feather dusters and the like.

Probably the most common shrimp in aquarium shops is the Banded Coral Shrimp, *Stenopus hispidus*. This species, with its huge claws, red and white stripes, and long, white antennae, is hardy and undemanding. On the reef, *Stenopus* is a cleaner, but this behavior is rarely exhibited in the aquarium, and the shrimp is content to feed upon bits of food missed by the fishes. Mated pairs of Banded Coral Shrimp are sometimes available. Having a mated pair is the only way to keep two of these shrimps together, as they will fight to the death otherwise. Studies indicate that females will accept any male in the neighborhood, however, if he is introduced immediately after she molts. Some aquarists claim to be successful at creating pairs by acquiring two specimens of unequal size. By carefully observing a group of shrimp in your dealer's tank, you may be able to discern a pair that stays in close proximity to each other without displaying aggression. The Golden-banded Coral Shrimp (*S. scutellatus*) is also available from time to time.

In nature, *Stenopus hispidus* often shares its territory with another cleaner shrimp, the Scarlet Lady, *Lysmata grabhami.*

Arrow Crab (*Stenorhynchus seticornis*): delicate in appearance, but a keen predator of bristleworms and crustaceans.

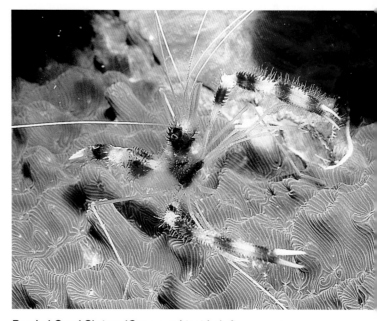

Banded Coral Shrimp (*Stenopus hispidus*): fine aquarium choice, but will battle its own kind if not kept in mated pairs.

(Another name often applied to this shrimp, especially to specimens from the Pacific, is *Lysmata amboinensis*.) Unlike *Stenopus*, the Scarlet Lady Shrimp is not aggressive toward members of its own species, and a dozen or more of these interesting shrimps could be kept in the same tank. Scarlet Lady Shrimp, also known as "Scarlet Cleaner" and "Eel Cleaner" shrimp, will eat a variety of common aquarium foods and usually subsist quite well by scavenging. They are avid cleaners, however, and will even alight on the hand of the aquarist, tugging at hairs and removing bits of dead tissue from around the fingernails. Fish that are, to the aquarist's eye, free from external parasites and wounds will nevertheless seek out the services of the Scarlet Lady Shrimp in the aquarium. Cleaning behavior is practiced by a number of fish and invertebrate species and has obvious advantages to both the cleaner and the individual being cleaned. Do not trust the Banded Coral Shrimp or other members of the genus *Stenopus* with other, smaller shrimps. I would not place a Scarlet Lady in a small tank with a large Arrow Crab either.

The Scarlet Lady Shrimp is in the Family Hippolytidae. Several other members of this family are available for the aquarium. *Lysmata wurdemanni*, for example, called the Peppermint Shrimp or Candycane Shrimp, is very common in Florida and the Caribbean. It is usually found around sponges or other encrusting invertebrates and exhibits cleaning behavior. Growing to about 1½ inches in length, it is transparent with bright red markings. It is apparently not difficult to catch, as specimens are seldom expensive. Several authors have recommended keeping a few Peppermint Shrimps in any reef tank because they regularly mate in captivity, producing an abundance of free-swimming larvae that can serve as a nutritious food for filter feeders. The larvae can also be reared to maturity.

Because of the abundance and diversity of life on the fore reef, there are many potential natural aquarium themes

Royal Gramma (*Gramma loreto*): a near-perfect reef species appropriate for a variety of Caribbean and Bahamas biotopes.

that might be drawn from this zone. Here are but two to stimulate your thinking. The first of these is more typical of reefs further south in the Caribbean, because its major inhabitant, the Royal Gramma, is very rare in Florida, despite its abundance from the Bahamas south to Venezuela.

Caribbean Fore-Reef Terrace Aquarium

THE DAZZLING ROYAL GRAMMA (*Gramma loreto*) lives in caves and under ledges on the sloping face of the fore-reef terrace. It is a gregarious species, with groups of up to 12 or more individuals sharing the same cave. A gently sloping wall of aquacultured live rock from Florida or the Caribbean would provide a perfect backdrop for a group of these fish. Half a dozen specimens would make a suitable population for a 75-gallon tank and might very well afford the opportunity to observe breeding behavior. Arrange the rock so that there are several caves near the center (or wherever you prefer the fish to congregate), and try to obtain at least one large, flat piece of rock that can be used to create

Indigo Hamlet (*Hypoplectrus indigo*): an interesting and unusual "Floribbean" sea bass for the larger reef system.

a ledge. Grammas have the amusing habit of hanging upside-down under rocky shelves. When visitors come to view the aquarium, you will be able to point out this interesting behavior, although the brilliant colors of the Royal Gramma could scarcely be more arresting. (Thirty years ago, this species was considered a rare jewel of the marine aquarium and carried an outrageous price tag. Today it is no less desirable, but is readily available at modest prices and is a reef fish suitable even for beginning aquarists.)

With a larger aquarium, say 125 gallons or more, a school of Blue Chromis (*Chromis cyaneus*) will inhabit the open water away from the rock slope occupied by the gramma clan. In such an aquarium design, a light-colored sandy bottom running the length of the tank could suddenly give way to a steeply stacked escarpment of live rock placed at one end. The rock should occupy only about one-third of the length of the tank. The gramma colony will associate itself with the rocks, and the chromis school will hover above the sand at the opposite end. Top the escarpment with an assortment of encrusting soft corals and sponges, and

attach several Purple Frilly Gorgonians (*Pseudopterogorgia*) to the rock face with underwater epoxy. This gorgonian is often seen projecting outward from the reef face.

Any of the shrimps mentioned earlier would be at home in this habitat, occupying nooks not in use by the grammas. Include a dozen or more snails for algae control, and perhaps a modest-sized sponge or two for additional color. If healthy sponges are available, consider including several Peppermint Shrimp, which seem to associate with sponges.

Instead of crustaceans, one might include a Blue Hamlet (*Hypoplectrus gemma*) if the tank is roomy enough. The hamlets mimic various species of damselfishes in order to go unnoticed by their intended victims. In the wild, *H. gemma* can be found hiding in schools of Blue Chromis, where its color and behavior dupes prey into ignoring the shoal of planktivorous damsels and allowing the hamlet to strike. Captive hamlets will quickly eat prized shrimps and crabs.

Lighting for this biotope must be quite bright near the top of the escarpment, and the gorgonians, though tolerant of lower light levels, should nevertheless receive adequate illumination. Depending on the final design, the surface area to be illuminated, and the water depth, either metal halide or fluorescent lighting could be used. With the former light source, patchy outgrowths of *Halimeda* could be placed here and there on the bottom. *H. opuntia* simply lies on the sand, while *H. incrassata* and *H. tuna* have a buried holdfast.

Deep Fore-Reef Wall Aquarium

THE DEEP FORE REEF will be rather dimly illuminated, owing to the attenuation of sunlight by the water column, and so provides inspiration for an aquarium in which the only photosynthetic organisms are colonies of coralline algae on live rock. Such a tank can be inexpensively illuminated, using just one or two fluorescent lamps; good choices would be those that have a significant blue component in

the spectrum. When illuminated with such lights, the water will have a definite bluish cast, well known to divers, but will not have the eerie "black light" effect created when the very blue actinic lamps are used alone. Combining one blue actinic lamp with one bulb of about 5,000 degrees K will create the desired effect.

Apart from crustaceans, such as a mated pair of Banded Coral Shrimp, this aquarium habitat can be used to showcase some of the reef's most spectacular inhabitants. The muted colors of coralline algae, running mostly to mauve, lavender, and cool pink, provide a striking contrast to the blue, yellow, and iridescent turquoise of the Queen Angel (*Holacanthus ciliaris*). Since this species attains about 18 inches in length in the wild, a roomy tank of at least 150, and preferably 300, gallons will be required to accommodate it for a full 20-year-plus lifespan. Although largely herbivorous, adult Queen Angels feed mostly on sponges, supplementing this diet with a variety of other encrusting invertebrates and algae. Large angel specimens can be difficult to acclimate to captive life, and it is therefore wise to obtain a juvenile specimen and allow it to grow up in the aquarium display. In this manner, it will become accustomed to feeding on a variety of aquarium foods more readily obtainable than its natural diet. At least one manufacturer of frozen foods markets a formula containing sponges. In my experience, this product is readily accepted by the Queen Angel and should form a portion of the diet of any captive specimen. Many fishes, including squirrelfishes (Holocentridae) and soldierfishes (*Myripritis* spp.), a grouper, or any of the smaller Atlantic moray eels would make compatible tankmates for the angelfish in a large system, but most of the sessile invertebrates discussed in this chapter will sooner or later fall prey to the angel's aggressive appetite, limiting

Queen Angel (*Holacanthus ciliaris*): a captivating species for a carefully planned large, deep fore-reef biotope aquarium.

Resplendent Angel (*Centropyge resplendens*): a rare little dazzler from Ascension Island in the middle of the Atlantic.

Cherub or Pygmy Angel (*Centropyge argi*): an endearing deeper-water species that will spawn in captive systems.

the choices for this aquarium to hermit crabs, sea urchins, algae-grazing snails and perhaps a small spiny lobster. But with so spectacular a fish in residence, who will notice?

If the urge to create a deep fore-reef aquarium appeals to you but a large tank lies outside your budget or space limitations, simply scale the same general design down to a 30-

Swissguard or Peppermint Basslet (*Liopropoma rubre*): a prized specimen for a deeper-water habitat with rocky refuge.

Blackcap Basslet (*Gramma melacara*): typically found on deep walls, but also occurs in shallower waters near some islands.

to 50-gallon aquarium. Instead of the Queen Angel, this tank could be occupied by a Cherub (or Pygmy) Angel, (*Centropyge argi*), which is found most commonly at depths greater than 100 feet, ranging from the Bahamas to the West Indies. The Cherub Angel also occurs in the Florida Keys, and companion species might include one or more garden eels, a shoal of iridescent Blue Chromis, or an attractive hamlet (*Hypoplectrus* sp.). If your desired habitat is meant to reflect the Caribbean, the Blackcap Basslet (*Gramma melacara*) would be a nice choice, albeit not for the budget-conscious. The Swissguard Basslet (*Liopropoma rubre*) and deep-water Caribbean basslets would make eye-catching tankmates; fishes from the deep fore reef can command breathtaking prices, directly related to the difficulty and danger of collecting at such depths.

Finally, another aquarium possibility would focus on the deep fore-reef microhabitat of Ascension Island, a tiny speck of the British Commonwealth lying about 9 degrees south of the equator, smack in the middle of the Atlantic between Brazil and the African coast. Here, and only here, lives the Resplendent Angel (*Centropyge resplendens*), an

electric-blue and yellow dazzler with obviously close genetic ties to *C. argi*. Rare in the trade, usually expensive, and beautiful enough to warrant a tank of its own, the Resplendent Angel has proved itself to be as hardy as its cousin.

Anyone who has traveled in this hemisphere knows that coral reefs in the tropical Atlantic are not restricted to Florida, and the dividing line between Atlantic and Caribbean waters is biologically rather arbitrary. (Visitors to various tiny Caribbean islands are often bemused to learn that the eastern side of the island is considered to be bathed by the Atlantic, while the west coast sits in the Caribbean.) The Bahamas, Bermuda, Puerto Rico, Haiti, the Dominican Republic, the Leeward Islands, the Windward Islands, the Turks and Caicos, Bonaire, Curaçao, Venezuela, and the eastern coasts of Mexico and Central America are all home to stony corals, invertebrates, and fishes that range far and wide in and around the Caribbean and tropical western Atlantic. Ascension Island and Brazil, both sources of marine aquarium specimens, are rather remote from my old Florida Keys haunts — Pigeon Key lies about 5,300 miles northwest of Ascension — but the marine life found

Rose Coral (*Manicina areolata*): tiny specimens often arrive on live rock.

Elkhorn Coral (*Acropora palmata*): massive, fast-growing species.

Branching Fire Coral (*Millepora alcicornis*): a hydrozoan and not a stony coral.

Finger Coral (*Porites porites*): rare lavender thin-finger or *divaricata* form.

Mustard Hill Coral (*Porites astreoides*): found at depths from 3 to 160 feet.

in these two locales are not totally foreign to each other.

While similarities exist among the faunas of all these wider Caribbean-Western tropical Atlantic waters, the aquarist bent on duplicating the view remembered from a snorkeling trip to, say, Bonaire, may have to be content with one or two species actually found there, fleshing out the aquarium display with species from Florida, the Gulf of Mexico, or elsewhere. This has more to do with the peculiarities of the aquarium trade than with the distribution of species. Most tropical Atlantic species sold by aquarium retailers come from wholesalers in Florida. These, in turn, may buy specimens from local collectors, may be collectors themselves, and may import species from other regions.

Fortunately, the habitats and aquarium designs de-scribed in this chapter as being typical of Florida are closely related to diverse locations throughout the Caribbean basin. Trendy restaurants in Miami now reflect the close ties between frost-free south Florida and its truly tropical island neighbors by featuring "Floribbean" cuisine on their menus. In the same spirit, you may opt for a "Floribbean" aquarium; it may not be scrupulously accurate, but I doubt that anyone will take umbrage at this concession to practicality. Purists, of course, will try to be as true to nature as possible, going to the extra effort (and expense) of finding sources of invertebrates and fishes from the same geographic locale. As in all aspects of this hobby, there is room both for the beginner and the diehard enthusiast bent on replicating a wild reef habitat in miniature.

Chapter Seven

The Gulf of Mexico

*In Quest of the Christmas Tree Worm and
Other Native Treasures and Oddities*

SCOURED BY SHRIMP TRAWLERS, dotted with oil rigs, and routinely churned by hurricanes, the Gulf of Mexico is not blessed with a reputation for pristine coral reefs, and despite its proximity, it is largely unappreciated by marine aquarium hobbyists in North America. For the aquarist with an eye for the unusual, however, it can be a source of unique and amazingly beautiful living organisms and materials for the captive reef.

Compared to the Florida Keys and the neighboring Caribbean, the Gulf of Mexico is a significantly different habitat, although some tropical species from the Keys area regularly migrate into Gulf waters, and sometimes one finds species in the Keys that are more commonly seen farther north. Because Gulf species are often included in imports of marine livestock from Florida to other parts of the United States, aquarists should be aware of the special habitats that such specimens represent. Collectors working the Gulf can supply the adventuresome aquarist with an array of unusual invertebrates and living materials to create extraordinarily attractive biotopes.

A sea mat from the northern Gulf of Mexico is regularly

Fascinating to behold, Atlantic Christmas Tree Worms, *Spirobranchus giganteus*, are often found embedded in live rock.

sold in aquarium shops and is commonly kept in tanks along with stony corals and other photosynthetic invertebrates. This is *Palythoa grandis*. The large, dark green polyps are very attractive, and the species is hardy in captivity. Most other northern Gulf species are not well suited to a tropical reef aquarium, but are excellent subjects for an aquarium intended to reflect their special habitat. A good example of such a community is the central Gulf area near Tampa, where a unique assemblage of invertebrates can be found. A characteristic species from this region is the Christmas Tree Worm, *Spirobranchus giganteus*. While this species is found throughout the West Indies and the world, it occurs abundantly only in the Gulf.

Worm Rock Colony

CHRISTMAS TREE WORMS are among a select group of reef invertebrates that always elicit a "What's that!?" response from first-time aquarium observers, and it is difficult not to be mesmerized by their stunning colors, perfect geometric structure, and curious habit of closing with lightning speed and unfolding with majestic grace. A truly different biotope can be created with a colony of this species as the invertebrate centerpiece.

The Christmas Tree Worm derives its common name (and its generic label) from the appearance of specialized structures, the radioles, that are used in both feeding and respiration. (The generic name comes from two words meaning "spiral gill.") The worm spends its life housed in a calcareous tube attached to a rock or coral head, extending the radioles into the surrounding water column. The radioles consist of a pair of tentacles with feathery appendages wound around them in a tapering spiral. When extended from the mouth of the tube, the radioles look like a pair of Christmas trees sharing the same stand. The brilliant colors and symmetrical appearance of these structures are responsible for the popularity of this annelid with aquarists. The worms are often gregarious, with individuals bearing

Peppering a colony of live *Porites* coral, these Indo-Pacific Christmas Tree Worms display a typical range of colors.

radioles of strikingly different colors growing side by side.

Spirobranchus giganteus occurs in both the Indo-Pacific and the Atlantic-Caribbean regions. Recognizing the source of a particular specimen is simple, as there are apparently two subspecies of this worm. Specimens from the Indo-Pacific are usually smaller (in terms of the length of the radioles) and are always embedded in living coral. Specimens from the Atlantic-Caribbean region are also associated with corals but are about twice as large as the Indo-Pacific form: the individual "Christmas tree" structures reach just over an inch in length.

It has been my observation that there is a different range of color variation between the two subspecies of *Spirobranchus*. Bicolor forms appear to occur more commonly in Atlantic-Caribbean worms, for example, while bright blue specimens appear to be more abundant in the Indo-Pacific type. The fact that the worms come in different colors may be an adaptation to avoid predation. The worm's most useful defense, however, is its ability to withdraw its radioles into its protective tube at the first hint of danger. The opening of the tube is capped with an *operculum* bearing fierce-looking horns. Close examination will show that the horns are nearly identical between the two subspecies, providing evidence of their relatedness.

According to references cited in Delbeek and Sprung (1994) the coral that harbors *Spirobranchus* in the Indo-Pacific is *Porites* (*Synaraea*) *rus*. The worms appear to require the presence of the coral for survival, and, unfortunately, the coral itself is not often successfully maintained by aquarists. These authors suggest that shipping and handling stresses lead to the poor survival rate of these specimens, commenting that *Porites*, and presumably *Spirobranchus* as well, proves hardy when supplied with sufficiently intense illumination and vigorous water movement. These specimens are not recommended for beginners, and dealers should be urged to import only a few. Obviously, improved handling techniques for them should be instituted. Specimens should be regarded as "corals" rather than as "worms" or "rocks" by those responsible for their collection and shipment. (This may result in better treatment, as *Porites* specimens are shipped alongside, and from the same sources as, corals that have high survivability in the aquarium.) Because *Porites* grows rapidly under natural conditions, few other organisms besides it and *Spirobranchus* are present on these specimens.

The Atlantic-Caribbean subspecies of *Spirobranchus giganteus* does not occur embedded in colonies of *Porites* coral in shallow, wave tossed-waters. In fact, while the worms are found scattered throughout the region (Kaplan, 1982), most specimens that are collected for the aquarium trade come from the middle Gulf of Mexico, miles from the nearest coral reef. The implications of this simple fact for the aquarium husbandry of these specimens are often overlooked. Further, unlike the Indo-Pacific specimens, worm rock from the Gulf harbors a wide variety of coralline algae and invertebrates — often in bright, attractive colors — in addition to the worms themselves.

A Collector's View

AS OF JANUARY 1, 1997, collection of any type of live rock product was banned in the waters off Florida. This prohibition includes Christmas Tree Worm colonies growing on rock. Some collectors stockpiled this material, however, and it is legal for such stocks to be sold. The number of specimens is very limited as of this writing, and hobbyists should be aware that a significant amount of "bootleg" (illegally collected) material has managed to reach the market. To avoid participating in violation of collecting laws, hobbyists should look for Christmas Tree Worm specimens that are attached to clam shells, which are legal to collect.

The supply of worm rock specimens should be restored in the near future, however, as the worms are starting to appear on aquacultured live rock. Roy and Teresa Herndon are professional collectors of aquarium specimens and pioneers in the aquaculture of live rock products, available through their company, Sea Critters, in Dover, Florida. The

While many larger fish cannot resist these feathery radioles, *Spirobranchus* worms can do well with smaller reef species.

Herndons report that Christmas Tree Worms are starting to appear on aquacultured rock, and Teresa says that *Spirobranchus* can also be induced to spawn in the aquarium by manipulating temperature and day length. This may result in the "farming" of this desirable species in the future.

The Herndons are widely known and respected both for the quality of rock and organisms that they sell and their willingness to share advice and assistance in the aquarium care of *Spirobranchus*:

"Our Christmas Tree Worm specimens are collected off the coast of Tarpon Springs, Florida (central west coast) in the Gulf of Mexico," says Roy. "We've found them as far south as Sarasota and as far north as Crystal River. Most of the divers work from St. Petersburg to Tarpon Springs. The depth we work is from 40 to 60 feet, although we've found worms at 25 to 90 feet. Water temperature ranges from 86 degrees F on the bottom in August to an uncomfortable 50 degrees F in January and February.

had success in keeping them over two years with no noticeable loss of their original beauty.) He stresses that lighting is minimal at the depths from which these specimens are taken. "We collect in 40 to 60 feet of water. The average water visibility at this depth is 15 to 20 feet. If you subject live rock from this depth to higher lighting in the aquarium, it will have a propensity to fade, although I have noticed that in a lot of cases the corallines will go through a 'metamorphosis' and regrow." One tank housing a Christmas Tree Worm display at Sea Critters is lit by a single fluorescent bulb and has no mechanical filtration — relatively dim with nothing to remove any particulate matter upon which filter feeders might dine. All of this suggests to me that the problems aquarists may experience with these specimens may be due to exposing them to very bright light in tanks that are better suited to the cultivation of shallow water, photosynthetic invertebrates. A tank intended for Christmas Tree Worms and species from the same habitat should *not* be intensely illuminated, or the worms should be placed in deep or shaded locations.

WATER QUALITY. Herndon also has the advantage of using natural seawater. Aquarists not living near the coast should make certain that they keep up with water changes

Rock-boring Urchin (*Echinometra lucunter*): common arrival, often tiny and unseen at first, on Gulf rock.

Spotfin Butterfly (*Chaetodon ocellatus*): as with other Atlantic butterflies, a species best left to the experts.

and/or trace element additions in the Gulf of Mexico aquarium. Many sponges are thought to accumulate trace elements, although it is an open question whether they require specific elements to survive and grow. Bear in mind that sponges — more species than enumerated here — are among the most important "co-fauna" found on aquacultured rocks from the Gulf.

Both the worms and the coralline algae found on these specimens deposit calcium carbonate skeletons. Therefore, maintaining pH at 8.4 and alkalinity greater than 3 milliequivalents per liter will be important to facilitate calcification. Additions of limewater should accomplish both these goals and assist in maintaining a calcium concentration around 400 ppm. Strontium, possibly an important ion in the calcification process, could be supplemented, but see the discussion on page 61. Iodide supplementation may stimulate growth in coralline algae, and possibly other organisms.

Cool water temperatures may also be important, and I would suggest that a Gulf of Mexico tank be maintained at about 70 to 75 degrees F. Filtration should be accomplished through the use of heavy protein skimming and live rock.

The Herndons' aquaculture beds produce a coralline algae-encrusted rock that would make both a good "base" and "topping" material for a Gulf of Mexico aquarium. Alternatively, the bottom cover could be a layer of aragonite sand or "live sand," pebbles, or a combination of these two. It is important to have invertebrates and fishes in the tank to help stir the sand. Gobies, brittle stars, and the snapping shrimp listed would be suitable for this purpose. In short, this aquarium would be set up and maintained as a Berlin-style coral aquarium (see page 31), but without the intense illumination and with much more supplemental feeding. If one were willing to invest in a chiller for more precise control of water temperatures, mimicking the seasonal temperature fluctuation found in the Gulf would probably also be of benefit.

Northward Ho! : Other Eastern U.S. Habitats

THE NORTHERN GULF OF MEXICO, the Flower Garden Banks in the western Gulf of Mexico, the Grand Strand of sandy beaches stretching from Fort Lauderdale to the shores of Delaware, the mid-Atlantic region from the Chesapeake Bay to Cape Cod, and the northern Atlantic coast of New England all offer an array of marine invertebrates, seaweeds, and small fish species that are suited to appropriately designed aquariums. I have devoted tanks to several of these habitats over the years. In fact, my first marine aquarium, at age 8, consisted of a mayonnaise jar outfitted with a "bubbler" powered by a worn-out air pump that my aunt had given me, housing two surf clams retrieved from Myrtle Beach, South Carolina. I had enough sense to bring along sufficient seawater and sand to provide a suitable habitat, but I hadn't thought to make provisions for filtration or a plankton substitute, and this venture was doomed to failure.

Today, there are many new opportunities for creating successful and interesting aquariums featuring the temperate

Gray Angel (*Pomacanthus arcuatus*): a showy Gulf and Caribbean species but too large and omnivorous for a tank with delicate invertebrates such as Christmas Tree Worms.

and cold water species of our Atlantic and Gulf coasts. Most people — even those who have lived all their lives on the coast — have no idea of the diversity and beauty of underwater life in their own region. The intrepid aquarist in these areas will mostly be on his own, scouring the tidepools and or taking to the water with snorkel or scuba. (Be sure you aren't in violation of any state or local fish and game laws.) Bait shops may also provide interesting specimens or may be able to put you in contact with someone who can help you collect or at least point you in the right direction. Local and regional field guides and natural history books will prove invaluable. Libraries, public aquariums, natural history museums, and local biology instructors are all excellent sources of information on saltwater habitats not covered in the aquarium literature.

A marine habitat tank that replicates one of these environments can be an eye-opener — and an especially rewarding challenge to the adventuresome aquarist.

Chapter Eight

Indo-Pacific Reefs: Diversity's Motherlode

Microhabitats and Recommended Species from the
Biological Treasure Trove of the Seas

T HE INDO-PACIFIC REALM is large and dynamic, encompassing the Earth's richest reef environment and stretching from Hawaii across the South Pacific to the Coral Sea, onward to the Indian Ocean and into the fabled Red Sea. It is immense and wonderfully complex, but its characteristic environments, at least for aquarium purposes, can be lumped into a few simple categories. This is partly because the availability of specimens is limited arbitrarily by the peculiarities of the aquarium trade in marine invertebrates and fishes. Collection of specimens for the aquarium trade tends to focus upon specific areas, and collectors tend to harvest only certain organisms for which there is an established market. The tendency to collect what is easily accessible also influences what may be available to aquarists. Thus, lagoon species, which can often be collected by wading at low tide, are more commonplace than species whose range is restricted to the outer-reef slope. Marine invertebrates are not strictly limited in their ability to exploit different microhabitats, of course, with many occurring over a wide area. Further, it is risky to create species lists when the lines delineating the species themselves begin to blur, and when characteristics once thought

to be diagnostic are shown to be fluid and dependent upon the local environment. Coral biologist J.E.N. Veron (1995) cites the example of a coral skeleton in his collection that possesses all the "classic" traits of *Favia* on one side and equally "diagnostic" traits of *Favites* on the other. Similarly, the classification of octocorals is in such a state of flux that the application of species names based on gross morphological observation, the usual approach taken by aquarists, is a futile exercise. Without precise information about the location from which a specimen was taken, even experts are hesitant to apply scientific names to soft corals. Therefore, while it can be useful to delineate the broad outlines of the communities found in an Indo-Pacific lagoon, as opposed to the outer-reef slope, the aquarist should not slavishly adhere to the species lists published here and elsewhere when attempting to recreate an Indo-Pacific microhabitat in the aquarium. What I am offering in this chapter is a set of guidelines to be used as a starting point. These guidelines should allow you to avoid adding specimens wholly unsuited to your aquarium design. Beyond that, you must exercise your creativity in designing a natural reef aquarium reflecting this fantastic realm.

Any effort to condense the variety of biotopes that might be found near even a small coral atoll in the Indo-

Impressive Giant Clam (*Tridacna gigas*) on Pacific reef slope.

Pacific will result in oversimplification. You cannot, however, encompass many habitat types in a single tank and so must choose an aquarium theme that imitates only one. Available species of invertebrates may be classified, for aquarium purposes, into a few key groups that are conveniently correlated with habitat preferences.

Among the most widely available cnidarians are the soft corals, sea mats, disc anemones, and large-polyped scleractinian (LPS) corals that inhabit shallow, inshore waters. The first habitat category, then, is the shallow, inshore environment. Important characteristics for this habitat are intense lighting (shallow water allows maximum penetration of solar radiation), moderate currents (inshore regions are protected by the reef from the pounding of the open sea), and organisms with a tolerance for elevated nutrient levels (lagoon waters tend to accumulate nutrients).

Because of their long-term popularity with hobbyists, I include the clownfish host anemones in a second habitat category, although different species of these anemones characteristically occur in different habitats.

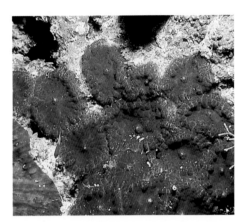

Purple corallimorpharians (*Rhodactis* sp.)

Striped mushroom coral (*Discosoma* sp.)

Rapidly gaining favor among reef enthusiasts are the small-polyped scleractinian (SPS) corals that predominate on the outer reef. Outer-reef fauna thus belong in the third category. In this habitat, water movement can be extreme, and nutrient levels are so low as to be nearly unmeasurable. Lighting needs can vary from high to low, depending upon

depth, although many SPS corals need very bright light.

One should utilize these groupings of cnidarians as the basis for the aquarium, because cnidarians are most often Pivotal Species (see Chapter Two). Cnidarians from different habitats have different requirements for lighting and water movement, and different degrees of tolerance for levels of nutrients and dissolved oxygen. In addition, the ability of cnidarians to engage in chemical warfare with each other, often in the absence of direct physical contact, has obvious implications for aquarium care. This, for example, is why clownfish host anemones should be given separate consideration from other cnidarians. These facts should be carefully considered as you compose your own list of proposed species for a new or redesigned Indo-Pacific reef aquarium.

The Shallow, Inshore Habitat

PRACTICALLY ALL of the invertebrates collected for the aquarium in the early days came from shallow water — it is easier to work in the lagoon than in deeper water, and scuba equipment is not often available to collectors in the developing countries that supply most of the specimens. Thus, species of macroalgae, corals, and anemones from this habitat have been in the trade for a long time. Any of the following groups would be at home in a shallow-water lagoon tank:

DISC ANEMONES (Order Corallimorpharia). Tentacles are absent from many of the Pacific disc anemones or "mushroom corals," of which there are several species from the genera *Rhodactis*, *Actinodiscus*, and *Discosoma*. All are flat, rounded polyps with very short columns. Mushroom corals typically do well in moderate light and can be placed near the bottom of the aquarium or in tanks where lighting is below 10,000 lux. Also called "false corals," corallimorpharians come in many colors, with blue-green, brown, and green being the most common. Some have blue or red pigments and are very striking. This pigmentation may change, however, if the lighting conditions in the tank are significantly different from those under which the specimen was growing in the ocean. Moderate currents are preferred, and elevated levels of nutrients are tolerated. As a general rule, the false corals are easy to keep and will grow and multiply in the aquarium.

Spreading mushrooms in a reef aquarium.

Large blue mushroom coral (*Rhodactis* sp.)

One false coral deserves special mention. This is the Elephant Ear, a species of *Amplexidiscus*. It is perhaps the largest of the false corals, reaching nearly a foot across. It can be spectacular, but it does have a propensity to eat small fishes that may be unwary of its stubby tentacles. Most other corallimorpharians rely either on photosynthesis entirely or upon small planktonic organisms for their food. Any species is a good choice for a tank depicting quiet waters with subdued light. Companions that thrive in sheltered areas with gentle currents might include *Trachyphyllia*, a hardy and often showy stony coral, one of the *Lobophytum* species, and *Pachyclavularia* sp., the beautiful Green Star Polyps.

Shallow, inshore waters do not often have a lot of vertical relief. Rather than a steep outer-reef escarpment, or even the gradual incline found where the lagoon gives way to the back reef, horizontal elements, such as a broad, sandy bottom or a lea of Turtle Grass, typify the inshore zone. This makes choosing an aquarium in which to mimic this habitat something of a challenge, as most tanks are rather tall and narrow, rather than shallow and expansive. Space considerations in the area where the tank will be placed may also limit the design possibilities. One can always have a shallow tank made to order, assuming one's pockets are sufficiently deep, or one can borrow techniques from artists and designers to give the illusion of expansiveness. Start with a reasonably wide tank — manufacturers now routinely offer designs that are 24 inches from front to back, and several standard tank sizes measure 18 inches, front to back. When the choice is available, opt for a shallower tank; simply by virtue of its proportions, such an aquarium will fool the eye. The principle is the same as that used by restaurants when serving soup: a broad, shallow container gives the illusion of greater volume than a tall, narrow one.

Use light-colored sand for the substrate and avoid building up a huge pile of live rock from side to side across the background. You do not really need that much rock for filtration, especially if a good bed of live sand is present. Use small groupings of rock to suggest patch reefs or outcrops, with plenty of open space in between. Limit the vertical elements to no more than is necessary to hide plumbing or other tank equipment. Choose a lighter background for the rear glass rather than black, which always suggests depth. Pale blue or the shade of green sometimes called "sea foam" will give the impression of peering through shallow water with rippled sand in the foreground appearing to stretch back to the horizon.

Yellow polyp colony (zoanthid species)

Bright, uniform lighting of high intensity, such as that supplied by metal halide lamps, not only provides energy for photosynthesis but eliminates shadows that suggest a confined space. Halides, in combination with water returns or powerhead pumps that disturb the surface of the tank, also create the highly desirable "glitter lines" of light sparkling across the sand and rock that one would see in shallow reef

Green Sea Mat or zoanthids (*Protopalythoa* sp.), one of many desirable colonial species.

waters. Any aquarium, almost by definition, constitutes a living trompe l'oeil — the painterly approach to tricking the human eye into seeing a scene as reality by intensifying and manipulating the elements present. For a shallow-water system, achieving the appearance of space must involve visual deception, but doing it right can bring a sense of reality missing from the average fish tank.

SEA MATS (Order Zoantharia). Sea mats are also called "colonial anemones," and most species look like a colony of small anemones connected at the base by a sheet of tissue that spreads over the substrate. One in particular is not so connected, being classified with the sea mats because it shares other anatomical traits with them. This is "*Parazoanthus gracilis*" (probably not a valid name for this zoanthid, which is most likely an undescribed species) sold as Yellow Polyp colony in shops. This is an excellent choice, and its bright lemon yellow color is unusual and attractive. (Some aquarium references call this organism *P. axinellae*, a Mediterranean sea mat.)

There are many other Pacific sea mats. These come in a variety of colors, but coloration is usually restricted to the center of the oral disc, with the column and tentacles being dull gray, brown, or greenish. Colors range from greens to blue and even pink. Without a technical reference book, the species are difficult to identify. I regularly see specimens that are green with orange centers, and a lovely pinkish purple form. All these Indo-Pacific sea mats probably belong to the genera *Isaurus*, *Palythoa*, and *Zoanthus*.

Often, corallimorpharian specimens have zoanthids present.

SOFT CORALS (Order Alcyonaria). While shallow-water hard-bottom habitats in the Florida Keys are frequently dominated by photosynthetic gorgonians, the photosynthetic alcyonarians occupy this niche in the Indo-Pacific. Photosynthetic soft corals are very popular as aquarium subjects and are amenable to captive propagation by simple vegetative reproduction. They generally fall into three groups, the leather corals, the pulse corals, and the stoloniferans.

Leather Coral (*Sarcophyton* sp.)

Flat Leather Coral (*Sinularia dura*)

Finger or Digitate Leather Coral (*Sinularia* sp.)

Colt Coral (*Alcyonium* sp.)

Leather Corals. *Sarcophyton* species, usually called leather corals, are among the most suitable of alcyonarians for aquarium care. In all of the leather corals, the body mass is brownish or yellowish in color, and the polyps are embedded in this skeletal mass. Leather corals generally prefer high light intensities and a stable, high pH. They often grow in abundance in shallow lagoons. These conditions are also favored by many green macroalgae, and leather corals look good in tanks with lots of green macroalgae

growth, as they are often a contrasting brown to yellow-brown in color. It is not unusual for the polyps of leather corals to remain contracted for several days after a change in water conditions, such as a move from one aquarium to the other. Close relatives of *Sarcophyton* include other leather corals in the genera *Lobophytum* (Devil's Hand Soft Coral or Cabbage Coral), with only a few short polyps; *Sinularia* (Lettuce or Cauliflower Soft Coral), in which the large skeletal elements are prominent, and *Alcyonium*, a bushy

Iodine is thought by many experienced aquarists to be essential for successful management of the pulse corals. Noel Curry, of Scientific Corals, suggests using Lugol's solution (5% iodine with 10% potassium iodide) along with a trace element supplement in aquariums housing *Xenia, Anthelia,* and their relatives. Dosing once a week is the usual approach, but the use of a reliable test kit to ensure that the iodine/iodide concentration remains at the natural seawater level of 0.06 ppm is recommended. Remember that more iodine will be consumed as specimens grow and multiply.

Soft and hard corals in Ningaloo Marine Park, Australia.

Pulsing Xenia: note polyps arising from thick stalks or trunks.

species that produces a lot of mucus when handled. Other regularly available genera include *Lemnalia* and *Litophyton.*

Pulse Corals. Several species of soft corals hold special interest for invertebrate enthusiasts because they may exhibit continuous pulsing movements. These are collectively referred to as "pulse corals," and may be species of either *Xenia, Heteroxenia, Cespitularia,* or *Anthelia.* In *Xenia,* the individual polyps arise from thick stalks or trunks and can be translucent in color, as well as brown, green, white, or a pale gold. In *Anthelia,* the feathery, cream, brown, or blue polyps are attached to a matlike base that anchors to a hard surface. *Heteroxenia* specimens are have two distinctly different types of polyps rising from stalks. All of the pulse corals may stop pumping when currents are too strong or when aquarium nutrient levels are not to their liking. The pulse corals are known to feed on nanoplankton, but there are suggestions that they may also rely on photosynthesis for growth.[1] Pulse corals are generally hardy and will reproduce readily in the aquarium.

Anthelia (*Anthelia glauca*): polyps arise from a matlike base.

---

[1] Charles Delbeek, personal communication.

Organ Pipe Coral (*Tubipora musica*): note hardened tubes.

Daisy Polyps or Palm Coral (*Clavularia* sp.): soft coral.

Consequently, regular testing, rather than the habitual addition of a certain amount of supplement, is necessary for long-term success.

Stoloniferans. Green Star Polyps, commonly called *Clavularia viridis* but probably a species of *Pachyclavularia*, is also called Starburst Soft Coral and is frequently misidentified as Organ Pipe Coral (*Tubipora musica*), another stoloniferan. In these alcyonarians, the skeleton is a rubbery, flattened sheet that encrusts a solid substrate. Each polyp resides in a short tube that projects upward from the basal sheet about ¼ inch. The polyps themselves are generally pale green with bright green centers or an overall lime color. When expanded, this is a very beautiful species. It is also, happily, one of the hardiest soft corals and can be highly recommended even to the beginner. Its only special requirements seem to be water current and very bright light, under which it will grow and spread. In the much harder to keep *Tubipora*, the wine-colored skeleton is heavily calcified and shows distinct layering.

STONY CORALS. The scleractinian corals seen in the aquarium trade fall neatly into two groups that may be easily differentiated. Small-polyped scleractinian (SPS) corals,

now the rage among advanced hobbyists because of the ease with which they may be propagated, are generally thought of as species of the outer reef. The delineation is not so sharp, and Veron (1986) notes that *Montipora*, *Pachyseris*, and *Leptoseris* can be found in extensive stands in deep lagoons with sediments present; even *Acropora* species can thrive in sandy- or rocky-bottom lagoon areas.

Typical inshore lagoon species have mostly large polyps, although the designation "LPS" for these species is not widely used. There are, of course, species of stony corals that occur over a range of habitats, and many of these may alter their growth form to take advantage of a particular microenvironment. This can make identification of species extremely difficult, and all identifications to the species level should be considered suspect. This is why, with few exceptions, only genera are mentioned here.

SPS Corals. These reef-building corals are the jewels of the reef ecosystem — occurring in every shade of pink, purple, lavender, blue, fluorescent green, and electrifying orange. Without them, the reefs themselves would not exist. Although they are somewhat challenging to the marine aquarist, given a proper environment, SPS corals will grow

Plate Coral (*Heliofungia actiniformis*)

Mushroom Coral (*Fungia scutaria*)

Flowerpot Coral (*Goniopora* sp.)

Open Brain (*Trachyphyllia geoffroyi*)

Meat Polyp (*Cynarina lacrymalis*)

Tooth Coral (*Lobophyllia* sp.)

rapidly and display amazing colors under the proper aquarium lighting.

Stony corals all produce a hard skeleton composed of calcium carbonate. They require excellent water quality, good water movement ("chaotic" is a term often used to describe the type of water movement favored by many corals), and suitable illumination. They are typically unforgiving of any lapse in temperature control, lighting, or water chemistry, and they should be regarded as suitable specimens only for aquarists who have already succeeded in keeping the hardier soft corals. Anyone attempting to keep SPS corals for the first time is encouraged to seek out captive-propagated fragments, which bring with them a greatly elevated chance of success. These fragments have already adapted to artificial lighting and aquarium conditions and do not carry the same risk of introducing coral diseases, bacteria, or parasites from the wild. They can grow with amazing rapidity and are an inexpensive way to learn the demands of keeping sensitive reef-building corals.

LPS Corals. Stony corals of the shallow-water lagoon habitat are often large, single polyps contained within a cone-shaped skeleton that sits partially buried, pointed end down, in a soft substrate. Asexual reproduction is less commonly seen in these species than in SPS corals and is seldom easy to induce without risking damage to the parent colony, which may become infected rather than heal. Sexual reproduction in lagoon species is less common in the aquarium. Lagoon corals are often species in which the sexes are separate, and therefore both male and female colonies must be present for spawning to occur. Lagoon corals are more tolerant of high nutrient levels, higher temperatures, and sluggish water movement than their cousins on the fore reef.

Heliofungia actiniformis (Plate Coral) needs a soft, sandy substrate and plenty of room. It is spectacular in a tank designed with its special needs in mind. It is the only commonly available coral capable of moving from place to place. Symbiotic shrimps, *Periclimenes holthuisi* and *Thor amboinensis*, are found on this coral in nature. It lives in shallow water subject to intense illumination.

Herpolitha (Slipper Coral, Hedgehog Coral) is a close relative of *Heliofungia* and needs similar conditions. Provide it with average light intensity and moderate, not forceful, current. It should be placed on the floor of the aquarium on sand, rather than perched upon a stack of live rock.

Goniopora (Flowerpot Coral, Sunflower Coral) is prolific in nature and commonly offered for sale, but many experienced reef keepers consider it a difficult species to maintain. A related genus, *Alveopora*, with 12 tentacles to *Goniopora*'s 24, is sometimes available. Despite the fact that these species are challenging, they may produce offspring — extratentacular buds — that survive and grow rather well. I have observed that *Goniopora* survives longest when no other cnidarians are present in the tank. Nevertheless, I cannot recommend this species to beginners until we know better how to keep it alive.

Trachyphyllia geoffroyi (Open Brain Coral) is a hardy and attractive species that is regularly imported. This coral is a single large polyp, a design that seems to be associated with ease of aquarium care. The skeleton is in the form of an inverted cone, often attached at the apex to a hard substrate when the coral is young, but later breaking off, allowing the coral to sit upright in soft sand or silt. As a result of this growth form, it is easily collected without damage, which may explain why aquarium specimens do so well. *Trachyphyllia* prefers the same conditions favored by false corals. *Cynarina* (Button Coral) is also a single large polyp and should receive the same care as *Trachyphyllia*. Another similar genus is *Lobophyllia*, recognizable by the "teeth" at the margin of the colony, which are lacking in *Trachyphyllia* or *Cynarina*.

Catalaphyllia jardinei (Elegant, Elegans, or Elegance Coral) is closely related to *Euphyllia* (see below). This is one of the most popular, hardy and spectacular stony corals. Like *Trachyphyllia*, this species is a single polyp that lives in mud and is easy to collect in an undamaged condition. In addition, the polyps can withdraw completely into the skeleton where they are adequately protected during transport, and the coral rarely arrives at its destination in damaged condition. It is highly prized and commands a premium price, but if I were planning to have only one coral, this would be my choice. Specimens can double in size in six months.

Several species of *Euphyllia* are available to aquarists, and all make good additions to the reef tank. All have rela-

Elegance Coral (*Catalaphyllia jardinei*)

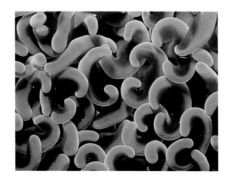

Anchor Coral (*Euphyllia ancora*)

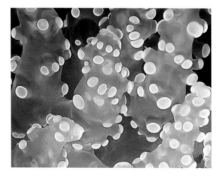

Frogspawn Coral (*Euphyllia divisa*)

Torch Coral (*Euphyllia glabrescens*)

Cup Coral (*Turbinaria peltata*)

Bubble Coral (*Plerogyra sinuosa*)

Fox Coral (*Nemenzophyllia turbida*)

Galaxy Coral (*Galaxea fascicularis*)

Trumpet Coral (*Caulastrea furcata*)

tively long tentacles and must not be placed close to other invertebrates, which they may sting. They need bright light. *Euphyllia ancora* (Anchor Coral, Hammerhead Coral, Hammer Coral, or Ridge Coral) has a curved extension at the end of each tentacle, giving the appearance of little hammers or anchors. *Euphyllia divisa* (Wall Coral, Frogspawn Coral, or Vase Coral) gets one of its colorful common names from the appearance of the tentacles. It sports numerous tubercles and white spots, suggesting a mass of frog's eggs when viewed at a distance. Although it is another good aquarium species, in my experience, specimens may die as a result of damage incurred during shipping. Torch Coral, *Euphyllia glabrescens*, looks like several cone-shaped torches attached at the apex. The elongated tentacles with pale, rounded tips extend from the torch like flames.

Turbinaria peltata (called Cup Coral, Chalice Coral, or

Wineglass Coral) is so named because the skeleton is shaped like a goblet with a fat stem by which the coral is attached to a hard substrate. Thin, brownish tissue covers the entire surface. It is important to avoid specimens that have merely been snapped off above the point of attachment. The large, flowerlike polyps are borne only on the inside of the "goblet." *Turbinaria* is interesting in appearance and easy to keep. Other species of *Turbinaria* are thinner and more delicate in appearance and are good aquarium subjects as well. Often, such specimens are an attractive mustard yellow color.

Plerogyra sinuosa (Bubble Coral) may be pale blue, brownish, or green in color. This is a commonly available and popular species and is often long-lived. A related genus, *Physogyra*, which looks very similar, is called Pearl Bubble Coral. These corals will do well in moderate light, but should be protected from strong currents of water.

Blastomussa, Nemenzophyllia, Galaxea, and *Caulastrea* are additional genera of lagoon corals that are available sporadically. Of these, *Caulastrea* is a personal favorite of mine, with both green and brown forms. *Galaxea,* though very beautiful, has astonishingly long sweeper tentacles that will "nettle" and eventually kill neighboring corals. (In the wild, it can take over large areas of inshore fringing reefs, and in the aquarium should be given at least 6 inches of buffer zone in all directions.)

FISHES FOR THE SHALLOW-WATER TANK. Shallow, inshore habitats in the Indo-Pacific harbor a variety of species collected for the aquarium trade, fishes as well as invertebrates, largely because they are easily accessible to collectors with minimal equipment. Especially good choices — just a sampling of an ever-increasing wealth of available species — for fishes to go along with the invertebrates from this environment include the following:

Pajama Cardinalfish (*Sphaeramia nematoptera*) is often found among *Acropora* colonies and will reproduce in captivity;

Yellowtail Damselfish (*Chrysiptera parasema*) associates with inshore corals, often in turbid, silty waters;

Firefish (*Nemateleotris magnifica*) prefers shallow water in Indonesia, but has been found on the deep outer reef in Hawaii;

Signal Goby (*Signigobius biocellatus*) digs a burrow in clear lagoons, usually accompanied by its mate;

Yellow Tang (*Zebrasoma flavescens*) and Sailfin Tang (*Z. veliferum*) graze the shallows where algae are abundant;

Hawaiian Neon or Four-Line Wrasse (*Pseudocheilinus tetrataenia*) and its cousin, the familiar Six-Line Wrasse (*P. hexataenia*), are found in a variety of habitats from shallow stands of coral to deep outer reefs;

Hawaiian Domino Damsel (*Dascyllus albisella*) lives in very calm, shallow water and often associates with the Hawaiian Sand Anemone. The anemone was once known as *Antheopsis papillosa,* but more recent studies have shown it to be *Heteractis malu,* which hosts Clark's Clownfish in Asian waters.

No list of shallow-water reef-tank compatible species from the Indo-Pacific would be complete without mentioning the Banggai Cardinalfish, *Pterapogon kauderni.* This shoaling species, known only from a remote location to the

Banggai Cardinalfish (*Pterapogon kauderni*)

Pajama or PJ Cardinalfish (*Sphaeramia nematoptera*)

east of Sulawesi in Indonesia, created a sensation at the Seventh Marine Aquarium Conference of North America in Louisville, Kentucky, in 1995, when Dr. Gerald Allen unveiled stunning photographs — the first ever presented of a species previously unknown to aquarists and modern ichthyologists. (Allen at first assumed it to be a new species, but eventually learned that it had been identified decades earlier and promptly forgotten.)

The specimens found by Allen happened to lie directly beneath a rustic outhouse on the end of a wooden dock, a fact that produced guffaws from the assembled multitude of marine enthusiasts. Never deterred in the pursuit of a beautiful fish, no matter how inglorious its habitat, aquarists thronged the podium at the end of Allen's talk, anxious to learn of a source for specimens. Now regularly available to hobbyists, the Banggai Cardinal has proved to be a bold, hardy aquarium fish, with striking black and silver coloration and a propensity to breed in captivity. It is a mouthbrooder. Larvae mature in the male parent's mouth; when released, they are developed enough to feed on newly hatched brine shrimp. The young are reported to be simple to keep, even fed solely on frozen foods, and can thus be raised even by the aquarist with limited facilities. Given its apparently limited range in the wild and fears that its native stocks could become depleted, this species could quickly become a captive-bred standard of the aquarium hobby. In all, this is a fascinating species and ideal for anyone eager to try his or her hand at captive breeding. (An appropriate habitat, sans privy, would be a sandy lagoon bottom with Turtle Grass and long-spined sea urchins.)

The Clownfish & Host Anemone Tank

CLOWNFISH AND THEIR ANEMONES are popular aquarium subjects, never failing to capture the attention of all who view them. Yet they are widely misunderstood. Before com-

mitting to creating an aquarium for them, one should consider their special needs.

THE HOST ANEMONES. Given its powerful stinging tentacles and its demanding care requirements, the anemone is the Pivotal Species in the aquarium community. Three families of anemones are represented among the clownfish hosts. One, Thalassianthidae, is of minimal interest. Of the remaining two families, Actiniidae is relatively easy to manage in the reef aquarium, while Stichodactylidae is rather difficult .

Family Actiniidae. Hardiness is a characteristic of the two actiniid anemones that host clownfishes and makes them good choices for the beginning aquarist who wants to set up a clownfish/host anemone tank. These are *Macrodactyla doreensis* and *Entacmaea quadricolor*. *Macrodactyla* is known to the aquarist as Long Tentacle Anemone, often abbreviated simply as LTA. The red column topped with bluish gray verrucae is distinctive, although in a proper habitat tank, the column will be buried, as it is in the ocean. The long tentacles — gray, bluish, or pinkish in color — often twist into a spiral shape, leading Fautin and Allen (1986) to call this the Corkscrew Anemone. It hosts only three clownfish species in nature, but in the aquarium will be accepted by others. Its range is also restricted, with the majority of specimens collected from Indonesia. LTA is a widely available clownfish host and is reasonably hardy, but it does need a suitable substrate in which to bury its column. Lacking this, it will wander around, fail to attach, and eventually die. It is most frequently found in mud, in water less than 15 feet deep. Mud implies moderate current, and shallow water suggests the need for bright illumination.

Entacmaea quadricolor, called the Bulb, Bubble Tip, or Maroon Anemone in the aquarium trade, holds the record

Skunk Clowns (*Amphiprion perideraion*) with huge Magnificent Anemone (*Heteractis magnifica*) on current-swept slope.

for clownfish species hosted, at 13. The inflated tips of the tentacles, looking something like the nipples on old-fashioned glass baby bottles, are characteristic. No other

Maroon Clown pair (*Premnas biaculeatus*) in their Bubble Tip Anemone (*Entacmaea quadricolor*): the female clownfish is always larger.

anemone has this feature. The bulbs occur more commonly on anemones that have clownfish in residence than on those that do not. There are two types of *Entacmaea*, which may have important implications for aquarium care. In shallow water, typically on the tops of reefs, a "clonal form" occurs. Generally less than 2 inches in diameter (across the oral disc), this form occurs in large aggregations, with individuals often so close together as to give the appearance of a single anemone. In deep water, the polyps are of the "solitary form," and can be over a foot across. Fautin and Allen (1986) refer to the shallow-water form as the clonal form because the aggregations are thought to arise as a result of vegetative division of individuals, leading to a collection of genetically identical offspring — clones of the original

anemone. The larger, deep-water form apparently does not divide in this fashion. (*Heteractis magnifica* shares this trait with *Entacmaea*.) Dunn (1981) points out that the relationship between size and type is not necessarily constant, with large specimens sometimes found in shallow water and small specimens occurring at greater depth (although any form of this anemone is rare below 60 feet).

Entacmaea is called the Maroon Anemone by some aquarium wholesalers because of its long-recognized association with the Maroon Clownfish, *Premnas biaculeatus*. Fautin and Allen report that this fish is found only in association with the deep-water, solitary form of the anemone, while the shallow-water, clonal form is preferred by the Cinnamon or Bluestripe Clownfish, *Amphiprion melanopus*. A rare color variety, in which the body is red with pink tentacles, is called Rose Anemone by aquarium dealers and commands a high price.

Dunn speculates that in *Entacmaea*, the larger individuals are responsible for sexual reproduction (which makes sense when one remembers that a larger individual has more resources upon which to draw in order to carry out the demanding job of producing eggs and sperm). It is known that sexes are separate in *Entacmaea*, and the female anemones brood eggs, which are fertilized by sperm carried on the water currents. Despite the fact that the two different types may arise as a result of differing environmental conditions at different depths, it appears that the clonal form reproduces readily by asexual reproduction, whereas the solitary form does not.

Family Stichodactylidae. This anemone family is the more difficult one to manage in the reef aquarium. *Heteractis aurora*, Beaded Sea Anemone, is perhaps the easiest of this group to identify, as the tentacles are ribbed with swellings that are often a contrasting color. It hosts seven clownfish species. *H. crispa*, Leathery Sea Anemone, hosts 11 clownfish species. It is sometimes confused with *H. malu*, which Fautin and Allen (1986) call Delicate Sea Anemone, but which in the aquarium trade is usually known as the Sebae or Singapore Sebae Anemone. *H. malu* hosts only Clark's Clownfish (*Amphiprion clarkii*), a species often incorrectly identified as *A. sebae*. (The true *A. sebae*, a much rarer species, associates in nature only with *Stichodactyla haddoni*, discussed below.) *H. crispa* has a decidedly firmer column than *H. malu*, but the latter is most easily recognized by the typically short tentacles, seldom over an inch in length, that are tipped in magenta. *H. magnifica*, Magnificent Sea Anemone, still goes by its old name of *Radianthus ritteri* in the aquarium industry, and is often called simply Ritteri Anemone. It is host to ten clownfish species, including *A. ocellaris* and *A. percula*, for which it is the most frequently suggested aquarium host.

Stichodactyla gigantea, the Giant Carpet Anemone of the aquarium trade, is host to seven clownfish species and can be separated from the other two *Stichodactyla* species by its noticeably longer tentacles, often strikingly colored. *S. haddoni*, Haddon's Sea Anemone, is called the Saddle Carpet in the aquarium trade, because of the affinity of the Saddleback Clownfish, *A. polymnus*, for this host. The very short tentacles are frequently of two colors, giving the oral disc a mottled appearance and distinguishing this species from the other two carpet anemones. Besides *A. polymnus*, five other clownfish species associate with this anemone. Merten's Sea Anemone, *S. mertensii*, is called Sri Lanka Carpet by aquarium dealers and is sometimes bright green in color. Its stubby tentacles, often more like little knobs, are uniform in color, although there may by a contrasting ring of purple

pigment encircling the mouth. This species (despite the use of *gigantea* as the species name for another carpet anemone) holds the oral disc size record for clownfish hosts — it can be over 3 feet in diameter.

Clownfish host anemones in the Stichodactylidae family have a mixed record of success in the aquarium, and the majority of specimens probably die before reaching anything approaching their natural lifespan. I know of one specimen of *H. malu* that survived 12 years in a hobbyist's aquarium, but this seems to be an exception. It succumbed to loss of water quality during a prolonged power outage, unfortunately, and barring this disaster might well be alive

Clark's Clownfish (*Amphiprion clarkii*) group, again with a clearly dominant female, in a Leathery Sea Anemone (*Heteractis crispa*).

today. The specimen more than doubled in size in a 55-gallon tank. The tank was filtered with an undergravel filter and a canister filter containing activated carbon and was illuminated with four 40-watt shop lights. Tank decor con-

CLOWNFISH HOST ANEMONES: DIFFICULT CHOICES

THOUGH THE CLOWNFISHES are generally a hardy lot, the anemones with which they associate in the wild are not. Some experienced aquarists have come to believe that most Pacific anemones are more difficult to maintain than even the sensitive small-polyped stony corals. Most aquarists should choose between *Entacmaea quadricolor* and *Macrodactyla doreensis* and leave the others to the experts. (Many species of clownfish will bond with anemones other than their native favorites if they have no other choice in the aquarium.) This list encompasses the more common species seen in the aquarium trade.

RECOMMENDED:

Entacmaea quadricolor (Bulb, Bubble Tip, Maroon, or Rose Anemone): Tentacles inflated at tips, with white band and pink tip (usually). Attaches to hard surface. In nature, this anemone hosts Maroon and Bluestripe Clownfishes. In the aquarium, it will also host Tomato and Clark's Clownfishes.

Macrodactyla doreensis (Long Tentacle Anemone, LTA): Column always red or salmon pink, with verrucae underneath oral disk. Buries column in substrate. Natural symbionts are Clark's and Pink Skunk Clownfishes. In the aquarium, it is often accepted by Maroon, Bluestripe, and Tomato Clownfishes as well.

EXPERT CARE REQUIRED:

Heteractis crispa (Leathery Anemone): Column tough, leathery and buried in substrate. Tentacles long and pointed, often purple. Hosts the Clark's, Bluestripe, True Percula, Pink Skunk, and Saddleback Clownfishes.

Heteractis aurora (Beaded Anemone, Aurora Anemone): Buries column in substrate. Tentacles with raised, white ridges. Only common aquarium clown hosted is Clark's.

Heteractis malu (Sebae Anemone, Singapore Sebae): Column and oral a disk uniform pale color, with stubby tentacles usually tipped in magenta. Hosts only Clark's Clownfish in nature; may host Tomato and Bluestripe Clowns in the aquarium.

Heteractis magnifica (Magnificent Anemone, Ritteri Anemone, Red Radianthus Anemone): Attaches to hard surfaces in good current and bright light; may wander if not happy. Column smooth, often colorful; tentacles always slightly inflated, with yellow or white pigment at tips. Hosts Clark's, Bluestripe, Ocellaris ("Percula"), True Percula, and Pink Skunk Clownfishes.

Stichodactyla gigantea (Giant Carpet Anemone): Tentacles longer than other carpet anemones and slightly pointed at tips. May be green, yellow-brown, blue, turquoise, or purple in color. Hosts Clark's, Ocellaris, and True Percula Clownfishes.

Stichodactyla haddoni (Haddon's Carpet, Saddle Carpet Anemone): Tentacles almost always two colors, imparting a mottled appearance. Hosts Saddleback and Clark's Clownfishes.

Stichodactyla mertensii (Merten's Carpet, Sri Lanka Carpet) Tentacles stubby, knoblike, uniform brown or occasionally bright green in color. Hosts Clark's and Ocellaris Clownfishes.

sisted of dead coral skeletons. It was typical for a fish-only tank of its day. Water changes were performed monthly, but nothing special was done in the way of husbandry for the anemone. The owner of the tank preferred to clean the coral skeletons each time he did a water change. As a result, algae was held to a minimum and nutrients were thus exported from the system. Perhaps that was important to the longevity of this specimen. Other aquarists of my acquaintance have not had such good luck with *H. malu*.

H. magnifica is in particular known for its habit of wandering all over the aquarium, often being killed or damaged when sucked into a powerhead or filter intake. It appears that the availability of light, planktonic food, and water movement are important to this species. The fact that it is often beautifully colored, that the most popular clownfish species, *A. ocellaris*, prefers this host, and that it is more commonly available than the other hosts for this clown, may explain why many aquarists are tempted to buy this species despite its reputation.

The carpet anemones pose other husbandry problems for the aquarist. Only *S. mertensii* is found on the reef proper, while *S. haddoni* and *S. gigantea* occur in sandy, shallow-water habitats. All three species require intense lighting, as can be noted from the presence of brightly colored pigments in many specimens. Insufficient light may be one reason for aquarium difficulties. Attention should also be paid to the nature of the substrate preferred by the anemone. *S. haddoni* and *S. gigantea* prefer clean sand, deep enough to allow the anemone to retract completely into the substrate when disturbed. The latter species is often found in water so shallow that the anemone is exposed at low tide, while the former prefers deeper water. *S. mertensii* lives on hard surfaces on the reef

slope. Also living buried in soft sediment are *Heteractis aurora*, *H. malu* and *H. crispa*, although the latter may also be found with the pedal disk attached to branching coral on the outer reef. The other two species are found in shallow, quiet waters. *H. magnifica* is always found attached to a solid ob-

Skunk Clownfish with Magnificent Sea Anemone (*Heteractis magnifica*)

ject in a fully exposed position, such as atop a coral head. Its requirements for light, oxygen, and turbulence are similar to those of SPS corals.

Another problem that may affect all stichodactylid anemones in the aquarium may be incompatibility with other species of cnidarians because of nettling. I have found, for example, that *H. magnifica* will not survive long in a typical reef aquarium containing an assortment of other cnidarians, despite conditions otherwise appropriate for its survival. Other aquarists report similar experiences. It is my tentative conclusion that aquarium hobbyists should 1) attempt to keep the stichodactylid anemones in a tank devoted solely to them and their clownfish symbionts, and 2) avoid these anemones until experience in maintaining other species with exacting requirements, such as SPS corals, is attained.

THE CLOWNFISHES. No other family has held such fascination for aquarists, divers and biologists alike as has the anemonefish, or clownfish, family. Anemonefishes are from the Pomacentridae (damselfish) family, but they are damselfishes that have evolved the unique habit of living in association with large sea anemones. An inkling as to how this relationship may have developed can be seen in the behavior of juvenile *Dascyllus* damselfishes, which also associate with anemones, but later, as adults, defend a territory consisting of a coral head. Adult anemonefishes are rarely found more than 3 feet from their host anemone.

This unique dependence upon a scarce resource, giant sea anemones, has resulted in an equally unique way of coping with the problems of reproducing the species while avoiding inbreeding. All anemonefishes start life as males. Sex in these fishes is not genetically predetermined. Soon after hatching, the larval fishes spend a period of time drifting with plankton, feeding upon other, smaller organisms.

At metamorphosis, a juvenile anemonefish must locate and successfully join an established family of its own species already in residence in a suitable host anemone. As if this were not a sufficient challenge for a fish less than 1 inch in length, the chosen anemone is sure to be the territory of a breeding pair of anemonefishes. The resident adult male fish will drive off new arrivals that do not meet his criteria for adoption. Assuming the newcomer is accepted, he may yet never have the opportunity to fulfill his biological destiny. The resident pair will consist of a large female and a much smaller male. He will nevertheless be larger than the juvenile males that constitute the remainder of the clan. The pair may live to be over ten years old, and will, during that time, produce thousands of offspring, only a tiny fraction of which will survive to maturity. Recruitment of unrelated juveniles insures that gene flow occurs among various pairs of fishes within a given area.

When the breeding female anemonefish dies, her former mate rapidly develops into a functional female, and one of the juvenile males now takes the role of adult breeding male. This arrangement guarantees that an anemone, once occupied, will never lack a source of eggs for contin-

Clark's Clowns with Carpet Anemone (*Stichodactyla* sp.)

Tomato Clown (*Amphiprion frenatus*) in Bubble Tip Anemone

ued propagation of the species. It also makes the process of acquiring mated pairs of anemonefishes for aquarium breeding purposes quite simple: any two juveniles placed together in an appropriate environment will often develop into a pair within several months. Perhaps 10 of 26 species of anemonefishes are available as captive-propagated specimens, with the Common Clownfish (*Amphiprion ocellaris*), Clark's Clownfish (*A. clarkii*), Tomato Clownfish (*A. frenatus*), and the Maroon Clownfish (*Premnas biaculeatus*), almost universally available. Wild-caught clowns of nearly all species are still to be found in the aquarium trade, but the majority do not ship well and are becoming less popular as more captive-propagated stock reaches the aquarium market.

Common, Ocellaris, or False Percula Clownfish (*Amphiprion ocellaris*)

Because they normally spend their lives in a restricted area near their host anemone, anemonefishes are "preadapted" to captivity. They are undemanding in their requirements, needing only appropriate water conditions and a suitable diet (a variety of readily available, small, meaty seafoods and some vegetable matter) to thrive, and even spawn, in aquariums as small as 30 gallons. The host anemone need not even be present. Many excellent books on anemonefishes exist, most with color photographs of each species (see Bibliography, page 313). Creating a microhabitat aquarium featuring any of the anemonefishes is a rewarding project, even for a novice aquarist. For those with sufficient experience to assume responsibility for a host anemone, here are two suggested designs for habitats featuring a clownfish-anemone pair as the focal point:

A REEF-TOP AQUARIUM FOR CLOWNFISH. An aquarium exhibiting the host anemone *Entacmaea quadricolor* (clonal form) with the clownfish *Amphiprion melanopus* would closely duplicate the top of a tiny pinnacle of reef in the Coral Sea. A tank of about 75 to 120 gallons would be ideal. (See Chapter Two for equipment suggestions for a 120-gallon system for SPS corals, appropriate also for the reef-top habitat.) Include only one anemone (leaving room for its eventual progeny), five tank-reared, juvenile clowns (which will eventually form a "family"), several *Tridacna maxima* clams (also found on reef tops), and an assortment of Indo-Pacific shrimps, including *Lysmata amboinensis* and *L. debelius*. SPS corals would also be at home in this aquarium. Choose specimens with pink or purple pigments, indicating that they came from shallow water, rather than relying on species identifications. Place the corals so that

ANEMONE CONSERVATION

WITH SOME BIOLOGISTS NOW SUGGESTING that marine anemones ought not to be collected for sale in the aquarium trade, pressure is mounting to find species and methods that assure survival in captivity. Based on the experience of two aquarium-maintenance businesses here in my hometown, I have concluded that the relatively hardy *Entacmaea quadricolor* (Bulb, Bubble Tip, Maroon, or Rose Anemone) may be the perfect candidate, especially the form found in shallow-water habitats. The specimens I have been keeping tabs on are all descended from a single individual originally purchased from my company and placed in one of our tanks, where it divided several times. The offspring were transferred to other aquariums, where they divided again. Thus, some of these anemones are second-generation, captive-propagated clones. The only common thread among these aquariums is that all of them are on the cooler side. Some *Entacmaea* specimens in other aquariums maintained by these same people have refused to divide, and many have not fared well generally.

Paletta (1993) reported a similar experience with the Rose Anemone form of *E. quadricolor*. He also gives a useful account of aquarium growth rate in this anemone. The specimen increased in size from about 1 inch to about 12 inches

Bubble Tip Anemone: the author's choice as the most appropriate species for most aquarists.

in a 20-month period, "with little direct feeding." Prior to splitting into daughter anemones, the specimen retreated to a dark area of the tank and exhibited reduction in tentacle size. Division required about two days to complete. I have spoken with three or four aquarists over the years whose Rose Anemone specimens retreated in this way. In every case, the aquarist assumed that a problem was developing and may have mistakenly inhibited reproduction by trying to move the anemone back into the light, adding various trace element supplements, feeding the anemone, etc. Paletta reported that he assumed the anemone was dying. I wonder how many people have removed a partially split *Entacmaea*, thinking the same thing and hoping to avoid polluting the tank with a dead anemone?

While it is difficult to trust conclusions from such a small sample, the implications of this information for the aquarium care of these anemones, and their potential captive propagation, is obvious. The rate of growth reported by Paletta is sufficiently rapid (1 inch to 5 inches in 8 months, without feeding) to make greenhouse propagation potentially worthwhile from an economic point of view. Dunn (1981) provides a way for us to distinguish the two forms, reporting that the siphonoglyph of the solitary, deep-water form is paired and symmetrical, while in the clonal form found in shallow water, there can be up to eight siphonoglyphs, asymmetrically arranged around the mouth.

Whether the other clownfish host anemones should be collected in large numbers should be given consideration. In the first place, authorities such as Fautin and Allen (1986) are quite certain that recruitment (survival of larvae to become adult anemones) is rather rare. Very few small individuals of any anemone species are observed in the field. Further, low recruitment rates are characteristic of species that are long-lived, and there are documented instances of captive anemones living to be quite old. Consider this passage in Larson and Cooper (1982):

"A fascinating account of an anemone living to sixty-six years of age was reported in the late 1800's. Sir John Dalyell collected an *Actinia* that eventually outlived him. During its productive lifetime it bore over 750 young, 150 of them born at the age of 50. With this in mind, it would be hard to guess the age of sea anemones that live peacefully in the uninhabited regions of the world's oceans."

Fautin and Allen conclude that many of the larger anemones they see in field studies are over a century in age. That such long-lived creatures often survive only a few months in captivity is strong evidence that aquarium hobbyists should become more adept at keeping them, or should avoid these specimens altogether in favor of species more likely to live out a natural lifespan in captivity. Any anemones attempted should be smaller specimens, since selection of larger individuals affords a lowered likelihood of successful husbandry, and since these individuals may represent the brood stock. Further, I recommend that aquarium hobbyists select only *Entacmaea* and *Macrodactyla* as the clownfish hosts of primary interest and avoid the much more difficult stichodactylid species. *Entacmaea* seems to me to be the most appropriate aquarium species. It is the most abundant host anemone in nature; it is widely distributed, occurring from the Red Sea to Samoa; it is host to many species of clownfish, and it has the potential for captive propagation through vegetative reproduction. In my experience, it settles into the aquarium readily, and unlike *Macrodactyla*, it does not require substrate into which to bury the column, preferring instead to attach to a rock or other solid object. This species clearly deserves more attention from aquarists capable of providing for its needs — good illumination and cooler water (70 to 75 degrees F). Noted amateur clownfish breeder Joyce Wilkerson points out that these fishes do not need an anemone in order to thrive and reproduce. She argues that clownfish make endearing and long-lived aquarium subjects, even without their hosts, and are perfectly suited to beginners' reef tanks where anemones typically fare poorly.

Maldives Clownfish (*Amphiprion nigripes*) with Magnificent Anemone (*Heteractis magnifica*).

Crocea Clam (*Tridacna crocea*): among the most colorful of the tridacnids.

they will not come into contact with the anemone's tentacles, or nettling is possible. Including a Six-Line Wrasse, *Pseudocheilinus hexataenia*, will help protect the giant clams from parasitic snails they may be harboring. A coral goby, such as *Gobiodon citrinus*, will makes its home in the branches of the SPS corals if placed in this tank. Schools of Orange-lined Cardinalfish, *Apogon cyanosoma*, emerge from hiding to feed in the open at night. Their inclusion would also be appropriate.

AN INSHORE AQUARIUM FOR CLOWNFISH. For a smaller system than the one just described, a suitable clownfish/host combination might be the host anemone *Macrodactyla doreensis* with tank-raised *Amphiprion clarkii* clownfish. Intense lighting, but moderate current, are the basic environmental prerequisites, along with a suitable layer of fine, soft sand for the anemone to bury in. A Monaco-style sand bed would be a natural choice. This habitat would also be home to the Mandarinfish, *Synchiropus splendidus*, and its cousin, the Spotted Mandarin, *Synchiropus picturatus*. (The latter requires a well-established system with good natural opportunities to forage over live rock and gravel for small live foods.)

Because many of the soft corals and other cnidarians found in the lagoon might nettle a clownfish host anemone, one must choose from other invertebrate groups to create a diverse community in this aquarium design. Sabellid worms are commonplace in this habitat, and several species of giant clams might be found here. *Tridacna squamosa* would be the most likely choice, since it prefers sheltered shallows.

Derasa or Smooth Giant Clam (*Tridacna derasa*)

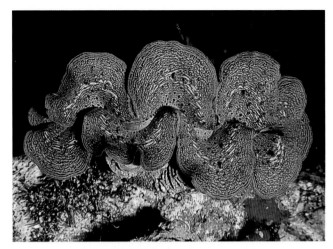

Maxima or Great Clam (*Tridacna maxima*)

Blue Maxima (*Tridacna maxima*)

Green Crocea (*Tridacna crocea*)

T. gigas, T. crocea, Hippopus hippopus, and *H. porcellanus* would also be appropriate, with *Hippopus* often found simply lying on the substrate. *T. gigas* and *T. crocea* are typically attached to a hard surface. The latter species frequently bores into coral heads, for example.

Overcollecting for food use has reduced the numbers of giant clams in the wild, and some are now protected throughout much of their natural range. Fortunately, hatchery-raised giant clams have become widely available. Of the eight species of giant clams found in the Indo-Pacific region, seven are available from hatcheries. These are *Tridacna derasa, T. crocea, T. squamosa, T. gigas, T. maxima, Hippopus hippopus,* and the recently described *H. porcellanus.* Another recently discovered species, *T. tevora,* has not yet appeared on the aquarium market as of the date of this writing.

Tridacnids are conveniently undemanding as reef invertebrates go, requiring primarily good lighting, sufficient calcium and the absence of predators. These clams have been shown to thrive on nitrate, and in well-aged, nutrient-poor systems with efficient protein skimming, the clams may actually need supplementation in order to grow. If there are fish in the tank, their feeding regimen will likely provide sufficient waste to supply tridacnids with the inorganic ions they need.

Startlingly pigmented black and white Maxima Clam (*Tridacna maxima*) in the wild.

Many aquarists who set up giant-clam microhabitats include a Hawaiian Neon or Four-Line Wrasse (*Pseudocheilinus tetrataenia*) or a Six-Line Wrasse (*P. hexataenia*) for control of tiny molluscan parasites that frequently hitchhike into the aquarium along with the tridacnid. These parasites resemble small grains of rice and are most frequently observed on the bottom of the clam near the byssal opening. They can and will kill clams if left unchecked.

Other fishes for a tank featuring tridacnid clams would be grazing tangs and mid-water planktivores like anthias, cardinals, damsels, or others mentioned in this chapter. Angelfishes (and other omnivorous foragers that spend the day picking at the reefscape) are not recommended as they will nip at the delectable tridacnid flesh. Even the seemingly harmless *Centropyge* species of dwarf angels will often nibble at a clam's mantle, causing it to retract and eventually wither and die. Stinging *Aiptasia* anemones can be troublesome; either move the clam or kill the *Aiptasia* (sealing each under a patch of aquarium epoxy putty can be effective if there are just a small number of these pests to subdue).

The mantle of *Tridacna* is filled with zooxanthellae, which form interesting patterns that no doubt account for their appeal to aquarists. Coloration of the mantle ranges from bright green to blue and purple. Each individual clam looks different, and many are quite beautiful.

The aquarium husbandry of all species of giant clams is the same. The clam relies upon its zooxanthellae for food. It absorbs both inorganic and organic nutrients from the water, probably for the primary benefit of the zooxanthellae. Such nutrients include both ammonia and nitrate. Nitrate removal can be dramatic, if large numbers of clams are introduced into the aquarium. Phosphates are also absorbed. Thus, *Tridacna* actually enjoys levels of nitrate and phosphate that would be considered unsuitable for a coral reef aquarium in general. Nevertheless, attention should be paid to water quality for

Staghorn Coral (*Acropora* sp.)

Encrusting Stony Coral (*Porites* sp.)

Closed Brain Coral (*Favites* sp.)

Staghorn Coral (*Acropora gemmifera*)

Captive-grown *Acropora* fragment

these clams, which require sufficient oxygen, a high, stable pH, and an alkalinity of 3.5 milliequivalents per liter (meq/L) or more. High-intensity lighting is also necessary. In addition, these clams need protection from irritants and parasites. The latter can be controlled, as mentioned above, by keeping a Six-Line Wrasse (*Pseudocheilinus hexataenia*) in the tank. All of the shallow-water clams are frequently encrusted with coralline algae, sponges, and other small invertebrates. Live rock organisms may establish themselves on the shells of clams, helping to create a natural look.

The Outer-Reef Habitat

OUTER REEFS OF THE INDO-PACIFIC are the home of the most widely available giant clam, *Tridacna derasa*, which is an adaptable species that can be recommended to any

aquarist. This is a good species to accompany SPS corals. Dartfishes, such as the Common Firefish, *Nemateleotris magnifica*, and the Purple Firefish, *N. decora*, occur here in pairs, and shoals of anthias hover in the strong currents. (See the discussion of anthias in Chapter Ten before attempting these fish, however.) The striking Purple Dottyback, *Pseudochromis porphyreus*, is often found in this habitat on drop-offs and fore-reef slopes. This and many other pseudochromids are now being propagated in hatcheries.

SPS CORALS. Small-polyped scleractinian corals reach their greatest abundance and vigor on the fore reef, where bright light, nutrient-poor conditions and strong turbulence are the rule. They are rapidly becoming popular with hobbyists in the United States, although European aquarists have been keeping and propagating them for years. In contrast with their large-polyped counterparts, SPS corals ex-

Beautiful tangle of Indo-Pacific staghorns and other corals: a habitat that demands an aquarist's keenest skills to replicate.

hibit a branching form and can be readily propagated by removing fragments and securing them to an appropriate substrate with underwater epoxy. Under proper care, the fragments readily develop into new colonies. SPS corals are usually hermaphroditic, and sexual reproduction is often simultaneous among the majority of the species in a given area, a phenomenon thought to be under the control of environmental factors such as temperature, photoperiod, and lunar cycles.

SPS corals include the genera *Acropora, Pocillopora, Seriatopora, Stylophora, Hydnophora, Pavona, Anacropora, Porites, Favites, Favia*, and *Goniastrea*. The first three have received the majority of attention, and there are many species in cultivation. *Favia* and *Favites* are two similar genera usually called Closed Brain Coral. These hardy corals, in which

[2] Bruce Carlson, remarks presented to the 1995 Southwest Marine Conference in Costa Mesa, California.

the individual polyps are grouped together to create a rounded, massive colony with a honeycomb surface, may be appropriate for a variety of aquarium microhabitats.

CORAL DISTRIBUTION AND AQUACULTURE. Dr. Bruce Carlson of the Waikiki Aquarium outlined the distribution, based on his observations, of corals in Fiji and Palau.[2] In the lagoon, where the water is rather turbid, were found *Plerogyra sinuosa, Euphyllia ancora, Heliofungia actiniformis, Goniopora, Pavona*, and *Favites*. In shallower, cleaner water, stands of *Anacropora*, preferring high light and low water movement, dominated. In Turtle Grass, *Catalaphyllia jardinei* and *Montipora digitata* were the commonest species. On the reef flat, *Seriatopora*, a widespread species, *Stylophora, Porites cylindrica, Goniopora, Caulastrea furcata, Acropora austera*, and *A. formosa* occurred. On the outer-reef slope, table forms of *Acropora* dominated.

(The Waikiki Aquarium has over 50 stony coral species in its public exhibits, many of which were cultured at the aquarium from tiny fragments collected in the sea. Dr. Carl-

Lyretail Anthias (*Pseudanthias squamipinnis*)

TIPS ON CORAL PLACEMENT

ONE OF THE MORE VEXATIOUS CHALLENGES, even for experienced reef keepers, is the appropriate placement of corals within the aquarium. Finding just the right level of light intensity and water motion can mean the difference between a specimen that thrives and grows, showing full polyp extension and brilliant coloration, and one that leads a lackluster existence, with polyps retracted or shrunken, dull coloration, and no growth.

Specific recommendations for each species of coral that an aquarist might encounter are not always easy to find, and many are still poorly documented in the literature available to hobbyists. Here are my own general rules for placing corals in the reef tank.

1. Corals (and anemones) in which the ends of the tentacles are pink or purple in color, and corals with a lot of pink in the tissue, such as the red form of *Trachyphyllia geoffroyi*, were likely collected in shallow water where they received very bright light. It is believed that the pink and purple pigments help to protect the coral from ultraviolet light.

2. Branching corals grow nearest the surface of the ocean, high up on the reef, where light and oxygen are max-

Trial and error may be the best instructor in learning to arrange specimens in a reef tank.

imally abundant. Massive, rounded corals grow at moderate depths. Platelike growth forms are characteristic of areas where light is lowest, resulting in the coral spreading out to expose maximum surface area to the sunshine.

3. Extreme variation in form in a single species can lead to confusion about which species are found where. For example, in *Pocillopora damicornis* from the Great Barrier Reef, a "colony from the reef flat has more in common with colonies of other *Pocillopora* species than it does with colonies of *P. damicornis* from other environments." (Veron, 1995) It is probably more useful to consider the nature of the growth form of a particular specimen, rather than its actual species designation, when deciding whether the specimen would be suitable for an aquarium depicting a limited microhabitat.

Trial and error, in the end, will be the best guide in many situations. If a coral seems not to be doing well, try another location with a different set of conditions. We must resist the temptation to constantly rearrange a tank, but judicious experimentation with a problem specimen can often yield surprising improvements.

son is noteworthy among professional aquarists and marine biologists for his willingness to involve aquarium hobbyists in his studies of coral reef biology.)

The collection of stony corals is prohibited in many countries, and the question of whether stony coral species should be collected for the aquarium is debated. Captive spawning of stony corals may be a very rare event. Stony corals do not as readily reproduce themselves by other means, as do soft corals, but vegetative reproduction of all the branching stony coral species is successful. Coral "farms" have sprung up all over the United States, ranging in size from what can be accommodated in a suburban basement to multiple greenhouses to a multimillion-dollar, high-tech facility in a 5,000-square-foot warehouse. Cultivation of coral fragments in trays placed in shallow water is being pursued in Palau and probably in other locations in the tropical Indo-Pacific. The supply of SPS corals, and many of the other species as well, may one day come exclusively from such sources, although at present there are not enough propagators to keep up with demand. Hobbyist interest is high, however, and this bodes well for the future of the captive-propagated coral market.

Spawnings of many coral species occur seasonally and predictably, with the waters surrounding the reef clouded with millions of eggs and sperm. But for every larval coral that finds a suitable spot and grows into a visible colony, billions die. An idea that takes advantage of this natural fecundity is the placement of artificial substrates, such as ceramic tiles, in hopes of collecting coral larvae that will grow into aquarium-sized colonies. The "seeded" tiles could then be transferred to grow-out aquariums in which conditions could be adjusted to optimize the rate of coral growth. The government of Guam is reported to be interested in seeing a coral industry of this sort attempted in its waters.

FISHES FOR THE OUTER-REEF HABITAT. Because they are mobile, fishes are not as restricted in their habitat preferences as are sessile invertebrates. Some rough habitat guidelines, however, are possible for the most commonly seen aquarium species. Among those species usually seen on the outer side of the reef are:

Most anthiid species, including *Pseudanthias hawaiiensis*, which lives under deep ledges in Hawaii, or *Serranocirrhitus latus*, inhabiting caves and ledges at greater than 90 feet in Micronesia;

Flame Hawkfish, *Neocirrhites armatus*, found on surge-swept areas in association with *Pocillopora* corals, and the

Bicolor Blenny (*Escenius bicolor*)

Flame Hawkfish (*Neocirrhites armatus*)

Longnose Hawkfish, *Oxycirrhites typus*, which associates with gorgonians, generally at depths greater than 100 feet;

Vanderbilt's Chromis, *Chromis vanderbilti*, schools above coral heads in at least 15 feet of water;

Many *Cirrhilabrus* wrasses, including Jordan's Fairy Wrasse, *C. jordani*, which is often found in the same habitat as the Longnose Hawkfish;

Potter's Angelfish, *Centropyge potteri*, endemic to Hawaii, is most abundant in waters greater than 15 feet, while its cousin, the Flame Angel, *C. loriculus*, inhabits dense stands of coral at 60+ feet in Hawaii, although it is found in shallow waters elsewhere in the Indo-Pacific, including Christmas Island;

The Bannerfish, *Heniochus diphreutes*, schools along drop-offs at 40+ feet and is one of the few members of the butterflyfish family suitable for the reef tank. Many butterflies will decimate the live coral population of a home aquarium, and some will even consume anemones with relish. The Bannerfish, by contrast, feeds on plankton;

The Purple Firefish, *Nemateleotris decora*, prefers depths of 90 feet or more.

The Regal Tang (*Paracanthurus hepatus*) is one of the few aquarium species that is collected from the turbulent waters of the outer-reef crest, where it lives among branching corals. Unfortunately, the difficulty of collecting in such treacherous waters has resulted in a high proportion of the catch being stunned with cyanide or other poisons. Exercise care in choosing a supplier for this species, and, if possible, do not bring the fish home until it has spent a week

Zebra Lionfish (*Dendrochirus zebra*): not for tanks with smaller fishes or shrimp

or two in your local dealer's tank and is exhibiting a healthy appearance and appetite.

Wide-ranging species of aquarium fishes include the following, which may be found in a variety of habitats both shoreward and seaward of the reef:

Zebra Lionfish, *Dendrochirus zebra*

Antennata Lionfish, *Pterois antennata*

Radiata Lionfish, *P. radiata*

Volitans Lionfish, *P. volitans*

Many *Centropyge* angelfish

Bicolor Blenny, *Ecsenius bicolor*

Fanged Blenny, *Meiacanthus atrodorsalis*

tractive colonies to the light, encouraging them to grow and spread. Try to construct at least one overhanging ledge or cave, especially if you plan to include fishes. Everything from plastic cable ties to Portland cement, depending upon the size of the aquarium and the rock-work, can be used to stabilize the structure.

To choose appropriate marine life for this habitat, consider the following suggestions:

Cnidarians

WHILE MOST CNIDARIANS require very bright illumination, there are several types that prefer shade or darkness.

ORDER CERIANTIPATHARIA (Tube Anemones and Black Corals). Tube-dwelling anemones (Family Cerianthidae) have no symbiotic algae and thus do very well in the deep-reef aquarium microhabitat. Cerianthids may be distinguished from true anemones in that the former have two sets of tentacles. The outer rows are quite long, and the inner ones, surrounding the mouth, are much shorter. Purple or brown tube anemones (*Ceriantheopsis americanus, Arachnanthus nocturnus*) are often available and live buried in substrate, lining the burrow with a tube made of a mucus secretion. When freshly collected, the tube is usually heavily encrusted with mud. This should have been re-

Tube anemone (Order Ceriantipatharia)

Black coral (Order Ceriantipatharia): often found on dimly lit deep fore-reef walls.

moved by the dealer before placing the anemone on display, as the mud can easily foul a tank. If this is not the case, however, gently and carefully remove the anemone from the tube and place it in the tank. It will soon construct a new tube and bury itself in the substrate. Tube anemones can catch small fishes and can sting other invertebrates. Make sure no other specimens are within reach of the anemone's tentacles when fully expanded, and avoid fishes such as clown-fishes, hawkfishes, and seaweed gobies, which may attempt to perch in the anemone's tentacles with fatal results. Feed tube anemones a small piece of frozen marine fish meat once a week. Cerianthids are nocturnal and may not expand their tentacles if kept under bright illumination.

Black corals, or antipatharians, look nothing like tube anemones, but are classified along with them because of similarities in the details of structure and embryology. They superficially resemble gorgonians, as they are colonial and sometimes treelike, and are stiffened by an axial skeleton. Black corals often grow in a form that resembles a left-handed corkscrew — the "anti" in their name is a reference to the observation that most other natural spirals are right-handed. Black corals were once collected for jewelry making in Hawaii and the Indo-Pacific, because the dense, hard axial skeleton of certain species can be polished and made into jewelry. Small ones in the aquarium trade have been called "spring corals" and are seen only occasionally.

ORDER SCLERACTINIA (Stony Corals). Only one stony coral commonly available to the aquarist is suitable for the deep-reef tank, but it is a beauty. This is *Tubastraea*, the Orange Polyp Coral. Bright orange colonies the size of a tennis ball are often collected from caves and underneath ledges. *Tubastraea* is easy to care for. Provide a good, strong current, directed sideways across the coral colony, not pointed straight at it. When the tentacles are extended, which can be stimulated by the addition of a small amount of food juices, feed each member of the colony on frozen plankton, brine shrimp, or a small piece of shrimp or fish. Feeding should be done in the evenings, two or three times a week. Aquarists who take care to treat *Tubastraea* in this way will be rewarded with the growth of new polyps over several months' time. This coral has reached 6 inches in diameter in careful hobbyists' tanks, and larvae have successfully established themselves to form new colonies.

Orange Polyp Coral (*Tubastraea sp.*)

Tubastraea micrantha

ORDER ALCYONARIA (Soft Corals). While *Tubastraea* is the only commonly available stony coral that can do without light, many soft corals are suitable for the dimly lit reef tank. Certainly the loveliest is the soft coral *Dendronephthya*, usually known as Tree or Flower Coral. Two species, *D. klunzingeri* and *D. rubeola*, are imported. Each appears to have been made from hand-blown glass. The loosely branched, fragile-looking colonies come in shades of pink and yellow-orange. Some species do poorly if exposed to bright light and may be challenging to keep. I suspect most failures are due to too infrequent feedings. Charles Delbeek has noted that this genus requires cool temperatures, a laminar current flow, and regular feedings of phytoplankton (cultured algae, "green water"). A related genus, *Scleronephthya*, needs shade and apparently feeds on detritus. This whole group of nonphotosynthetic animals has proved impossible to keep for many aquarists. Research on Red Sea species of *Dendronephthya* and *Scleronephthya* indicates that they feed most heavily on phytoplankton. Clearly they are being starved to death in too-new or too-

Tree Coral (*Dendronephthya* sp.)

Tree Coral (*Dendronephthya* sp.)

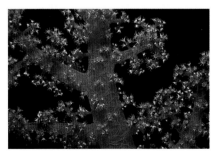
Tree Coral (*Dendronephthya* sp.)

Red gorgonian with white polyps, perhaps *Ellisella* sp.

Deep-water gorgonian (unidentified)

clean reef aquariums.) A breakthrough in satisfying their feeding needs will be required before they can be recommended to anyone other than experienced reef aquarists.

ORDER GORGONACEA (Gorgonians). Most of the gorgonian species of interest are in Family Ellisellidae, the deep-reef gorgonians, such as the typical genus *Ellisella*. These gorgonians are usually red with white polyps and are nonphotosynthetic. They are confined to deep (60 feet or more) water, and are sometimes available for the aquarium.

Wilkens and Birkholz (1986) discussed these gorgonians briefly and reported that their experiences with them in the aquarium ranged from frustrating to easy. All nonphotosynthetic types required top-notch water quality, good currents, and twice-daily feedings to thrive and grow, along with an absence of filamentous algae. There was one notable exception, a *Eugorgia* species that was described as "the hardiest of all imported species for the aquarium." Judging from the picture of this specimen, it is the one commonly known as Red Tree Gorgonian, often imported from the Indo-Pacific. I, too, have found this to be an easy species.

Nonphotosynthetic gorgonians are frequently brightly colored — orange, red, pink, or yellow — often with polyps

of a contrasting color. They do not require light and in fact will not thrive if the light is too bright. They also require cool water, no warmer than about 75 degrees F. Feeding twice daily on a plankton substitute, such as live brine shrimp nauplii and phytoplankton, is essential. (In the ocean, there are usually two plankton "swarms" each day, controlled by the daylight cycle and the ebb and flow of the tides.) Like the soft coral *Dendronephthya*, nonphotosynthetic gorgonians extract a great deal of effort from the aquarist in exchange for the enjoyment of their beautiful colors. Most gorgonians, therefore, are suitable only for the advanced aquarist willing to dedicate the necessary time to their proper care and habitat.

Red Finger Gorgonian (*Mopsella*), which is sparsely branched like a dead tree, red with white polyps, is a hardy species that might be suitable for a first effort at keeping these organisms.

Inspect all gorgonians carefully for damage before purchasing. If the colored tissue is missing entirely in some places, but the polyps are expanded and the other areas of the specimen appear in good shape, the gorgonian is probably in good health. If the colored tissue is missing at the

Yellow-polyped gorgonian (unidentified)

Acalycigorgia sp., a deep-water soft coral off Sulawesi

tips of the branches, prune off the internal skeleton just above the point where the colored tissue stops, using a pair of sterilized scissors. Underwater epoxies, such as Devcon, AquaStik, or SeaRepair can be used to attach gorgonians to rocks for stability or decorative effect.

A rather impressive aquarium could be created using deep-water or cave-dwelling cnidarians alone; however, there are other creatures that are suitable also.

Sponges

MANY SPECIES OF SPONGES that are collected for the aquarium do best in shady locations, as they are easily "swamped" if algae growth (which is stimulated by light) gets started on them. Sponges have a porous body, and it is through the pores that they feed and acquire oxygen. If algae or detritus are allowed to accumulate, clogging the pores, the sponge will suffocate and die. Various species of sponges are imported from both the Indo-Pacific and Caribbean regions, but try to locate the beautiful blue *Adocia*. This sponge is sometimes imported from Indonesia.

There are three basic requirements in the care of

sponges. Make certain that the sponge is never removed from the water. If it is, air may be trapped inside, and the sponge will slowly die from within. Second, never allow detritus or algae to accumulate on the surface of the sponge, as noted above. Third, supply good current. Sponges feed on very small particles and may absorb dissolved organic materials, such as proteins, from the water. No special feeding is necessary if the aquarium already supports sessile invertebrates. The physiology of sponges is poorly understood, but it is known that some species extract certain trace elements from the water. Regular partial water changes should provide sufficient trace elements.

Sponges will do well in the aquarium and may reproduce if these simple requirements are met. Several kinds may grow voluntarily on the decor and glass after the aquarium has been in operation for a while. The ability of some sponges to reproduce vegetatively is legendary: a standard college biology lab demonstration involves chopping up a living sponge in a blender, placing the puree in an appropriate environment, and observing how the sponge reaggregates and regenerates over the next few weeks. According to Stanley Brown of the Breeder's Registry, this technique

Wild palette: sponges and other deep-reef invertebrate life of the Indo-Pacific.

individually or can be found on live rock specimens. All are very easily kept and need no special feeding. *Sabellastarte* may toss off its crown of tentacles in response to poor water quality. If these conditions are promptly corrected, however, the worm will regrow its "feathers" in a few months' time. Interestingly, it is thought that some sabellids also cast off their tentacles in preparation for reproduction. This event may manifest itself as a milky cloud flowing from the opening of the worm's tube. Such a cloud of eggs or sperm will provide food for other filter-feeding invertebrates in the tank and could result in development of additional worm specimens. In my aquariums, *Sabella melanostigma,* or a similar species, reproduces itself readily. I have not determined if this occurs via sexual or vegetative means, but I have seen this worm growing in lovely colonies in many hobbyists' tanks.

can be employed successfully in the aquarium. Only certain species of sponges respond favorably to the procedure, however, and identification of sponges can be extremely difficult. Trial and error with available species is one approach to bringing sponges into cultivation for the aquarium hobbyist market.

Worms

ALL OF THE COMMONLY AVAILABLE TUBEWORMS will thrive without any special lighting and can thus be included in the deep-water tank. Available species include *Sabellastarte sanctijosephi*, which comes from Hawaii, and *Spirobranchus giganteus*, which is found on reefs throughout the world. (See the discussion of the latter species, however, that appears on pages 182-191.) Various other tubeworms, including *Sabella melanostigma, S. elegans, Spirographis, Spirobranchus tetraceros*, and many more, are either imported

Fanworms often form colorful, gregarious clusters.

Echinoderms

NEARLY ALL ECHINODERMS prefer at least a shady spot in which to retreat from time to time. This is especially true of brittle, serpent, basket, and feather stars, which are active mainly at night. Deep-water species of serpent stars are often bright red in color. Brittle stars and serpent stars (Class Ophiuroidea) are not fussy eaters, although serpent stars, in particular, should occasionally be fed a small piece of fish or shrimp. Most of the time, these organisms will feed on stray bits of this and that, which they locate during their nocturnal excursions around the tank.

Feather stars (Class Crinoidea), on the other hand, and the similar but distantly related basket stars (Class Ophiuroidea), are much more fragile. These specimens are not recommended for the aquarium.

With some exceptions, "regular" starfish (Class Asteroidea) are to be avoided in a tank filled with sessile invertebrates, as they have the habit of eating anything and everything. The exceptions, however, are quite desirable, and make attractive additions. These include the Blue Starfish (*Linckia laevigata*) and two species of *Fromia* — the Little Red Starfish (*F. elegans*) and the Orange Marble Starfish (*F. monilis*). Check an appropriate photographic reference to identify these species; a mistaken ID can result in having a starfish that will feed on other specimens in your tank.

Sea urchins (Class Echinoidea) are vegetarians and are sometimes placed in the aquarium for algae control. However, urchins are really out of place in the deep-reef habitat. They generally are found in shallower waters where their food source occurs.

Among the sea cucumbers (Class Holothuroidea), an especially attractive genus is that of the sea apples, *Pseudocolochirus,* of which there are two or three species or color types imported for the aquarium. Sea cucumbers are either burrowers or filter feeders. The latter are best suited to the deep-water aquarium and can be recognized by the fact that their tentacles are feathery and densely branched, not shaped like little goblets or otherwise. Sea apples are conspicuously colored, advertising to potential predators that their flesh is toxic. Their eggs have been called "poisonous candy" for fish by Sprung and Delbeek (1994). Aquarists should be aware of potential problems that these organisms can pose for fish housed in the same aquarium. Otherwise, they are interesting animals and can be long-lived in captivity if adequately fed. Other species of filter-feeding cucumbers appear in shipments from time to time. Some are quite colorful. Occasionally seen is a small, bright yellow species, often called "Little Yellow Cucumber," that reproduces itself in the aquarium. Filter-feeding cu-

Feather Star (Class Crinoidea): not recommended.

Blue Starfish (*Linckia laevigata*): a viable choice.

Sunburst Anthias (*Serranocirrhitus latus*): superb aquarium species, uncommon but well worth the extra effort to find.

cumbers may slowly starve if tank-generated plankton or added plankton substitutes are insufficient. The telltale sign of inadequate feeding is a reduction in the size of the animal. Since food requirements are a function of size, the Little Yellow Cucumber does well, probably because of its comparatively minuscule demand for food.

Burrowing cucumbers feed like earthworms, ingesting the substrate and digesting the edible matter therein. Most are found where rich sediments abound, as in grass beds. They are thus better choices for the shallow-water aquarium than for a deep-reef habitat.

Mollusks

ANYONE SERIOUSLY INTERESTED IN MOLLUSKS in the aquarium should purchase a good seashell identification book and learn to recognize the various species. Accurate identification is of utmost importance with mollusks, since their habits and diets vary widely. I have seen harmless species displayed side by side with predatory types in dealers' tanks. With perhaps 100,000 species of mollusks in the sea, one could spend a lifetime simply observing them under aquarium conditions. Herbivorous grazers, from the trochid and turbinid families, are frequently imported for algae control in the aquarium. These are easily, and now almost universally, included in all types of invertebrate aquarium displays. At the other extreme are species — such as most of the nudibranchs — so rigidly specialized in their feeding habits that they are impossible to maintain in a home aquarium. In between are a host of other mollusk species, including some that would make beautiful, intriguing aquarium subjects for the hobbyist willing to do the background work and provide what the species needs to survive.

Fishes

SOME OF THE MOST POPULAR aquarium fishes are found in deeper waters. The Flame Angel, *Centropyge loriculus*, is an excellent choice for the deep-reef aquarium. It is usually collected off Christmas Island in the Indo-Pacific. The Longnose Hawkfish, *Oxycirrhites typus*, an Indo-pan-Pacific species found at depths ranging from 30 to 300 feet, is confined to depths of about 90 feet in Micronesia. It is another good choice. Many species of cardinalfishes, Family Apogonidae, live in caves during the daytime, emerging at night to feed. Various species of cardinalfishes are seen in aquarium shipments. *Serranocirrhitus latus*, the Sunburst Anthias, is a superb choice for a deep-reef or cave tank. It is usually found in small groups near caves, to depths over 200 feet, and is available to hobbyists sporadically.

A deep-reef slope, wall or cave habitat can be a startling and beautiful departure from the typical shallow-water marine tank. It demands much less in the way of sophisticated lighting, but can require real dedication to specialized feeding schedules and water changes. Advanced aquarists who are ready for the challenge of delving deeper into the unknown may want to consider this biotope. In terms of color and form, denizens of deeper waters are among the most bizarre and fascinating in the reef environment.

Longnose Hawkfish (*Oxycirrhites typus*): commonly available and an appropriate choice for the deep-habitat aquarium.

Chapter Ten

Marine Fishes

Species That Can Make, Break — or Terrorize — a Captive Reef

WITHOUT HERBIVOROUS FISHES, there might not be any coral reefs. Algae can easily outcompete the reef-building corals for light and growing space. This has been demonstrated by fencing off sections of reef and observing how the balance shifts when herbivorous fishes are excluded. These days, one usually finds a healthy complement of fishes sharing reef aquariums with invertebrates. The old school mostly kept fishes out or to a minimum to prevent nitrate build-up; the new view is that corals need some nitrate and tiny bits of food missed by the fish population, that herbivorous fishes are very useful in combating algae, and that almost every tank looks much more "alive" and natural with at least a small population of active fish. Although some aquarists may have eyes only for the corals, to most observers the fishes make the aquarium complete.

It might seem odd to devote a relatively limited portion of a book about coral reef aquariums to the most conspicuous of the reef's residents. Fishes, the traditional emphasis of marine aquarium keeping, present special challenges to the aquarist. Their high levels of activity require

inputs of food to the system, and this ultimately means a higher level of pollutants. Fish also compete with all the other living organisms in the aquarium for available oxygen. Perhaps most importantly, fish exhibit behaviors that can be troublesome, and they can develop personalities that seriously threaten the peace and security of an aquarium microenvironment. Territoriality, aggression, and the need for a special social milieu may all be important factors in determining the degree to which a particular fish species adapts to captive life. I urge all marine aquarists to research the special needs of any fish species of interest before obtaining specimens that may disrupt or even destroy a delicately balanced reef biotope.

Another reason for placing primary emphasis upon invertebrates rather than fishes is that on the coral reef, invertebrates often fulfill the same ecological roles as do plants in a terrestrial habitat. It is the invertebrates, not the fishes, that determine the specific characteristics of a particular reef microhabitat, and invertebrate distribution is largely determined by water depth and topography. Given a particular kind of reefscape, one can expect to find certain fishes there. This, for example, is why juvenile fishes might be found in Turtle Grass beds while their adult counterparts are on the fore reef.

Blackcap Basslet (*Gramma melacara*): a Caribbean species especially suited to wall or deep-water aquascapes.

Considering the great diversity of marine fishes, I have found it helpful to use the family groupings that biologists employ. As a rule of thumb, if a trait is typical of one member of a particular fish family, it is a safe bet that the other members of this family exhibit that same trait. All tangs, Family Acanthuridae, are largely vegetarian in their dietary habits, for example, and are generally benign in a reef tank. The parrotfishes, Family Scaridae, on the other hand, have formidable jaws and teeth — designed to crush coral — and for this and other reasons should be entirely shunned as aquarium subjects. Knowing the family traits of a species new to you is a powerful starting point in assessing its potential for being a good reef aquarium fish.

Exercise Caution

An important subset of fish families are those that will not bother corals, anemones, and other cnidarians, but may feed on mollusks, worms, shrimps, other crustaceans, and/or smaller fishes, if the food item is small enough for the fish to swallow. A member of any of these families is not to be trusted with any active organism that will fit into its mouth. Therefore, although the following families are generally hardy in captivity, exercise caution in choosing specimens from them for your reef microhabitat:

Squirrelfishes and Soldierfishes (Holocentridae)
Groupers and Basses (Serranidae)*
Dottybacks (Pseudochromidae)*
Hawkfishes (Cirrhitidae)*
Cardinalfishes (Apogonidae)*

(*Includes members that may grow too large or that may be too aggressive for a typical mixed-community reef aquarium.)

Many fishes in the following families will feed on invertebrates or upon other fishes, and their incorporation into the aquarium display will make the task of creating a "complete" ecosystem more difficult. Certain ones, notably triggerfishes, may be very aggressive toward tankmates and even tank decorations. Many species in these families also grow rather large:

Lionfishes and Scorpionfishes (Scorpaenidae)
Angelfishes (Pomacanthidae)
Butterflyfishes (Chaetodontidae)
Triggerfishes (Balistidae)

Copperband Butterflyfish (*Chelmon rostratus*): a sometimes finicky eater, but a favorite of many advanced reef keepers.

Pennant Bannerfish (*Heniochus diphreutes*): an ideal schooling butterflyfish for reef aquariums, hardy and mild-mannered.

Masked Butterflyfish (*Chaetodon semilarvatus*): elegant, relatively easy to feed, and an excellent aquarium candidate.

Exquisite Butterflyfish (*Chaetodon austriacus*): beautiful, but an obligate coral eater, likely to die in the home aquarium.

Rabbitfishes (Siganidae)
Puffers (Tetraodontidae)
Wrasses (Labridae)

Scorpionfishes and rabbitfishes all bear venomous spines that can cause a painful, and possibly dangerous, sting if carelessly handled. Several species of scorpionfishes or lionfishes are available commercially. These differ only in size and color patterns, and all require the same care. Feed them every two or three days with frozen or live marine fishes and other seafoods (e.g., lancefish, shrimps). Foods derived from the ocean are of utmost importance in the diet of lionfishes, which will not live out their normal lifespan if fed exclusively on freshwater fish, such as live goldfish. Dwarf lionfish (genus *Dendrochirus*) rarely exceed 6 inches in length and feed mostly on crustaceans and other mobile invertebrates that they hunt at night, preferring to spend the day sleeping, often upside-down under a ledge. Members of the genus *Pterois*, such as the commonly available *P. volitans*, eventually reach a length of 18 inches or more by feeding largely on other fishes. Small *Pterois* specimens grow quickly and can live for ten years or more in captivity. Because of

their venomous nature, careful consideration should be given to inclusion of these species in the home aquarium, despite their hardiness.

Similarly, one must consider the special needs of certain groups of fishes and make sure that these needs can be met. A classic example of a popular group with exacting requirements is the seahorse family. Pipefishes and seahorses (Syngnathidae) must have great care devoted to them in the aquarium, owing to their specialized feeding requirements. Seahorses require live foods, and finding a continuous source of the appropriate food may be difficult. Brine shrimp and amphipods are two possible choices. Some dealers stock live adult brine shrimp, but few have amphipods available. To culture these live foods at home requires considerable space.

Fishes Compatible with Reef Aquariums

TAKING INTO ACCOUNT THE ABOVE WARNINGS, we can now examine the fish species that are best suited to home aquariums. Listed below are the families of fishes

CAPTIVE-PROPAGATED SPECIMENS

MANY OF THE FAMILIES IN THE LIST of "Fishes Compatible With Reef Aquariums" are amenable to captive propagation, and aquarists are urged to seek out such specimens. Captive propagation is finally becoming a growing source for marine aquarium hobbyists (see Chapter Thirteen). Already, several hatcheries and prop-

Caribbean Neon Gobies

agation "farms" produce an abundance of specimens in a variety unheard of just a few years ago. The following captive-propagated species are all available: most species of clownfish, Neon Goby, Lime-striped Goby, Citron Goby, Seaweed Goby, Neon Dottyback, Orchid Dottyback, Purple Dottyback, Royal Dottyback, Diadema Dottyback, seven species of giant clams, disc anemones, sea mats, many soft corals, stony corals, Peppermint Shrimp, and dozens of macroalgae.

Entrepreneurs are working on other species, with jawfish, gobies, basslets, dottybacks, blennies, dragonets, dwarf angelfishes, and all types of corals receiving serious attention.

The list of potentially suitable species for small-scale aquaculture projects is even longer, and includes additional fish families, as well as shrimps, mollusks, and possibly even large anemones. The future for captive-propagated specimens for the aquarium trade looks very bright, indeed.

encompassing the majority of recommended species. Groups marked with an asterisk (*) have members with specific needs that must be met in captivity, and so should be limited to aquarists who have acquired some experience. In addition, some of the individual species within the marked families may have special needs that cannot be met in captivity and therefore may not be suitable for the aquarium.

Fairy Basslets (Grammidae)
Sea Basses (Serranidae)*
Anthias (Anthiidae)*
Dottybacks (Pseudochromidae)
Hawkfishes (Cirrhitidae)*
Cardinalfishes (Apogonidae)*
Tangs (Acanthuridae)*
Dwarf Angels (Pomacanthidae)
Wrasses (Labridae)
Clownfishes and Damselfishes (Pomacentridae)
Dragonets (Callionymidae)*
Blennies (Blenniidae)*
Jawfishes (Opistognathidae)*
Gobies (Gobiidae and Microdesmidae)*

FAIRY BASSLETS.
Examples of aquarium-compatible fairy basslets include: Royal Gramma (*Gramma loreto*) and the Blackcap Basslet (*G. melacara*), both from the Atlantic-Caribbean region. Captive propagation should be possible for either of these nest-building fishes, but efforts to date have not succeeded in rearing the larvae past metamorphosis.

Royal Gramma (*Gramma loreto*): a dazzling, hardy, highly desirable reef species for beginners' tanks and a variety of Caribbean biotopes.

SEA BASSES. The Swissguard Basslet (*Liopropoma rubre*), is but one of many small serranids suitable for the aquarium. Ranging from south Florida and the Bahamas to the Yucatán, this species is found at depths ranging from 10 to 150 feet. It prefers a cool, dimly illuminated aquarium with suitable hiding places among the live rock. It feeds on small, meaty foods and is hardy in captivity. The related Candy Basslet (*L. carmabi*) is less frequently seen, primarily because it is found at greater depths, ranging from 45 to 200 feet, in the waters from the Florida Keys to Bonaire. It reaches only 2 inches in length. Both species are solitary and are simultaneous hermaphrodites, and although captive propagation has not been reported, the potential is high (Hunziker, 1995). The larger basses, including the groupers, may be trusted with sessile invertebrates, but because of their size, waste production, and appetite for smaller fishes and shrimps, they are generally not recommended for most typical reef aquariums.

ANTHIAS. The Anthiidae, or anthias family, contains many beautiful species, and with special care, some of the more commonplace ones can be maintained in a coral reef aquarium. There are also, however, many anthias that are impossible to acclimate to captivity. The best course of action for the beginning aquarist is to avoid this group altogether.

Experienced hobbyists wishing to try anthias should start with one of the better known species, such as *Pseudanthias squamipinnis*. This species has many common names, but we will use Lyretail Anthias. Feeding on zooplankton in the warm waters from East Africa to the Great Barrier Reef, the Lyretail Anthias can reach 6 inches in length. It lives in schools of ten to many hundreds of individuals. Each school

Lyretail Anthias (*Pseudanthias squamipinnis*): a gorgeous Indo-Pacific species that does best in shoals in larger aquariums with frequent feedings.

has its own rigid social hierarchy. Swimming at the highest point in the school is the brightly colored, territorial, alpha male. Below him is a group of large females about to undergo their sex change into males. All anthias hatch as females and develop into males as they mature. This pattern of development, called protogynous hermaphroditism, is found in many reef fishes, notably many small serranids, to which anthias are closely related. The remaining 90% of the anthias school consists of actively reproducing females and juveniles.

When fish approach the time of their sex change, they attempt to create territories for themselves so as to attract females for breeding. The alpha male may prevent them from doing so, and these so-called "bachelor" males form a group of hangers-on, down at the lowest position in the school. If the alpha male should meet an unfortunate fate,

Purple Dottyback
(*Pseudochromis porphyreus*)

Orchid Dottyback
(*Pseudochromis fridmani*)

Diadema Dottyback
(*Pseudochromis diadema*)

Neon Dottyback
(*Pseudochromis aldabraensis*)

Bicolor Dottyback
(*Pseudochromis paccagnellae*)

Sunrise Dottyback
(*Pseudochromis flavivertex*)

one of the bachelors will move to the "head of the class" within a few days. The primary drawback to successful aquarium husbandry of these fish is the space requirements dictated by their social pattern. Kept in schools in a suitably large tank, however, they are spectacular creatures. Esterbauer (1995) recommends stocking the tank with a group of ten or more 2-inch specimens, as these will be juvenile females and the school can develop its own social hierarchy naturally, as the females mature. As the school develops, new members, always smaller individuals, can be added.

Solitary anthias often refuse to eat and will soon starve. Feed them small living foods and gradually wean them to frozen substitutes. A smaller species, *Pseudanthias hawaiiensis*, lives in deep water and makes a superb aquarium fish, with the best specimens coming from Hawaiian collectors.

DOTTYBACKS. Among the Pseudochromidae, or dottybacks, the Purple Dottyback (*Pseudochromis porphyreus*), Diadema Dottyback (*P. diadema*), and Bicolor Dottyback (*P. paccagnellae*) are readily available and inexpensive aquarium inhabitants. These three species come from the Indo-Pacific. Several other beautiful dotty-

Coral Hawkfish (*Cirrhitichthys oxycephalus*): caution advised.

backs come from the Red Sea and the Persian Gulf. From the former location, the Sunrise Dottyback, (*P. flavivertex*) and the Orchid Dottyback (*P. fridmani*) are the most attractive. The Neon Dottyback (*P. aldabraensis,* often misidentified as *P. dutoiti*) comes from the Persian Gulf and is extraordinarily beautiful, with bright orange coloration highlighted by stripes of intense blue.

All of these dottybacks are in commercial production in Puerto Rico. Two males will not get along, but a mated pair, or a male and several females, may share the same aquarium if it is large and provided with ample live rock as shelter. The Orchid Dottyback is an especially good choice for grouping and breeding, as it is both beautiful and less fiesty than most other common dottyback species and will spawn under good aquarium conditions. Many other fairy basslets, anthias, serranids, and pseudochromids will likely prove amenable to captive propagation, both by hobbyists and commercial breeders.

HAWKFISHES. Several of the hawkfishes are suited for the reef aquarium, although they have a reputation for preying on ornamental shrimp and herbivorous hermit crabs. Two popular and generally well-behaved species are the Longnose Hawkfish (*Oxycirrhites typus*) and the Flame Hawkfish (*Neocirrhites armatus*). The former is colored in a red and white checkerboard pattern and is often found associated with gorgonians and sea fans; the latter is bright red with a black stripe on the dorsal fin and a black ring around the eye and is often observed perched on a coral head. Neither of these fishes will do damage to corals. Mixing larger specimens of either species with smaller shrimp could be a recipe for trouble, however. Both are found on the outer reef.

CARDINALFISHES. Specimens of some of the many species of cardinalfishes are available from time to time. Among the most desirable is *Sphaeramia nematoptera*, usually called the Pajama Cardinal. It lives in shallow lagoons

and is often imported from the Philippines. The so-called Banggai Cardinal, *Pterapogon kauderni*, recently rediscovered by Dr. Gerald Allen and now available commercially for the first time, is a strikingly beautiful silver and black species that makes an ideal reef-tank fish. Many cardinalfishes are nocturnal planktivores and should have a shady ledge under which to spend the day. Both the Pajama and Banggai Cardinal often break this general rule in the aquarium, spending their days in open water. Keeping them in groups is most rewarding. They may, like the hawkfishes, feed on small shrimps, so caution is advised. All species are mouthbrooders, making captive propagation a likely prospect, since the young develop to a large size before being spit out by the adult. This family has received insufficient attention from aquarists.

Yellow Tang (*Zebrasoma flavescens*): the quintessential reef fish, grazing on algae and peaceful with all but other tangs.

TANGS. The Yellow Tang, *Zebrasoma flavescens*, is one of the ten most popular marine aquarium species and is a good representative of the acanthurids, or tangs. This species is

Regal Tang (*Paracanthurus hepatus*): an electric blue, easy-going herbivore, too often the victim of cyanide collectors.

Powder Blue Tang (*Acanthurus leucosternon*): strikingly beautiful, but best reserved for more advanced aquarists.

found in Hawaii, Micronesia, and Japan, but most aquarium specimens come from the Hawaiian Islands. Bright color, hardiness, and low cost make this species a mainstay.

The Yellow Tang is lemon yellow in color, becoming paler with a distinctive mid-lateral white stripe at night. Members of the *Zebrasoma* genus live singly or in loose aggregations that are active by day, foraging along the reef crest for algae, which forms the bulk of their diet, with a small percentage of invertebrate organisms consumed incidentally. Providing appropriate plant foods in the aquarium is a simple matter. Some marine tanks, especially fish-only systems, grow abundant filamentous algae, often sufficient to meet the requirements of an adult Yellow Tang. Natural algae growth can be supplemented by a variety of frozen foods with seaweeds as their primary component, and both flake foods and fresh greens, such as romaine lettuce, will also be accepted. Ocean-derived foods are best, however.

The Yellow Tang has developed an undeserved reputation for susceptibility to infestations by *Cryptocaryon* and *Amyloodinium* parasites. Most likely, this is due to a lack of understanding of this species' basic needs. Stress that can re-

sult from improper conditions typically results in an outbreak of parasites. Apart from water conditions appropriate to any tropical marine aquarium, the Yellow Tang should be given plenty of swimming space, tankmates of its own species, and adequate nourishment. An aquarium smaller than 4 feet in length is probably too confining for any tang species. Keeping five specimens together in a 6-foot-long aquarium would be an appropriate display. Yellow Tangs can be aggressive toward one another if not kept in a group. A lone individual may harass other species housed in the same tank. Similarly, if a pair is housed together, one may constantly pick on the other. These tangs often exhibit stubborn territorial instincts, and weaker or smaller specimens can easily be chased, abused, and driven to starvation. In my experience, keeping groups of five or more individuals together usually dissipates the sparring satisfactorily. It may help to start by purchasing younger fish of equal size.

As mentioned earlier, many tangs are vegetarian grazers. Their food is relatively low in nutrients, and the fish expends a lot of energy just moving around from place to place in search of it. This is why it is important to give the Yellow

Tang ample algal fare and, ideally, to provide the fish with access to food all day long. Smaller individuals, especially, can suffer the effects of malnutrition in a surprisingly short time. It is wise to choose specimens that are at least 3 inches in diameter.

When provided with appropriate conditions, the Yellow Tang is rarely bothered by parasite infestations. If symptoms are detected, however, it is important to administer treatment promptly, as these fish may be rapidly killed by oxygen starvation if the gills are infested. Treatment with copper sulfate is effective outside the reef system. Another pest is common only on tangs. This is Black Spot, an infestation of dark-colored flatworms that burrow into the fish's skin. The condition is especially obvious against the bright background of the Yellow Tang's body and makes the infested individual look as if it has been sprinkled with pepper. Bathing the fish in a parasiticide is an effective remedy. Consult references for the appropriate procedure.

Public aquarium records indicate that tangs can live five to seven years. Given attention to their simple requirements, there is no reason why home hobbyists should not be able to maintain the Yellow Tang for a similar period.

Yellow Tangs sometimes spawn in huge aggregations that gather periodically at precise locations around their home reef. Thus, it may be unlikely that captive spawning of this species can be achieved. Fortunately, this colorful and hardy fish is abundant. Barring the imposition of collecting restrictions in Hawaii, the Yellow Tang should remain popular for many years to come.

The Regal Tang, *Paracanthurus hepatus*, is a distinctive true-blue color with a yellow tail. A sickle-shaped black bar on the side completes the dramatic appearance of this handsome fish. It is found almost exclusively in association with the stony coral *Pocillopora eydouxi* on the seaward side of the reef. When disturbed, the fish has a habit of wedging itself into the coral, lying flat on its side. Its propensity

The Flame Angel (*Centropyge loriculus*): highly desirable, but a potential nibbler on corals and *Tridacna* clam mantles.

Potter's Angel (*Centropyge potteri*): strikingly hued and best-suited to established reefs with ample quantities of live rock.

to do this in the aquarium has given pause to more than one novice aquarist. Unfortunately, too many of these fish

Long-finned Fairy Wrasse (*Cirrhilabrus rubriventralis*): show-stoppingly beautiful and one of many reef-compatible wrasses.

delicate invertebrates. However, the dwarf angels in the genus *Centropyge* offer possibilities. Good choices are the Pygmy Angel (*Centropyge argi*), the only Florida-Caribbean species; the eastern Atlantic species Resplendent Angel (*C. resplendens*); the Flameback Angel (*C. acanthops*); and several Pacific species, typified by Potter's Angel (*C. potteri*) and the Flame Angel (*C. loriculus*), both from Hawaii. Potter's Angel is a Hawaiian endemic, meaning it is found nowhere else. All of these angels do best in well-established reef aquariums with ample grazing opportunities on live rock. Be forewarned: some individuals can become nuisances, nibbling at the mantles of *Tridacna* clams or generally worrying certain corals to the point that they refuse to open fully.

have been collected in the wild by poisoning an entire coral head. As a result, this fish is a good candidate for having been exposed to cyanide, so know your dealer before you purchase. The Powder Blue Tang, *Acanthurus leucosternon*, is another species often collected with cyanide. Because it commands a high price, good judgment is required when choosing a specimen.

Combtoothed tangs, in the genus *Ctenochaetus*, are sought after by aquarists because they feed on detritus and unicellular algae. The Chevron Tang, *C. hawaiiensis*, and the Kole or Goldeye Tang, *C. strigosus*, are widespread in the Indo-Pacific. High-quality specimens come from Hawaii.

ANGELFISHES. Some angelfishes (Pomacanthidae) are almost exclusively vegetarian and can be kept with the majority of invertebrates. Most others are omnivorous and cannot be trusted not to sample a bit of almost anything they encounter. In my view, none of the larger angelfish species should be attempted by the beginner; most are at least somewhat challenging to keep and all can make shreds of

WRASSES. Among the wrasses (Labridae), the majority of species are carnivores that feed on invertebrates such as crustaceans, echinoderms, worms, and mollusks.

Blue Devil Damsel (*Chrysiptera cyanea*): colorful but scrappy.

As is the case with the larger angelfishes, sizable wrasses are not to be trusted in the reef tank. Smaller wrasses, however, may not pose a threat, and many are ideally suited to the reef aquarium. Some widely available "safe" wrasses include: two closely related species called the Six-Line

Blue-Green Chromis (*Chromis viridis*): iridescent and meek.

Wrasse (*Pseudocheilinus hexataenia*), and the Hawaiian Neon or Four-Line Wrasse (*P. tetrataenia*); several smaller species from the genus *Halichoeres*, such as the hardy Yellow or Golden Coris Wrasse (*H. chrysus*); and the fairy wrasses (genus *Cirrhilabrus*). Fairy wrasses (sometimes called social wrasses) should be kept in groups consisting of a single male and several females.

CLOWNFISHES AND DAMSELFISHES. Clownfishes and damselfishes (Pomacentridae) are often the first fishes kept by a beginner. They are hardy and beautiful and will accept a variety of foods. There is so much interest in clownfishes that I have devoted an entire section to them (see pages 204-214). Damselfishes that do not associate with anemones occur in many reef habitats.

Pomacentrids are generally territorial species. To minimize disputes, keep only one kind of damselfish per tank. For some, such as the "humbug" damsels in the genus *Dascyllus*, if you keep several individuals of the same species together, each fish must be provided with its own cave or coral head. This spot will be vigorously defended by the resident damselfish, even unto death.

Perhaps the most popular of the damselfishes is the Blue Devil (*Chrysiptera cyanea*). This fish can be kept in groups, if one pays attention to sex ratios. On the reef, its natural grouping is a single male and several females and juveniles. Overall body color of both sexes is a stunning electric blue. Females and juveniles have a black spot on the posterior base of the dorsal fin and colorless tail fins. Males lack the black spot and have bright orange-yellow tails. This is one of the few damselfish species that display obvious external sexual differences. In the Philippines and Japan, the male Blue Devil lacks both the black spot and the orange tail.

Chromis are damselfishes that form shoals in open water over reefs, where they feed on plankton. An excellent choice is the Blue-Green Chromis (*C. viridis*), a native of Indo-Pacific waters.

The Mandarinfish (*Synchiropus splendidus*): exquisite colors but a species that does best in a well-established aquarium.

Spotted or Psychedelic Mandarin (*Synchiropus picturatus*): never stock more than one male mandarin per aquarium.

Red-lipped Blenny (*Ophioblennius atlanticus*)

Canary Blenny (*Meiacanthus ovaluensis*)

Saber-toothed Cleaner Mimic (*Plagiotremus rhinorhynchos*)

DRAGONETS. Only two attractive dragonets are commonly imported for the aquarium. Both are bottom-dwelling fishes, with docile habits and exquisite coloration. The Mandarinfish (*Synchiropus splendidus*) and the Spotted Mandarin (*Synchiropus picturatus*) are ideal specimens for the reef tank. In all dragonets, the male can be distinguished from the female by the greatly elongated first spine of the dorsal fin, and his larger size. One can keep mandarins of the same species together as trios consisting of one male and two females, and one can keep the two mandarin species together, but one should *never* put two male mandarins of the same species together in the tank. They will fight until one is killed. Mandarins are seldom bothered by other fishes, perhaps because they are poisonous if eaten. Its gaudy coloration lends credence to this supposition. Mandarins feed on copepods and do best in a well-established aquarium. They often starve in new reef tanks and are not for beginners.

BLENNIES. Combtoothed blennies, typified by the Red-lipped Blenny (*Ophioblennius atlanticus*) from Florida, and the Bicolor Blenny (*Ecsenius bicolor*) from Indonesia and Australia, feed largely on microalgae. Either species will even eat "red slime" algae, which many other fishes dislike. The Bicolor Blenny is usually dark brown with an orange abdomen and tail, and the Red-lipped Blenny is brown, with distinctive bright red lips. "Eyelash" blennies (genus *Cirripectes*) also help rid the aquarium of microalgae. They can be recognized by their cirri, which resemble eyelashes.

The saber-toothed blennies do not feed upon algae, but rather upon small bottom-dwelling crustaceans. They swim actively, largely free from fear of predators, because they all have poisonous fangs. Any fish foolish enough to grab one of these blennies will have the inside of its mouth bitten painfully and repeatedly, and will usually spit out the feisty "meal." This trait is used only in defense, however, and the blenny will not bite other fish unless harassed. Saber-toothed blennies of the genus *Meiacanthus* are also called lyretail blennies, because of the shape of their tail. The two saber-toothed blennies most often available to aquarists were once considered subspecies of the same species, *M. atrodorsalis*, but are now viewed as distinct. The Canary Blenny, *M. ovaluensis* is bright yellow and is found only around the Fiji Islands. The more wide-ranging *M. atrodorsalis* is baby blue with a pale green tail and has a black line running through the middle of the dorsal fin and continuing through the center of the eye. It is given a variety of common names in the aquarium trade, including the especially confusing name Eyelash Blenny. Probably because of their poisonous fangs, the color patterns of many of the saber-toothed blennies are mimicked by other fishes, which thereby gain protection from predators.

Another case of mimicry in blennies is well-known and involves two undesirable members of the saber-toothed blenny clan. *Plagiotremus rhinorhynchos* and *Aspidontus taeniatus* both mimic not only the coloration but also the movements of the cleaner wrasse, *Labroides dimidiatus*. When an unsuspecting fish approaches one of these masqueraders expecting to be cleaned of parasites, the blenny instead takes a bite from its unfortunate victim. Ironically, *A. taeniatus* has actually been observed receiving the services of the same cleaner wrasse that it mimics. Some observers also report them feeding heavily on tubeworms and fish eggs.

JAWFISHES. Jawfishes are thought to be related to the basslets, but their classification is still being debated. They are excellent aquarium fishes, although inclined to be jumpers. There are jawfishes that grow much too large to be included in a tank with invertebrates such as shrimps, but these are rarely available, owing to their drab coloration or large size or both. New species are being discovered all the time, but they are rarely imported. All require a deep layer of substrate composed of particles ranging in size from grains of sand to small pebbles in which to dig their characteristic

Purple Firefish (*Nemateleotris decora*): a shy but elegant fire goby and ideal choice for the quiet Indo-Pacific reef.

Common Firefish (*Nemateleotris magnifica*): best kept singly or in mated pairs, without overly aggressive tankmates.

Golden-headed Sleeper Gobies (*Valenciennea strigata*): live in pairs and can be a challenge to keep well-fed.

The Signal Goby (*Signigobius biocellatus*): a fish that appears to mimic a crab and that will perish if separated from its mate.

burrows. Further, they cannot be kept with large anemones or other stinging cnidarians, because these will eventually catch and eat the jawfish. So why keep them at all? Simple: there is nothing as charming as a group of jawfishes, each hovering just above its vertical burrow, with large, expressive eyes alert to every movement. Each fish builds itself a pile of shells and gravel at the entrance to the burrow, and each spends quite a bit of time raiding the pile of its neighbor.

There are two species of jawfish collected for the aquarium. One of these, the Blue-spotted Jawfish (*Opistognathus rosenblatti*), endemic to the Sea of Cortez, is infrequently seen and should not be kept in groups. Far more readily available is the Yellow-headed Jawfish (*O. aurifrons*) from Florida and the Caribbean. Yellow-headed Jawfish can be kept singly or in groups (a group is more fun to watch) in any size aquarium that will accommodate the number of fishes desired. They will excavate vertical burrows in the substrate, about twice as deep as the fish is long. They feed on planktonic organisms snatched from the water column and accept a variety of fresh and/or frozen foods, such as adult brine shrimp, mysis shrimp, bloodworms, and blackworms. Jawfishes are mouthbrooders, with the male carry-

ing the eggs until they hatch, and they have spawned and been reared successfully in captivity.

GOBIES AND DARTFISHES. The goby group contains the greatest number of species in tropical seas. Virtually all gobies are peaceful, small fishes that feed on small benthic or planktonic invertebrates. Rather than attempt to describe all the gobies that one might find in aquarium shops, I will mention one or two representatives of each of the groups into which the goby clan is divided. Ichthyologists have grouped gobies into two families, but for aquarium purposes, I will consider five artificial groupings.

Family Microdesmidae, the dartfishes, includes two aquarium groups — fire gobies and torpedo gobies. Certainly the most familiar of these are the fire gobies. The Common Firefish (*Nemateleotris magnifica*) is found in several locations in the Indo-Pacific region. It has a cream-colored body, with a brilliant flame red tail, and hovers in midwater with its elongated dorsal fin held erect. Among the torpedo gobies, the Blue Gudgeon (*Ptereleotris heteroptera*) is typical. It is an elongated species, shaped like a torpedo, and is solid baby blue with a single black splotch in the fork of the tail. This species will spend more time out in the open if kept in a group. Singles often hide. They do not squabble among themselves, as is sometimes the case with the firefish. The Blue Gudgeon is a good jumper; cover the aquarium carefully.

Among the Gobiidae, or true gobies, we find, for aquarium purposes, three subgroups: a huge general grouping of goby species, the signal gobies, and the fascinating prawn gobies.

The Neon Goby (*Gobiosoma oceanops*) was among the first marine fishes to be spawned in captivity. Today, thousands of them are hatchery-produced. Just over an inch in length, black in color with brilliant blue and white horizontal stripes, the Neon Goby is at home even in a small tank. Pairs can be obtained by keeping a group of juveniles together and allowing them to pair off as they grow. This species is a cleaner. Related species, the Lime-striped Goby (*G. multifasciatum*) and the Red-headed Goby (*G. puncticulatus*) are also available as captive-propagated specimens.

Much larger than the Neon Goby, the 6-inch Golden-headed Sleeper Goby (*Valenciennea strigata*) lives in pairs in a cave that is constructed by the fish under a rock or other structure. Older specimens (both males and females) develop long filaments extending upward from the anterior end of the dorsal fin. These gobies (as well as several other *Valenciennea* species that are imported from time to time) constantly dig in the sand, "chewing" the grains to obtain small crustaceans and worms upon which

Rainford's Goby (*Amblygobius rainfordi*): an endearing sand-sifter and just one of a huge array of fascinating gobies.

Yellow Watchman Goby
(*Cryptocentrus cinctus*)

they feed. Interestingly, these gobies are known to communicate with each other via signals produced by the mouth. Since ichthyologists have reclassified this group, *Valenciennea* is no longer technically a "sleeper" goby (Family Eleotridae). Perhaps a suitable new common name would be Golden-headed Talking Goby, in honor of their communication capabilities.

Signal Gobies, which are closely related to *Valenciennea*, may also signal to each other with their mouths, but that is not where the common name comes from. The huge eyespots on the dorsal fins inspired the name Signal Goby for the single species *Signigobius biocellatus*. This goby apparently mimics, of all things, a crab. When threatened, the goby extends its dorsal fins to display its eyespots, which, together with the dark blue pectoral and pelvic fins, are intended to give the impression of a large, aggressive crab. The goby even mimics the sideways movement of a crab. On the reef, *Signigobius* is usually found in mated pairs and should only be kept as such in the aquarium. Deprived of its mate, a solitary individual will soon die. These gobies sort the substrate to obtain food, but will also take food from midwater. They are sometimes imported from Australia, but are never common. Both the Golden-headed Sleeper and the Signal Goby ought to be regarded as species requiring experienced care, as many tend to starve to death in smaller systems without sufficient fare to forage out of the substrate.

The remaining group of gobies demonstrates one of the most remarkable adaptations to be found in the sea. These are the prawn gobies, of which there are several species. I will describe only one, the Yellow Watchman Goby (*Cryptocentrus cinctus*), which is yellow in color with blue dots all over the body. Watchman gobies all have large eyes that are located high on the head. The coloration and appearance of this goby is enough to make it attractive to the aquarist, but the relationship that these gobies have with certain species of prawns (actually alpheid shrimps) is truly amazing.

Prawn gobies live in areas of loose rubble, sand, and gravel, but are unable to dig a burrow into which they can escape from predators. That duty is carried out by the prawn, which has specially modified claws for digging. A prawn and a pair of gobies may share the same burrow, or a single goby may occupy the burrow, but the prawn is always present. The goby feeds on small organisms exposed by the excavations of the prawn. So what does the hard-working prawn get from the association? A pair of eyes. The prawn is nearly blind and thus cannot see the approach of a predator. When the goby swims out of the burrow, hovering just above or in front of it, the prawn trails behind, always keeping one of its antennae in contact with its roommate. If danger threatens, the goby flicks its tail to warn the prawn, and both dart back to the safety of the burrow. The association must be of great benefit to both, since over 25 species of prawn gobies and at least 8 species of associated prawns are known. Always be sure the association is established in the dealer's aquarium before purchasing these species. Some of the associations are specific; not just any

Prawn gobies (*Cryptocentrus cinctus*) with their prawn: the nearly blind alpheid shrimp excavates food and a burrow for all three, while the fish watch for approaching predators.

prawn and goby pair will take up with each other. Some observers report these gobies thriving without their shrimp, but I recommend that aquarists not buy the goby without the prawn. Unable to dig and faced with the lack of a burrow, the goby may refuse to eat and thus slowly starve in the aquarium.

NO FEAR TAXONOMY

DROP BY A GARDEN CENTER and you will hear terms like *Chrysanthemum, Rhododendron,* and *Philodendron* used by all types of gardeners without hesitation. Visit a marine aquarium shop and you will quickly appreciate that many people seem to find scientific names for fishes and invertebrates daunting. Frankly, I find this a bit baffling. Why are the proper names for plants easy for the average person to use but not the scientific names for aquarium fishes and invertebrates?

Possibly, nonscientists are afraid of appearing foolish through mispronunciation, although one should remember that even professionals may pronounce the same name slightly differently. Even if you start out

***Goniopora lobata* is commonly called both Flowerpot Coral and Sunflower Coral.**

mangling a few names, most seasoned marine hobbyists and scientists will know what you mean and will uniformly thank you for at least trying to use the legitimate name rather than some of the fanciful and localized common labels that emerge from the pet trade.

Taxonomy, the science of naming and classifying living organisms, often receives a bad rap because people see it as an endless preoccupation with trivial details and confusing hierarchical classifications. In fact, taxonomy is the foundation for all other biological science. Not only does the cataloging of organisms reveal the diversity of the living world, but also it opens the way for all of us to talk intelligently about our observations. A molecular geneticist in New York can compare observations about a species of clam with a marine ecologist in Palau with the assurance that the object of their observations is the same organism.

Recognizing species is an important, indeed the primary, function of taxonomy. Species are populations of actually or potentially interbreeding organisms that do not share genetic material with other, similar populations. All perceptive hobbyists are constantly expanding their memory bank of species, learning to recognize and pin a name on an ever-increasing profusion of fishes and invertebrates. Most of us start out using the common names, but the dedicated aquarist will eventually come to recognize and rely on the utility and beauty of scientific names and taxonomic relationships.

When aquarists become more fluent in the use of the correct scientific names of the organisms they work with, we will all be better off. Why? Because scientific names make our communications about these organisms more precise. The species that I refer to as Flowerpot Coral may be called Sunflower Coral by someone else, but the scientific name, *Goniopora lobata,* is unambiguous. This is the beauty of taxonomy; every organism that has been formally described by a biologist has but one scientific name, and this name is used throughout the world to refer to that particular organism. So whether one is in Bangkok or Boise, *Goniopora lobata* refers to the same animal. Conversely, "Flowerpot Coral" could mean something entirely different to two individuals, depending upon local usage.

As aquarists gain more experience with maintaining marine fish and invertebrates and share their observations with each other, the importance of having a precise understanding about just which organism is being discussed can hardly be overestimated. Many times a species that is easy to keep has a relative that is similar in appearance but is challenging or impossible to maintain. The large family of butterflyfishes is a perfect example; knowing and being able to use the correct scientific name can be a powerful aid in avoiding those species within a given family that are doomed in most aquariums.

***Forcipiger flavissimus*, commonly known as the Long-nosed Butterflyfish.**

Each scientific name consists of two parts. The first part identifies the genus (plural, genera), or group, to which the organism belongs. Thus, *Forcipiger flavissimus* and *Forcipiger longirostris* are two species of butterflyfishes within the same genus. The second part of the name identifies the species. *F. longirostris* is thus "the long-snouted forceps-carrier." (Indeed, the snout of this butterflyfish is much longer than that of the Long-nosed Butterflyfish, *F. flavissimus.*) Taken together, the two parts

of the scientific name identify a specific organism.

Several rules apply to the use of scientific names:

1) The genus name can stand alone to represent all members of the genus, e.g., *Forcipiger*. However, the species name can never stand alone. For example, *flavissimus*, by itself, is meaningless unless both parties to the conversation or communication know the context.

2) The genus and species names are always italicized. The genus is capitalized and the species name is always begun with a lower-case letter.

3) When a list of species within a single genus is being presented, the generic name is spelled out the first time it is used. Thereafter, it may be abbreviated, as in "*Forcipiger flavissimus* and *F. longirostris* both occur in the Indo-Pacific."

4) Biologists group genera to form families. Family groupings are often convenient for the aquarist, since members of a given family share similar traits. Family names are capitalized, but not italicized, and always end in "idae." The family name is taken from the generic name of the most common or best known member of the family. Thus, the butterflyfish family is Chaetodontidae, from *Chaetodon*, the genus to which most butterflyfishes are assigned. *Forcipiger* also belongs to this family, along with *Chelmon, Chelmonops, Coradion, Heniochus, Hemitaurichthys*, and all other genera of butterflyfishes.

Apart from the elimination of confusion, scientific names can, if understood, supply valuable information about the organisms to which they refer. The Long-nosed Butterflyfish's name, *Forcipiger flavissimus*, means "the most-yellow forceps-carrier."

Several conventional methods are used by biologists to create scientific names. Knowledge of these may help the aquarist in understanding something about the organism and may make pronunciation easier. Often, an organism is named in honor of a person. The species name ends in "i" if the honoree was male, or "ae" if the honoree was female. *Periclimenes pedersoni*, thus, is the name for Pederson's Cleaning Shrimp. The "i" always carries the long vowel sound, i.e., "PEE-der-sun-eye," and the "ae" ending is always pronounced as a long "e," as in *Allomicrodesmis dorotheae* ("Dorothea's fish that is similar to *Microdesmis*"), where the species name is pronounced "door-o-THEE-ee." The place where the species was discovered may be used in the name, and this is usually indicated by the ending "ensis." The species *Pomachromis guamensis,* therefore, is found around Guam, and is pronounced "GUAM-en-sis."

Beyond clear communication, a further goal of taxonomy is to bring a sense of order to the seemingly chaotic profusion of organisms that have evolved on our planet. Even the process of naming species is a process of describing relationships, as species are grouped into genera, genera into families, and families into larger and larger groups, called taxa, according to these steps:

Species
  Genus
    Family
      Order
        Class
          Phylum
            Kingdom

Forcipiger longirostris, **commonly known as the Black Long-nosed Butterflyfish.**

With each successive step, the taxon becomes more encompassing. When a particular line of development is especially rich in diversity, intermediate taxa — such as subclass, superorder, or tribe — are included. Plotting the pattern of relationships for an organism creates a "phylogenetic tree" — the story of the descent of that particular organism, or rather its genes, through time.

For the beginning marine aquarist, taxonomic names and relationships can seem bewildering and intimidating. In time, you will come to appreciate how all of this can make you a better aquarist and enrich your enjoyment of this hobby. "To the dull mind," Ralph Waldo Emerson once wrote, "nature is leaden. To the illumined mind, the whole world burns and sparkles with light." For those of us who spend our lives working with and contemplating the world of the coral reef, taxonomy is part of what enlightens us and helps us see this sparkling world with greater clarity and deeper appreciation.

Chapter Eleven

Disease in the Reef Aquarium

Prevention, Acclimation, and the Simple Realities
of Keeping a System Healthy

MARINE FISH have amazingly tough constitutions. I have seen them survive wounds of the sort seen in B-grade horror movies: an eye torn from the head, body parts shredded to ribbons, appendages mangled to mere stumps. Fish jump and crash into the glass canopy above them with surprising force. Imagine running at full speed into a plate-glass door. I've found fish lying on the floor, covered in lint, nearly crisp from desiccation, only to have them recover completely after being returned to the aquarium. So why do marine fish have a reputation for extreme delicacy and susceptibility to disease? Probably because too many aquarists fail to anticipate problems and are then unprepared when they arise. Despite the frustration that often results from attempts to cope with disease outbreaks in marine aquarium fish, more than 90% of the deaths could probably be avoided.

The basic rules for disease prevention and control are simple:

1. All new fish must be placed in a separate isolation tank for a minimum of two weeks prior to introducing them into an established display aquarium. Period. No exceptions.

Health care on the reef: cleaner shrimp and gobies groom a Nassau Grouper, seeking parasites and dead flecks of skin.

2. If disease becomes evident in an established reef aquarium, there is no known way to treat the problem successfully without removing the fish to a separate tank.

3. Only one medication is widely effective, widely available and easy to use: copper. For best results, however, it must be administered in a separate tank.

Note the repeated admonition of "separate tank." Without this essential tool, you must choose between having a reef system with no fish or with the virtual certainty of losing the entire tank of fish at some point. No sense hiding this unpleasant truth. Now for the good news: there is only one disease syndrome that you need to worry about (with a couple of exceptions). I use the term "syndrome," because two very similar parasite infestations account for the vast majority of sick marine aquarium fishes: *Cryptocaryon irritans* (white spot, marine ich) and *Amyloodinium ocellatum* (oodinium, marine velvet, coral reef disease). Both produce the same symptoms, and both respond to the same treatment regime.

Whether or not the dealer carries out his or her own quarantine procedures, it is still best to place newly acquired fishes in their own tank, apart from the main display tank, for at least two weeks. There, one can observe them for signs of disease and treat them appropriately. Treatments cannot

labored breathing as with *Amyloodinium*, and, in particular, produce such copious external mucus that they appear to be sloughing off layers of skin. Commercial preparations containing formalin and malachite green are an effective treatment, but copper is not. Clownfishes should be treated immediately upon discovery of the problem, which usually manifests itself within a day or two after the fish arrive in the retail shop. Hatchery-produced clownfishes are seldom affected by *Brooklynella*, probably due to higher standards of sanitation in the facilities, compared to conditions to which wild clowns are exposed while awaiting export to this country.

Other Parasites

MARINE FISHES ARE SUBJECT TO INFESTATION with various kinds of flukes, worms, and crustacean parasites. These problems are much rarer in home aquariums than the hobbyist literature might lead one to suppose. Further, hobbyists are not likely to be able to treat such problems effectively. In the case of external parasites, professional help will usually be required to determine not only the identity of the parasite, but also an appropriate treatment. Internal parasites are, for all practical purposes, untreatable.

Only one external worm parasite is common. It is also easily treatable. This is Black Spot disease of tangs. The agent is a small flatworm that burrows under the fish's skin, making it appear as if the fish has been dusted with black pepper. Yellow Tangs are frequently reported as having this problem; their coloration makes an infestation especially obvious. A dip in a bucket of seawater containing a solution of picric acid formulated for the purpose is an effective remedy. The medication is commercially available. Most of the time, the dealer, rather than the hobbyist, will be the one carrying out this treatment, as fish showing the black spots will be avoided by customers.

Bacterial Infections

MARINE FISH CAN ALSO BECOME DISEASED as a result of a bacterial infection. Effective treatment of bacterial diseases requires 1) identification of the causative organism; 2) antibiotic sensitivity testing; and 3) appropriate dosage and route of administration of antibiotics in a timely manner. Small wonder that attempts by the hobbyist to treat bacterial infections usually fail. Antibiotic preparations available in aquarium shops are likely to be inappropriate for the disease they purport to treat and are often too stale to retain potency. In addition, they generally are supplied in a form inadequate for proper administration and come with dosage recommendations that are far below therapeutic levels. According to the manufacturers' recommendations, virtually all of these medications should simply be added to the water, but this route of administration is seldom able to achieve a high enough dose to do the fish any good.

Widespread use of antibiotics by hobbyists is also to be discouraged because of the likelihood of creating resistant strains of bacteria. The subtherapeutic dosage and lack of targeted administration suggested on the packages of these medications is, ironically, the perfect scenario for developing resistance.

Fish that are suffering from a problem that is not amenable to copper treatment (or one of the other minor problems mentioned earlier) should be euthanized, or the assistance of a veterinarian should be sought. In any event, the infected specimen must be isolated from its tankmates.

One possible exception to the use of antibiotics is for the prevention of infection in wounded specimens or those that have suffered skin damage (from jumping out of the tank, for example). If the wound is localized and not near the gills, antibiotics are not needed. Simply painting the damaged area with a swab dipped in a mixture of one part ordinary mercurochrome and one part aquarium water is usually effective in preventing infection. However, for a more generalized treatment, a broad-spectrum antimicrobial compound, such as one in the nitrofurazone family, at 50 mg per gallon every other day for a week, may be effective.

The United States Food and Drug Administration is currently considering restricting the availability of antibiotics to home aquarists. In my view, this action will not create a significant burden.

Acclimation

THE PROCESS OF INTRODUCING A FISH to new water conditions is called acclimation. Probably every aquarist is aware that some sort of procedure is necessary, and everyone has a preferred method. However, my experiences with hundreds of marine fishes indicate that most of the usual methods are of little benefit if the intent is to get the fish slowly accustomed to the new water. Most acclimation procedures call for about an hour's time for the transition. This is simply not sufficient for the fish to make the necessary physiological adjustments if water conditions in the new location are significantly different from those to which the fish was previously exposed.

Efforts to maintain specimens in good condition will be thwarted if they have not been packed properly for travel from the shop to your home. Even when the customer lives near the shop, attention to details can make the difference between a fish arriving in the hobbyist's tank in the best possible condition and arriving in severe stress. One of the most accomplished aquarists I know is Jackson Andrews, whom I first met while he was with the National Aquarium in Baltimore. He is now Director of Operations and Husbandry at the Tennessee Aquarium in Chattanooga. While at the National Aquarium, he was responsible for collecting operations in the Florida Keys that stocked the aquarium's giant coral reef fishes exhibit. Here was an opportunity to experiment with

Slow-drip acclimation: a bagged specimen gradually adjusts to temperature, pH, and specific gravity of a new system.

different shipping techniques and to keep track of the results in terms of the size of the fish, the species, mortalities, and so forth. The study accumulated a lot of data, but Andrews summed it up in one sentence: "The more water there is in the shipping container, the lower the fish mortality."

Along with plenty of water, specimens should always be given ample room in the shipping container. In my experience, a 3-inch fish needs about a half gallon of water,

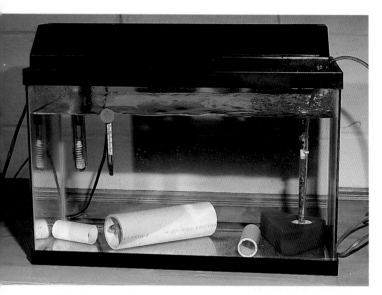

Simple quarantine set-up: 10-gallon tank and cover, heater, thermometer, air-driven filter, and PVC hiding places.

and an equal amount of pure oxygen, in the shipping bag. To ship fish long distances by air freight or for an overnight car trip, they should be packed in at least two layers of plastic bags. These are placed in an insulated container and surrounded with loosefill (Styrofoam "peanuts") to absorb shocks and to help keep the temperature stable. Packed this way, they will survive a surprisingly long time in perfect shape. (My record is 69 hours.)

Over the years, I have developed some specific recommendations for handling recently shipped fish. First, it is important to stop and think about the nature of the journey the fish has made from the dealer's tank to your home. If the dealer is ten minutes away, the water in the transport bag will of course be in better condition than if the journey has lasted several hours. If the specimen appears to be in severe distress, open the bag, pour out as much of the shipping water as possible and then dump the fish into your holding tank immediately. This may add to its stress, but it will be of greater value in the long run to get the specimen

into good water as soon as possible. (Never add shipping water to your system or even to your quarantine system.)

If the specimen does not exhibit signs of stress, as is most often the case, the water used for transporting it should be tested with the same equipment in use on the aquarist's holding tank. If these tests show that temperature, pH, and specific gravity of the transport water are similar to conditions in the holding aquarium, release the fish (separated from its shipping water) into its temporary quarters. If, however, there are significant differences in water conditions, do not add to the fish's stress unnecessarily with a sudden transfer.

The first step should be to equalize the temperature between the transport container and the holding/quarantine tank. An increase in temperature is easier for the fish to handle than a decrease. Therefore, if the bag is cooler than the tank, which is the most common situation, float the unopened bag in the tank for a half hour or so to allow the shipping water to warm to the tank temperature. However, if the tank is cooler than the bag, it is better to turn up the thermostat and warm the holding tank to a temperature equal to or up to 2 degrees F greater than that of the bag before proceeding. Once the temperature has equalized, open the transport container and drop in an airstone. Adjust the airflow so that a good stream of bubbles is produced, but not so much as to slosh the fish around in the bag (this will only increase its stress). Carbon dioxide builds up in the shipping water as a result of the fish's respiration. If the concentration of CO_2 becomes high enough, the fish will die of respiratory distress, even if there is abundant oxygen present in the water. Fish in respiratory distress usually exhibit rapid, shallow opercular movements. Aeration of the water in the bag eliminates a lot of CO_2 quickly, but check the transport water for ammonia. It may be present if the fish's journey has been a long one and will become more toxic to the fish as the pH rises due to aeration of the water. If ammonia is present, transfer the fish into ammonia-free water immediately.

Once the fish is in the holding tank, it will probably appear somewhat disoriented for a few minutes and will soon seek shelter and hide. At this point, turn out the room lights and walk away. Leave the new arrival alone for 24 hours to allow it to become accustomed to its new environment in peace. Offer fresh or frozen food after the first 24 hours. Some fish will start eating promptly; others may take three or four days to settle down and start feeding. Observe the fish carefully for signs of disease: scratching, rapid breathing, sores or lesions, lethargy, etc. After the third day, healthy fish should be normally active and searching for food. If disease symptoms are apparent, take appropriate treatment measures. Check pH, ammonia, and nitrite in the holding tank, and make appropriate adjustments if necessary. Otherwise, continue feeding for two weeks, then move the fish into the display tank.

Ideal handling of a fish that must be moved: avoid nets in favor of traps or wide-mouthed containers into which the target specimen is gently guided.

Handling Marine Fishes

FISHES ARE SUSCEPTIBLE to skin infections if they are roughly handled. Try not to use a net to catch a fish. Instead, if right-handed, hold a wide-mouth clear plastic container in your left hand and use your right hand or a net to herd the fish into the container. This takes practice but saves fish lives. Traps are available for those who lack the dexterity. Traps are essential for removing a fish from an established tank with lots of rockwork, where the risk of damaging invertebrates while chasing the fish is very high. As a last resort, hook and line may be used. Experienced aquarium fishermen report that the hook size must be chosen with care, and, of course, the barb must be removed from the hook.

IN SUMMARY, all wild marine fishes must be placed in a separate tank for at least two weeks before being introduced to an established display aquarium. It is likely that any disease problem (probably caused by one of two microscopic parasites) will become apparent during this time. Treatment for either problem with copper sulfate is straightforward and usually effective, provided the aquarist learns to recognize when a fish is in trouble. More exotic problems, with one or two exceptions, are probably beyond the abilities of the home hobbyist to manage without professional help. In particular, bacterial infections may require the assistance of a veterinarian. Fortunately, the most difficult diseases to treat are the rarest. Aquariums that are maintained under good conditions are rarely troubled by disease outbreaks, and the fish in them often live longer than if in the sea.

Chapter Twelve

Feeding the Captive Reef

Nutrition Basics and Balances in the Marine Aquarium

THE ANGLERFISH LIES IN CAMOUFLAGE, motionless except for a fleshy lure that twitches at the end of a modified fin spine. A smaller fish approaches, spies the bait, and poises to strike. Suddenly, the anglerfish explodes into life and engulfs its prey in a cavernous mouth . . .

A harmless-appearing blenny from the genus *Plagiotremus* suddenly darts toward a trusting angelfish that mistook it for a friendly cleaner wrasse, and the tiny attacker rips a mouthful of scales and flesh from the angelfish, then retreats instantly to the safety of a crevice in the reef . . .

The Psychedelic Mandarin of the Family Callionymidae hops deliberately from rock to rock, pecking at tiny crustaceans more in the manner of hummingbird than fish. It is so slow and gaudy that it appears a perfect target for larger predators passing by, but the dragonet has been reported to protect itself from bolder fishes by exuding toxic secretions when disturbed. Such a weapon would do no good, of course, if the fish were swallowed instantly, so this family has evolved an unmistakable coloration pattern that warns predators to avoid them . . .

Poised to strike: a lionfish (*Pterois volitans*) focuses on a potential target in its typical feeding posture over a reef.

Elsewhere on the reef, there are wrasses that appear to specialize in stealing food from other fishes, lionfishes that hunt in teams, and tangs that thrive on the vitamin-rich feces of other fishes . . .

Watching the feeding behaviors of reef animals is one of the great pleasures to be derived from a marine aquarium. Understanding the feeding behavior of fishes and invertebrates in the wild and providing acceptable captive diets is fundamental to the long-term health of aquarium specimens. The quality and quantity of the rations you feed will have a major bearing on the longevity not only of the individual tank inhabitants but on the sustainability of the entire microhabitat you have created. Unlike the sea, the aquarium is a closed system. Food inputs, therefore, must be closely controlled to minimize pollution and carefully chosen to supply an adequate diet for the variety of species in your captive reef.

Among the interlocking relationships that bind the organisms of the reef environment into an ecosystem, the most obvious interaction is that between predator and prey. At every trophic level, and in every corner of every habitat, there is a constant ebb and flow of energy between a multitude of producers and a hierarchy of consumers. Ultimately, solar energy feeds the reef. It is trapped in sugar molecules via photosynthesis. When photosynthetic organisms are consumed, part of the energy is liberated for the needs of the consumer. Photosynthetically stored solar energy is the bullion in the vault, and food webs constitute the currency market. One needs but to witness the sometimes bizarre adaptations organisms have achieved to obtain food to understand why authors often point to the dynamic of "eat or be eaten" as the most compelling illustration of Darwin's notion of "survival of the fittest."

Experienced marine aquarists are typically familiar with the feeding peculiarities of certain fish families, but invertebrates have collectively evolved an even more extensive repertoire of techniques. As with fishes, camouflage, ambush, poison, parasite removal, and raw aggressiveness characterize invertebrates from across the taxonomic spectrum. A host of more specialized predator-prey relationships has been identified among the organisms of the reef, as well. A given species of nudibranch, for example, typically feeds on a single prey species or at most on a very limited range of food items. (As an "obligate" predator, it is genetically programmed to survive on one particular prey species.) Precise, rather poorly understood interactions between the nudibranch and its food species prevent the mollusk from overexploiting the resources in its vicinity. Many of these nudibranchs look remarkably like their prey species, and some even commandeer body parts from their prey, such as the nematocysts from stinging hydroids, and utilize them.

The Lettuce Sea Slug (*Tridachia crispata*) from Florida and the Caribbean takes the utilization of foreign body parts a step further, extracting the living chloroplasts (subcellular structures that carry out photosynthesis) from the tissues of the *Caulerpa* algae upon which it feeds, transferring them to specialized frills of tissue running along its back. The slug thereupon becomes a photosynthetic "plantimal," subsisting for several weeks by merely basking in the sun. The slug's tissues apparently do not provide an adequate envi-

ronment for the long-term functioning of the chloroplasts, however, as they must be replenished every few weeks. Nevertheless, this adaptation does result in conservation of the food source, probably allowing a much larger population of slugs to survive in a given location than would be the case if the *Caulerpa* were consumed in the usual manner. The slug, in turn, does not have to expend as much energy to obtain nourishment and can thus devote more resources to growing larger and becoming more fecund.

I have spent quite a bit of time observing *Tridachia* in the field on my excursions to Florida. One bay just north of Marathon supported a particularly rich population of this mollusk. It was easy to find three or four on each of the rounded boulders at the base of the seawall. The rough rocks provided a perfect purchase for the holdfasts of *Caulerpa floridana*, which formed a lush carpet in the relatively calm, shallow water. Many of the individual slugs were about the size of my forefinger, at least ten times the mass of the typical sea slug or nudibranch. As I watched one, it moved slowly away from the *Caulerpa*, leaving behind a colorless "scar" where the juices of the seaweed had been sucked out. Crawling a few centimeters, emerald green photosynthetic frills undulating hypnotically, the *Tridachia* settled down to bask on the highest point of the boulder, only a few inches under the surface. Thus exposed, it might easily fall prey to predators if not for its unpleasant secretions.

Feeding Fishes

OF ALL THE FACTORS that occupy the interest of average aquarists in the course of caring for their charges, perhaps none is given less attention than the quality of the fishes' diet. In a well-established natural marine aquarium, there will be an abundance of small organisms, such as microcrustaceans and algae, that can serve as food for the fish. While these foods are perhaps the best kind of nourishment

Supplementary feeding of dried algae or fresh greens is required for captive tangs in systems without heavy algal growth.

for captive fishes, they generally cannot be relied upon to sustain the fish population indefinitely. An input of food from outside the aquarium ecosystem will be necessary. The quantity of food given to fish is certainly important, but equally or even more important is the quality of the diet from a nutritional standpoint.

Authors differ on the subject of feeding marine fish. Certainly one does not need to feed fishes as often as some aquarium owners do. This is only in part because of the availability of food organisms within the aquarium. Another reason is the importance of keeping the water nutrient-poor. Added foods are a major source of nitrate, phosphate, and dissolved organic carbon, and the concentration of these substances in the water should be kept to a minimum. Further, marine fish appear to have lower caloric needs in the aquarium, because they are not swimming against strong ocean currents and thus receive less exercise. Overfeeding can result in accumulations of waste products that impair the fishes' health, especially in a fish-only system with heavy dependence on artificial biological filtration and little pro-

Always in season and readily available, freeze-dried foods offer the aquarist an excellent substitute for fresh or live foods.

FREEZE-DRIED FOODS. Freeze-drying preserves almost as much nutritional value as freezing, although certain vitamins may be lost in the process. Many freeze-dried aquarium foods contain only crustaceans, such as krill or brine shrimp. These foods are high in protein and are very convenient, but should not form the staple diet for marine fish. Use them as a supplement to other foods.

DEHYDRATED AND FLAKE FOODS. Dehydration has been used to preserve foods for centuries. While many essential nutrients are lost or destroyed in the dehydration process, dried foods are still nutritious. Moreover, they are cheap, convenient, and certain to be stocked by any aquarium shop. Choose flake foods that are specifically made for marine fishes. Reputable manufacturers include ingredients that supply nutrients essential to the fishes for which the food was formulated. While some aquarists are scornful of flake foods, associating them with the goldfish-bowl set, many accomplished reef keepers supplement their mainstay rations of frozen and fresh foods with regular pinches of high-quality flakes. *Spirulina*, a blue-green alga cultivated both for captive fishes and health-food devotees,

is especially appealing to ravenous grazers like tangs and makes a convenient, nonpolluting food source for the reef tank. Despite the cost savings that accrue when such flake foods are bought in quantity, it is best to purchase only a small amount at any time. Opened flake foods may lose food value or even develop mold or bacterial growth. Dried seaweed is seldom sold in aquarium shops but can be found in specialty-food stores. Look for nori, a seaweed that is used in making sushi. It consists of dried macroalgae and comes in both sheets and shreds. (The price of nori can be astronomical in some supermarkets — seek out a neighborhood Asian market for the best prices.) Vegetarian fishes, such as tangs, angelfishes, rabbitfishes, and certain damselfishes and blennies love this product, and it is a more natural and nutritious food for them than garden vegetables.

FOOD ADDITIVES. With growing awareness that certain nutrients are essential for the long-term health of marine fishes and that these nutrients may be lacking from commercial fish foods, a new category of products for the marine hobbyist has made its appearance. These are food additives, designed to replace important nutrients that some fish foods lack. Several of these products are advertised to contain essential fatty acids, vitamin C and vitamin B$_{12}$. Certain fatty acids are recognized to be vitally important in the nutrition of marine fishes. Vitamin C deficiency has been linked to a condition called Head and Lateral Line Erosion (see below). Vitamin supplementation of aquarium foods is likely to increase and improve in the future, but regard with skepticism any cure-all that recommends the addition of vitamins directly to the aquarium water.

HANDLING AQUARIUM FOODS. All foods should be purchased in small quantities that will be used within a reasonable period of time (one month or less) and should be stored in the freezer or refrigerator to facilitate maximum retention of nutritional value. The same goes for food additives. Keep all foods tightly sealed, as oxygen from the air can break down valuable vitamins, and moisture intrusion can lead to spoilage. Spoiled foods can be recognized by a foul odor; mold growth produces a musty smell. Discard spoiled or moldy foods immediately. Keep frozen foods solidly frozen, thaw out only what is needed, and do not refreeze completely thawed food. Many aquarists are concerned about transmitting disease to their fishes via fresh or frozen seafoods. This is extremely unlikely. In nature, sick or injured fishes are often eaten by other fishes with no ill effects. Disease outbreaks in the aquarium can usually be traced to less than optimal water quality or some other condition that creates stress for the fishes and leaves them susceptible to infection. Feeding a fresh, wholesome, balanced diet is one way to prevent disease outbreaks.

Most of the foregoing is simple common sense. We are all taught the importance of clean, fresh, wholesome food in maintaining our own health. But many people have the notion that fishes do not conform to these nutrition basics. Certainly some species are specialized in their dietary needs, but the majority of marine fishes eat a variety of foods. It goes without saying that on the reef all the foods are fresh, whether algae or coral polyps are on the menu. The cost of food is only a fraction of the cost of setting up your aquarium, so paying attention to the fishes' diet is a wise investment in maintaining your captive ecosystem.

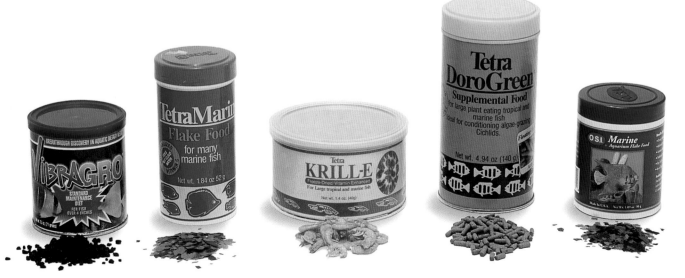

Dried and freeze-dried rations provide both convenience and concentrated nutritional values and can supplement other foods.

Nutrition-Related Problems

HEAD AND LATERAL LINE EROSION (HLLE) has long been known to affect captive marine fishes. This condition, characterized by erosion of the skin tissue along the lateral line and around the face, is seen especially in tangs, angelfishes, and clownfishes. In the past, a variety of remedies were tried, all to no avail, based upon the mistaken assumption that the condition was due to bacterial infection brought on by poor water quality. Research has shown that HLLE results, at least in part, from ascorbic acid (vitamin C) deficiency (Blasiola, 1988). Blasiola was able to induce the condition in the Regal Tang (*Paracanthurus hepatus*) by feeding a diet deficient in this nutrient. Restoration of the vitamin to the diet reversed the progress of the erosion. A biologist on the staff of my company believes that a low-grade bacterial infection may accompany HLLE and that this infection should be treated with antibiotics along with an improved diet. (Lowered resistance to infection can accompany HLLE, which may explain why antibiotics sometimes help.)

Prevent HLLE by feeding fishes fresh foods high in vitamin C and adding supplements that contain this vitamin to frozen and dried foods. Vitamin C is notoriously difficult to preserve by traditional storage methods, hence the need for fresh foods and/or supplements. Green algae was excluded from the test aquariums in Blasiola's study and was added to the diet along with ascorbic acid to reverse the erosion. Those fishes that feed largely or exclusively on algae in the wild appear to be prime candidates for HLLE in the aquarium.

Sprung (1991) has also presented anecdotal evidence that elimination of induced electrical charge by grounding the aquarium was instrumental in reversing HLLE in an angelfish.

FATTY-ACID DEFICIENCY is a slow and insidious form of malnutrition that can affect large, predatory fishes such as lionfishes. The marine fish that form the bulk of the diet of these species are rich in highly unsaturated fatty acids (HUFAs). HUFAs are essential to the health of many aquarium fishes. Feeding lionfishes exclusively on freshwater baitfish, a common practice, condemns the lionfish to an early death. To avoid the problem, feed ocean-derived foods, including fish, and use a supplement that supplies HUFAs. Cod-liver oil has been used successfully as a supplement, and Selcon, a dietary-supplement mix developed for the aquaculture industry, also gives good results.

UNBALANCED DIET. Another example of what I suspect is malnutrition in aquarium fish affects puffers, porcupine fish, and spiny boxfish. I have seen cases in which these fish lose the ability to eat, specifically the ability to move the jaws, sometimes accompanied by loss of the teeth. In every case, the fish had been fed freeze-dried krill exclusively for several months before the problem developed. This is not evidence that krill is bad for fish. It is evidence, however, that an unbalanced diet can lead to problems. In nature, fishes such as these feed on a wide variety of invertebrates and smaller fishes. It is not surprising that they would suffer problems from a diet consisting of a single food. In each of these cases, the fish eventually died of starvation or became so debilitated that they were euthanized. This makes me wonder how many other problems in aquarium fish could be traced to an improper or inadequate diet.

I offer these three simple recommendations for avoiding nutritional problems:

1) Find out the natural diet of the species intended for the aquarium, and attempt to duplicate it closely.

2) Feed marine fishes the widest possible variety of foods, within the context of the natural diet.

3) Use living, fresh, and frozen foods as the bulk of the diet, and rely on other forms of commercially prepared food only occasionally.

Starvation

SOME FISHES MAY STARVE not from receiving an inadequate diet but from being fed in a manner that is inappropriate to the fish's lifestyle. Yellow Tangs, along with their various cousins in the Acanthuridae, graze on algae, and this behavior is almost constant during the daylight hours. A vegetarian diet is not nutrient dense, so the fishes must eat a lot to supply their caloric needs. A "pulsed" feeding schedule, where food is available only once or twice daily, does not suit these species' needs. If the aquarium has little algae growth apart from corallines, cultivation of seaweeds should be undertaken, with the aim of producing enough to keep the tangs occupied all day, every day. Tiny tangs the size of a quarter may starve in only a short period of time; in fact, the delicacy of juvenile tangs, with or without adequate food, is probably best dealt with by avoiding specimens under 2 inches in length.

Similarly, fishes that feed on very tiny crustaceans, including dragonets, *Chromis*, anthiids, and *Heniochus*, cannot obtain enough food to satisfy their requirements when the tank is flooded with food only periodically. Dragonets seem to need a natural population of tiny crustaceans, usually found in a large, mature tank with lots of live rock and live sand, to thrive. Others in this category can be fed finely chopped prepared foods, administered by some form of automated dispenser, or they can be offered live, newly hatched brine shrimp. Morsels that these fish obtain when the other tank inhabitants receive a daily feeding round out their diet.

The Shedd Aquarium in Chicago succeeds with a planktivorous freshwater species, the Mississippi paddlefish (*Polyodon*), by allowing newly hatched brine shrimp to drip slowly from a reservoir into the tank all day long. The shrimp are kept in suspension by aerating the reservoir, and the drip is controlled with an arrangement similar to that used by physicians for administering intravenous solutions.

Juvenile fishes and those with retiring habits may also starve in the aquarium if the correct environmental cues are absent. Small *Pomacanthus* angels, such as the juvenile Koran Angels (*P. semicirculatus*), may be too intimidated in their new home to feed adequately. Dwarf angels (*Centropyge*) may also exhibit this syndrome, as may adult butterflyfishes (Chaetodontidae). Even triggerfishes, usually thought to be aggressive, may refuse to eat if they do not feel safe. Any new specimen in this category should be observed carefully. If the fish has not eaten after three days in your holding tank and is housed with other new specimens, consider providing it with private quarters. Most of the time this will result in the resumption of feeding. After the fish has had an opportunity to become accustomed to captivity, it can be moved to the display aquarium.

Feeding Invertebrates

ADDING ORGANIC MIXES to the aquarium to "feed" invertebrates is a mistake. Photosynthetic invertebrates seem to require only light to satisfy their needs, and nonphotosynthetic species derive at least some nourishment from the bacteria and other microorganisms that "grow by themselves" in the tank. Also, if fishes are housed in the same aquarium, invertebrates will dine abundantly on the leftovers of their foods. In some cases, growth of invertebrates may be more rapid if outside foods are added, however. This knowledge might be of use, for example, in "farming" these species, as it would be desirable to optimize their growth rate. If there is reason to experiment with feeding a particular invertebrate to enhance its growth, follow these guidelines:

1) Carry out experiments in a separate tank housing only the species of interest. (It is foolish to carry out feeding experiments in an established display aquarium.)

2) Keep careful records.

3) Remember that added food will inevitably be mineralized in the aquarium, and the nutrient-ion content of the water in the experimental tank will rise. Appropriate measures to offset this trend will be necessary.

Recently, the subject of feeding corals previously thought to thrive only on good light has attracted the attention of a number of marine hobbyists and experimenters. Nutritional recommendations for these invertebrates are sure to evolve in coming years, with fresh and frozen planktonic supplements very likely to emerge as important for many species. Nonetheless, the heavy-handed addition of various "invert" potions has polluted many a reef tank, and the aquarist is cautioned to use great care in trying new coral-feeding regimens. Live foods, as discussed next, are biologically interesting in their own right, with the least potential to throw an aquarium system out of balance.

Live-Food Cultivation

PHYTOPLANKTON CULTURES. Microalgae, believe it or not, are the aquarist's friend. Readers may take a moment to recover from the shock, since microalgae are widely regarded as the bane of the reef aquarium's existence. I earlier offered advice on the control of these organisms (in Chapter Five) and now I say that they are beneficial. Why?

The term "microalgae" is, of course, a broad category. Included are everything from single-celled free-swimming organisms that show a weird mix of plant and animal characteristics to filamentous and mat-forming types that can indeed become a scourge. Cyanobacteria, the so-called "slime algae," are perhaps the most notorious, and the methods for control of algae growth in the aquarium are primarily directed at these species. Diatoms, golden-brown cells encased in silica, dinoflagellates of the free-living variety (as opposed to the symbiotic zooxanthellae), and a few

species of filamentous green algae (*Cladophora* being a commonly encountered example) may also cause problems. At least two species commonly regarded as macroalgae, *Valonia* and *Bryopsis*, can sometimes grow uncontrollably and may frustrate all attempts at eradication, only to finally disappear as unexpectedly as they arrived.

The vast majority of algae, however, are benign species that form the basis of the entire marine food web. In the aquarium, especially an aquarium in which nonphotosynthetic filter-feeding invertebrates are housed, these kinds of microalgae, collectively called phytoplankton, must be provided in order to achieve success. As Gerald Heslinga recently wrote, "Phytoplankton are the basis for the aquaculture food chain."[1] Fortunately, cultivation of phytoplankton can be quite simple, if the aquarist follows a few guidelines.

Isochrysis, *Dunaliella*, and *Chlorella* are three species of phytoplankton often grown in laboratories and hatcheries as food for marine organisms. Rotifers, for example, are fed phytoplankton. Should you attempt your own phytoplankton culture, it is important to 1) work with pure cultures of known identity; 2) maintain the purity of the culture(s) via sterile techniques; and 3) keep records of feeding regimens, culture density when fed, and similar data. An explanation of these techniques is beyond the scope of this book, but hobbyists who are interested in pursuing this form of phytoplankton culture should consult such sources as Bold and Wynne (1978).

On the other hand, if the only interest is in producing a mixed culture of "green water" for feeding a tank of fanworms or soft corals, then one of the experimental techniques mentioned below may be the best route to that goal.

ROTIFERS. Rotifers are strange multicellular, but microscopic, invertebrates that have been used for years as a source of food for larval marine fishes, such as clownfishes. The

---

[1] Gerald Heslinga, personal communication.

species most often cultivated for this purpose is *Brachionus plicatilis*. This organism, which is easily maintained on a diet of cultured phytoplankton such as *Isochrysis*, might be regarded as the foundation of the marine fish aquaculture industry. Explicit instructions for culture of *Brachionus* can be found in Moe (1989), and various other references.

BRINE SHRIMP. The brine shrimp, *Artemia salina*, is a common inhabitant of highly saline environments and is available year round to aquarists, either as live adult shrimp or as resting cysts. Newly hatched brine shrimp, called nauplii, are an old-fashioned staple food for all types of aquariums. The resting cysts, or "eggs," are widely available. To hatch nauplii, place about 2 tablespoons of synthetic seawater mix in a clean quart jar and fill with RO water. Add about ¼ teaspoon of cysts, then aerate vigorously. The cysts will hatch in about 24 to 48 hours, depending upon temperature. The nauplii are attracted to light, and a flashlight can be used to lure them to a convenient spot from which they may be siphoned out, strained through a fine mesh net, and fed to the aquarium.

To rear adult brine shrimp, a large shallow container, such as a child's wading pool, is filled with old aquarium seawater and allowed to sit in a brightly lit area until the water turns green, indicating a thriving population of microalgae. To speed up the process, add a pinch of houseplant fertilizer to supply nitrate and phosphate for the algae. Nauplii are then added. They will feed on the algae and grow to adult size (about ½ inch) in about three weeks.

AMPHIPODS. Amphipods are the tiny, transparent, shrimplike creatures that are sometimes seen scuttling around on the rocks in the aquarium, feeding on detritus. They are about ¼ inch in length. To culture them as food for the aquarium, set up a tank with a heater and a large, box-type power filter or a canister filter. Fill the filter compartment with a large sponge block or polyester filter pads. Pack in as much of this material as possible without restricting water flow. Now fill the tank with water containing detritus siphoned from an existing aquarium—the more, the better. Start the filter running, adjust the heater to 75 degrees F, and add a few amphipods, also collected from an established aquarium. In about a month, the filter material will be teeming with amphipods, which can easily be harvested by removing some of the material and swishing it in a bucket of clear seawater. Pour this through a net to concentrate the amphipods, then feed them to the aquarium.

Experimental Techniques

A HOST OF MARINE SPECIES can probably be used as live foods. Copepods, for example, and especially their larvae (nauplii), appear to be important components of the natural diet of marine fish larvae. Copepods and other small crustaceans may form the bulk of the diet for adult dragonets, such as *Synchiropus picturatus*. These tiny crustaceans often undergo spontaneous population explosions in mature aquariums established by the methods outlined in this book. When such an explosion occurs, one can harvest a few hundred of the organisms and transfer them to a separate container in an attempt to establish a culture. Supplying them with algae, detritus, and other organic matter removed from the display aquarium should result in a successful copepod "farm." Mass culture of a single copepod species is also possible, using techniques similar to those developed for *Brachionus* rotifers.

Aquarists living near the seashore, or able to visit the ocean with regularity, should attempt to establish cultures of natural plankton. As with the cultivation of copepods taken from the aquarium, the approach to working with natural plankton can be simple or more refined. Simply collect seaweed or other flotsam from the beach just after the tide recedes — you'll want material that hasn't been exposed too long. Placing this material in a bucket or tank of seawater will result in a remarkable culture of marine invertebrates that can be best appreciated only with the aid of a microscope. As well as being a source of live food, this type of plankton farm can be entertaining and instructive if it can be examined periodically under magnification. (A good microscope, like a good pH meter, should be considered an essential tool for a serious marine aquarium hobbyist. Magnification in the range of about 10X to 100X is most useful. The instrument need not be expensive. Used microscopes can sometimes be found in pawn shops or in surplus-property auctions held by colleges. If the lenses are not scratched, a used scope can be a real bargain.)

A sprig of seaweed the size of the parsley garnish on your dinner entrée is sufficient to establish a marine protozoan culture in a quart of seawater. Simply fill a jar with water directly from the ocean, drop in the seaweed, or perhaps a chunk of wood encrusted with small invertebrates, and place the jar in indirect sunlight. Aeration will result in a different sort of community of microorganisms than would be the case without it, but is not necessary for producing food organisms. Even the death and decay of the seaweed or other life forms will not spell catastrophe, because this will, in turn, feed another cycle of growth for other kinds of plankton. Examination of the container every day will reveal a changing pattern of life. You might even choose to remove an especially useful species to its own tank or jar for mass cultivation.

One need not collect the original starter material from the Tropics in order to use the organisms as food for tropical invertebrates. I know of at least one case in which such a plankton farm from the Chesapeake Bay was used successfully to rear the Mandarinfish, *Synchiropus splendidus*.[2] For feeding a typical invertebrate aquarium, I recommend using a 10-gallon tank for the farm, although one can have dozens of plankton aquariums in quart jars on a windowsill as well.

A more refined, albeit very expensive, approach to the use of plankton in marine aquariums is to go out to sea in a boat periodically and tow a plankton net through the currents. The resulting catch is returned to a holding tank or tanks on shore and subsequently used for feeding. While elegant (some hobbyists even time the plankton tow to match natural spawning cycles of fish and invertebrates in order to duplicate the natural conditions), this option is clearly available only to the dedicated marine enthusiast who lives near a coast.

Supplementation

MARINE FISHES AND INVERTEBRATES require certain elements in order to grow and reproduce. These include food components, such as proteins, fats, and carbohydrates, as well as calcium, strontium, iodine, and other minerals. Trace elements and vitamins may be required by some species, although little is known about the food requirements of the majority of marine organisms. Experience has taught reef aquarium enthusiasts that supplementation of some important elements enhances the growth rate of coralline algae, corals, tridacnids, and other specimens.

CALCIUM. Natural seawater contains approximately 412 mg/L of calcium. This chemical element is required by all forms of life, but is especially important to organisms that secrete a calcium carbonate skeleton, or that have calcium carbonate as a component of the exoskeleton. These include certain species of macroalgae, corals, mollusks, tubeworms, crustaceans, and echinoderms that extract calcium from the water. (Calcium chemistry in the aquarium is discussed in Chapter Five.)

STRONTIUM. Strontium is present in natural seawater at a concentration of 7.9 mg/L. A test kit for strontium is

---

[2] Julian Sprung, personal communication

depleted by the use of protein skimmers, as ... ral absorption by living organisms. Some ... solution of potassium iodide to supplement ... gh commercially prepared iodine supple-... y available. Test kits for iodine are available and make dosing this element much less a matter of hit or miss. One professional aquaculturist[3] has advised me that in his experience with *Xenia* soft corals, it is crucial to maintain an iodine concentration in the range of 0.06 to 0.08 ppm. Colonies of the species "crash" when iodine levels fall below this threshold.

TRACE ELEMENTS. All chemical elements are present in natural seawater, and a variety of these are known to be required ... nds of marine life. Those that are present ... n of 1 ppm or less are called "trace ele-... r of supplements are available that can be ... , ostensibly to replenish those elements ... from the water by biological processes ... ation. Each manufacturer touts its special, ... la. I urge the aquarist, however, to resist ... e ad campaigns. Some of these products ... but some may also be deleterious, their efficacy not having been scientifically evaluated in most cases. No additive can substitute for water testing, careful observation of the health of your stock, and good maintenance, including regular water changes, as a formula for success.

(Bibliography, page 315).

IODINE. Iodine is present in natural seawater at a concentration of 60 micrograms per liter (60 parts per billion). It is essential to all organisms, but is especially necessary for macroalgae, soft corals, and crustaceans. If shrimps die during the process of molting, suspect a deficiency of iodine.

---

[3] Noel Curry, personal communication

Introduction

Ecology & the Aquarist

*Weighing the Environmental Costs
and Benefits of Keeping Reef Aquariums*

IT WAS BACK TO PIGEON KEY FOR ME, freshly minted master's degree under my arm, when I was fortunate enough to receive an appointment as an instructor in the University of Tennessee's general biology program. This was a huge course, required of many freshmen, and a team of 3 instructors and some 60 graduate assistants was needed to give lectures, labs, and exams for over 1,500 students. As the youngest instructor and the only one without a doctorate, I was assigned to handle the less desirable tasks: greenhouse work, culturing algae and protozoans to supply the demonstration labs, and caring for several aquariums. If this had been the football team, I would have been the water boy, but I loved it.

In addition to having a busy teaching schedule, going on weekend

A delicate reef habitat of the Florida Keys, with Common Sea Fan (*Gorgonia ventalina*) and Spanish Hogfish (*Bodianus rufus*). Above: aquarists' button protesting the use of cyanide in the collection of fishes.

A fore-reef slope in the Red Sea: a wealth of challenges for the captive propagator.

As for sexual reproduction, aquarium release of larvae that were sexually produced in the wild has been reported many times, often with subsequent successful larval development. Sea hares, a group of shell-less, herbivorous mollusks, are cultured for laboratory use, as are various echinoderms (the group that includes starfish, brittle stars, sea urchins, sea cucumbers, and feather stars). Propagation of some species of crustaceans has been problematic, but I am willing to bet that a commercial aquaculturist specializing in food shrimps could succeed with the aquarium shrimps as well. The Peppermint Shrimp, *Lysmata wurdemanni*, from Florida and the Caribbean, is readily amenable to sexual propagation in the aquarium. The future, therefore,

ular invertebrates currently in production. The number of species that might potentially be cultured, however, is remarkable. One of the best consequences of the interest in reef tanks has been the discovery that the reproduction of many species is not only possible, but sometimes unavoidable. Certain sponges have grown in my tanks with no special care, along with at least three species of sedentary worms, one of which is large and showy enough to have some commercial potential. Among the cnidarians, aquarists have found that virtually all mushroom polyps, sea mats, and soft corals, along with many stony corals and at least one of the clownfish host anemones (Paletta, 1993), can be vegetatively propagated in the aquarium, with unassisted reproduction of some species quite commonplace.

looks bright for tank-cultured aquarium animals. I would like to see more hobbyists involved in this aspect of the hobby. If one has the space, growing soft corals for a local dealer could even become a secondary income source.

If we wish to continue to enjoy and learn from marine aquariums, we must be responsible stewards of the natural environments from which aquarium specimens originate. Most aquarists appear to share this view.

Once the aquarist has mastered basic techniques and has a good grasp of the ecology of the reef environment, it is time for the most enjoyable and rewarding part of the hobby: observing the growth, development, and reproduction of the aquarium's inhabitants over time. Marine invertebrates, such as corals and anemones, have remarkably long lifespans, and a number of fish species that make good aquarium subjects can live more than 10 years, offering long-term enjoyment of a carefully designed marine habitat.

This part of the book contains information you need to follow the aquarium hobby into the future. As mankind increasingly encroaches upon the living space of other species, more and more organisms will have as their only refuge zoos and aquariums. Several small freshwater fishes now exist solely as aquarium subjects, and this may unfortunately be true one day of some stony corals. Carefully maintained hobbyist aquariums collectively constitute a reserve of captive specimens — and the labor to care for them — unmatched by all public aquariums combined.

Eliminating irresponsible practices, emphasizing captive propagation, and bringing the hobby of marine aquarium keeping to a level of maturity on a scientific par with, for example, horticulture, pose significant challenges to hobbyists and professional aquarists alike.

We aquarists face a peculiar dilemma. On the one hand, by exposing more people to the wonders of life around the world's coral reefs, we are raising the consciousness of a public that seldom or never comes face to face with living marine organisms. Further, we collectively encourage the preservation of reef ecosystems by providing a ready market for sustainably harvested fishes and invertebrates and for organisms farmed in emerging countries. The most noteworthy recent example is the *Tridacna* clam, now being cultivated by indigenous peoples in various parts of Micronesia and the South Pacific. This constitutes an important step in restoring a group of species that had been, for all intents and purposes, economically extinct. There is growing evidence that cultivated stony and soft corals might be used in restoration of damaged reefs, and aquarium hobbyists are at the forefront of this embryonic aspect of aquaculture.

On the other hand, there are those who see this hobby as a threat to reef ecosystems. Our apathy concerning the use of cyanide to collect aquarium specimens in the Philippines and Indonesia is but one example of behavior that has fueled this point of view. This problem has been confronted in the aquarium literature for over 20 years, but millions of cyanide-poisoned specimens continue to flow into the United States each year because many hobbyists do not care enough to question the sources from which dealers obtain their specimens.

In 1995, I founded the American Marinelife Dealers Association in an attempt to gain recognition in the marketplace for those retailers and wholesalers who have made the extra effort to avoid contributing to the ghastly trade in cyanide-caught reef fishes. Since that time, nearly 100 dealers have joined the cause.

I recently went to Washington, DC, to attend a meeting of aquarium industry leaders, public aquarium professionals, and representatives of conservation organizations. This international committee is developing a plan to insure that marine aquarium specimens harvested in the future are collected in environmentally sound, sustainable ways (or are produced in farms and hatcheries) and are properly cared for from reef to retail sale. This is a huge task, but the future of our hobby and industry is at stake.

While acknowledging that we ought to be doing a better job of policing and educating ourselves, we must also remember that captive reef keeping can be part of the solution. In the chapters that follow, I suggest a two-pronged approach for hobbyists to consider: supporting the emergent captive-breeding industry, and helping to educate the purveyors of live reef organisms by refraining from purchasing specimens that have been collected in unsustainable ways or have very little chance for survival in the aquarium. I do not ask that everyone agree with my positions on these issues, only that you consider that your aquarium buying habits can have important consequences for a reef 10,000 miles from your own back door.

Chapter Thirteen

Captive-Propagated Fishes & Invertebrates

The Livestock Supply of the Future

SURPRISINGLY FEW OF THE THOUSANDS of hobbyists with whom I have become acquainted are aware of the number and variety of captive-propagated marine species now available. Most express disbelief at the ease with which a diverse assemblage of invertebrates can be cultivated. A few still think breeding marine fishes is impossible. However, we are witnessing the beginning of a trend that, I think, will ultimately result in the captive culture of most of the marine species sold for aquariums. This will come not only because of expansion of the number of species that can be propagated, but also because hobbyists will focus more and more of their attention on these species, for several reasons.

First, captive-propagated marine fish and invertebrates are far better suited to aquarium life than their counterparts harvested from the wild. Second, such specimens will cost less. Although captive-propagated marine life now often costs more than a comparable wild specimen, the prices will inevitably come down as demand among hobbyists increases, making economies of scale possible for the hatcheries. Also, dealers will learn that they can take a smaller

markup on cultivated livestock, because they will lose fewer specimens, costs of transport may be less, and requirements for maintaining the stock in good condition will be clearly documented and understood. Price reduction resulting from such savings has already happened in the freshwater segment of the aquarium industry and has made it a mass-market business. This must also happen in the marine segment if it is to grow and mature.

The species that will be the keys to this revolution will not be the large angels, wrasses, and triggers so often seen in artificial, fish-only displays. Rather, basslets, gobies, blennies, damsels, dwarf angels, and anemonefishes, along with the many other species that grow to moderate size and reproduce under aquarium conditions, will dominate the market. Why? Because these are the species that can be successfully accommodated in a small, inexpensive system of 50 gallons or less for their entire lifespan. These will be the marine world's equivalent of the widely available guppies, platies, tetras, barbs, dwarf cichlids, and danios of the freshwater hobby. They are also the ones upon which hatchery efforts are most intensely focused.

Similarly, the fact that a collection of soft corals and disc anemones can be maintained successfully in a 10-gallon system costing about a hundred dollars to set up ensures that

Swarming juvenile Maroon Clownfish (*Premnas biaculeatus*), propagated in captivity at C-Quest Farms in Puerto Rico.

there is potentially a much larger market for reef aquariums than at present. When people learn what can be done with a 30-gallon tank, provided a few simple techniques are mastered, dealers will sell more of them, along with the livestock to go in them. This can only help the industry, and it will be captive-propagated livestock that will form the base of this new economic pyramid.

Marine Fish Aquaculture

HOBBYISTS OFTEN ASSUME, since they often have only the experience of freshwater enthusiasts upon which to draw, that the problem with the propagation of marine fish is in enticing a suitable pair to spawn. This is seldom the case, although determining the sex of a fish can sometimes be a problem. Aquarium spawnings of marine fish are actually rather commonplace, and even include species that are

A remarkable crop of Neon Dottybacks (*Pseudochromis aldabraensis*) reared at William Addison's C-Quest facilities.

extremely delicate aquariums subjects. For example, Stan Brown of the Breeder's Registry has a photograph depicting spawning by captive Orange-spotted Filefish (*Oxymonacanthus longirostris*). This species is generally impossible to acclimate to aquarium life, but there they are, placing adhesive eggs on the tank glass. I have observed *Cirripectes* blennies spawning and guarding eggs in aquarium-store holding tanks.

For those species that cannot be induced to spawn in the normal manner, the marine aquaculturist has other options. Eggs and sperm can be stripped from adult fish collected from the ocean, and fertilization can take place in the laboratory. Using this technique, Martin Moe was not only able to culture both the French and Gray Angelfishes (*Pomacanthus paru* and *P. arcuatus*), but also to produce a hybrid of the two species. Moe's fishes were too costly to compete with wild-harvested specimens, but this might not be the case for other species.

No, the problem is not in getting fertilized eggs. The problem is in rearing the offspring past a certain critical point. Marine fish eggs hatch into larvae that are scarcely more than a swimming brain and spinal cord. Many are so small that they are at the lower limit of human visual acuity. Immediately after hatching, the larvae are attached to yolk sacs that provide nutrition, but once these are exhausted, an appropriate food must be available, suspended in the water column, or the larvae will starve. Providing an appropriate substitute for the rich oceanic soup called "plankton" is the primary challenge of the aquaculturist.

The most commonly used plankton substitutes are discussed in Chapter Twelve and include unicellular algae, rotifers, and brine shrimp nauplii. Experiments with more exotic fare have become popular with the proliferation of interest in captive propagation. Mollusk larvae have been used with success, and the larvae of other invertebrate groups, especially arthropods and echinoderms, should prove to be among the most useful. Eggs or sperm may also be used directly as food, and can often be extracted easily from a donor organism. Sea urchins, for example, can be induced to extrude gametes by administering an injection of potassium chloride. Larval echinoderms can also be produced in a laboratory culture, using techniques in widespread use in research laboratories. The size of the food organism is important, although there may be a variety of other factors that determine whether larval marine fishes can survive to metamorphosis on one diet or another. This is an area ripe for extensive research, as very little is known about the ecology of fishes during this critical period of life. Collection or cultivation of natural plankton is another approach often taken in the search for an appropriate larval fish food. A good beginning point for anyone wanting to research this aspect of marine biology is Smith (1977).

A recent survey of 51 public aquariums (Walker, 1996) shows that, for larvae produced as a result of aquarium spawnings, 43% of all species could be reared beyond metamorphosis. Almost half (48%) of the successful rearings were at one institution, suggesting that more species could be reared through the delicate metamorphosis period if the effort is made, and that laboratories that develop techniques that work for one species may have later success with another.

Striped Mushroom Anemone (*Actinodiscus* sp.): much in demand and easily propagated, organisms like these are excellent candidates for small-scale captive reproduction by hobbyist-breeders.

Propagation of Marine Invertebrates

CULTURE OF MARINE INVERTEBRATES from sexually produced larvae offers challenges similar to those faced by the fish culturist. Obtaining larvae is rarely the issue; many species can be induced to shed gametes, and the natural method of fertilization in reef invertebrates is frequently the chance meeting of gametes cast into the open sea. Spawning behavior is timed to maximize the chances of such a meeting, or it may be accomplished through the release of chemicals that lure sperm to eggs. "Sperm" or "male" gametes are, by definition, the smaller, motile member of the pair, while "eggs" or "female" gametes are larger, contain a food supply for the larva, and are incapable of locomotion. Of course, there are exceptions, and the terms "male" and "female" can become blurred in the world of marine invertebrates and algae.

Nevertheless, invertebrate larvae, once obtained from captive or wild spawnings, may prove as difficult to feed as fish larvae are. For example, many attempts by aquarists to rear the popular Banded Coral Shrimp (*Stenopus hispidus*) have failed, despite the fact that a pair will produce a clutch

proximately 100,000 fish per year and is now aggressively marketing directly to pet shops throughout the United States, using overnight door-to-door air freight shipments.

After helping establish the state-of-the-art Micronesian Mariculture Demonstration Center (MMDC) to propagate giant clams in Palau, Gerald Heslinga is now setting up a beachhead in the Hawaii Ocean Science and Technology Park, Kailua-Kona, to bring his breeding programs closer to home. Producing six species of *Tridacna*, his company, Indo-Pacific Sea Farms, also offers started colonies of *Acropora* (in shades of lavender, green, blue, gold, and purple), *Pocillopora*, *Seriatopora*, and *Caulastrea*, as well as various *Sarcophytons* and a neon green *Nephthea*-type soft coral. Marketing to the United

Pioneering reef-fish breeder Bill Addison at his
C-Quest facilities near Juana Diaz, Puerto Rico.

States is done through Reef Science International, of San Ramon, California. (MMDC's pioneering methods and broodstock have paved the way for similar clam-propagation programs elsewhere in the South Pacific.)

Opened in 1996, Oceans, Reefs and Aquariums of Palm Beach, Florida, is planned as among the largest marine aquaculture facilities in the world, with 18,240 square feet of space and the potential to produce 1,000,000 clownfish per year. This new venture plans to expand that capacity in the future, as well as to add additional species to its repertoire, according to its president, Richard Davis.

In recent years, live rock produced by dumping quarry rock at sea and allowing it to become colonized by marine organisms has arrived in the hobbyist market. Roughly 30 businesses are "cultivating" rock in the Gulf of Mexico, and one has a similar enterprise in the Florida Keys. Several mil-

lion pounds of rock are under cultivation. Licenses to conduct these operations were granted as part of new regulations under which the harvest of "natural" live rock in Florida was phased out as of the beginning of 1997. A side benefit to hobbyists is that Atlantic-Caribbean species of stony corals, formerly protected, may now be sold, provided they occur on cultivated live rock.

One of the beauties of aquaculture is that it can also be done successfully from an inland location, which has the effect of moving the supply of fish closer to the people who constitute the market. Thus, my own home region, the Tennessee Valley, now has its own large-scale marine aquaculture business, Wildlife Ecosystems of Cleveland, Tennessee. Dr. Marc Clark established the 12,000-square-foot facility in 1994. Besides clownfish and some of the other "standard" species, Wildlife Ecosystems cultivates corals, clams, macroalgae, and other invertebrates. The company also operates a farm in the Solomon Islands that produces stony corals and tridacnids by growing out small individuals in trays placed in the lagoon.

The collective investment in these facilities is in the range of tens of millions of dollars, clear evidence that, at least for these entrepreneurs, the future of the marine aquarium hobby lies in captive-propagated livestock.

SMALLER, HOME-BASED BUSINESSES. Marine aquaculture businesses operated from a basement or spare outbuilding belonging to a dedicated hobbyist are becoming more common. Perhaps the first was Tropicorium, owned by Richard Perrin. At his home in Michigan, Perrin farms soft and stony corals and gorgonians in greenhouses that once held tropical plants. An expansion of the 36,000-gallon Michigan operation to, among other things, propagate tridacnid clams, is underway in Florida, with plans for a 3-to-4-million-gallon facility.

Noel Curry, president of Scientific Corals, reasoned that if Perrin could succeed in the chilly climate of Michigan, a coral farm in a suburb of Atlanta might also be successful. Curry sells only specimens he has propagated, ranging from pulsing *Xenia umbellata* to a purple-tipped *Acropora*, altogether about a dozen species.

From his small quarters in Murrieta, California, Steve Tyree's Dynamic Ecomorphology company is distributing thousands of captive-propagated stony coral fragments and colonies from various small coral farms. In addition to a selection of dozens of species of *Acropora*, *Montipora*, *Pavona*, *Stylophora*, and others, Tyree offers custom-pre-pared started fragments of rare and hard-to-obtain corals.

Out in Idaho, Geothermal Research Enterprises, under owner LeRoy Headlee, is reportedly farming marine invertebrates and "tank-raised live rock" in greenhouses warmed by water from natural hot springs.

Up in Chicago, Joe Lichtenbert runs Reef Propagations out of his basement, selling several thousand tank-raised clownfishes every year to local shops. (Joe claims to be "the only marine aquaculturist in the country who has made a profit," although Bill Addison counters, with typical good humor, that "this is only true if Joe pays himself an hourly wage of 50 cents.")

This listing can hardly claim to be all-inclusive, but rather is offered to illustrate the growing vitality of the captive breeding movement in North America.

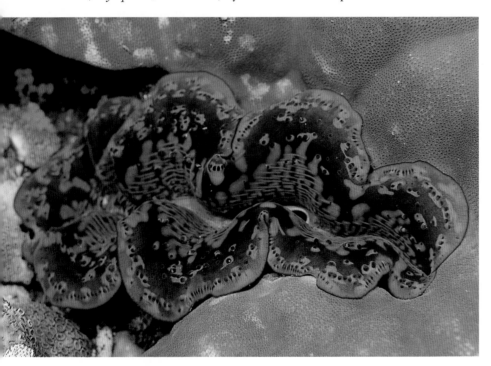

One of the most noteworthy success stories in reef aquaculture, giant clams like this *Tridacna maxima* have been rescued from near extinction by captive breeding.

BACKYARD MARICULTURE is not for the faint of heart, nor, indeed, for the lazy. The proliferation of such cottage industries, however, helps to ensure that species the big companies may ignore, including unique varieties of stony and soft corals, will remain available to aquarium hobbyists, even if wild stocks of these species become depleted or are placed off-limits. I wish them all, together with the other bold adventurers that will soon enter this new industry, the very best of luck. All marine hobbyists should recognize the importance of these ventures to the future of the home aquarium hobby, and should support these fledgling businesses by seeking out and purchasing captive-propagated specimens whenever possible.

A difficult-to-feed species, the Red-finned Batfish (*Platax pinnatus*) typically perishes within months in home aquariums.

these two extremes. These may constitute the majority of species in old, stable ecosystems such as the Great Smoky Mountains. When their habitat is disturbed in some way, perhaps by a forest fire, the pattern of species that results as the ecosystem recovers from disturbance often reveals the basic strategy of these "middle of the road" species. Nature rarely, if ever, fits precisely into human-defined categories.

What does this have to do with reef aquariums? Only that the species that usually do best in captivity are either r-selected species or those k-selected species whose habitat requirements are clearly understood. Aquarium hobbyists, particularly novices, should be aware that some species are on the market whose chances of survival in captivity are slim. Just because a specimen is swimming in a dealer's tank does not mean that it will continue to accommodate itself to an artificial habitat as readily as might another species swimming alongside it. Attempts to categorize marine aquarium fishes to identify those that typically have a high likelihood of survival and those that do not have been met with varying degrees of acceptance by hobbyists and those in the industry. While few disagree that life-history information should be made widely available, the idea of categorizing species into broad "suitable" or "unsuitable" lists is controversial. Oversimplification in such listings can easily lead to misunderstandings.

On the other hand, it does seem appropriate to create some rules of thumb that could make it easier for hobbyists to decide whether a species should or should not be attempted. Whether or not dealers use such categories to choose which species to stock, market forces, driven by hobbyists' collective buying decisions, will ultimately determine whether or not a given species remains in the aquarium trade. This is an alternative far preferable to attempts by government regulators to control the importation of aquarium specimens, if the experiences of other countries are any indication. In Germany, the government's re-

these species, a lifetime is measured in centuries. The giant redwood is an oft-mentioned example.

It is tempting to draw conclusions about the implications for human behavior such observations suggest. One must remember, however, that both strategies succeed, because the criterion for success is longevity of the *species*, not of the individual.

Some species, of course, fall somewhere in between

sponse to environmentalists' complaints about the continued importation of certain butterflyfishes was to place off limits the entire Family Chaetodontidae. But this was an oversimplification. Despite their general reputation for delicacy, some of the best aquarium species are butterflyfishes. These appropriate species, unfortunately, were also included in the ban. Hobbyists and dealers in the United States are justifiably concerned that any government regulators here will be equally myopic. Hence some are opposed to the kind of listmaking found in this chapter.

Nevertheless, I believe we must begin the educational process somewhere. Herewith are nine categories of selected species that I prefer to designate "of special concern" to hobbyists. In each case, one or more aspects of their ecology currently render them less easily maintained in a typical home-based aquarium. Consider these facts carefully before purchasing these species.

All of the obligate cleaners, such as this Hawaiian Cleaner Wrasse (*Labroides phthirophagus*), are best left in the wild.

Category 1

The species is protected in its native habitat.

IT SHOULD BE OBVIOUS that all collecting of aquarium specimens must be done in accordance with local environmental regulations, but hobbyists should be aware that some protected species are still collected. I suspect Caribbean stony corals are subject to poaching. My company has received numerous requests for sea dragons, such as *Phycodurus eques*, and *Phyllopteryx taeniolatus*, which are protected in their native Australia. Other members of the Family Syngnathidae, to which sea dragons belong, pose special problems for aquarists (see Category 8). Perhaps the most commonly seen species that may be poached from restricted waters is the Garibaldi Damselfish (*Hypsypops rubicunda*), found in the kelp forests off the southern California coast. This is a cool-water species that is often inappropriately maintained. If one were considering an aquarium display depicting the

fauna of the kelp forest, one might then inquire as to the legal availability of this species. It is out of place, however, in the warm water of a tropical reef tank. The King Angelfish (*Holacanthus passer*) is protected in a portion of its home range, but aquarium specimens are legally collected in other areas. (Hence the importance of knowing where a specimen originated.) The aquarium-fish hobby has a generally good reputation for not trading in illegal species, and I think we can all play a role in never encouraging the collection of banned or questionable livestock.

Category 2

Removal of this species is demonstrably detrimental to other reef species, i.e., this is a "key" species in its habitat.

SPECIES THAT EXHIBIT CLEANING BEHAVIOR, and that are locally rare, may fall into this category. Key species are often the subjects of ecological research, but I know of no study that examines the impact of collection of cleaner species, for example, for the aquarium trade. Perhaps of more concern than mere removal is the fate of such species once collected. If a potentially key species is also one that fails to survive readily in captivity, a stronger argument for abstaining from collecting it can be made. Obligate cleaners, such as the Hawaiian Cleaner Wrasse (*Labroides phthirophagus*) seldom survive for long in the aquarium. Further, this species is endemic, meaning it is found only in the Hawaiian archipelago.

The Magnificent Anemone (*Heteractis magnifica*) is seldom amenable to aquarium care and represents another example of a potentially key species. Since the population of clownfishes in a given area is directly tied to the abundance of these anemones, reducing the anemone population may have consequences for the clownfish population, especially since the anemones are slow-growing, long-lived, and have few offspring.

Category 3

*The species grows too large for the
typical home aquarium.*

MANY SPECIES OF SHARKS AND RAYS (Order Elasmobranchi), for example, grow too large for standard home aquariums. Unsuspecting aquarists, when faced with the question of what to do with an overgrown shark, often turn to public aquariums for help. Only rarely is the public aquarium able to accommodate the specimen. Other big predators pose similar problems. Always find out the adult size of any prospective aquarium specimen.

Many sharks are k-selected species that mature late and have few young. Because of their important role at the top of many food chains, sharks are receiving a growing amount of attention from marine ecologists. Look for shark fishing, as well as collection of live sharks for aquariums, to receive regulatory scrutiny in the near future.

Among the sharks often sold for aquariums are the leopard sharks (*Triakis* spp.) the wobbegongs (*Orectolobus* spp.) and, most commonly, the Nurse Shark (*Ginglymostoma cirratum*). Nurse Sharks, so named because they produce a sucking sound when feeding (like the sound of a child nursing) are frequently sold to aquarium shops shortly after birth, when they are about 24 inches in length. In a few years' time, the fish will have grown to a 4-foot specimen that is unable to turn around in a 300-gallon tank. Nine-foot Nurse Sharks are not uncommon in the waters of the Caribbean and Florida.

Rays are members of the shark clan adapted to life on the bottom. Spotted rays (*Taeniura* spp.) and stingrays (*Dasyatis americana*, for example) need broad expanses of sandy bottom and may grow to several feet in diameter. Stingrays, of course, have venomous spines they use for defense, another potential deterrent to the home hobbyist (see Category 5).

Category 4

The species is aggressive and territorial.

ANYONE, OF COURSE, can end up with a fish like this. The King Angelfish (*Holacanthus passer*) can cause problems, as can many members of Family Balistidae, the triggerfishes. Any large triggerfish has powerful jaws and sharp teeth. As they grow, their aggressive tendencies become more apparent. The Queen Triggerfish (*Balistes vetula*) is among the largest — and nastiest — of its family. I know of one diver who lost a thumb to a Queen Trigger in the Florida Keys. Another trigger with a nasty disposition is the Undulated Triggerfish (*Balistapus undulatus*).

Aggressive fish must often have an entire aquarium devoted to them, but do frequently have the advantage of being extremely hardy and undemanding. If this is your goal, so be it, but keep your hands out of the tank.

Category 5

The species is venomous.

"VENOM" REFERS TO A POISON that is introduced into the body of another organism by means of a weapon of some kind — fangs, for example, or a stinger. Like aggressiveness, the possession of venom does not make a species unsuitable for aquarium life, but this trait must be considered by any prudent person. The presence of small children in the home might rule out the keeping of venomous species.

Lionfishes, Family Scorpaenidae, are splendid aquarium fishes, even though they have venomous spines. Genera in this family include *Dendrochirus*, *Pterois*, and *Inimicus*.

A closely related subfamily, Synanceiinae, the stonefishes, includes species that have caused human deaths. Contact with the dorsal spines of a *Synanceia* species has been known to result in such excruciating pain that victims have amputated their own limbs to achieve relief.

Less frightening are the foxfaces, Family Siganidae, including species of *Siganus* and, most commonly in the aquarium trade, *Siganus vulpinus*, the Common Foxface. These herbivorous grazers are armed with venomous dorsal spines. Contact feels much like a bee sting, according to reports from victims. Similarly, the Coral Catfish (*Plotosus lineatus*) shares with some of its freshwater cousins the possession of a barbed, venomous pectoral fin spine. Black with longitudinal yellow stripes, these fish are cute as juveniles, when they gather into a school. As they grow, they change color to a drab gray, become solitary and aggressive, and are not cute at all.

Among invertebrates, the Blue-ringed Octopus (*Hapalochlaena lunulata* and *H. maculosa*) can administer a deadly bite, as can many species of cone snails (*Conus*). Many other *Conus* species can sting, though not fatally. Brightly colored mollusks that

show up in Indo-Pacific shipments should always be handled with care until positive identification can be made. Several sea urchins are capable of delivering a venomous "bite" with specially modified appendages. Because of the appearance of these structures, venomous urchins are sometimes labeled "Flower Urchins" in the trade. They should be handled with extreme caution. The long-spined sea urchins (*Diadema* spp.) are prickly, but impaling oneself with a spine, though painful, is hardly a serious injury. *Diadema antillarum* specimens are protected from collection in some areas.

Some fish are not venomous, but they *are* toxic, meaning that their flesh, if eaten, is harmful to the predator. Among these are the puffers, Family Tetraodontidae, which number human beings among the species that have died from consuming their flesh. So, too, do the dragonets, Family Callionymidae, protect themselves from harm. Neither of these families is prone to cause problems in the aquarium,

Worthy of care but not for children's tanks are venomous species such as this Tassled Scorpionfish (*Scorpaenopsis oxycephala*).

however, and several species are widely kept. On the other hand, boxfishes and trunkfishes, Family Ostraciidae, all are able to exude a toxin that is deadly even to themselves in the confines of an aquarium. Toxin secretion is a response to stress, so careful consideration should be given to including these species in a community aquarium. Cowfishes (*Lactoria* spp.) are among the most commonly imported members of this clan.

Another kind of "venom" is the ability to produce an electric shock. The Electric Ray (*Narcine brasiliensis*) reaches only 18 inches, but reportedly can generate a shock sufficient to knock down a human.

Category 6

The natural lifespan of the species is brief.

INCLUSION OF THIS CATEGORY has more to do with consumer education than with reef conservation. Species with a brief lifespan are often r-selected and are so abundant that removal of a few specimens from a given area will have little significance. A short lifespan can actually be advantageous in an aquarium species, as such species typically grow rapidly, mature early and have many offspring. This is what has made killifish, including annual types that live only a few months, popular with a segment of the freshwater aquarium hobby. Nevertheless, many hobbyists are disappointed to find out after the fact that the seemingly untimely death of a specimen is normal for that species. The species most often generating these kinds of complaints, and their approximate natural lifespans, are:
- Octopuses: survive 1 to 3 years, depending upon the species; females invariably die after the young hatch.
- Seahorses: survive 1 to 3 years; require appropriate live foods.
- Nudibranchs and sea slugs: smaller species usually live a year at most; may be very difficult to feed.

Truly flamboyant, most nudibranchs, such as *Chromodoris bullocki*, have extremely short lifespans, even in the wild.

Category 7

Special requirements for this species, usually dietary needs, cannot be met by the home aquarist. Appropriate conditions for keeping this species are not yet defined.

THIS IS THE LARGEST CATEGORY and contains the greatest number of species regularly seen in the aquarium trade. These species should not be dogmatically regarded as "impossible." Rather, they should be regarded as appropriate subjects for research into methods for their successful captive husbandry. Who should or should not be permitted to acquire such species for this purpose, of course, remains an open and politically touchy question.

Chief among the species with specialized dietary requirements are the butterflyfishes, Family Chaetodontidae. While there are butterflyfishes that adapt readily to aquarium diets, the species listed in Table 14-1 (page 296) usually do not. Most of them feed on stony-coral polyps or other sessile invertebrates and will starve rather than accept an unfamiliar food. The Short-bodied Blenny (*Exallias brevis*) and the Orange-spotted Filefish (*Oxymonacanthus longirostris*) share this trait with the butterflyfishes.

Other tastes are more exotic. Mimic blennies (*Plagiotremus* spp.) feed by dashing out and tearing bits of flesh from other fishes. Some have evolved elaborate disguises, usually contriving to look like harmless species. For the wrasses listed in Table 14-1, food items are as varied as polychaete worms, benthic invertebrates, and parasites picked from the bodies of other fishes. The Red-finned Batfish (*Platax pinnatu*s) often lives around mangrove roots where it feeds on a multitude of encrusting invertebrates. While this species may sometimes learn to feed on shrimp or other foods in the aquarium, it seldom lives longer than a few months. The Clown Sweetlips (*Plectorhinchus chaetodontoides*), which mimics a toxic invertebrate and is perhaps toxic itself, feeds at night on a variety of living invertebrates and generally refuses to eat in the aquarium. The dietary requirements of angelfishes apparently include

Evolved to feed on calcareous sponges, this nudibranch (*Notodoris minor*) is destined to starve in captive systems.

a large proportion of benthic invertebrates, sponges in particular, and some species may not fare well without these foods. In some cases, specimens collected as large juveniles seem to adapt best to aquarium diets, while smaller or larger individuals do not. The Rock Beauty (*Holacanthus tricolor*) fits this description. This may be because the natural dietary preferences of the juvenile differ from those of the adult. Another sponge-eating fish that does not survive well under aquarium conditions is the Moorish Idol (*Zanclus cornutus*). A specimen maintained in my office died after about a year, for no apparent reason, despite appropriate water conditions and a varied diet, including a commercial food claimed to contain marine sponges. Shrimpfishes are tiny and generally spend their lives hanging nose down among the spines of a sea urchin. They require minuscule live foods to survive. Some species of parrotfishes feed by biting off chunks of living coral, digesting the polyps and excreting coral sand. Others feed only on leafy sea grasses. Neither type survives well on captive diets.

An interesting subset of this group of species are those that public aquariums were unable to maintain successfully for a year or more. (Hutchins, et al., 1994) This list is reproduced as Table 14-2 (page 298). Note that the same species appear again and again on lists such as this, irrespective of the compiler.

Invertebrates with specialized food needs include most nudibranchs and sea slugs. Flamingo tongue snails (*Cyphoma* spp.) all feed exclusively on gorgonians.

As explained in Chapter Twelve, some fishes may not adapt to aquarium life because the appropriate social milieu cannot be provided. This may be one reason why cleaner wrasses, such as the common *Labroides dimidiatus*, so often fail to thrive. Similarly, tilefishes (Family Malacanthidae) fare poorly because in nature they are seldom far from their burrow in the sand, into which they dart immediately at any sign of danger. The often-imported Purple Tilefish

Table 14-1

Fishes with Special Dietary Needs

Blenniidae		**Haemulidae**	
Aspidontus spp.	Mimic Blennies	*Plectorhinchus chaetodontoides*	Clown Sweetlips
Exallias brevis	Short-bodied Blenny	**Labridae**	
Plagiotremus spp.	Mimic Blennies	*Anampses* spp.	Tamarin Wrasses
Centriscidae		*Labroides phthirophagus*	Hawaiian Cleaner Wrasse
Aeoliscus spp.	Shrimpfishes	*Labropsis* spp.	Tube-Lip Wrasses
Centriscus spp.	Shrimpfishes	*Macropharyngodon* spp.	Leopard Wrasses
Chaetodontidae		*Paracheilinus* spp.	Flasher Wrasses
Chaetodon aureofasciatus	Golden-striped Butterflyfish	*Pseudojuloides* spp.	Pencil Wrasses
C. austriacus	Exquisite Butterflyfish	*Stethojulis* spp.	Stethojulis Wrasses
C. baronessa	Eastern Triangular Butterflyfish	**Malacanthidae**	
		Hoplolatilus purpureus	Purple Tilefish
C. bennetti	Bennett's Butterflyfish	**Monacanthidae**	
C. citrinellus	Speckled Butterflyfish	*Oxymonacanthus longirostris*	Orange-spotted Filefish
C. guentheri	Guenther's Butterflyfish	*O. halli*	Red Sea Orange-spotted Filefish
C. guttatissimus	Spotted Butterflyfish		
C. larvatus	Orange-Face Butterflyfish	**Muraenidae**	
C. marcellae	French Butterflyfish	*Rhinomuraena quaesita*	Blue, Black Ribbon Eels
C. melapterus	Arabian Butterflyfish	**Platacidae**	
C. meyeri	Meyer's Butterflyfish	*Platax pinnatus*	Red-finned Batfish
C. nigropunctatus	Black-spotted Butterflyfish	**Pomacanthidae**	
C. octofasciatus	Eight-striped Butterflyfish	*Centropyge boylei*	Boyle's Angelfish
C. ornatissimus	Ornate Butterflyfish	*C. multifasciatus*	Multi-barred Angelfish
C. plebeius	Blue-blotched Butterflyfish	*Desmoholacanthus arcuatus*	Bandit Angelfish
C. quadrimaculatus	Four-Spot Butterflyfish	*Holacanthus tricolor*	Rock Beauty Angelfish
C. rainfordi	Rainford's Butterflyfish	*Pygoplites diacanthus*	Regal Angelfish
C. reticulatus	Reticulated Butterflyfish	**Scaridae**	
C. speculum	Ovalspot Butterflyfish	*Bolbometopon.* spp.	Parrotfishes
C. triangulum	Triangular Butterflyfish	*Cetoscarus* spp.	Parrotfishes
C. trichrous	Tahiti Butterflyfish	*Scarisoma* spp.	Parrotfishes
C. tricinctus	Three-striped Butterflyfish	*Scarus* spp.	Parrotfishes
C. trifascialis	Chevron Butterflyfish	**Zanclidae**	
C. trifasciatus	Redfin Butterflyfish	*Zanclus cornutus*	Moorish Idol
C. zanzibariensis	Zanzibar Butterflyfish		

(*Hoplolatilus purpureus*) easily injures itself in repeated, futile attempts to seek shelter when it is confined.

Examples of invertebrates for which the home aquarium environment may be too confining are the pelagic sea jellies, most species of squid, and the Chambered Nautilus (*Nautilus pompilius*).

Species such as the Common Cleaner Wrasse (*Labroides dimidiatus*) bridge the gap between the category of species that are at the moment "impossible," or nearly so, to those that clearly can be kept alive in captivity for long periods, but which require an unusually large investment of time and effort from the aquarist.

Category 8

The species can be maintained only if its special requirements are met; such requirements can be provided in a home aquarium setting, given sufficient effort.

WITH THESE SPECIES, the problem is usually one of providing an adequate diet. The Achilles Tang (*Acanthurus achilles*) is an exception. Since it inhabits very turbulent water and grazes heavily on algae, it often fares poorly in aquariums with low water movement. On the other hand, its cousin, the Lipstick Tang (*Naso lituratus*), must have brown algae, such as kelp, included in its diet in order to survive long term.

Frogfishes (Family Antennariidae) all feed by enticing prey into the range of their cavernous mouths with a "fishing pole" that is actually a modified fin ray. Antennarids require regular feeding with live marine fish.

Callionymids, such as the popular Psychedelic Mandarin (*Synchiropus picturatus*) or Mandarinfish (*Synchiropus splendidus*), feed exclusively on tiny benthic invertebrates and should be placed into a well-established system with an abundant natural population of benthic copepods.

Species of *Amblygobius*, including *A. decussatus*, the Cross-hatched Hover Goby; *A. rainfordi*, Rainford's Goby; and *A. phalaena*, Phalaena's Hover Goby; along with *Valenciennea strigata*, the Golden-headed Sleeper Goby; *V. puellaris*, the Diamond Goby; and *Signigobius biocellatus*, the Signal Goby, all feed by taking up a mouthful of substrate and "chewing" it, expelling the sand through the gill covers and extracting the small invertebrates and algae therein. Care must be taken to insure that the aquarium has a sufficiently "live" substrate to fulfill the needs of these species.

Similarly, jawfishes (Family Opistognathidae) are among the most desirable of aquarium species, but must be provided with a deep substrate in which to excavate a burrow. Lacking a burrow, jawfishes spend all their time hiding and thus starve. Seahorses and pipefishes (Family Syngnathidae) are also difficult to keep if not provided with abundant, living foods.

Creatures typically found in deep water, such as the Pinecone Fish (*Monocentrus japonicus*) and the flashlight fishes (*Photoblepharon* and *Anomalops*) seem to require darkness and living foods. These fishes are sometimes collected

A typical corallivore, Rainford's Butterflyfish (*Chaetodon rainfordi*) should be shunned by knowledgeable marine aquarists.

Table 14-2

Marine Fish Species Not Successfully Maintained by Public Aquariums

Blenniidae

Aspidontus spp.	Mimic Blennies
Exallias brevis	Short-bodied Blenny
Plagiotremus spp.	Mimic Blennies

Chaetodontidae

Chaetodon austriacus	Exquisite Butterflyfish
C. baronessa	Eastern Triangular Butterflyfish
C. bennetti	Bennett's Butterflyfish
C. melapterus	Arabian Butterflyfish
C. meyeri	Meyer's Butterflyfish
C. octofasciatus	Eight-striped Butterflyfish
C. ornatissimus	Ornate Butterflyfish
C. plebeius	Blue-blotched Butterflyfish
C. triangulum	Triangular Butterflyfish
C. trifascialis	Chevron Butterflyfish
C. zanzibariensis	Zanzibar Butterflyfish

Labridae

Anampses spp.	Tamarin Wrasses
Labroides phthirophagus	Hawaiian Cleaner Wrasse
Macropharyngodon spp.	Leopard Wrasses
Pseudojuloides spp.	Pencil Wrasses
Stethojulis spp.	Stethojulis Wrasses

Monacanthidae

Oxymonacanthus longirostris	Orange-spotted Filefish

Pomacanthidae

Centropyge boylei	Boyle's Angelfish

Serranidae

Pseudanthias pascalis	Purple Queen Anthias

and exported to the aquarium trade because they possess luminescent organs that hobbyists find intriguing. But they require husbandry at a level more commonly found in public, rather than private, aquariums.

Among the butterflyfish family are a few species that are neither easy nor impossible, with a curiously high number of species in which some individuals will adapt to the aquarium and some will not. The following butterflyfishes are slow to acclimate to aquarium conditions and may require careful attention for two months or more, some failing even then to flourish: *Chaetodon capistratus* (Foureye), *C. collare* (Red-tailed), *C. ephippium* (Saddleback), *C. ocellatus* (Spotfin), *C. sedentarius* (Reef), *C. striatus* (Banded), *Chelmon rostratus* (Copperband) and *Chelmonops truncatus* (Truncate Coralfish). Of these, the Caribbean species (Foureye, Spotfin, Reef, Banded) are readily maintained in public aquariums, suggesting that the problem may be one of confinement or the need for a particular social milieu. The schooling, planktivorous species of *Heniochus*, including the Pennant Butterflyfish (*H. acuminatus*), may also be difficult if not kept in a group and provided with live foods.

Planktivorous fish species may or may not be easily adaptable to the aquarium, depending upon the size of the food items pursued. Smaller species, such as many anthiids, may need not only an appropriate plankton substitute but also the correct social environment. Other anthiids, however, make very good aquarium specimens. This family is one that a novice should skirt, returning later as a seasoned hobbyist. Much depends upon the choice of species and the care with which specimens are collected and handled.

Among the invertebrates that require special husbandry are those that feed on plankton. These include sponges, nonphotosynthetic soft corals, such as *Dendronephthya*, nonphotosynthetic gorgonians, such as *Mopsella*, and the stony coral *Tubastraea*. Filter-feeding echinoderms include the delicate crinoids, or "feather stars," and the basket stars, close relatives of brittle stars. Apparently, the problem with many of these species is not in finding a satisfactory food. Cultured unicellular algae, brine shrimp, and microinvertebrates can be used to feed them. The trouble arises in providing adequate quantities, perhaps at frequent intervals, to meet the needs of larger specimens, such as the basket stars. There is also the danger of starvation when food cultures fail to perform as anticipated.

Badly overcollected in some areas, giant clams (*Tridacna* spp.) are best acquired as captive-bred rather than wild-harvested.

The Blue Ribbon Eel (*Rhinomuraena quaesita*), being shy and difficult to feed, has a poor survival record in captive systems.

A few other difficult invertebrate species are regularly imported for reef tanks. These include the stony corals *Heliofungia actiniformis* and *Goniopora* spp. Neither seems to fare well for the majority of hobbyists, although there are some reports of successes.

One can argue that the requirements for all photosynthetic invertebrates, stony corals in particular, are exacting. But I am suggesting that certain species lie at the outer extreme of fastidiousness, even for the experienced aquarist, and are best avoided.

Category 9

The species is hardy in the aquarium and its care requirements are understood, but problems resulting from methods of collecting and handling are frequent.

THIS FINAL CATEGORY is the most controversial, because the species included are among the best aquarium animals. After many years of working with imported marine fish and talking to hundreds of people who have tried, with varying degrees of success, to maintain marine aquariums, I have

Table 14-3

Marine Fish with a High Likelihood of Problems
Resulting from Improper Collecting and Handling Techniques

Acanthuridae		**Pomacanthidae**	
Acanthurus nigricans	Powder Brown Tang,	*Centropyge bicolor*	Bicolor Angelfish
A. leucosternon	Powder Blue Tang	*C. bispinosus*	Coral Beauty Angelfish
Paracanthurus hepatus	Regal Tang, Hippo Tang	*Pomacanthus imperator*	Emperor Angelfish
		P. navarchus	Majestic Angelfish
Balistidae		*P. xanthometapon*	Blueface Angelfish
Balistoides conspicillum	Clown Triggerfish		
		Pomacentridae	
Labridae		*Amphiprion* spp.	Clownfishes*
Coris aygula	Threespot Wrasse	*Premnas biaculeatus*	Maroon Clownfish*
Choerodon fasciatus	Harlequin Tuskfish		
Novaculichthys taeniourus	Dragon Wrasse	**Serranidae**	
Thalassoma lunare	Moon Wrasse, Lunar Wrasse	*Calloplesiops altivelis*	Comet

*Wild-caught specimens only.

noted that an unreasonable number of people fail with some very popular species. It is my view that most of the time, these fish are subjected to stressful conditions during collection (often, perhaps, with cyanide) and subsequent holding and shipment. The list is presented as Table 14-3 (above). **My advice to hobbyists concerning this group: only purchase these fish from a supplier whose reputation you know and trust completely.** It is tempting to suggest that these species should be avoided altogether, in an effort to thwart the cyanide trade. This, however, would only penalize those competent collectors, wholesalers, and dealers who make the extra effort to bring high-quality specimens of these species to the American market.

A few comments are in order regarding these species: Powder Blue Tangs, Regal Tangs, Emperor Angelfish, Harlequin Tuskfish, Coral Beauties, and Dragon Wrasses from localities other than the Philippines and Bali do very well and typically command a much higher price than their less-healthy counterparts. Wild clownfishes, except for the mated pairs often exported from Australia, arrive in very poor condition and are usually suffering from *Brooklynella* infestation (see Chapter Eleven). While these fishes can be treated and often recover, many do not. It seems wasteful, therefore, to continue to remove them from the ocean when captive-propagated specimens of all popular clownfish species are now widely available and inexpensive.

Although the Tables in this chapter will cause controversy, my motivation for assembling and including them is to spare at least one novice aquarist the consternation of watching a splendid, exotic animal slowly die despite his or her best, most conscientious efforts to keep it alive. No "hobby" should exact such a price.

Epilogue

L AST FATHER'S DAY, my Mom bought my Dad a new microscope. From a drawer in my office, I was able to resurrect some slides, pipettes, and other related paraphernalia. I also found a wooden box, filled with prepared microscope slides I had made and used when I taught biology. They were all common things, textbook things, like *Hydra* and *Cyclops*, that are used all the time by biology instructors. But to Dad, they were anything but commonplace.

"All my life, I've read about these varmints, but this is the first time I've actually seen them," he told me. He had collected his own pond water and looked at the usual household specimens, but he was now getting his first look at these creatures from a biological culture lab.

Dad was 83 at the time. For over 35 years, it had never occurred to me that he hadn't had a chance to make these kinds of observations. After all, it was I who had gone away to school. He had had no education beyond high school. As a boy, he was an avid amateur scientist, with a chemistry lab in the basement and the microscope his father had given him. He had just turned 17 by October of 1929 when the stock market crashed, and with it any hopes he had of going to college and studying science. Now we sat, he and I, engrossed as we had been on the day so long ago when he had given me my first microscope. This time, I lectured

while he peered into the eyepiece, enthralled — another of life's pathways come full circle.

There are intriguing similarities between aquarium ecosystems and controlled terrestrial environments. A garden pond, for example, when properly executed becomes simply a very large planted freshwater aquarium. Vascular plants remove wastes and help to minimize algae growth; fishes feed on insects and plant matter, grow fat, and spawn, producing larvae that feed on microinvertebrates. The processes of biological filtration, denitrification, and assimilation are played out here as they are in the aquarium.

Controlled terrestrial environments, from the terrarium, or "Wardian case," to greenhouses, conservatories, and landscaped "natural" gardens, all exhibit features that coincide with circumstances found in aquariums. Encasement in a glass box is one reason why parasite infestations that seem insignificant in vast ocean ranges can be devastating in the aquarium. The parasites, like their hosts, are confined to an unnaturally circumscribed environment. The open sea, to a microorganism, is boundless and infinite in scope. In a relatively tiny aquarium, even one containing hundreds of gallons of water, parasite numbers can reach plague proportions quickly. Similarly, plants confined to a greenhouse may suffer infestations of insects that are seldom a serious problem for plants grown in the open. And just as the aquarist must sometimes resort to copper medication in the aquarium, even the most devoted organic gardener must sometimes resort to chemicals or emergency biological controls rather than offer up the contents of the greenhouse to certain devastation.

Each kind of captive ecosystem — aquarium, pond, greenhouse, or garden — is governed by rules set down in ancient evolutionary pathways. All life is related, and each living thing, bacterium or brontosaurus, adheres to the principle of adaptation shaped by natural selection. The differences among ecosystems are in degree, not kind. Sometimes, I fear, we humans fail to respect this. For the first time in history, we have the ability to alter the very essence of the biosphere. Our activities have opened the ozone layer, exposing the Earth to unnatural levels of ultraviolet radiation. We have harvested nearly all of the redfish population of the Gulf of Mexico in a few years because of a food fad. We dump trillions of gallons of precious freshwater, laden with pollution, sewage, and silt, into the streams, rivers, and oceans of the world. The litany of examples of our foolish disregard for the sanctity of the world's ecosystems goes on and on. Yet, the same technology that permits us to destroy also permits us to build.

Take, for example, an obscure little catfish called the Smoky Madtom (*Noturus baileyi*). Thought to be extinct since the 1950s, this endangered species, one of many in the once-pristine streams of the southern Appalachians, was rediscovered in Monroe County, Tennessee, in the 1980s. Since then, efforts to restore the fish to Abrams Creek in the Great Smoky Mountains National Park, the site of its original discovery, have been successful. Fertile eggs were collected, reared in an aquarium, and transplanted to the creek. Last spring, nests of breeding male Smoky Madtoms were once again found in Abrams Creek for the first time in nearly three decades. Humans do have the power to effect positive change.

Marine aquarium keeping, as a hobby or a profession, is beginning to have its own breeding success stories. We now stand at the threshold of a revolution. Freed from total dependence upon wild creatures as stock-in-trade, an expanding hobby will see a larger and larger proportion of species supplied through some form of cultivation. Someday, perhaps, only new species — and there are still thousands of them on the reefs of the world that would make good aquarium subjects but that have not yet been introduced to the trade — will be harvested. Once techniques for the care of such a species are understood, it could then be cultured by some presently known, or yet to be discovered, technique. Adapting wild species to cultivation is nothing new, it is business as usual in the horticulture industry.

A short drive from my vegetable patch is a complex of greenhouses and laboratories where plant-tissue culture techniques that were the stuff of pure research when I was in college are put to practical use daily. Orchid species that once were harvested from the rain forests of Central America are cultivated for the florist industry. And new species are brought into the horticultural trade every year as a result of botanical forays into the wild. This is how marine biology and the ornamental marinelife industry must work together in the future.

Nevertheless, we amateurs must not, in our excitement, trample down the whole meadow, just to pluck a few wildflowers. We have reached a point where our efforts can mean much more than trendy decor for the den. Reports on restoration of damaged reefs through transplantation of coral fragments taken from healthy reefs are many (Guzman, 1993; Harrison & Wallace, 1990; Rinkevich, 1982; Rinkevich, 1995; Sato, 1985). Coral transplantation may well be the best approach to reef restoration that preserves biodiversity. Studies reveal that coral larvae reared in the laboratory can survive well when returned to the reef. Juvenile corals survived better when their environments were controlled, thereby protecting them from sedimentation, grazing by predators, and encroachment by filamentous algae. Acclimating small fragments of corals in the laboratory resulted in reduced mortality and prompt regeneration.

In a restoration experiment in Costa Rica, more than 80% of directly transplanted coral fragments ("healthy" reef to "damaged" reef, with no intervening laboratory stay) were alive and growing after three years. Suppose that the fragments had been removed to the laboratory, allowed to recover and to begin growing again under the watchful eye of a technician able to provide them with optimally controlled conditions, and then moved to the transplant site. The success rate could approach 100%.

The strategy of cultivating small individuals of a target species under controlled conditions before restoring the species to wild habitat appears to work for madtoms and mountain streams, for corals and reefs, and probably for any habitat restoration project. What mankind can foolishly destroy, we can sometimes wisely rebuild. Being a part of that continues to fill me with excitement.

Selected Sources

A Sampling of Information Sources for Reef Aquarists

INTERNET SITES

Perhaps the best source of information for a beginner is a consultation with an experienced aquarist in his or her neighborhood. On the Internet, almost anyone in the world might be in your "neighborhood." Below are a few of the sites I have found useful. (This is necessarily only a partial list. Each of the sites has multiple links to other sites of interest.)

American Marinelife Dealers Assn.
www.amdareef.com
Aqualink Aquaria Web Resources
www.aqualink.com
Breeder's Registry
www.breeders-registry.gen.ca.us
Compuserve Aquaria/Fish Forum
petsforum.com
Coral Reef Alliance
www.coral.org
Coral Reef Aquaculture Sites
farmedcoral.homestead.com
International Marinelife Alliance
www.imamarinelife.org
Marine Aquarium Council (MAC)
www.aquariumcouncil.org
#Reefs (Reef Aquarium Forum)
www.reefs.org
Reef Central
www.reefcentral.com

Reef Relief
www.reefrelief.org
U.S. Government Coral Reef Task Force
coralreef.gov

BOOKS

The Aquatic Bookshop
P.O. Box 2150
Single Springs, CA
(530) 622-7157
Web site: www.byobs.com/aquaticbookshop
Large offering of frehwater and marine aquarium titles.

Fish Books
Raymond M. Sutton, Jr.
P.O. Box 330
Williamsburg, Kentucky 40769
(606) 549-2288
Natural history books with both recent works and antiquarian titles for serious collectors.

Freshwater & Marine Aquarium Books
P.O. Box 487
Sierra Madre, CA 91025
(818) 355-1476
Anthologies from the pages of FAMA Magazine.

Gary Bagnall Bookseller
3100 McMillan Rd.
San Luis Obispo, CA 93041
(805) 542-9295
Old aquarium magazines, books, and other arcana.

Green Turtle Publications
P.O. Box 17925
Plantation, FL 33318
Classic marine handbooks by Martin A. Moe, Jr.

Microcosm Ltd.
P.O. Box 550
Charlotte, VT 05445
(802) 425-5700
Web site: www.microcosm-books.com
Aquarium and natural history books.

Odyssey Publishing
11558 Rolling Hills Drive
El Cajon, CA 92020
(619) 579-8405
Books for aquarists and divers on Indo-Pacific natural history.

Sea Challengers Natural History Books
35 Versailles Court
Danville, CA 94506
(925) 327-7750
Web site: www.seachallengers.com
Outstanding selection of natural history books for divers, snorkelers, and marine hobbyists.

T.F.H. Publications, Inc.
One T.F.H. Plaza
Neptune City, NJ 07753
(732) 988-8400
Web site: www.tfh.com
Large offering of freshwater and marine aquarium titles.

Two Little Fishies
4016 El Prado Boulevard
Coconut Grove, FL 33133
(800) 969-7742
Web site: www.petsforum.com/twolilfishies
Books and videos for marine aquarists.

PERIODICALS

Aquarium Fish Magazine
Russ Case, Editor
Fancy Publications
P.O. Box 6050
Mission Viejo, CA 92690-6050
(949) 855-8822
Web site: www.animalnetwork.com/fish

Aquarium Frontiers On-Line
Terry Siegel, Editor
Web site: www.animalnetwork.com

Aquarium Sciences and Conservation
Chapman & Hall
400 Market Street, Suite 750
Philadelphia, PA 19106
Web site: www.thomsonscience.com
e-mail: chsub@itps.co.uk

Freshwater and Marine Aquarium
Patricia Crews, Editor
144 West Sierra Madre Boulevard
Sierra Madre, CA 91024
(818) 355-1476
Web site: www.mag-web.com/fama

Journal of MaquaCulture
Stanley Brown, Editor
P.O. Box 255373
Sacramento, CA 95865-5373
e-mail: fishxing@netcom.com

Marine Fish Monthly
Boyce Phipps, Editor
3243 Highway 61 East
Luttrell, TN 37779
e-mail: pubcon@worldnet.att.net

Ocean Realm
Charlene deJori & Cheryl Schorp, Editors
4067 Broadway
San Antonio, TX 78209
(210) 824-8099

Practical Fishkeeping
Steve Windsor, Editor
EMAP Pursuit Publishing
Bretton Court
Bretton, Peterborough
PE3 8DZ United Kingdom
011-44-1733-264666

SeaScope
Thomas A. Frakes, Editor
Aquarium Systems, Inc.
8141 Tyler Boulevard
Mentor, OH 44060
Web site: www.aquariumsystems.com

Tropical Fish Hobbyist
One T.F.H. Plaza
Neptune City, NJ 07753
(732) 988-8400
e-mail: info@tfh.com
Web site: www.tfh.com

MARINE AQUARIUM SOCIETIES

NATIONAL

Marine Aquarium Societies of North America (MASNA)
c/o Nancy Swart, President
31 Lagoon Drive
Hawthorn Woods, IL 60047
(847) 438-3917
e-mail: n_swart@msn.com
Web site: www.masna.org

REGIONAL

**Chesapeake Marine Aquaria Society
(CMAS - Chesapeake)**
c/o Tom Walsh, President
4220 Erdman Ave.
Baltimore, MD 21213
Web site: www.cmas-md.org/

**Chicagoland Marine Aquarium Society
(CMAS - Chicagoland)**
c/o Dennis Gallagher, President
1455 Nottingham Lane
Hoffman Estates, IL 60195
(847) 882-8594
Web site: www.cmas.net

**Cleveland Saltwater Enthusiasts Assn.
(C-SEA)**
c/o Peter J. Chefalo, President
3041 Lincoln Blvd.
Cleveland Heights, OH 44118-2033
(216) 371-8344
e-mail: pjc4@po.cwru.edu
Web site: www.geocities.com/clevelandsaltwater

Dallas/Fort Worth Marine Aquarium Society (DFWMAS)
c/o Brad Ward, President
P.O. Box 1403
Bedford, TX 76095-1403
Brad Ward, President
e-mail: award@airmail.net
Web site: www.dfwmas.com

Florida Marine Aquarium Society (FMAS)
c/o Charles Keller, President
3280 S. Miami Ave.
Miami, FL 33129
e-mail: charles.keller@coulter.com
(305) 380-4804
Web site: www.gate.net/~tbc/fmas.html

**Marine Aquarium Society of Los Angeles County
(MASLAC)**
840 N. Valley St.
Burbank, CA 91505-2736
Catherine Lee, President
e-mail: catherlee@yahoo.com
Web site: www.maslac.org

Marinelife Aquarium Society of Michigan (MASM)
1167 Tracilee Drive
Howell MI 48843
(517) 548-0164
John Dawe, President
e-mail: johndawe@umich.edu
Web site: www.masm.org

Marine Aquarium Society of Toronto (MAST)
33 Rosehill Ave.
Toronto, Canada M4T-1G4
(416) 925-1033
e-mail: flamehawk64@hotmail.com

Orlando Reef Caretakers Assn. (ORCA)
c/o John White, President
2100 Harrell Rd.
Orlando, FL 32817
(407) 482-0074
e-mail: jwhite@magicnet.net

Oklahoma Marine Aquarium Society (OMAS)
c/o Eric West, President
8044 Forest Glen Rd.
Claremore, OK 74017
(918) 266-7685
e-mail: westeric@hotmail.com
Web site: www.omas.org

Puget Sound Aquarium Society (PSAS)
c/o Bryan Petersen, President
15127 NE 24th, Suite 320
Redmond, WA 98052
e-mail: bryanp@nela.net
Web site: home.att.net/~psas.seattle/

Wasatch Marine Aquarium Society (WMAS)
537 E. 750N
Ogden, UT 84404
Mark Peterson, President
(801) 296-1563
e-mail: mrpslc@deseretonline.com
Web site: www.xmission.com/~mikeb/wmashome.html

Western Michigan Marine Aquarium Club (WMMAC)
26694 66th Ave
Lawton, MI 49065
(616) 624-6667
Web site: www.wmmac.org

CONTACTS

American Marinelife Dealers Association (AMDA)
P.O. Box 9118
Knoxville, TN 37940-0118
Web site: www.amdareef.com
A group of marine-aquarium retailers and suppliers, founded by author John H. Tullock, dedicated to responsible marine aquarium keeping and to promoting education and sustainable use of reef resources. AMDA members avoid drug-damaged livestock and species that are impossible to maintain, while offering captive-propagated specimens whenever possible.

Breeder's Registry
P.O. Box 255373
Sacramento, CA 95865
Web site:
www.breeders-registry.gen.ca.us
Publishes the Journal of MaquaCulture, devoted to marine life breeding, and maintains a database of captive-propagation observations.

Center for Marine Conservation
1725 De Sales Street NW
Washington, DC 20036
(202) 429-5609
Web site: www.cmc-ocean.org
Activist organization dedicated to protecting marine mammals, endangered species, and environments. Quarterly newsletter: Marine Conservation News.

The Coral Reef Alliance
64 Shattuck Square, Suite 220
Berkeley, CA 94704
(510) 848-0110
e-mail: coralmail@aol.com
Web site: www.coral.org
Independent, nonprofit membership organization working to address the problems of coral reef destruction worldwide.

The Cousteau Society
870 Greenbrier Circle, Suite 402
Chesapeake, VA 23320-2641
(800) 441-4395
e-mail: cousteau@infi.net
The late Capt. Jacques-Yves Cousteau's nonprofit educational and research organization; publishers of Calypso Log and, for children, Dolphin Log; bimonthly reports on environmental topics.

International Marinelife Alliance-USA
2800 4th Street North, Suite 123
St. Petersburg, FL 33704
(813) 896-8626
e-mail: prubec@compuserve.com
Web site: www.imamarinelife.org
Grassroots environmental group with a history of trying to control the use of cyanide in fish collection through monitoring and by teaching net-catching techniques to Third World fishermen.

Ocean Voice International
P.O. Box 37026
3332 McCarthy Road
Ottawa, ON Canada K1V 0W0
(613) 521-4205
Web site: www.conveyor.com/oceanvoice.html
Canadian-based group working to end cyanide collecting and other reef-damaging practices.

AUTHOR & EDITOR

Comments about this book and suggestions for future editions are invited.

John H. Tullock
American Marinelife Dealers Assn.
P.O. Box 9118
Knoxville, TN 37940
Web site: jhtullock.home.mindspring.com
e-mail: jhtullock@mindspring.com

Microcosm Ltd.
P.O. Box 550
Charlotte, VT 05445
e-mail: jml@microcosm-books.com
Web site: www.microcosm-books.com

Bibliography

Adey, Walter H., and Karen Loveland. 1991. *Dynamic Aquaria*. New York: Academic Press.

Allen, Gerald R. 1980. *The Anemonefishes of the World: Species, Care and Breeding*. Mentor, OH: Aquariums Systems.

Allen, Gerald R., and Roger C. Steene. 1987. *Reef Fishes of the Indian Ocean*. Neptune City, NJ: TFH Publications.

Alvarez, A.A. 1995. "Dead corals in exchange for live fish exports?" *Marinelife* 2 (1): 9.

Axelrod, H.R., and W.E. Burgess. 1985. *Saltwater Aquarium Fishes*. Neptune City, NJ: TFH Publications. pp. 32-33.

Axelrod, H.R., W.E. Burgess, and C.W. Emmens. 1985. *Exotic Marine Fishes*. Loose-leaf edition with supplements. Neptune City, NJ: TFH Publications.

Barnes, R.D. 1974. *Invertebrate Zoology*. 3rd ed. Philadelphia: W.B Saunders.

Bearman, Gerry, ed. 1989. *Seawater, Its Composition, Properties, and Behavior*. New York: Pergamon Press.

Bellwood, David R. 1981a. "Cyanide, part 1." *Freshwater and Marine Aquarium* 4 (November 1981): 31.

_____. 1981b. "Cyanide, part 2." *Freshwater and Marine Aquarium* 4 (December 1981): 7.

Blasiola, G.C. 1988. "Description, preliminary studies, and probable etiology of head and lateral line erosion (HLLE) of the palette tang (*Paracanthurus hepatus*) and other Acanthurids." In *Proceedings of the Second International Congress of Aquariology*, Monaco: Musée Océanographique. Abstracted in *SeaScope* 5 (summer 1988).

Bold, H.C., and M.J. Wynne. 1978. *Introduction to the Algae*. Englewood Cliffs, NJ: Prentice-Hall.

Burke, Maria. 1994. "Phosphorus fingered as coral killer." *Science* 263 (25 February 1994): 1086.

Colin, P.L. 1978. *Caribbean Reef Invertebrates and Plants*. Neptune City, NJ: TFH Publications.

Committee on Marine Invertebrates, Institute of Laboratory Animal Resources, Assembly of Life Sciences, National Research Council. 1981. *Laboratory Animal Management: Marine Invertebrates*. Washington, DC: National Academy Press.

Cook, Gregory. 1995. "The small-polyp stony coral reef aquarium." *SeaScope* 12 (fall 1995).

Curtis, Helena. 1983. *Biology*. 4th ed. New York: Worth Publishing.

Dakin, Nick. 1995. "State of the art marines." *Practical Fishkeeping* (June 1995): 70-73.

Debelius, Helmut. 1989. *Fishes for the Invertebrate Aquarium*. Mentor, OH: Aquarium Systems.

Delbeek, J.C., and Julian Sprung. 1994. *The Reef Aquarium*, Vol. 1. Coconut Grove, FL: Ricordea Publishing.

Dempster, Robert P., and Melvin S. Donaldson. 1974. "Cyanide — tranquilizer or poison?" *Aquarium Digest International* 2 (4): 21.

Dunn, Daphne Fautin. 1981. "The clownfish sea anemones: Stichodactylidae (Coelenterate: Actinaria) and other sea anemones symbiotic with pomacentrid fishes." *Transactions of the American Philosophical Society* 71 (1): 15-28.

Esterbauer, Hans. 1995. "*Pseudanthias squamipinnis*." *Tropical Fish Hobbyist* 43 (July 1995): 50.

Fautin, Daphne, and Gerald Allen. 1986. *Field Guide to Anemonefishes and Their Host Sea Anemones*. Perth: Western Australian Museum.

Frakes, Thomas. 1993a. "Red Sea reef 'mesocosms' in Monaco." *SeaScope* 10 (fall 1993).

_____. 1993b. "Nitrate menace?" *SeaScope* 10 (winter 1993).

_____. 1994. "Monaco aquarium revisited." *SeaScope* 11 (summer 1994).

_____. 1995. "Live rock aquaculture." *SeaScope* 12 (spring 1995).

Gosliner, Terence M., David W. Behrens, and Gary C. Williams. 1996. *Coral Reef Animals of the Indo-Pacific*. Monterey, CA: Sea Challengers.

Guzman, H.M. 1993. "Transplanting coral to restore reefs in the eastern Pacific." In *Rolex Awards Book*. New York. pp. 409-411.

Hall, K., and David R. Bellwood. 1995. "Histological effects of cyanide, stress and starvation on the intestinal mucosa of *Pomacentris coelestis*, a marine aquarium fish species." *Journal of Fish Biology* 47: 438-454.

Harrison, P.L., and C. C. Wallace. 1990. "Reproduction, dispersal, and recruitment of scleractinian corals." In *Coral Reefs*, edited by Z. Subinsky, 133-207. New York: Elsevier.

Haywood, Martyn, and Sue Wells. 1989. *The Manual of Marine Invertebrates*. Morris Plains, NJ: Tetra Press.

Herwig, Nelson. 1980. "Disease prevention and control." *Freshwater and Marine Aquarium* 3 (April 1980): 14.

_____. 1980. "Disease prevention and control." *Freshwater and Marine Aquarium* 3 (May 1980): 12.

Heslinga, G., T.C. Watson, and T. Isama. 1990. *Giant Clam Farming*. Honolulu: Pacific Fisheries Development Foundation (NMFS/NOAA).

Holliday, Les. 1989. *Coral Reefs*. Morris Plains, NJ: Salamander Books.

Hoover, John P. 1993. *Hawaii's Fishes*. Honolulu: Mutual Publishing Company.

Humann, Paul. 1994. *Coral Reef Identification: Florida, Caribbean, Bahamas*. Jacksonville, FL: New World Publications.

_____. 1994. *Reef Creature Identification: Florida, Caribbean, Bahamas*. Jacksonville, FL: New World Publications.

_____. 1995. *Reef Fish Identification: Florida, Caribbean, Bahamas*. Jacksonville, FL: New World Publications.

Hunziker, Ray. 1995. "Rare basslets for the reef aquarium." *Tropical Fish Hobbyist* 43 (July 1995): 62.

Hutchins, M., R. Weise, K. Willis, and J. Bowdoin. 1994. "Marine fishes TAG lists difficult fishes, seeks AZA review." *AZA Communiqué* (November 1994).

International Marinelife Alliance. 1995. *Marinelife* 2 (1): 16.

Jaubert, J. 1995. Remarks presented to the Seventh Marine Aquarium Conference of North America. Louisville, KY, 16 September 1995.

Kaplan, E.H. 1982. *A Field Guide to Coral Reefs of the Caribbean and Florida*. Boston: Houghton Mifflin.

_____. 1988. *A Field Guide to Southeastern and Caribbean Seashores*. Boston: Houghton Mifflin.

Larson, R.J., and J.W. Cooper. 1982. "Phylum Cnidaria." In *Encyclopedia of Marine Invertebrates*, edited by J.G. Walls, 29-126. Neptune City, NJ: TFH Publications.

Littler, Diane S., Mark M. Littler, Katina E. Bucher, and James N. Norris. 1989. *Marine Plants of the Caribbean: a Field Guide From Florida to Brazil*. Washington, DC: Smithsonian Institution Press.

Magruder, William H., and Jeffrey W. Hunt. 1979. *Seaweeds of Hawaii*. Honolulu: Oriental Publishing Company.

McLanahan, J. 1973. "Growth media — marine." In *Handbook of Phycological Methods*, edited by J.R. Stein, 25-51. Cambridge: Cambridge University Press.

Michael, Scott W. 1997. "Fishes for the marine aquarium: beautiful wrasses." *Aquarium Fish Magazine* 9 (3): 18-33.

Moe, Martin A., Jr. 1989. *The Marine Aquarium Reference: Systems and Invertebrates*. Plantation, FL: Green Turtle Publications.

Morris, Percy A. 1973. *A Field Guide to Shells*. Boston: Houghton Mifflin.

Myers, Robert F. 1989. *Micronesian Reef Fishes*. Guam: Coral Graphics.

Paletta, Michael. 1993. "Anemone propagation." *SeaScope* 10 (winter 1993).

_____. 1996. "Bleaching of small-polyp stony corals in aquaria." *SeaScope* 13 (fall 1996).

Rinkevich, B. 1982. "*Stylophora pistillata:* ecophysiological aspects in the biology of a hermatypic coral" (in Hebrew with English summary). Ph.D diss. Tel Aviv University.

_____. 1995. "Restoration strategies for coral reefs damaged by recreation activities: the use of sexual and asexual recruits." *Restoration Ecology* 3 (4): 241.

Robinson, Steve. 1981. "Who needs drugs? Confessions of an organic fish collector." *Freshwater and Marine Aquarium* 4 (July 1981): 14.

Roessler, Carl. 1986. *The Underwater Wilderness: Life Around the Great Reefs*. New York: McGraw-Hill.

Rubec, P.J. 1986. "The effects of sodium cyanide on coral reefs and marine fish in the Philippines." In *The First Asian Fisheries Forum*, edited by J.L. Maclean, L.B. Dizon, and L. V. Hosillos, 297-302. Manila, Philippines: Asian Fisheries Society.

_____. 1987. "Fish capture methods and Philippine coral reefs. IMA Philippines visit. part 2." *Marine Fish Monthly* 2 (7): 26.

_____. 1988. "Cyanide fishing and the International Marinelife Alliance net training program." *Tropical Coastal Area Management* 3 (1).

Rubec, P.J, and V. Pratt. 1991. "A project to develop and implement a test to detect fishes captured with cyanide." *Sea Wind* 5 (1): 19.

Sato, M. 1985. "Mortality and growth of a juvenile coral *Pocillopora damicornis* (Linnaeus)." *Coral Reefs* 4: 27-33.

Shimek, R.L. 1995. "What benefit does strontium supplementation offer the reef aquarium?" *Aquarium Frontiers* 2 (1): 7.

Simkiss, K. 1964. "Phosphates and crystal poisons of calcification." *Biological Reviews* 39: 487.

Smit, George. 1986a. "Marine aquariums, is it time for a change? part 1." *Freshwater and Marine Aquarium* 9 (January 1986): 35.

_____. 1986b. "Marine aquariums, is it time for a change? part 2." *Freshwater and Marine Aquarium* 9 (February 1986): 12.

Smith, Deboyd L. 1977. *A Guide to Marine Coastal Plankton and Marine Invertebrate Larvae.* Dubuque, IA: Kendall/Hunt.

Spotte, Stephen. 1979. *Seawater Aquariums.* New York: John Wiley & Sons.

_____. 1992. *Captive Seawater Fishes.* New York: John Wiley & Sons.

Sprung, Julian. 1991. "Reef notes." *Freshwater and Marine Aquarium* 14 (October 1991) : 72.

_____. 1994. "Reef notes." *Freshwater and Marine Aquarium* 17 (October 1994): 114.

Sprung, Julian, and Charles Delbeek. 1990. "New trends in reef keeping." *Freshwater and Marine Aquarium* 13 (December 1990): 8.

Stawikowski, Rainer. 1993. *The Biotope Aquarium.* Neptune City, NJ: TFH Publications.

Steene, Roger C. 1990. *Coral Reefs: Nature's Richest Realm.* Bathurst, Australia: Crawford House Press.

Sterba, Gunter. 1983. *The Aquarium Encyclopedia.* Cambridge: MIT Press.

Strynchuk, Justin. 1990. "An insight into the mating habits of the banded coral shrimp." *Freshwater and Marine Aquarium* 13 (October 1990):42.

Taylor, W. Randolph. 1960. *Marine Algae of the Tropical and Subtropical Coasts of the Americas.* Ann Arbor: University of Michigan Press.

Tullock, John. 1980. "Rearing the dwarf octopus." *Freshwater and Marine Aquarium* 3 (March 1980): 30.

_____. 1982. "Light in the marine aquarium." *Freshwater and Marine Aquarium* 5 (April 1982): 7.

_____. 1989. "Reef tank on a shoestring." *Marine Fish Monthly* 4 (November 1989): 33.

Veron, J.E.N. 1986. *Corals of Australia and the Indo-Pacific.* North Ryde, Australia: Angus & Robertson.

_____. 1995. *Corals in Space and Time: The Biogeography and Evolution of the Scleractinia.* Sydney, Australia: UNSW Press.

Walker, Stephen. 1996. "Propagation of marine fishes in North American zoos and aquariums." *Annual Report on Conservation and Science.*

Wells, Susan M., ed. 1988. *Coral Reefs of the World,* 3 Vols. Cambridge: United Nations Environment Programme/ International Union for Conservation of Nature and Natural Resources.

Wilkens, Peter. 1994. Letter to the editor. *Aquarium Frontiers.* (winter 1994): 3.

Wilkens, Peter, and J. Birkholz. 1986. *Invertebrates, Tube-, Soft-, and Branching Corals.* Wuppertal, Germany: Englebert Pfriem Verlag.

Wood, Elizabeth. 1983. *Corals of the World.* Neptune City, NJ: TFH Publications.

_____. 1992. "Trade in tropical marine fish and invertebrates for aquaria: proposed guidelines and labeling scheme." Report for the Marine Conservation Society.

Zann, Leon P. 1988. *Marine Community Aquarium.* Neptune City, NJ: TFH Publications.

Photography & Illustration Credits

PHOTOGRAPHERS

Photographs are credited by page number and by position on the page as follows: (T)Top, (C)Center, (B)Bottom, (TL)Top left, (BL)Bottom left, etc.

PAUL HUMANN: Front Cover, 14, 16, 17, 18, 19, 85(L), 92, 93, 98, 99, 101, 102, 104, 114, 118, 133, 134, 143, 144, 145, 156, 157, 158(TR), 159, 161, 162, 163, 164(T), 165, 166, 168, 169, 170, 171, 172, 175, 176, 179(B), 180, 181, 182, 184, 185, 186, 187, 188, 189, 190(T), 192, 194(T), 197(TL), 200(TL), 202(BC), 205, 206, 207, 209, 210, 211, 212, 216, 217(BC), 218 (T), 221, 224(B), 225(T), 228(B), 229(B), 230, 231, 232, 236(R), 237, 238(B), 240(R), 242(B), 244(T), 246(L), 248, 250, 251, 252, 254, 278, 288, 293, 299

SCOTT W. MICHAEL: 15, 21, 22, 31, 35, 80, 88, 149, 153, 158(CL, BL), 160, 164 (B), 167, 174, 179 (T), 190(B), 194(B), 195, 196, 197(TR, BL, BR), 198, 199, 200(TC, BL, BC, BR), 201(L, R), 202(TL, TC, TR, BL, BR), 203, 213, 214, 215, 217(BL, R), 218(B), 220, 222, 224(T), 225(C, BL), 227(L), 228(T), 229(T), 234, 235, 236(L), 238(TL, TC, TR, CL, C, CR), 239, 240(L), 241, 242(TL, C), 243, 244(C,B), 245(T), 246(R), 247, 249, 257, 258, 259, 260, 280, 282, 283, 284, 286, 287, 290, 291, 294, 295, 297, 300, Back Cover(T)

MARK SASAHARA: 49, 50, 51, 52, 53, 57, 58, 59, 61, 62, 65, 75(L), 86, 87, 89, 91, 94, 95, 108, 109, 115, 120, 123, 124, 130, 131, 132, 137, 255, 263, 265, 266, 267, 273

JOHN GOODMAN: 38, 55, 63, 66, 67, 68, 69, 70, 71, 72, 73, 74, 75(R), 76, 77, 78, 79, 116

JANINE CAIRNS-MICHAEL: 85(R), 200(TR), 201(C), 217(TL, TC), 225(BC, BR), 226, 227(R)

FOSTER BAM: 142, 154, 177, 178, 191, 274, Back Cover(B)

MICHAEL PALETTA: 36, 97, 112, 113, 219

NORBERT WU: 24, 148, 245(B), Back Cover(C)

CORAL REEF ECO-SYSTEMS: 46, 47

STEVE LUCAS (Courtesy of Exotic Aquaria): 40, 42

DAVID BARTS (Courtesy of Robert M. Fenner): 28

JOHN HUGGARD: 32

STEVE TYREE: 33

ILLUSTRATIONS

RICK ALLEN: 37 (Filtration system reproduced with permission from *Practical Fishkeeping* magazine, June '95, UK.)

LORI BAKER: 82, 84, 146-7, 150, 151, 152-3

CORBIS-BETTMANN: 26

JOSHUA HIGHTER: 48, 127

SYSTEMS & BIOTOPES

CHAD SIMON, Research Assistant: 64-79

Index

About the Author

JOHN H. TULLOCK is an ecologist and one of North America's leading proponents of environmentally sound aquarium keeping. A native of Tennessee, Tullock received the Master of Science degree from the University of Tennessee in 1979. He later did graduate work in ichthyology under Dr. David Etnier, who is perhaps best known for his discovery of the snail darter. He has taught college-level biology and managed a research laboratory.

Tullock and a group of partners founded Aquatic Specialists in 1987, which grew to become one of the largest direct-to-consumer national suppliers of marine fish, invertebrates, and live rock. In 1994, he left the board of the company to pursue a career as a writer and consultant to the aquarium trade. He is the author of six books and numerous magazine articles, which have appeared in *Aquarium Fish* magazine, *Aquarium Frontiers Online* magazine, *Freshwater and Marine Aquarium* magazine, and other publications. He has been a consultant to the World Wide Fund for Nature in connection with the Marine Aquarium Council and is currently pursuing research relating to the development of environmental policy.

Tullock is the founder of the American Marinelife Dealers Association, an organization of aquarium-industry businesses that promotes environmentally sustainable practices and education for conservation awareness. In 1997, he was invited to present a paper on the aquarium industry and the environment at the Global Biodiversity Forum in Montreal, Quebec. He also serves on the board of Conservation Fisheries, a nonprofit organization that rears endangered and threatened species of native American aquatic life for habitat restoration and species-recovery projects.

In addition to his marine aquarium interests, Tullock is an avid gardener, cook and outdoorsman, with a particular fondness for exploring the Cumberland and Appalachian Mountains near his home in Knoxville, Tennessee.